American Indian History

American Indian History

Volume 1

Aboriginal Action Plan—
Oliphant v. Suquamish Indian Tribe

edited by

Carole A. Barrett
University of Mary

Salem Press, Inc.
Pasadena, California   Hackensack, New Jersey

02-948

∞ The paper used in these volumes conforms to the American National Standard for Permanence of Paper for Printed Library Materials, Z39.48-1992 (R1997).

Essays originally appeared in *Ready Reference: American Indians* (1995), *Great Events from History: North American Series, Revised Edition* (1997), and *Racial and Ethnic Relations in America* (2000). New material has been added.

Library of Congress Cataloging-in-Publication Data
American Indian history / edited by Carole A. Barrett.
    p. cm. — (Magill's choice)
Includes bibliographical references and index.
    ISBN 1-58765-067-3 (set : alk. paper) — ISBN 1-58765-068-1 (vol. 1 : alk. paper) — ISBN 1-58765-069-X (vol. 2 : alk. paper)
    1. Indians of North America—History. I. Barrett, Carole A. II. Series.
E77 .A496 2003
970'.00497—dc21
                                                            2002007731

First Printing

PRINTED IN THE UNITED STATES OF AMERICA

CONTENTS — VOLUME 1

Contents

Contents

Contents

PUBLISHER'S NOTE

American Indian History joins two other publications in the Magill's Choice series of core teaching tools for public, school, and college libraries: *American Indian Biographies* (1 volume, 1999), covering 329 Native North Americans from the sixteenth century to the present day, and *American Indian Tribes* (2 volumes, 2000), with surveys of the ten major culture areas of North America and nearly 300 tribes and nations. To these 636 essays we now add 224 more, covering the major events and developments in the history of Native Americans of North America, from the earliest prehistoric traditions through the activism and legislation of the present day.

The essays in these two volumes are drawn from three previous Salem Press publications: *Ready Reference: American Indians* (3 volumes, 1996), winner of the American Library Association's Outstanding Reference Source Award; *Great Events from History: Revised North American Series* (4 volumes, 1997); and *Racial and Ethnic Relations in America* (3 volumes, 1999). In addition, 16 essays were newly commissioned for this publication and appear nowhere else.

Arranged alphabetically by keyword, each of the essays addresses a turning point in the history of the indigenous peoples of present-day Canada and the United States in their struggle to maintain their autonomy and lifeways after European contact. Essays range in length from 250 to 3,000 words and cover battles, treaties, legislation, court cases, protest movements, organizations, and institutions from the Bureau of Indian Affairs to tribal courts. Here students will find chronological narratives of not only the basics—the Powhatan Wars, the Pueblo Revolt, the Riel Rebellions, the Sand Creek Massacre, the Battle of the Little Bighorn, the Indian Bill of Rights—but also trends and developments that reveal more about the Native American experience, from the Carlisle Indian School to the Trail of Tears and William Cody's wild west shows. In addition, each of ten major prehistoric traditions is surveyed in a series of essays filed under "Prehistory," from the Arctic through the Northwest Coast to the Southeast. The set's 100 illustrations include photographs, engravings, and 29 maps for locating events, tribes, routes, and the ever-retreating boundaries of "Indian Territory."

Each essay is arranged in a ready-reference format that calls out the following elements at the top: *name of the event or topic* by keyword; *date or dates* of its occurrence, founding, or existence; *locale* where the event took place (or where it had its effect); *tribe or tribes* involved; *category or categories*, such as nineteenth century history or protest movements, to which it belongs; and finally a brief synopsis of the topic's *significance*. These reference features are followed by a full narrative of the event or topic. Articles longer than 1,000 words conclude with bibliographies of sources for further study on the topic; bibliographies of articles 2,000 words or longer include annotations. These bibliographies have been updated for *American Indian History*.

Several appendixes and indexes at the end of volume 2 function as research tools for the student: a Gazetteer of Historic Places; a list of more than 100 Historic Native Americans, with their birth and death dates, alternative names, and significance; a directory of Museums, Archives, and Libraries; a list of Organizations, Agencies, and Societies; a Time Line of major events in the history of Native Americans (including some not covered in separate essays); a list of Tribes by Culture Area; a general Bibliography of sources for further study; and a list of Web Resources, with their sponsoring institutions, Web addresses, and a brief description of their usefulness. Topics addressed in the text are fully accessible through five indexes: a Categorized Index, a Geographical Index, a Personages Index, a Tribes Index, and a full Subject Index. Finally, the front matter to both volumes contains the full list of contents for ready reference.

A few comments must be made on certain editorial decisions. Terms ranging from "American Indian" to "Native American" to "tribe" are accepted by some and disapproved of by others. We have used American Indians for the title of this set, as it is today the most widely accepted collective name for the first inhabitants of North America and their descendants. (It might be noted that some American Indians essentially find all such collective terms equally offensive.) We have allowed authors to use either "American Indian" or "Native American" in their articles rather than impose a term editorially, recognizing that individual writers have their own preferences. Similarly, we have used the title "Inuit" for the article on that Arctic people, but the term "Eskimo" also appears in the set, as it has a long tradition of scientific usage and encompasses a variety of Arctic peoples to whom "Inuit" does not adequately apply.

Contributors were also free to use singular or plural designations for tribal names. Spellings of tribal names, however, have been standardized throughout the set. We have attempted to use names and spellings that are both accepted by the tribes themselves and widely recognized. Parenthetical notes are occasionally provided to identify alternative names for tribes; although such alternative names ("Fox" and "Mesquakie," for example) do not always signify exactly identical groups, they are intended to help readers recognize the tribe being discussed.

The editors wish to acknowledge the invaluable guidance and assistance of Professor Carole A. Barrett of the University of Mary, who specializes in American Indian studies. She selected the essays and recommended the new essays, all of which were commissioned and are found here. In addition, we wish to thank the contributing writers, without whose expertise such breadth of coverage would not be possible.

CONTRIBUTORS

Carole A. Barrett, Editor
University of Mary

McCrea Adams
Independent Scholar

Thomas L. Altherr
Metropolitan State College of Denver

Tanya M. Backinger
Jackson Community College

Carl L. Bankston III
Tulane University

S. Carol Berg
College of St. Benedict

Warren M. Billings
*Louisiana State University, New
  Orleans*

Cynthia A. Bily
Adrian College

Suzanne Riffle Boyce
Independent Scholar

John A. Britton
Francis Marion University

Daniel A. Brown
*California State University,
  Fullerton*

Gregory R. Campbell
University of Montana

Byron D. Cannon
University of Utah

Ward Churchill
University of Colorado at Boulder

Thomas Clarkin
San Antonio College

David Coffey
Texas Christian University

Richard G. Condon
University of Arkansas

David A. Crain
South Dakota State University

LouAnn Faris Culley
Kansas State University

S. Matthew Despain
University of Oklahoma

Paul E. Doutrich
York College of Pennsylvania

T. W. Dreier
Portland State University

John L. Farbo
University of Idaho

Anne-Marie E. Ferngren
Oregon State University

John W. Fiero
University of Louisiana at Lafayette

Michael Shaw Findlay
California State University, Chico

C. George Fry
University of Findlay

Lucy Ganje
University of North Dakota

Lynne M. Getz
Appalachian State University

Marc Goldstein
Independent Scholar

Nancy M. Gordon
Independent Scholar

Larry Gragg
University of Missouri, Rolla

Kelley Graham
Butler University

William H. Green
University of Missouri, Columbia

Arthur Gribben
Pierce College

Eric Henderson
University of Northern Iowa

Howard M. Hensel
United States Air Force Air War College

R. Don Higginbotham
University of North Carolina at Chapel Hill

C. L. Higham
Winona State University

Kay Hively
Independent Scholar

Russell Hively
Independent Scholar

Carl W. Hoagstrom
Ohio Northern University

John Hoopes
University of Kansas

William E. Huntzicker
University of Minnesota

Andrew C. Isenberg
University of Puget Sound

M. A. Jaimes
University of Colorado at Boulder

Joseph C. Jastrzembski
Minot State University

Albert C. Jensen
Central Florida Community College

Bruce E. Johansen
University of Nebraska at Omaha

Jane Anderson Jones
Manatee Community College

Leslie Ellen Jones
Independent Scholar

Charles L. Kammer III
The College of Wooster

Richard S. Keating
United States Air Force Academy

Abraham D. Lavender
Florida International University

Thomas T. Lewis
Mount Senario College

John L. Loos
Louisiana State University

William C. Lowe
Mount St. Clare College

Richard B. McCaslin
High Point University

Paul Madden
Hardin-Simmons University

Lynn M. Mason
Lubbock Christian University

Thomas D. Matijasic
Prestonsburg Community College

Steve J. Mazurana
University of Northern Colorado

Maurice Melton
Andrew College

Howard Meredith
University of Science and Arts of Oklahoma

David N. Mielke
Appalachian State University

Laurence Miller
Western Washington State University

Bruce M. Mitchell
Eastern Washington University

Michael J. Mullin
Augustana College

Molly H. Mullin
Duke University

Bert M. Mutersbaugh
Eastern Kentucky University

Michael V. Namorato
University of Mississippi

Gary A. Olson
San Bernardino Valley College

Patrick M. O'Neil
Broome Community College

Martha I. Pallante
Youngstown State University

William A. Paquette
Tidewater Community College

Francis P. Prucha
Marquette University

Jon Reyhner
Montana State University, Billings

William L. Richter
Cameron College

Moises Roizen
West Valley College

Fred S. Rolater
Middle Tennessee State University

Mary Ellen Rowe
Central Missouri State University

Richard Sax
Madonna University

Glenn Schiffman
Independent Scholar

Rose Secrest
Independent Scholar

Michael W. Simpson
Chimanade University

David Curtis Skaggs
Bowling Green State University

Glenn Ellen Starr
Appalachian State University

David L. Sterling
University of Cincinnati

Pamela R. Stern
University of Arkansas

Ruffin Stirling
Independent Scholar

Leslie Stricker
Park University

Glenn L. Swygart
Tennessee Temple University

Stephen G. Sylvester
Montana State UniversityùNorthern

Robert D. Talbott
University of Northern Iowa

Harold D. Tallant
Georgetown College

Gale M. Thompson
Delta College

Leslie V. Tischauser
Prairie State College

Brian G. Tobin
Lassen College

Spencer C. Tucker
Virginia Military Institute

Mary E. Virginia
Independent Scholar

Gregory Walters
University of Ottawa

David E. Wilkins
University of Colorado at Boulder

Raymond Wilson
Fort Hays State University

Sharon K. Wilson
Fort Hays State University

Susan J. Wurtzburg
Lincoln University

Clifton K. Yearley
State University of New York at Buffalo

COMPLETE LIST OF CONTENTS

Volume 1

Volume 2

American Indian History

Aboriginal Action Plan

Date: January 7, 1998
Locale: Canada
Tribes involved: Pantribal in Canada
Categories: National government and legislation, Twentieth century history
Significance: The Aboriginal Action Plan sought to improve living conditions for aboriginal Canadians through an emphasis on partnerships, aboriginal self-government, and other recommendations of the Royal Commission on Aboriginal Peoples. They included recognition of, apologies for, and reconciliation over past injustices and abuses suffered by many aboriginal Canadians, often at the hands of the federal government.

The Canadian Aboriginal Action Plan, released on January 7, 1998, focused on aboriginal communities and the tasks of reconciliation and renewal as recommended by the Royal Commission on Aboriginal Peoples. The plan had four main objectives: renewing partnerships, strengthening aboriginal governance, developing a new fiscal relationship, and supporting strong communities, people, and economies. The first objective, the renewal of partnerships, included a statement of reconciliation, community-based healing of sexual and physical abuse in the residential schools, public education to help nonaboriginals better appreciate aboriginal peoples, and a coordinated approach to addressing the problems of aboriginals living in urban settings. The second objective was strengthening aboriginal governance through such steps as affirming treaty relationships, commemoration of the historic treaties, a new independent claims body, cost-shared Metis enumeration, funding for aboriginal women's organizations, establishment of an aboriginal center of excellence to assist groups in promoting self-government, and professional development strategies in lawmaking, environmental stewardship, and resource management. The third objective was developing a new fiscal relationship through a more stable, accountable relationship that promotes greater self-reliance, new financial standards for governments to comply with generally accepted accounting procedures, support for development of First Nations sources of revenue including taxation, statistical training for aboriginal groups to promote data collection and information exchanges, as well as an aboriginal peoples survey following the 2001 national census. The fourth objective was supporting strong communities, people, and economies through a five-year strategy to develop aboriginal human resources, providing for an increase in the number of houses on reserves and a remedy for the shortage of water and sewer facilities. Other specific goals of the strategy included expanded aboriginal policing services, an aboriginal Head Start program available on reserves, reduced welfare dependence, increased access of aboriginal businesses to capital and markets, the creation of urban aboriginal youth centers, education reform, and greater focus on prevention, treatment, and care of diabetes.

See also: Declaration of First Nations; Indian Act of 1989; Indian-white relations: Canadian.

Gregory Walters

Acoma, Battle of

Date: December, 1598-February, 1599
Locale: Acoma Pueblo, New Mexico
Tribe involved: Acoma (Keres),
Categories: Colonial history, Wars and battles
Significance: After this first major Puebloan uprising against the Spanish invaders, defeat and the Spaniards' cruel punishment of the survivors kept the Puebloans from attempting another rebellion for many decades.

In May, 1598, Don Juan de Oñate, appointed by the Spanish authorities as governor and captain general of all the kingdoms and provinces of New Mexico, reached the Rio Grande valley with a large contingent of priests, soldiers, settlers, and servants as well as two nephews, Vincente and Juan de Zaldivar. Although many Puebloans fled in terror before the invaders, those who remained received Oñate and his men hospitably. In each pueblo he entered, Oñate declared that he had come to protect the Indians and save their souls, and he demanded that they swear allegiance and vassalage to their new rulers, the Spanish king and the Catholic church. At the pueblos of Ohke and Yunque, he drove the Indians from their homes and moved his own people in, leaving King Phillip's new subjects to survive as best they could in the countryside.

By October, Oñate had reached Acoma Pueblo, where, after the usual ceremony of swearing allegiance to king and church, the inhabitants were asked to give generously of their food, robes, and blankets. Oñate then con-

Acoma Pueblo, photographed by Ansel Adams in 1941 or 1942. (National Archives)

tinued on to the Zuñi and Hopi pueblos. In early December, Juan de Zaldivar and thirty soldiers, following Oñate, arrived at Acoma and demanded to be provisioned, ignoring the Indians' pleas that they had nothing left to spare. The Indians then attacked, killing Zaldivar and twelve of his men.

Oñate, vowing to avenge this serious blow to Spanish authority, called a general meeting to plan for the punishment of Acoma. He consulted the friars, who agreed that this was a "just war" under Spanish law, since the Puebloans had sworn obedience and vassalage to the Spanish crown and were therefore royal subjects who were now guilty of treason. On January 21, 1599, Vincente de Zaldivar and his forces reached Acoma, where they found the Puebloans ready to defend themselves. The Indians, fighting with arrows and stones, were no match for men armed with guns; after two days of bitter fighting, Acoma was defeated, with more than eight hundred of its people dead. The pueblo was destroyed, and some five hundred men, women, and children were captured. Those who did not immediately surrender were dragged from their hiding places and killed.

On February 12, Oñate himself decreed the punishment of the captives: All men over twenty-five had one foot cut off and served twenty years in slavery; all men between the ages of twelve and twenty-five and all women over twelve served twenty years in slavery; the old men and women were given to the Querechos (Plains Apache) as slaves; the children under twelve were given to Fray Alonso Martinez (father commissary of the

Church) and to Vincente de Zaldivar; two Hopi men, at Acoma when the battle began, had their right hands cut off and were sent back to Hopi as an object lesson.

See also: Indian-white relations: Spanish colonial; Pueblo Revolt; Zuñi Rebellion.

LouAnn Faris Culley

Adobe Walls, Battles of

Date: November 26, 1864, and June 27, 1874
Locale: Texas
Tribes involved: Cheyenne, Comanche, Kiowa
Categories: Nineteenth century history, Wars and battles
Significance: The confrontations at Adobe Walls reflect a pattern of ongoing conflict between whites and Plains Indians that culminated in the decisive defeat of the latter in the Red River War.

There were two engagements in present-day Hutchinson County, Texas, near Adobe Walls, which were the ruins of a trading post built in 1843 by William Bent and abandoned before 1864.

The first clash occurred when Colonel Christopher "Kit" Carson was told to attack the winter camps of the Kiowa and Comanche, who were threatening federal posts in New Mexico. Carson moved down the Canadian River into Texas with 14 officers and 321 enlisted men of the First New Mexico Cavalry, as well as 75 Ute and Apache allies, two howitzers, and a wagon train. On the morning of November 26, 1864, he attacked a Kiowa encampment with his mounted troops, leaving the infantry with the wagons. The ensuing alarm brought several thousand Kiowa and Comanche warriors to confront Carson, who established a defensive position at Adobe Walls. Sporadic attacks by Kiowa and Comanche were disrupted primarily by Carson's howitzers, and at dusk he retreated to reunite his command. The next day he continued his withdrawal, having lost three killed and fifteen wounded but having inflicted perhaps a hundred casualties on his opponents. Carson was praised for extricating his force from their predicament.

The second engagement occurred nearly ten years later in 1874, after white buffalo hunters built a trading post near Adobe Walls. Angry clashes led to an attack by about seven hundred Kiowa, Comanche, and Cheyenne,

Quanah Parker, the Comanche Chief who led the second Battle of Adobe Walls in 1874 as white buffalo hunters devasted the bison herds at the base of his people's economy. (National Archives)

led by Quanah Parker and Lone Wolf, on the post, which was occupied by about two dozen men and one woman. The warriors were told by a shaman that they could not be harmed, but heavy casualties led to the failure of their assault on June 27, 1874. After five days of siege, the hunters had lost four men, while the number of defenders had increased to about a hundred. The attackers, who had lost several dozen, withdrew. This escalating pattern of violence led to the Red River War, during which Adobe Walls was abandoned for good in August, 1874.

See also: Apache Wars; Kickapoo uprisings; Long Walk; Navajo War; Red River War.

Richard B. MacCaslin

Alaska Native Brotherhood and Alaska Native Sisterhood

Date: Beginning 1912
Locale: Alaska
Tribes involved: Haida, Tlingit, Tsimshian, other southeast Alaskan tribes Sisterhood
Categories: Civil rights, Organizations, Religion and missionary activities, Twentieth century history
Significance: Founded to fight social and political discrimination against Alaska Natives, the Alaska Native Brotherhood is the oldest modern Alaska Native or American Indian organization in the United States.

With the stated goal of winning citizenship for Alaska Natives, twelve men and one woman formed the Alaska Native Brotherhood (ANB) in Sitka in

1912. One member was Tsimshian; the rest were Tlingit. A companion organization, the Alaska Native Sisterhood, is variously reported to have been established in 1915 or 1923. Within a decade there were chapters, called camps, throughout southeastern Alaska.

The founders of the Alaska Native Brotherhood were heavily influenced by Presbyterian missionaries, and in addition to promoting native civil rights, the organization urged the abandonment of traditional native languages and customs. In the 1960's, it reversed itself on this latter issue and was instrumental in the revival of many Haida and Tlingit traditions.

In the area of civil rights the ANB was active in the pursuit of voting rights and citizenship for Alaska Natives. In 1922, an ANB leader and attorney, William Paul, successfully defended his great-uncle Chief Shakes against the felony charge of voting illegally. Thus, Alaska Natives won the right to vote two years before Congress passed the Indian Citizenship Act in 1924.

The brotherhood led a series of boycotts against businesses that discriminated against natives and in 1945 lobbied successfully for the passage of the Antidiscrimination Act by the territorial legislature. It also successfully lobbied Congress to extend the 1934 Indian Reorganization Act to include Alaska. This contributed significantly to economic development in southeastern Alaska by enabling several native villages to apply for federal loans to purchase fishing boats and canneries.

The brotherhood mounted the first organized efforts to secure land rights for Alaska Natives. Its efforts were a precursor to the Alaska Native Claims Settlement Act of 1971.

See also: Alaska Native Claims Settlement Act; Fish-ins.

Richard G. Condon

Alaska Native Claims Settlement Act

Date: December 18, 1971
Locale: United States
Tribes involved: Aleut, Eskimo, Inuit
Categories: National government and legislation, Twentieth century history
Significance: Native Alaskans receive compensation in return for relinquishing their claims to lands they historically occupied.

The Alaska Native Claims Settlement Act (ANCSA) was signed into law by President Richard M. Nixon on December 18, 1971. It represented the culmination of a long struggle over native land claims that was compounded by the immediate need to construct a pipeline to carry oil from Prudhoe Bay to Valdez through lands claimed by Native Alaskans. The ANCSA granted forty-four million acres of land and $962.5 million to Native Alaskans in exchange for the relinquishment of their claims to the remaining nine-tenths of the land in Alaska. The law provided for an equitable distribution of funds among the three primary native groups (the Aleuts, Inuits, and Eskimos) and allowed first village corporations and then the regional native corporations, formed by the ANCSA, to select their lands. The Alaska Federation of Natives, speaking for the Alaskan native groups, accepted the settlement by a vote of 511 to 56, despite concerns about how it would affect traditional native patterns of hunting and fishing.

Land claims had long been a disputed issue between Native Alaskans and the U.S. government. A Supreme Court ruling in 1955 declared that the Fifth Amendment to the Constitution did not protect native land rights. When Alaska became the forty-ninth state of the Union in 1959, it was granted the right to select 103.3 million acres of land over the next twenty-five years without any acknowledgment of claims by Native Alaskans. Between 1959 and 1969, the state claimed nineteen million acres. By comparison, Native Alaskans owned only five hundred acres and had restricted title to another fifteen thousand acres. Since the state claimed nearly 28 percent of Alaskan territory, fears arose that there would be little valuable land remaining to satisfy native claims, and native opposition to state land claims intensified.

Competing Parties. Some Native Alaskans believed that proposed use of their lands by the state or federal government would violate traditional rights enjoyed by the native inhabitants. The Atomic Energy Commission, for example, sought to use Cape Thompson as a nuclear testing site; it was situated near an Eskimo village, with a population of three hundred, at Point Hope and the ancestral lands the villagers used for hunting. Another issue under dispute was the proposed Rampart Dam, a hydroelectric project that was to be built on the Yukon River in the north-central region of the state. Opponents of the dam argued that it would damage wildlife breeding grounds, displace twelve hundred natives from seven small villages, and endanger the livelihood of five thousand to six thousand others who depended on salmon in that area. Finally, the state was beginning to legislate hunting restrictions on state-owned land, which natives believed would threaten their traditional way of life. In the early 1960's, native groups began to take action to protect their interests. Between 1961 and 1968, Alaskan natives filed claims protesting the state's use of 337 million acres of Alaskan territory.

In 1960, Native Alaskans constituted roughly 20 percent of the Alaskan population. For those living in native communities or villages, life consisted of subsistence hunting and fishing, which necessitated access to large amounts of land. Many were seasonally employed and lived in poverty. Seventy percent had less than an elementary education, and only ten percent had received a secondary education. Owing to disease, alcoholism, and impoverished conditions, the life span of Native Alaskans was about thirty-five years of age, half the national average. Many Native Alaskans believed that existing laws, rather than protecting them, stripped them of rights to lands that they claimed. They generally did not consider either the state or the federal government to be supportive of their concerns.

Two other groups who entered the contest over land claims were developers and environmentalists. Developers desired the construction of more fisheries and canneries, as well as highways and industries that would enable Alaska's natural resources to be fully developed. Environmentalists sought protection of certain lands as parks, natural wilderness areas, and wildlife refuges. By 1966, land disputes had become so hotly contested that Secretary of the Interior Stewart Udall ordered a freeze on all transfers of land claimed by the natives until a mutually acceptable agreement could be reached.

Following the discovery at Prudhoe Bay, on the North Slope of Alaska, of one of the largest oil fields ever found, the federal government proposed that a pipeline be constructed across the state to transport the oil to Valdez, a city easily accessible for loading petroleum because of its position as a year-round ice-free port on Prince William Sound. The proposed route of the eight-hundred-mile Trans-Alaska Pipeline included twenty miles of land that was claimed by Native Alaskans, who feared that construction of the pipeline would likely lead to other infringements of their land claims. By this time, however, the Alaska Native Brotherhood and the Alaska Federation of Natives, among other native groups, were well organized to press for their interests. It became evident that the land issue would have to be resolved before the pipeline was built.

Government Intervention. Walter Hickel, Udall's successor as secretary of the interior, extended the land-freeze in 1970. A federal restraining order halted the project until a settlement could be reached. Because developers and oil companies were anxious to get the project under way, pressure was applied to settle the issue quickly. Other interested parties anticipated benefits from the construction of the pipeline, which promised lower petroleum prices to the federal government, revenue to the state, land preservation to environmentalists, and previously denied rights to natives, particularly title to land that they believed was theirs. British Petroleum, one of the interested parties, agreed to lobby for a bill that would protect native land interests. A joint Senate-House conference committee drew up the final bill, which gained widespread support. It passed Congress and was signed into law by Nixon on December 18, 1971.

The ANCSA resolved the long-standing dispute regarding native rights to land in Alaska. Native land claims were extinguished in return for title to forty-four million acres that included mineral rights, as well as $962.5 million in additional compensation. Twelve regional corporations were established between 1972 and 1974 (to which a thirteenth was added for natives not living in Alaska) in order to manage the funds and organize land selection. Every Alaskan native became a member of a regional corporation, in which he or she was given one hundred shares of stock. In addition, about 220 village corporations were formed to oversee the distribution of land at the local level. Native reservations were abolished, and sixteen million acres of land were set aside for selection by the village corporations.

The village corporations were allowed to select their land over a three-year period and the regional corporations over four years. Beneficiaries of the land claims were required to be one-quarter native Alaskan (either Inuit, Aleut, or Eskimo) and had to be born on or before December 18, 1971. While the land selection involved a lengthy process, native corporations eventually selected 102 million acres instead of the allotted 44 million. For twenty years after the passage of the act, Native Alaskans were not permitted to sell their stock to non-natives, and their undeveloped land was not to be taxed. In 1987, Congress passed the "1991 amendments," which preserved the tax-exemption benefits on undeveloped lands indefinitely and allowed new stock to be issued to Native Alaskans born after December 18, 1971.

The ANCSA was, in many respects, a watershed in the history of Native Alaskans that promised to change their way of life permanently. The act began the transformation of Alaskan native cultures from a subsistence economy based on traditional hunting and fishing patterns to one based on ownership of modern business-for-profit ventures. Many Native Alaskans embarked on a difficult transition from life on reservations to membership in native corporations that undertook a variety of commercial enterprises.

These corporations invested in banking, hotels, fisheries, real estate, and mineral exploration. Some were successful and some were not. Nevertheless, the acquisition of land and income gave Native Alaskans a position of influence in state politics that they had never had before.

See also: Alaska Native Brotherhood and Alaska Native Sisterhood; Fish-ins.

Anne-Marie E. Ferngren

Sources for Further Study

Anders, Gary C. "Social and Economic Consequences of Federal Indian Policy." *Economic Development and Cultural Change* 37, no. 2 (January, 1989): 285-303. Includes discussion of the effects of the ANCSA on the Alaskan Natives.

Arnold, Robert D., et al. *Alaska Native Land Claims*. Anchorage: Alaska Native Foundation, 1978. A comprehensive discussion of the act and its significance.

Berger, Thomas R. *Village Journey: The Report of the Alaska Native Review Commission*. New York: Hill & Wang, 1985. A critical account of the effects of the ANCSA on Native Alaskans.

Berry, Mary Clay. *The Alaska Pipeline: The Politics of Oil and Native Land Claims*. Bloomington: Indiana University Press, 1975. Describes the influence of the construction of the pipeline on the passage of the ANCSA.

Case, David S. *Alaska Natives and American Laws*. Fairbanks: University of Alaska Press, 1984. A detailed description of the historical interaction of Native Alaskans and U.S. law.

Flanders, Nicholas E. "The ANCSA Amendments of 1987 and Land Management in Alaska." *The Polar Record* 25, no. 155 (October, 1989): 315-322. Discusses the modifications of the ANCSA by the 1991 Amendments.

Mitchell, Donald Craig. *Take My Land, Take My Life: The Story of Congress's Historic Settlement of Alaska Native Land Claims, 1960-1971*. Fairbanks: University of Alaska Press, 2000. Discusses the legal and regulatory history of ANCSA.

Strohmeyer, John. *Extreme Conditions: Big Oil and the Transformation of Alaska*. New York: Simon & Schuster, 1993. Illustrates the impact of the petroleum industry and law on native peoples.

Albany Congress

Date: June 19-July 10, 1754
Locale: Albany, New York
Tribes involved: Iroquois Confederacy
Categories: Colonial history, National government and legislation, Treaties
Significance: To resolve Iroquois land and trade complaints, colonial delegates draft the Plan of Union.

In June, 1753, the Mohawk leader Hendrick declared the Covenant Chain— a term used to symbolize the Iroquois Confederacy's alliance with New York and the other colonies—to be broken. Hendrick's action shocked colonial and imperial officials. From their perspective, Hendrick's timing could not have been worse. Tensions between the French and English were increasing, and British officials had based their military strategy for North America on an Anglo-Iroquois alliance. Just when the Iroquois alliance was most needed, the Mohawks had voided the centerpiece of Britain's military strategy for North America. Something had to be done, and that something was the Albany Congress of 1754.

Hendrick's declaration represented a culmination of events dating back a decade. In 1744, the Onondaga, believing they were ceding the Shenandoah Valley to Virginia, agreed to the Treaty of Lancaster. Virginians, however, used this treaty to claim the entire Ohio region. Over the next decade, Virginian officials opened nearly three hundred thousand acres of land to settlement through land companies such as the Ohio Company of Virginia. King George's War (1739-1748) temporarily delayed settlement. Once the war ended, however, the Ohio Company renewed its efforts at settling the region. French officials responded by sending Captain de Céleron into the Ohio Valley in 1750. French soldiers also began building forts in the region. One such outpost, Presque Isle, was in the heart of Iroquoia. When the Iroquois asked for assistance in removing the French from Presque Isle, Virginian officials refused to help. By the early 1750's, the Mohawks and other Indian groups felt themselves trapped between the English and French.

Need for Negotiation. Following Virginia's response to the Iroquois, members of the Board of Trade recommended that King George II call a congress to address Indian complaints about colonial behavior. In September, 1753, the Board of Trade notified colonial governors that King George II wanted all colonies having a relationship with the Iroquois to attend a conference that was to resolve existing Iroquois complaints about land and trade with the colonists. The resulting Albany Congress was unlike any other Anglo-Iroquois conference. It was the first intercolonial-Indian conference called by London officials.

The proposed conference met with the approval of Massachusetts governor William Shirley and the Pennsylvanian Benjamin Franklin. However, the lieutenant governors of New York and Virginia were less enthralled with the board's directive. New York lieutenant governor James De Lancey could not escape the conference. Robert Dinwiddie of Virginia, however, failed to send a representative to Albany. Still, when the conference began in June, 1754, representatives from nine colonies attended.

The delegates met at Albany for specific reasons. It was the historic meeting place for Iroquois-European conferences. Albany was the site of one of the two council fires the English and Iroquois maintained. As one of the anchors of the Covenant Chain, official business could be conducted and ratified there. It was also the closest city to the frontier that delegates could reach by boat.

Hendrick, chief of the Mohawks, who in 1753 declared the Covenant Chain—the Iroquois Confederacy's alliance with New York and other British colonies—to be broken as a result of Iroquois attacks against westward-expanding settlers. The Albany Congress was designed to allow the British to make peace with their long-standing Iroquois allies in the face of mounting French-British tensions. Mohawk leaders such as Hendrick hoped that the congress' proposed Plan of Union would allow all British colonists to speak with a single voice, thus alleviating Iroquois-settler tensions, but the plan was rejected. (Library of Congress)

Agenda. When representatives met at Albany, they needed not only to address Iroquois complaints but also to prepare for war. Delegates saw the two issues as interrelated. On June 19, 1754, they created a seven-person committee to prepare James De Lancey's opening speech to the American Indians. Five days later, the representatives created a second committee to consider "some Method of affecting the Union between the Colonies." This latter delegation produced the Plan of Union associated with the Albany Congress. It did so, however, "as a Branch of Indian Affairs." Mohawk leaders such as Hendrick hoped confederation would allow the colonists to speak with a single voice. Some delegates agreed. They thought colonial confederation would alleviate the problems of which the Iroquois complained. Therefore, the Albany Plan of Union was designed primarily as a mechanism for conducting Indian affairs.

Besides improving colonial policy toward the natives, representatives thought colonial confederation would improve their military preparedness and help them defeat New France. There were mutual security reasons for confederation. Politicians did not prepare their plan to tamper with each colony's internal autonomy.

Common wisdom maintains that Benjamin Franklin is the father of the colonial confederation. There is, however, some evidence to suggest that Thomas Hutchinson of Massachusetts wrote the plan. If Hutchinson was the author, then American Indian affairs were probably an important influence on the Plan of Union, because Hutchinson was a member of the original subcommittee appointed to study American Indian affairs. Franklin was not.

Proposals. Whoever the author was, the Plan of Union contained specific proposals. It created a unicameral legislature, to be called the Grand Council. This council would consist of forty-eight representatives chosen from the lower houses of the colonies. Representation in the Grand Council was limited to members of the lower houses of assembly in the colonies because it was assumed that only directly elected representatives had the right to tax the colonists. Initially, representation in the Grand Council would be based on the population of each colony. After three years, representation would be based on the revenue a colony generated for the confederation, so as to reward participation. In both its name and the number of delegates, the Plan of Union paid homage to the Iroquois League.

The new government also would have a president general. This executive would receive his salary directly from England, so the president general would be independent of the colonial legislatures. This proposal recognized the problems confronting the relationship between governor and lower house in colonial America.

The proposed confederation government had eight functions. One of the most important was the right to direct all Indian treaties for the colonies. The government also would make declarations of war and peace toward the natives, make all land purchases from the natives in the name of the king, and regulate trade with the natives. Purchased land would reside outside the existing boundaries of established colonies. The government would direct the creation of settlements in the territory, would rule them in the name of the king, and would be responsible for the defense of the frontier.

The Plan of Union also gave the proposed government the ability to tax. The Grand Council could enforce an excise tax on luxury goods. The government would secure additional money by regulating the Indian trade. Traders would be required to carry licenses and post bonds of good behavior before being allowed to trade with the natives. Traders were to purchase these licenses and bonds from the confederation government. Trade would be restricted to specific forts, built just for that purpose. It was hoped that by regulating trade with the Indians, many of the problems associated with the traders would be curtailed. Finally, the government would receive quitrent from colonists as they settled lands newly purchased from the Indians. Politicians thus pursued colonial confederation as a method of addressing Indian affairs.

Rejection. The Albany delegates approved the Plan of Union on July 10 and adjourned to take the proposals back to their respective colonies. Not one colonial legislature accepted the plan. Legislators in seven colonies voted the Plan of Union down. The other six legislatures let the issue die away during the Seven Years' (French and Indian) War. Each colonial legislature had specific reasons for rejecting the Albany Plan. Some politicians feared that the plan gave too much power to the governor. Others feared the creation of a president general. Still others believed that the confederation government threatened the western lands included in their original charters.

Colonial legislators were not the only ones to repudiate the Plan of Union. The Board of Trade rejected it too, believing the idea of a Grand Council to be cumbersome. They wanted a smaller council, with delegates chosen by the royal governors. They also thought that the Albany Plan gave too much power to colonial assemblies. From the Board of Trade's perspective, the Albany Congress was a failure.

If the Albany Congress was a failure, it was an important one. The congress showed how different England and America had grown since the Glorious Revolution in the 1680's. The Seven Years' War would strain the imperial-colonial relationship even more. The failure of delegates to the Albany Congress to address Iroquois complaints directly forced the home government to become an active participant in colonial-Indian relations. The result was the creation of an Indian superintendent system. This new system, begun in 1755, made imperial policies, not colonial desires, the primary focus of Anglo-Iroquois dialogue in the years to come.

See also: French and Indian War; Indian-white relations: English colonial; Iroquois Confederacy; Iroquois Confederacy-U.S. Congress meeting; Paxton Boys' Massacres; Proclamation of 1763.

Michael J. Mullin

Sources for Further Study

Alden, John R. "The Albany Congress and the Creation of the Indian Superintendencies." *Mississippi Valley Historical Review* 27, no. 2 (September, 1940): 193-210. Describes how the Albany Congress led British officials to create the Indian superintendent system.

Gipson, Lawrence Henry. "The Drafting of the Albany Plan of Union: The Problem of Semantics." *Pennsylvania History* 26, no. 4 (October, 1959): 291-316. Argues that Thomas Hutchinson was responsible for writing the Albany Plan of Union.

Hopkins, Stephen. *A True Representation of the Plan Formed at Albany*. Providence, R.I.: Sidney S. Rider, 1880. Hopkins, who represented Rhode Island at the Albany Congress, details the issues that delegates discussed concerning Indian affairs.

Mullin, Michael J. "The Albany Congress and Colonial Confederation." *Mid-America* 72, no. 2 (April-July, 1990): 93-105. Discusses the role of Indian affairs at the Congress.

Newbold, Robert C. *The Albany Congress and Plan of Union of 1754*. New York: Vantage Press, 1955. A summation of the scholarship on Albany at the time.

Shannon, Timothy J. *Indians and Colonists at the Crossroads of Empire: The Albany Congress of 1754*. Ithaca, N.Y.: Cornell University Press, 2000. Argues that the Albany Congress was actually the moment of shifting European-Indian relationships from independent commerce to an imperialist model, based on hierarchy and governed by a distant authority rather than face-to-face.

Alcatraz Island occupation

Date: 1969-1971
Locale: Alcatraz Island, San Francisco Bay
Tribes involved: Pantribal in the United States

Categories: Protest movements, Twentieth century history

Significance: The takeover of Alcatraz Island symbolized the awakening of American Indian peoples to cultural and political concerns, even though its stated goal, the establishment of a Center for Native American Studies, was not realized.

The occupation of Alcatraz Island in San Francisco Bay by an organization calling itself Indians of All Tribes was a high-profile act of self-empowerment by native American people. In 1962, the United States government closed operations of the federal penitentiary situated on the island. There were actually two subsequent occupations of the island by young American Indian people. First came a short-lived effort in 1964, then the highly publicized takeover of 1969 which lasted until June of 1971, when federal marshals and other law enforcement officials removed all American Indians left on the island.

The occupying Indians wanted the island to be transformed into a center for Native American studies. This would involve the practice of traditional tribal spirituality; people would be trained in song, dance, and healing ceremonies. It would also be a place of training in scientific research and ecology. Also, it was to become an Indian training school whose purpose would be to teach the use of modern economics to end hunger and unemployment.

The Indians of All Tribes organization desired transfer of Alcatraz as surplus federal property, in the same manner that facilities such as Roswell Air Force Base in New Mexico, the Stead Air Force Base in Nevada, the Madera Radar Station, and Camp Parks were transferred to such profit-making organizations as Philco-Ford, Radio Corporation of American (RCA), and Litton.

Negotiations were carried out with Robert Robinson of the National Council on Indian Opportunity representing the United States. In March of 1970, the government's counterproposal included these ideas: a new name for the island, possibly from the Ohlone language; monuments commemorating noted American Indian people placed on the island park; a cultural center and museum built as an integral part of the park plan; and a number of Indians professionally trained as park rangers by the National Park Service. The federal government balked at the idea of locating an institution of higher learning on the island, noting that the first tribally controlled college was already being established at Many Farms on the Navajo Reservation and that a number of Native American studies courses were being offered at universities across the nation. This proposal was rejected by the Indians of All Tribes, and the negotiations broke down. On June 11, 1971, federal marshals arrested everyone on Alcatraz Island.

The takeover of Alcatraz Island served as a symbol in re-awakening American Indian people, as self-determination continued to replace federal policies of relocation and termination.

See also: American Indian Movement; Indian Civil Rights Act; Indian-white relations: U.S., 1934-2002.

Howard Meredith

All-Pueblo Council

Date: Established 1922
Locale: New Mexico
Tribes involved: Pueblo
Categories: Native government, Organizations, Twentieth century history
Significance: The All-Pueblo Council defended the integrity of Pueblo lands, communal life, and tribal traditions in the face of federal legislation threatening Pueblo reservation lands.

The All-Pueblo Council was established in response to the proposed Bursum bill of 1922. This legislation resulted from decades of controversy over land that had been purchased since 1848 by Hispanic and white settlers from the Pueblo Indians of New Mexico. In 1913, the United States Supreme Court ruled in the Sandoval case that the Pueblo Indians came under federal jurisdiction as wards of the government and therefore did not have the authority to sell their lands. Occasional violence broke out as Pueblos challenged the right of white settlers to be on former Pueblo lands. In 1922, Secretary of the Interior Albert B. Fall, a former New Mexico senator, asked New Mexico senator Holm O. Bursum to introduce legislation to confirm the land titles of all non-Pueblo claimants and place Pueblo water rights under the jurisdiction of the state courts. The intention of Fall and Bursum was to settle the controversy over Pueblo lands in favor of Hispanic and white settlers and to prevent further violence.

Sympathetic whites, including the General Federation of Women's Clubs, artists from Santa Fe and Taos, and sociologist John Collier, organized a movement to stop the Bursum bill. After Collier alerted the Pueblos to the danger of the bill, they responded by calling an All-Pueblo Council, which met on November 5, 1922, at Santo Domingo. The 121 delegates drafted "An Appeal by the Pueblo Indians of New Mexico to the People of the

United States." They claimed that the Bursum bill would destroy their communal life, land, customs, and traditions. A delegation from the All-Pueblo Council went with Collier to Washington, D.C., to testify before the Senate Committee on Public Lands. The Bursum bill was defeated in Congress as a result of the public outcry against it. In 1923, a compromise bill, the Public Lands Act, was passed; it empowered a board to determine the status and boundaries of Pueblo lands.

See also: Gadsden Purchase; Indian-white relations: U.S., 1871-1933; Pueblo Revolt; Zuñi Rebellion.

Lynne M. Getz

Allotment system

Date: 1887-1934
Locale: United States
Tribes involved: Pantribal in the United States
Categories: National government and legislation, Nineteenth century history, Reservations and relocation, Twentieth century history
Significance: Intended to assimilate Indians by making them small farmers, the allotment system instead led to a massive loss of Indian land.

Allotment—the division of tribal lands among individual Indians—became the dominant theme in federal Indian policy in the years between 1887 and 1934. During the 1880's many whites who regarded themselves as "friends of the Indians" came to believe that Indians could be saved from extinction only by assimilation into American society. Tribal loyalties and cultures were seen as barriers to this end. Reformers hoped that by carving up reservations and making small farmers of the Indians, they could effectively detribalize and assimilate the Indians into American culture. This policy also attracted support from those who wanted to open up tribal lands for settlement or exploitation. There were precedents for this policy. In the first half of the nineteenth century, several eastern states had broken up state-recognized reservations by dividing land among tribal members, and a number of the removal treaties of the 1830's made provision for allotments to individual Indians who wished to remain east of the Mississippi.

In 1887 Congress enacted the General Allotment Act, also known as the Dawes Severalty Act (for Senator Henry Dawes of Massachusetts, one of its proponents). The act gave the president authority to allot reservation lands in "severalty" (to individual Indians). As a general rule, heads of families would receive 160 acres, single Indians less. Title to the allotments would be held in trust by the government for twenty-five years to enable allottees to acquire the necessary skills, and the land could not be sold during the trust period. Once an Indian took up an allotment, he became an American citizen. Land not required for distribution could be sold off or opened to white settlement, with the proceeds intended to support assimilationist policies. It was suggested that the Indians, freed from tribal domination, would develop as small farmers and so be capable of taking their place in American society. The Five Civilized Tribes of Indian Territory, along with a few others, were originally exempted from the act, but in the 1890's Congress established a commission headed by Senator Dawes to negotiate allotment and thus the abolition of their tribal governments.

The actual process of allotment was complex and went on for more than forty years. Along the way Congress made several modifications: In 1900, the leasing of allotments before the end of the trust period was allowed; in 1902, heirs of allottees were

An 1879 advertisement for white settlement on land bought by the U.S. government from the Creek, Chickasaw, Choctaw, and Seminole in 1866 (the government's original intent was that the land be settled by other Indians and former slaves). (Library of Congress)

permitted to sell their lands with the permission of the secretary of the interior; and in 1906, the Burke Act delayed citizenship until the end of the trust period (also permitting the secretary of the interior to cut short the trust period for Indians deemed competent to manage their own affairs).

The system did not work as intended. Many Indians came from nonagricultural tribal backgrounds and were reluctant to become farmers. Others found their allotments too small to support a family or of little agricultural value. Whites often encouraged Indians to lease or sell their lands, sometimes resorting to intimidation or outright fraud. It often proved easy to separate Indians from allotments.

The foremost result of the allotment policy was a drastic reduction in the amount of land controlled by Native Americans, from 138 million acres in 1887 to 52 million acres when the policy ceased in 1934. Of the amount lost, 60 million acres had been declared "excess land" and disposed of by the government to non-Indians. By 1934, two-thirds of Native Americans were either landless or without enough land to provide subsistence. The policy weakened tribal cultures and fostered the growth of a large bureaucracy in the Bureau of Indian Affairs.

By the late 1920's, doubts about the allotment system were growing. An investigation led by Lewis Meriam shocked many when its findings were published in 1928 as *The Problem of Indian Administration* (better known as the Meriam Report). The report detailed dismal conditions and poverty among American Indians and identified the allotment system as the major source of Indian problems. In 1934, the Indian Reorganization Act stopped the process of allotment and allowed the reorganization of tribal governments.

See also: Burke Act; Friends of the Indian organizations; General Allotment Act; Indian Reorganization Act; Meriam Report.

William C. Lowe

Sources for Further Study

Greenwald, Emily. *Reconfiguring the Reservation: The Nez Perces, the Jicarilla Apache, and the Dawes Act.* Albuquerque: University of New Mexico Press, 2002.

Hoxie, Frederick E. *A Final Promise: The Campaign to Assimilate the Indians, 1880-1920.* Lincoln: University of Nebraska Press, 1984.

Kinney, J. P. *A Continent Lost, a Civilization Won: Indian Land Tenure in America.* 1937. Reprint. Baltimore: The Johns Hopkins University Press, 1991.

McDonnell, Janet A. *The Dispossession of the American Indian, 1887-1934.* Bloomington: Indiana University Press, 1991.

Otis, Delos S. *The Dawes Act and the Allotment of Indian Lands.* Edited by Francis Paul Prucha. Norman: University of Oklahoma Press, 1973.
Washburn, Wilcomb E. *The Assault on Indian Tribalism: The General Allotment Law (Dawes Act) of 1887.* Philadelphia: J. B. Lippincott, 1975.

American Indian

Date: Colonial times-present
Locale: Americas and West Indies
Tribes involved: Pantribal
Categories: Terminology
Significance: An "American Indian" is broadly defined as a member of any of the aboriginal peoples of North, Central, or South America and the West Indies. Peoples covered under this definition are also generally considered part of a group once widely referred to by anthropologists as "Mongoloid" in reference to certain physical characteristics and facial features.

The term "American Indian" is an obvious misnomer on two counts: First, the word "American" refers to explorer Amerigo Vespucci, for whom the Americas were named by European explorers. Second, the word "Indian" refers to inhabitants of the Indian subcontinent (South Asia), which explorer Christopher Columbus mistakenly thought he had reached when he arrived in the Americas in the late 1400's.

As colonization of the Americas by Europeans progressed, the term continued to be used by the European immigrants, regardless of its inappropriateness. The early European explorers and colonists were not interested in exploring differences among native cultures; they simplistically perceived the hundreds of distinct indigenous cultures of North America as a singular primitive, barbaric, and uncivilized entity. "American Indian," or "Indian," became the standard term used by Europeans and European Americans simply through common usage. Many indigenous peoples, in their own languages, call themselves "the people" or "human beings," emphasizing their distinctive qualities among all living creatures, to which they believe themselves related.

In the mid-twentieth century, "Native American" became a widely used alternative collective name. By the 1990's, however, the popularity of this term had also waned, and many native people found American Indian to be relatively acceptable, even preferable. Some American Indians find all terms such as American Indian, Native American, and Amerind to be equally objectionable, as all owe a debt to European views and, at worst, to the racism of dominant American society. The most accurate—and most widely accepted—way to identify a person or tradition is simply to refer to the specific tribe or group to which the person or tradition belongs. When referring to the many indigenous cultures collectively, "American Indians" is still widely used, essentially because no consensus has been reached on a preferable term.

See also: Amerind; Federally recognized tribes; Indian; Native American; Tribe.

Michael W. Simpson

American Indian Defense Association

Date: Established 1923
Locale: United States
Tribes involved: Pantribal in the United States
Categories: Organizations, Twentieth century history
Significance: Organized by social reformer and later Bureau of Indian Affairs commissioner John Collier, the American Indian Defense Association (AIDA) was the primary advocate for tribal revitalization.

The American Indian Defense Association (AIDA) was organized in New York City in May, 1923, by white reformers sympathetic to Indian causes. Under the leadership of John Collier, the AIDA's founder and first executive secretary, the organization consisted primarily of wealthy, liberal Californians who joined hands in opposition to a proposed bill addressing land disputes in the Northwest that might have resulted in the loss of Pueblo lands. Led by Collier, members of the AIDA were critical of the General Allotment Act of 1887, pleading for the maintenance of Indian tribal integrity.

In 1922, Collier explicitly stated the AIDA's goals. The association was to aid in the preservation of Indian culture, including a revitalization program of Indian arts and crafts. It sought to entitle Indians to social and religious freedoms and to rejuvenate tribal governments. Provisions were also made for safeguarding Indian civil liberties. Furthermore, Indians were to be entitled to federal aid in the form of Farm Loan Bank credits, public health services, and other federal assistance programs. To break its monopoly over Indian programs, Collier suggested reform of the Bureau of Indian Affairs. Through congressional lobbying, publication of pamphlets, and advice to Indian tribes, Collier and the AIDA labored to influence federal Indian policy and to improve conditions on Indian reservations.

In its first decade, the AIDA grew to more than 1,700 members. Headquartered in Washington, D.C., the organization maintained branches in cities throughout the country. During the 1920's, executive secretary Collier became the nation's leading advocate of Indian rights. With the election of President Franklin D. Roosevelt in 1932, Indian reform organizations furnished candidates for appointment as commissioner in the Bureau of Indian Affairs, Collier foremost among them. Although Collier was considered controversial because of his communist sympathies and his confrontational nature, Roosevelt nevertheless appointed him commissioner in 1933. Under Roosevelt, Collier initiated his own Indian New Deal, whereby governmental Indian policy shifted away from assimilation and toward tribal revitalization. Collier's culminating triumph was passage in 1934 of the Indian Reorganization Act, the heart of the Indian New Deal. The American Indian Defense Association consistently supported Collier and the Indian New Deal, although the association was frequently critical of its application.

In 1936, the American Indian Defense Association merged with the National Association on Indian Affairs, becoming the Association on American Indian Affairs (AAIA). By the 1990's, the AAIA was headquartered in New York City. There it maintained a staff of employees and had thousands of members nationwide with an annual operating budget of more than $1 million. The AAIA provided legal and technical assistance in health, education, economic development, the administration of justice, and resource utilization to United States tribes. In addition, the AAIA maintained the American Indian Fund, published the newsletter *Indian Affairs*, and occasionally published books.

See also: Indian New Deal; Indian Reorganization Act.

Mary E. Virginia

American Indian Higher Education Consortium

Date: Established 1972
Locale: United States and Canada
Tribes involved: Pantribal in the United States

Categories: Education, Organizations, Twentieth century history

Significance: The American Indian Higher Education Consortium promotes tribally controlled colleges and monitors state and federal legislation affecting Indian higher education.

The American Indian Higher Education Consortium (AIHEC) was formed by six tribal college leaders in 1972 to protect the interests of tribally controlled colleges in the United States and Canada. The overall goal of the organization is to ensure survival of tribal colleges, maintain Indian control of the colleges, and secure an adequate funding base. The consortium promotes culturally meaningful training for college administrators and teachers working in the tribal colleges; it promotes and encourages the preservation and teaching of American Indian, Inuit, and Alaska Native languages, cultures, and traditions; and it encourages programs that are consistent with the inherent rights of tribal sovereignty and self-determination.

AIHEC came about at a time when Indian people were identifying common goals and establishing issue-oriented organizations that promoted sovereignty and represented both tribal and pantribal needs. Because of the complex issues connected with the implementation of the Tribally Controlled Community College Act of 1978, AIHEC has become a vital force in monitoring political and legislative issues connected with American Indian higher education at the state and federal levels. AIHEC also functions as a national forum to promote Indian higher education and recognition of the tribal college movement.

AIHEC provides considerable support to the tribal college infrastructure and sponsors annual conferences at which administrators, faculty, and students from the various colleges meet to participate in training workshops, seminars, and a variety of intercollegiate activities. AIHEC also publishes *Tribal College: Journal of the American Indian Higher Education Consortium*, which focuses on issues of Indian higher education and provides a forum to address Indian research issues. In an effort to raise money and establish endowments, AIHEC created and oversees the American Indian College Fund, intended to promote personal, corporate, and foundation gift-giving to support the tribal college movement. Through the various activities of AIHEC, the Indian tribal colleges are connected by a national organization that promotes their well-being while respecting their inherent sovereignty.

See also: Carlisle Indian School; Indian Education Acts; Indian Self-Determination and Education Assistance Act; Kennedy Report; National Congress of American Indians.

Carole A. Barrett

American Indian Movement

Date: Established 1968
Locale: United States
Tribes involved: Pantribal in the United States
Categories: Organizations, Protest movements, National government and legislation, Native government, Twentieth century history
Significance: Creates public awareness of injustices to Indians; struggles for American Indian treaty rights; encourages self-determination among native peoples.

The American Indian Movement (AIM) was founded by Chippewas Dennis Banks and George Mitchell in Minneapolis, Minnesota, during July, 1968. Taking its initial ideas from the Black Panther Party, AIM sought to protect urban Indians from police abuse and to create programs promoting community self-sufficiency. Inspired by the 1969 takeover of Alcatraz Island, however, the movement adopted an agenda centered on indigenous spiritual traditions, land recovery, and treaty rights.

AIM's credibility in "Indian country" was truly established in early 1972, when Russell Means led a large caravan to tiny Gordon, Nebraska, protesting the fact that two local whites who had brutally murdered an Oglala Lakota from the nearby Pine Ridge Reservation were charged only with manslaughter. As a result, the culprits became the first white men in Nebraska history to be imprisoned for killing an Indian.

In November, 1972, AIM played a key role in a spectacular seizure of the Bureau of Indian Affairs (BIA) headquarters in Washington, D.C. This was followed, in January, 1973, by a major confrontation between AIM and police in the streets of Custer, South Dakota, which left the county courthouse in flames (the issue again concerned official inaction after the murder of an Oglala). In February, 1973, while supporting Lakota treaty rights, AIM undertook a lengthy armed standoff with federal authorities at Wounded Knee. Afterward, the Federal Bureau of Investigation mounted a grim campaign of repression against "insurgents" on Pine Ridge.

Over the next three years, AIM's leadership was largely tied up in what one federal official admitted was "an effort to destroy these radicals via the judicial process." Meanwhile, more than sixty AIM members and supporters were murdered on the reservation, many of them by a federally sponsored entity calling itself "the Goon Squad," and more than three hundred others suffered serious physical assault.

On June 26, 1975, AIM's efforts to defend itself led to a massive firefight that left an Indian and two FBI agents dead. Three AIM members—Bob

02.948

Poster urging support for the American Indian Movement in New York City. (Library of Congress)

Robideau, Dino Butler, and Leonard Peltier—were charged with murdering the agents. Butler and Robideau were acquitted by an all-white jury after a U.S. Civil Rights Commission representative testified that they had merely responded to a government-induced "reign of terror" on Pine Ridge. Peltier, however, was convicted and sentenced to a double life term in a controversial process that a federal appellate court later described as "fraught with FBI misconduct."

By 1977, AIM had entered an extended period of relative dormancy, although it did go on to organize or participate in such events as the 1978 Longest Walk, the 1980 Black Hills Survival Gathering, the Yellow Thunder Camp occupation of 1981-1985, and the anti-Columbus demonstrations of the early 1990's.

Although it may never reconstitute itself in a form exhibiting the power it once displayed, some analysts believe that the movement had achieved its major objectives by 1975. "AIM instilled a deep sense of pride and resistance to oppression among Indians which was greatly lacking at the time," Vine Deloria, Jr., observed, "and for that we owe it a real debt." Lakota traditionalist Birgil Kills Straight concurs: "Whatever else may be said," he maintains, "AIM acted as the shock troops of Indian sovereignty at a time when we needed them most."

See also: Pine Ridge shootout and Peltier killings.

Ward Churchill

Sources for Further Study

Churchill, Ward, and Jim Vander Wall. *Agents of Repression: The FBI's Secret Wars Against the Black Panther Party and the American Indian Movement.* Boston: South End Press, 1988.

Deloria, Vine, Jr. *Behind the Trail of Broken Treaties: An Indian Declaration of Independence.* 2d ed. Norman: University of Oklahoma Press, 1987.

Johansen, Bruce, and Roberto Maestas. *Wasi'chu: The Continuing Indian Wars.* New York: Monthly Review Press, 1979.

Matthiessen, Peter. *In the Spirit of Crazy Horse.* 2d ed. New York: Viking Press, 1991.

Smith, Paul Chaat, and Robert Allen Warrior. *Like a Hurricane: The American Indian Movement from Alcatraz to Wounded Knee.* New York: New Press, 1997.

Weyler, Rex. *Blood of the Land: The U.S. Government and Corporate War Against the First Nations.* 2d ed. Philadelphia: New Society Publishers, 1992.

American Indian Policy Review Commission

Date: Established 1975
Locale: United States
Tribes involved: Pantribal in the United States
Categories: National government and legislation, Twentieth century history
Significance: This federal commission, after two years of study, published an extensive report calling for major reforms of U.S. Indian policy.

The American Indian Policy Review Commission (AIPRC) was established in 1975 as a follow-up to the Indian Self-Determination and Education Assistance Act, passed in the same year. The commission was chaired by Senator James Abourezk of South Dakota (it is sometimes referred to as the Abourezk Commission). The commission's findings were published in 1977 in its multivolume report. The report opposed assimilationist policies and recommended continuing the 1968 initiative for the establishment of permanent government units in the federal system to protect and strengthen tribal governments.

Among the factors that led to the establishment of the commission was the activism and unrest sweeping American Indian communities in the early 1970's. According to Vine Deloria, Jr., and Clifford M. Lytle, the 1973 occupation of Wounded Knee in particular was a catalytic event in the decision to create a new commission to reexamine the government's Indian policy.

The AIPRC included Indian representatives in various positions; they were selected according to partisan tribal politics of the time. Indians dominated the staff; a significant number of contracted consultants were also native individuals. In addition to there being five Indian commissioners and thirty-one (out of a total of thirty-three) Indian task force members, the commission included six members of Congress. Inevitably, complicated political dynamics plagued the commission behind the scenes.

The final report of the AIPRC generally followed the line of Indian militants who had previously been excluded from positions on commissions and task forces. The extensive document listed more than two hundred recommendations. It claimed that the relationship between American Indian tribes and the United States was political and was established via treaties, according to international law. The commission recommended that two fundamental concepts should guide all future federal policy: First, Indian tribes are sovereign political bodies having the power to enact laws and enforce them within reservation boundaries; second, the relationship between the tribes and the United States "is premised on a special trust that must govern the conduct of the stronger toward the weaker." The AIPRC report also stated that the right to choose a form of government is an inherent right of any Indian tribe.

No actual social reform directed toward improving the lot of American Indians took place following publication of the AIPRC report. Moreover, Congress soon afterward abolished the standing Indian Affairs Subcommittees that operated under the Department of the Interior. Eventually a Senate Select Subcommittee on Indian Affairs was authorized by Congress to sort out the many AIPRC recommendations.

The commission was not without criticism from both ends of the political spectrum. Some (including the commission's vice chair, Representative Lloyd Meems) criticized it for going too far. Others have argued that, although the commission had good intentions in its promotion of self-determination, its recommendations in reality represented a continuation of the paternalistic relationship between the U.S. government and the tribes.

See also: Indian Self-Determination and Education Assistance Act; Wounded Knee occupation.

M. A. Jaimes

Sources for Further Study
American Indian Policy Review Commission Task Force. *Report*. Washington, D.C.: U.S. Government Printing Office, 1977.

Clarkin, Thomas. *Federal Indian Policy in the Kennedy and Johnson Administrations, 1961-1969.* Albuquerque: University of New Mexico Press, 2001.

Deloria, Vine, Jr., ed. *American Indian Policy in the Twentieth Century.* Norman: University of Oklahoma Press, 1985.

Deloria, Vine, Jr., and Clifford M. Lytle. *American Indians, American Justice.* Austin: University of Texas Press, 1983.

_____. *The Nations Within: The Past and Future of American Indian Sovereignty.* New York: Pantheon Books, 1984.

Robbins, Rebecca L. "Self-Determination and Subordination: The Past, Present, and Future of American Indian Governance." In *The State of Native America,* edited by M. A. Jaimes. Boston: South End Press, 1992.

American Indian Religious Freedom Act

Date: August 11, 1978
Locale: United States
Tribes involved: Pantribal in the United States
Categories: Civil rights, National government and legislation, Religion and missionary activities, Twentieth century history
Significance: The U.S. Congress recognizes its obligation "to protect and preserve for American Indians their inherent right of freedom to believe, express, and exercise traditional religions."

Throughout most of U.S. history, the federal government has discouraged and abridged the free exercise of traditional American Indian religions. The federal government provided direct and indirect support to a variety of Christian denominations who sought to Christianize and "civilize" American Indians. In 1883, bowing to pressure from Christian churches, the federal government forbade "the savage and barbarous practices that are calculated to continue [American Indians] in savagery, no matter what exterior influences are brought to bear on them." The Sun Dance, rites of purification, other religious ceremonies, and the practices of medicine men were forbidden. Violators could be prosecuted and receive ten days in jail if they continued their "heathenish practices." Such a law restricting freedom of religion was possible because tribes were regarded as distinct political units separate and apart from the United States, and so were not covered by the protections of the Constitution or the Bill of Rights.

In the 1920's, there was a crusade for reform in federal American Indian policy, and there were outspoken concerns for the support of freedom of religion for American Indian peoples. In 1933, John Collier was appointed Commissioner of Indian Affairs under Franklin Roosevelt. On January 31, 1934, he circulated a pamphlet entitled *Indian Religious Freedom and Indian Culture* among employees of the Indian Service. This pamphlet, which stressed that "the fullest constitutional liberty, in all matters affecting religion, conscience, and culture" should be extended to all American Indians, established policies for Indian Service employees to follow. Collier directed unequivocally, "No interference with Indian religious life or ceremonial expression will hereafter be tolerated. The cultural liberty of Indians in all respects is to be considered equal to that of any non-Indian group." Two weeks later, Collier issued a second order, which dealt with religious services at government-operated schools. It had been common practice to require students in government schools to attend church services. This new policy statement, "Regulations for Religious Worship and Instruction," prohibited compulsory attendance at services, although it did allow religious denominations to use school facilities for services. Religious instruction was permitted one hour per week in the day schools; however, parents had to give written permission for their children to attend. This policy was especially controversial, because these regulations extended to representatives of native religions as well as to Christian missionaries.

These policy statements were not well received by missionaries who had been active on various reservations, and many regarded Collier's move to protect American Indian religious freedoms as a direct attack on the churches and Christianity. Collier was accused of being an atheist and of being antireligious. Criticism of Collier was especially strong among Protestant missionary societies and included attacks from Christian Indians who decried this return to the old ways as subverting American Indian progress. Nevertheless, Collier insisted that American Indians be granted complete constitutional liberty in all matters affecting religion, conscience, and culture, and he asserted that religious liberty extended to all people, not just Christians.

Native Religious Freedom. Most tribal governments endorsed Collier's policy of religious freedom, and, on many reservations, there was a revival of the older spiritual traditions. However, federal and state laws have not endorsed or permitted freedom of religion for American Indians consistently. Certain state and federal laws and policies prevented the free exercise of religion for many American Indian people. A large area of concern was that many areas that were considered to be sacred lands by the tribes had passed from Indian control to state or federal jurisdiction. Access to such sacred sites often was limited or not permitted. The use of peyote in Native American Church ceremonies was a contentious issue because peyote is a restricted substance due to its hallucinogenic properties. The use of eagle feathers in a variety of rituals was another source of friction with federal officials, because eagles were protected under endangered species laws. There also have been occasions of interference in religious ceremonies by government agents and curious onlookers. American Indian people had little recourse to remedy these situations, and tribal governments had no powers of prosecution or enforcement.

As a result of continuing problems with the free exercise of traditional American Indian religions, Congress passed a broad policy statement, Senate Joint Resolution 102, commonly known as the American Indian Religious Freedom Act (AIRFA), on August 11, 1978. After noting the U.S. right to freedom of religion and the inconsistent extension of that right to American Indian people, Congress acknowledged its obligation to "protect and preserve for American Indians their inherent right of freedom to believe, express, and exercise the traditional religions of the American Indian, Eskimo, Aleut, and Native Hawaiian, including but not limited to access to sites, use and possession of sacred objects, and the freedom to worship through ceremonial and traditional rites." AIRFA also required all federal agencies to examine their regulations and practices for any inherent conflict with the practice of American Indian religions. These agencies were required to report back to Congress and recommend areas in which changes in policies and procedures were needed to ensure that American Indian religious freedoms were protected.

The American Indian Religious Freedom Act is a key element in self-determination and cultural freedom in the United States. However, even with passage of this act, Native Americans have continued to experience problems in access to sacred sites and the use of peyote. The right of Native Americans to use peyote is an unsettled issue in both federal and state courts. Although peyote is subject to control under the Federal Comprehensive Drug Abuse Prevention and Control Act, a number of states exempt its use in Native American Church ceremonies. Some courts uphold the right of Native Americans who are church members to possess and use peyote; other courts do not. Likewise, American Indians are not guaranteed access to sacred sites that are located outside the bounds of Indian lands, even when these lands are under federal control.

The United States Supreme Court has ruled that AIRFA is a policy statement only, and it does now allow American Indians to sue when federal agencies disregard native religious practices or when agencies pursue plans that will have an adverse impact on Native American religion or beliefs. In 1987, in *Lyng v. Northwest Indian Cemetery Protective Association*, the United States was granted the right to build a logging road through federal lands that were central to the traditional religions of the Yurok, Karuk, and Talowac tribes. In 1990, the United States Supreme Court ruled, in *Employment Division, Department of Human Resources of Oregon et al. v. Smith*, that the state of Oregon could prohibit a member of the Native American Church from using peyote, because that state regarded peyote as an illegal substance. These Supreme Court decisions make clear that if federal or state agencies fail to comply with the policies established in AIRFA, American Indian people have no legal recourse to sue or claim adverse impact on their religion. The extension of full religious freedom to Native American people is an evolving concept in U.S. jurisprudence, and the American Indian Religious Freedom Act constitutes an important philosophical foundation toward ensuring the free exercise of religion and access to sacred areas.

See also: Carlisle Indian School; *Employment Division, Dept. of Human Resources of the State of Oregon et al. v. Smith*; *Lyng v. Northwest Indian Cemetery Protective Association*; National Council of American Indians; *Native American Church v. Navajo Tribal Council*; Society of American Indians.

Carole A. Barrett

Sources for Further Study

Deloria, Vine, Jr., ed. *American Indian Policy in the Twentieth Century*. Norman: University of Oklahoma Press, 1985. These essays interpret American Indian policy through important legal decisions. One essay explores AIRFA and its ineffectiveness in protecting access to sacred sites.

Deloria, Vine, Jr., and Clifford Lytle. *The Nations Within: The Past and Future of American Indian Sovereignty*. New York: Pantheon Books, 1984. A thorough examination of the Collier years and their impact on later American Indian poetry.

Echo-Hawk, Walter E. "Loopholes in Religious Liberty. The Need for a Federal Law to Protect Freedom of Worship for Native American People." *NARF Legal Review* 14 (Summer, 1991): 7-14. An important analysis of what AIRFA should provide in the way of legal protection of religious freedoms for American Indian peoples.

Josephy, Alvin M. *Now That the Buffalo's Gone: A Study of Today's American Indians*. Norman: University of Oklahoma Press, 1984. Contains a chapter on American Indian efforts to retain their spirituality and provides American Indian perspective on this issue.

Long, Carolyn N. *Religious Freedom and Indian Rights: The Case of Oregon v. Smith*. Lawrence: University Press of Kansas, 2000. Part of the Landmark Law Cases and American Society series, this is the first book-length study of *Oregon v. Smith*, focusing on the case's sharp differences from previous opinions on First Amendment freedom of religion rights.

Amerind

Date: 1970's-present
Locale: Americas and West Indies
Tribes involved: Pantribal
Categories: Terminology
Significance: The term "Amerind" is a neologism combining the words "American" and "Indian." It came into common usage during the 1970's. A result of tribal activism meant to counter racism toward native peoples, this term was chosen as an alternative to "American Indian" and "Native American."

The people to whom this term refers include members of any of the aboriginal peoples of North America, Central America, South America, and the West Indies. Europeans and European Americans have continually sought to lump all the original inhabitants of the Americas into a convenient single group. "Amerind" represents an attempt to refer to native groups collectively with a term that could be considered (to use a post-1970's term) politically correct. Yet although the term may be descriptive and less inaccurate than others, it falls short of the redefinition needed when referring to the multitude of distinct original cultures of North America.

There are more than five hundred groups of indigenous peoples in the United States alone, each with its own name for itself, and each with a unique tribal specific cultural heritage and political legacy. Who a people are can be defined only in terms of specific environment, language, customs, traditions, taboos, and so on. Until modern Americans recognize the distinctive elements inherent in each indigenous community, any new terms such as "Amerind" will be viewed by scholars as empty generalizations. Such terms, although convenient, are more a reflection of American cultural bias than they are descriptive of the nature, quality, or diversity of the original inhabitants of the Americas.

See also: American Indian; Federally recognized tribes; Indian; Native American; Tribe.

Byron D. Cannon

Apache Wars

Date: February 6, 1861-September 4, 1886
Locale: Southwest
Tribes involved: Apache
Categories: Nineteenth century history, Wars and battles
Significance: The incursion of white settlers into the Southwest leads to armed conflicts with indigenous Chiricahua Apaches.

After the signing of the Treaty of Guadalupe Hidalgo in 1848, large portions of northern Mexico were ceded to the United States. As a result of the acquisition of these new lands, numerous white settlers began moving into the newly formed Arizona and New Mexico territories. Much of this region was the traditional range of various Apache groups, particularly numerous bands of Chiricahua, Coyotero, and Mimbreño Apache. Many of these groups practiced raiding, taking goods from others as an extension of their traditional methods of subsistence. Raiding increased in frequency as more white settlers moved into Apache territory.

In 1861, an Apache raiding party (thought to have been Coyotero Apache, not Chiricahua) kidnaped a boy who had been a member of a group of white settlers. The U.S. military reacted quickly by ordering Lieutenant George Bascom to investigate the incident and, if necessary, to take action against the "hostiles" that were thought to have committed the raid. On February 6, 1861, Bascom, possibly as a result of an invitation to the Chiricahua, persuaded Cochise, the principal chief of the eastern Chiricahua, and some of his family and followers, to come in for a peace parley. During the early stages of what has been termed the Bascom affair, Cochise, speaking on behalf of the eastern Chiricahua, tried to convince Bascom that it was not Chiricahua Apache who had conducted the raid. Bascom had Cochise and several of the chief's relatives arrested. Cochise later escaped. Bascom, as an act of reprisal for the kidnaping and Cochise's escape, ordered the execution of the chief's relatives.

Although conflicts between white settlers and Apache groups had occurred before 1861, this incident is generally viewed by historians as the starting point of what has come to be called the Apache Wars. Numerous armed conflicts involving various Apache groups occurred from 1861 to 1886 on both sides of the U.S.-Mexican border. For example, in retaliation for the execution of his relatives, Cochise organized a surprise attack on the Gidding party at Stein's Peak near Doubtful Canyon. Cochise killed nine of the settlers but lost sixty of his warriors in the attack. Numerous battles ensued in the years that followed. In July, 1862, Cochise and his father-in-law Mangas Coloradus and other Chiricahuas were attacked by infantry under the command of "Star Chief Carleton." During the battle, Mangas Coloradus was wounded. Mangas Coloradus survived the wound, but in January, 1863, he was covertly executed and beheaded after he had attempted to surrender and sue for peace with captain Edmond Shirland of the California Volunteers. This sentence was delivered without any official record of a fair trial.

Post-Civil War Hostilities. In the year 1865, the Apache Wars reached a pinnacle. With the end of the American Civil War the attention of the United States military, along with the bulk of its forces, shifted west to land traditionally occupied by Native American tribal groups. Action taken against the Apache by the Mexican military was also increasing. In late winter of 1865, for example, Mexican Federales from Sonora attacked and killed thirty-nine Apaches. Mexican forces, combined with pressure exerted by U.S. military forces in the American Southwest, caused Cochise and other Apache leaders to remain constantly on the run. In 1866, Cochise was driven by U.S. forces into hiding in Mexico, where he continued to harass white settlers by periodically crossing the border to conduct surprise attacks. These skirmishes continued until October 10, 1872, when Cochise finally signed a truce with the Americans at Cochise's camp in the Dragoon mountains in southern Arizona. Cochise died two years later.

For a decade, Geronimo, a Bedonkohe/Chiricahua shaman from northern Mexico, fought white incursion into his people's land until he was finally captured and removed to Florida, shortly before this picture was taken. (National Archives)

Other Apache leaders, however, refused to abide by the truce of 1872 and continued

Apache leaders Geronimo and Nana meeting with General George Crook and his men toward the end of the Apache Wars, probably in 1886. (Library of Congress)

their attacks on settler groups. Farther west, Geronimo, a Bedonkohe/ Chiricahua shaman from northern Mexico, was fighting his own wars against both Mexican and U.S. forces. By 1861, the U.S. Army was firmly established in southern Arizona. Forts Bowie and Apache had been built to assist the army in protecting the increasing numbers of settlers who continued to enter the Arizona territory. In 1871, the Camp Grant Massacre destroyed an entire Apache camp.

General Cook and Geronimo. In 1872, General George Cook, who had a reputation among Washington politicians for decisiveness in his dealings with Indian groups, took command of the Southwest operation. From 1872 until 1886 and his dismissal, Cook's career was dominated by attempts to keep Geronimo in check. In 1877, Geronimo, along with family members and other Chiricahuas, was arrested by Cook's men. Geronimo and his people were subsequently resettled on the reservation at San Carlos. Sometimes referred to as "Hell's Forty Acres," San Carlos proved to be an inhospitable environment lacking sufficient water and game for Apache survival. The army, in an attempt to conciliate the Apache, introduced corn agriculture to the reservation. The Chiricahua were traditional hunters and gatherers and attempts at agriculture, especially on arid reservation land, soon failed. Four years later, many Apache—including Geronimo—fled the reservation. From 1881 until his surrender at Skeleton Canyon in 1886, Geronimo fought numerous battles with both U.S. and Mexican forces. He also continued raiding white settlements. During this period of time Geronimo surrendered several times to the U.S. military. Late in the year 1881, for example, Geronimo was recaptured by General Cook and taken to Fort Apache. Geronimo and his followers were again taken to the reservation. Nothing had changed; the Apache could not make a sufficient living on the reservation, so they eventually fled to Mexico.

In April, 1882, Geronimo returned to San Carlos and conducted a raid. There he killed the chief of police and captured several Mimbreño Apache (former followers of the Apache leader Victorio), whom Geronimo forced to go back to Mexico with him. In May, 1883, Cook decided to pursue Geronimo by taking several units of infantry and cavalry into Mexico. On May 15, after several days of strenuous marching through Mexico's Sierra Madre, Cook attacked the camp of a group of Mimbreño Apache headed by Apache Chief, Chato. Although the battle itself was indecisive, it had become evident that the military was not going to give up its pursuit of Geronimo. In the days that followed the battle several chiefs of the Mimbreño Apache, including Chato, Loco, and Nana, surrendered to Cook. In March, 1884, Geronimo, by now a revered Apache leader, surrendered to Cook. This surrender and the subsequent confinement on the reservation, like the others, did not last. Geronimo fled and surrendered two more times.

Historians generally agree that Cook's goal was to secure a lasting peace with Geronimo and other Apaches. Cook's inability to keep Geronimo under the purview of the U.S. government, however, forced military and political leaders in Washington, D.C., to remove Cook from his command. General Nelson Miles was sent to replace Cook. General Miles was not as sympathetic to the plight of the Apache as had been General Cook. General Miles immediately sent out a force of approximately five thousand soldiers to seek out and capture Geronimo and his small band (estimated to be about twenty-four in number). On September 4, 1886, Geronimo, along with twenty-three members of his band of Chiricahuas (mostly women and children), surrendered for the final time at Skeleton Canyon—about sixty-five miles from Apache Pass, where the first skirmish of the Apache Wars had been fought. After Geronimo's surrender General Miles had all Chiricahuas in the immediate vicinity arrested, including the scouts that had been used by the army to track down Geronimo. Geronimo, his followers, and the former Apache scouts were placed in rail cars and transported east to a reservation in St. Augustine, Florida. With Geronimo's surrender and his removal to Florida, the Apache Wars ended.

See also: Adobe Walls, Battles of; Fort Atkinson Treaty; Gadsden Purchase; Indian-white relations: Spanish colonial; Indian-white relations: U.S., 1871-1933; Kickapoo uprisings; Long Walk; Medicine Lodge Creek Treaty; Taos Rebellion.

Michael Shaw Findlay

Sources for Further Study

Cole, D. C. *The Chiricahua Apache, 1846-1876: From War to Reservation.* Albuquerque: University of New Mexico Press, 1988. A general history of Chiricahua with special attention to cultural conflicts with Euro-Americans.

Griffen, William B. *Apaches at War and Peace: The Janos Presidio, 1750-1858.* Albuquerque: University of New Mexico Press, 1988. Details the emergence of the Mexican presidio system and the subsequent relocation and resettlement of various Apache groups in southern New Mexico, Arizona, and northern Mexico.

_____. *Utmost Good Faith: Patterns of Apache-Mexican Hostilities in Northern Chihuahua Border Warfare, 1821-1848.* Albuquerque: University of New Mexico Press, 1989. Summarizes historical accounts of hostilities between the Chiricahua Apache and Mexican military forces in Northern Mexico.

Kraft, Louis. *Gatewood and Geronimo.* Albuquerque: University of New Mexico Press, 2000. Focuses on the events leading up to Geronimo's surrender.

Skimin, Robert. *Apache Autumn.* New York: St. Martin's Press, 1993. A historical novel that describes the Apache Wars.

Stockel, Henrietta H. *Survival of the Spirit: Chiricahua Apaches in Captivity.* Las Vegas: University of Nevada Press. Describes the history of Chiricahua captivity.

Articles of Agreement

Date: 1730
Locale: North America
Tribes involved: Cherokee
Categories: Colonial history, Treaties
Significance: Although not a major treaty between Indians and the English, the Articles of Agreement were unique in that they were engineered by one man and that the Cherokees went to England to sign it.

During the late 1720's, it became evident that stronger ties were needed between the English colonists and the Cherokee Nation. The increasing conflict between France and England over interests in North America necessitated that each country have the loyalty of Indian tribes.

Colonel George Chicken, English commissioner of Indian Affairs, obtained Cherokee loyalty. In 1728, when he left the Cherokee, several French emissaries began working within the tribe. The French influence among the Cherokees had become so great by 1730 that an alarmed English government dispatched Sir Alexander Cumming for the purpose of bringing the tribe into sure alliance. Upon Cumming's arrival in the province, a council of the entire Cherokee Nation was called to meet at Keowee, and allegiance was sealed with the English. The Cherokees' Nequasse crown, a construction of opossum fur and feathers, and some scalps and feathers were laid at Cumming's feet along with a request that they be delivered to the king of England. Six Cherokee chiefs were selected to accompany Cumming to England. A seventh chief, plus Indian trader Eleazer "Old Rabbit" Wiggins and an interpreter, joined them at the Port of Charleston on May 13, 1730. They set sail, landing in Dover in June. The seven Indians remained in England for three months, visiting all the important places and inciting curiosity among the English. They were presented to King George II on September 7 and gave him the crown and artifacts; each signed the Articles of Agreement, a treaty of friendship and commerce.

The treaty consisted of a preamble of friendship and devotion along with the following six provisions:

(1) The English and Cherokee shall live in peace and trade with each other. The Indians and English may live wherever they please, but the English are forbidden to live near the Cherokee towns. (For that pledge the Cherokees were given two pieces of white cloth, dyed red.)

(2) The Cherokee pledge to fight against any enemy of the English, white or red. (For that pledge the Cherokees were given twenty guns.)

(3) The Cherokee pledge not to interfere with other Indians trading with the English. (For that pledge the Cherokees were given four hundred pounds of gunpowder.)

(4) The Cherokee will not be permitted to trade with any other white nation nor allow any other nation to build forts or cabins, or even plant corn near them. (For that pledge the Cherokees were given five hundred pounds of shot and five hundred pounds of bullets.)

(5) The Cherokee will return any runaway "Negro slaves" to the English. For each returned slave, a reward of a gun and coat will be paid. (For that pledge the Cherokees were given ten thousand gun flints and six hatchets.)

(6) The English government, through English law, is responsible for the trial and punishment of an Englishman should he kill a Cherokee and a Cherokee if he should kill an Englishman. (For that pledge, the Cherokees were given twelve dozen spring knives, four brass kettles, and ten dozen belts.)

The 1730 Articles of Agreement had little influence on the entire Cherokee tribe. It was signed by only seven of their chiefs; to be binding on the entire tribe it needed the signatures of all chiefs. The seven chiefs returned to their people and told of the greatness and splendor of England, contrasting it to the primitiveness and struggles of the Cherokee people. As a result of this visit and treaty, the English acquired five years of allegiance from the Cherokee people.

See also: Cherokee legal cases; *Cherokee Phoenix; Cherokee Tobacco* case; Cherokee War; Indian Removal Act; Indian-white relations: English colonial; Indian-white relations: U.S., 1775-1830; Indian Removal Act; Trail of Tears; Yamasee War.

David N. Mielke

Bacon's Rebellion

Date: May 10-October 18, 1676
Locale: Eastern Virginia
Tribes involved: Doeg, Pamunkey, Susquehannock
Categories: Colonial history, Wars and battles
Significance: Colonial planters rise up against both Virginia's governor and Native Americans, causing destruction and death.

Instability was inherent in the rapid growth of the English population in Virginia after 1640. Competition for political power and social position increased after 1660, as the earlier settlers entrenched themselves in local political offices. Land hunger was also a problem: Since the end of the second Powhatan War in 1646, the Powhatans had held the land north of the York River, which had the effect of hemming in English expansion. Landownership was a requirement for the vote as well as the key to personal fortune. Later settlers, many of whom had come to Virginia as indentured servants, found high land prices and limited opportunities, and they began to view the land held by the Powhatans as the answer to their problem. At the same time, the return of the Susquehannocks to the northern Chesapeake area meant the extension of their war with the Iroquois into that area. That European settlers would be caught in the crossfire of this war was inevitable, and also helped fuel frustrations.

A prosperous economy might have counteracted unstable political and social conditions, but Virginia's economy stagnated after 1660. Chronic overproduction of an inferior quality of tobacco, aggravated by restrictive features of the Navigation Acts, drove the price of tobacco down. Expensive experimentation with methods of diversifying the economy and the need for defense measures against the Dutch and the natives resulted in high taxes. In 1674, the colonists were further taxed to send agents to London to lobby against proprietary land grants. Circumstances conspired to exacerbate the planters' miseries, and Governor Sir William Berkeley's ineffectual leadership led to a general disaffection toward the government. Berkeley's own comfortable circumstances, derived in part from a profitable monopoly in the fur trade with local tribes, seemed to prove his indifference to the planters' troubles.

The events immediately leading to the rebellion grew out of a dispute between a planter and members of the Doeg tribe in June, 1675. After forces of Virginians pursuing the Doegs murdered numbers of friendly Susquehannocks on two separate occasions, the natives increased the intensity of their raids throughout the fall and winter. Governor Berkeley angered the planters in the frontier settlements when he countermanded the order for a force to proceed against the marauding warriors. In keeping with Berkeley's overall American Indian policy, the Assembly committed the colony to a defensive war, and the governor ordered the erection of a chain of forts on the frontier. Berkeley's solution was no solution in the planters' view, as the forts would add to the burden of taxation and hemmed in further settlement. The settlers' worst fears about Berkeley had been confirmed.

The Planters' Uprising. In April, an impatient group of upcountry planters persuaded one of their number, Nathaniel Bacon, Jr., to lead a band of volunteers against the natives. What followed on May 10 was a war of extermination, in which Native Americans of all tribes, friendly or hostile, were killed. Bacon, the son of an English gentleman and related to Berkeley through marriage, had not arrived in Virginia until 1674, but he had already been appointed to the Council of State. Governor Berkeley refused Bacon's request for a commission to raise volunteers and sent several letters warning him against becoming a mutineer. Unable to head off Bacon with his force of three hundred men, Berkeley, on May 26, 1676, declared him a rebel. On the same day, the governor dissolved the Long Assembly and called for the first general elections in fifteen years, promising that the new Assembly would deal with the American Indian threat and any other grievances.

Bacon's success in killing some natives prompted the residents of Henrico County to send him to Jamestown as one of their new burgesses, but the governor ordered his capture before he could take his seat. Bacon confessed his error and received a pardon from the governor. Several days later, he slipped off to Henrico.

The June Assembly met for twenty days and passed a series of acts dealing with the prosecution of the war with the natives and with various local problems, especially concerning the misuse of political power. Although Bacon has often been credited with pushing through reform legislation, he did not return to Jamestown until June 23, when the session was nearly over. Arriving with five hundred armed men, he terrorized the governor and the burgesses into granting him a commission to fight the natives.

As soon as Bacon marched toward the falls of the James River, Berkeley again proclaimed him a rebel and tried to raise a force against him. Failing in his attempt, Berkeley fled to the eastern shore, leaving Bacon in control of the western shore. Upon arriving in Middle Plantation, Bacon issued a manifesto, the Declaration of the People, that accused the governor of numerous offenses against the colonists and called for his surrender. While Bacon then proceeded to seek out and fall upon the friendly Pamunkey Indians, Berkeley returned to Jamestown and, having reached agreement with Bacon's garrison, took possession of the capital. Several days later, Bacon arrived with six hundred troops and besieged the town. The faintheartedness of Berkeley's men forced the governor to concede the town. Bacon burned it on September 19. A little more than a month later, the rebellion fell apart at the news of Bacon's sudden death of the "bloody flux" and "lousey disease," possibly dysentery.

On January 29, the royal commissioners John Berry, Francis Moryson, and Herbert Jeffreys arrived from England, along with a thousand British soldiers, to investigate the uprising and restore order. Berkeley nullified the royal pardons that they brought for the rebels and ordered the execution of twenty-three men. His extreme cruelty was criticized by the commissioners, and Sir Herbert Jeffreys formally took over the government in April upon Berkeley's recall by the Crown. Although Bacon was dead, the disorder and protest would not end until 1683, with the reconfiguring of imperial government in Virginia.

See also: Indian slave trade; Metacom's War; Powhatan Confederacy; Powhatan Wars.

Warren M. Billings, updated by Kelley Graham

Sources for Further Study

Fausz, J. Frederick. "Merging and Emerging Worlds: Anglo-Indian Interest Groups and the Development of the Seventeenth-Century Chesapeake." In *Colonial Chesapeake Society*, edited by Lois Green Carr et al. Chapel Hill: University of North Carolina Press, 1988. Details the changing English view of the Native Americans in the Chesapeake from "noble savages" to important trading partners.

Horn, James. *Adapting to a New World: English Society in the Seventeenth-Century Chesapeake*. Chapel Hill: University of North Carolina Press, 1994. A scholarly but lively study of the extent to which English colonists in the Chesapeake were influenced by their homeland in their attitudes about race, authority, and other matters.

Middlekauff, Robert. *Bacon's Rebellion*. Chicago: Rand McNally, 1964. A good collection of the primary documents associated with the uprising, beginning with Berkeley's American Indian policy and concluding with the official report submitted to London.

Tate, Thad W., and David L. Ammerman. *The Chesapeake in the Seventeenth Century: Essays on the Anglo-American Society*. Chapel Hill: University of North Carolina Press, 1979. An essential collection of articles addressing race relations, class structure, and the demographics of the seventeenth century Chesapeake. Includes a historiographic discussion of Bacon's Rebellion.

Washburn, Wilcomb E. *The Governor and the Rebel*. Chapel Hill: University of North Carolina Press, 1957. A classic study of the small details of the uprising; generous in its forgiveness of Governor Berkeley.

Webb, Stephen Saunders. *1676: The End of American Independence*. Cambridge, Mass.: Harvard University Press, 1985. Places the rebellion in a larger context, as a prerevolutionary condition, while providing a detailed study of the events of 1676-1677.

Bannock War

Date: 1878
Locale: Idaho and Oregon
Tribes involved: Bannock, Paiute, Sheepeater, Umatilla
Categories: Nineteenth century history, Reservations and relocation, Wars and battles

Significance: The Bannock War ended a series of resistance efforts by the northern mountain tribes of the Idaho/Oregon/Wyoming area and resulted in permanent relocation to reservations.

The Bannocks, a northern mountain branch of the Paiute language group, originally occupied the mountain areas of southern Idaho and northwestern Wyoming. In the 1850's they had accepted treaties that limited their area to southern Idaho. During the 1850's, raids by Bannock, Shoshone, Paiute, and others occurred often along the trails to Oregon and California. By the 1860 Pyramid Lake and 1863 Bear Paw campaigns and the victories of George Crook in the Snake War of 1866-1868, European Americans were in control of the area and the Bannock had peacefully begun drawing meager rations that amounted to two and a half cents per person per day. They supplemented this with their traditional hunting and gathering.

The 1877 escape attempt by their northern neighbors, the Nez Perce, caused considerable upset among the Bannock, but they did not join the resistance that year. The immediate cause of the Bannock War of 1878 was the issue of digging camas roots on the Camas Prairie, located about 90 miles southeast of Fort Boise. The right to dig camas roots had been guaranteed by earlier treaties, but hogs owned by white settlers were now eating many of the roots. In May, a Bannock wounded two whites, an event that led to the creation of a two-hundred-man war party under Buffalo Horn. This unit was defeated by Idaho volunteers, and Buffalo Horn was killed in June. The warriors moved to southeastern Oregon and joined Paiute from the Malheur Agency under the leadership of Chief Egan and medicine man Oyte. The regular army units from Fort Boise were mobilized under General Oliver O. Howard. A chase through southern Idaho and eastern Oregon ended with the defeat of the Indians at Birch Creek, Oregon, on July 8, 1878. Some of the Indians escaped to the Umatilla Agency near Pendleton, Oregon, where Chief Egan was killed by the Umatillas, and the rebels were betrayed and captured. Another smaller group of Bannock had escaped and were captured east of Yellowstone Park in September, 1878.

A subsidiary war developed with the smaller Sheepeater group in the extremely rugged Salmon River Mountains of central Idaho. The fifty warriors eluded the cavalry under Captain Reuben Bernard and defeated another unit under Lieutenant Henry Catley, but persistent tracking forced their surrender in October, 1878.

The Paiute reservation at Malheur in southeastern Oregon was terminated and the Paiute prisoners were placed on the Yakima reservation in central Washington. The Bannock were held at various military posts for a time and then returned to their reservation on the Snake River in southern Idaho, where the Sheepeaters soon joined them. Except for some outbreaks by the Ute to the south, this ended the northern mountain Indian wars.

See also: Bear River Campaign; Indian-white relations: U.S., 1871-1933; National Indian Association; Nez Perce War; Snake War.

Fred S. Rolater

Bear River Campaign

Date: 1863
Locale: Idaho
Tribes involved: Bannock, Shoshone
Categories: Nineteenth century history, Wars and battles
Significance: Like the Sand Creek Massacre, the Bear River Campaign exemplified the antagonistic nature of military leadership when state militias replaced federal troops in the West during the Civil War.

At the beginning of the Civil War (1861-1865), some 2,500 federal troops under General Albert Sydney Johnston left Utah to fight in the East. Utah Territory, like the West in general at the time, was placed militarily under a volunteer state militia. The regarrisoning of Utah fell to the volatile California businessman and former Mexican-American War veteran Colonel Patrick Edward Connor. Connor organized his California volunteers, numbering about a thousand, and marched them to Salt Lake City in 1862 to assume the task of policing the Overland Mail Route across Utah. Connor held even more contempt for American Indians than he did for the Mormons, and both experienced his fiery temper and decisive, vicious action. At one time Connor had a number of Indians hanged or shot, leaving their bodies exposed as an example.

At the time, the Shoshone and Bannock held a somewhat amicable relationship with the Mormon settlers, but occasionally they committed depredations on the Oregon and California trails as well as on the mail and telegraph routes—enough to cause Connor to muster his energies against them. Connor dispersed his forces throughout the region in an attempt to control the Indians, yet reports of belligerent activity continued. Incensed, Connor determined to deliver a decisive blow to the Shoshone and Bannock.

In the dead of winter, he marched a detachment of three hundred men, mostly cavalry, northward from Salt Lake City to attack the village of Shoshone leader Bear Hunter on the Bear River near Preston, Idaho. At daybreak on January 27, 1863, the Shoshone were in wait as Connor pressed his attack. About two-thirds of Connor's men forded the ice-choked Bear River and commenced a frontal assault on the village, but they met heavy resistance. Connor sent detachments to flank the village, thus trapping the Indians in the large ravine where they were wintering. As troops sealed off any escape routes, others swept over the rims of the ravine, pouring a murderous volley into the encampment. The Shoshone fought back desperately, having no alternative. Most were slain defending their positions. Others, who attempted to escape, were shot trying to swim the icy river. By mid-morning the fight was over.

Connor's troops counted 224 bodies, including that of Bear Hunter, though the death toll was higher. The troopers destroyed the village (seventy lodges), seized 175 ponies, and captured more than 150 women and children, who were then left in the razed village with a small store of food. Connor's losses were only 14 dead, 53 wounded, and 75 with frostbite. Connor's attack upon the village gained him the War Department's praise as well as quick promotion to brigadier general. Today the Bear River Campaign is perceived in much the same light as the Sand Creek Massacre: as an act of pointless, excessive bloodshed.

See also: Bannock War; Indian-white relations: U.S., 1871-1933; National Indian Association; Nez Perce War; Snake War.

S. Matthew Despain

Beaver Wars

Date: 1642-1685
Locale: Northeastern woodlands, from the Hudson River west to the Great Lakes and from the Ohio River north to Ontario
Tribes involved: Huron, Iroquois Confederacy
Categories: Colonial history, Wars and battles
Significance: The Iroquois Five Nations challenge the French-Huron trade monopoly, leading to large-scale intertribal warfare.

During the seventeenth century, the principal mode of subsistence for the Iroquois changed from farming to trapping. After the Iroquois had traded successfully with the Dutch for several decades, a seemingly insatiable demand for furs to make fashionable top hats for European gentlemen had depleted the Iroquois' source of beaver pelts. Meanwhile, the French had become allies with the Algonquians and Hurons to the north, establishing a lucrative monopoly on the fur trade in the upper Great Lakes. Acting as middlemen, the Hurons bought huge quantities of furs from the Ottawa, then sold them to the French. Seeking an expedient solution to the problem of a diminishing supply of furs, the Iroquois began attacking Huron villages and intercepting and confiscating fur shipments along trade routes, provoking a series of conflicts known as the Beaver Wars.

The name "Iroquois" refers both to the members of the Iroquois Confederacy, or League of Five Nations (Senecas, Cayugas, Onondagas, Oneidas, and Mohawks), and to their language. Consolidation of the league in 1570 (although it had existed informally for several decades before that) helped end centuries of warring among these neighboring tribes and protected them from attacks by surrounding tribes. Although known throughout the woodlands as fierce warriors, the Iroquois had met European advances into their territory peacefully and created profitable alliances, such as their trade agreement with the Dutch at Albany.

In 1608, French explorer Samuel de Champlain established Quebec at a deserted Iroquois site on the St. Lawrence River. In the area, the Huron Confederacy of four tribes and their Algonquian allies began a trade agreement with the French that was coveted by the Iroquois. This rivalry increased long-existing hostility between Hurons and Iroquois.

In July, 1609, Champlain, two soldiers, and sixty Algonquians and Hurons followed a war party of two hundred Mohawks along what is now called Lake Champlain. In the traditional manner, both sides agreed to engage in battle in the morning. Iroquois warriors preferred close-in fighting with wooden clubs and leather shields, and were accustomed to using bows and arrows only for ambushes. As the battle began, both sides advanced, but the French remained hidden among the Hurons. Advancing closely, the French fired their guns, killing two Mohawk chiefs instantly and mortally wounding the third. Many Mohawks died and a dozen captives were taken, one of whom was tortured during the victory celebration. This dramatic battle was the Iroquois' first encounter with Europeans and their dreadful weapons. Their humiliation left the Iroquois with a fierce hatred of the French. A few weeks later, Henry Hudson arrived at Albany to initiate the Dutch fur trade, which eventually brought guns to the Iroquois.

Wars of Attrition. In the next three decades, the Hurons and Iroquois lost many warriors in battle. The Jesuit priests who brought Christianity to

Quebec also brought European diseases. By 1640, through warfare and epidemics, only ten thousand Hurons remained, less than half of their previous number. However, they retained their alliance with the French. Iroquois offers of peace with the Hurons were dissuaded by the French. In 1640, five hundred Iroquois approached a French village to negotiate for peace and trade a French captive for guns. When French offers were not acceptable, the council disbanded and the Iroquois began planning for war.

Early Iroquois warfare was guerrilla-style fighting by small bands, so the beginning date of the Beaver Wars is difficult to determine, but an attack by a Seneca war party on the Huron village of Arendaronon in 1642 is marked as the first event. Iroquois also raided the Algonquian village of Chief Iroquet on the Ottawa River, capturing and later releasing Father Isaac Jogues.

In 1645, the French bargained for peace, using Iroquois captives. The Iroquois wanted to share the middleman role with the Hurons and continue trading with the Dutch. At the council, the great Mohawk orator Kiotsaeton appealed to the French, Hurons, and Algonquians, presenting fifteen wampum belts. He translated the symbolic messages coded in the shell beads. After the council, Father Jogues and Father Paul Le Junne continued to support the peace effort.

Months later, some Mohawks reported to Huron chief Tandihetsi about secrecy and intrigue involving the possible exclusion of the Algonquians. The chief had a wife and many relatives among the Algonquians. Finally, a trade-related treaty was made, honored for a time, then broken when a huge shipment of furs passed down the Ottawa River and the Iroquois were given no share. In retaliation, the popular Father Jogues was killed when he returned to visit a Mohawk village.

European presence in North America affected Iroquois social and cultural systems that had provided earlier stability. Ecological balance was upset by the high demand for beaver pelts; economic balance, by the shift from farming to trapping; and political balance, by rivalries among tribes. The Iroquois had become dependent upon the Dutch for food, metal tools, weapons, and ammunition. Since the primary commodity was beaver pelts and the agreement had been broken, the Iroquois began attacking Huron villages and intercepting travel along their trade routes, confiscating whole shipments of pelts. In times of warfare, one gun was well worth the price of twenty beaver pelts.

Huron Defeat. By March, 1649, the Iroquois had declared open warfare, and a thousand Iroquois set out for the Huron homeland. The starving Hurons, fearing annihilation, burned their villages and escaped into the woods, some to a Jesuit encampment, others divided into clan groups. Eventually, several thousand Hurons were adopted into the five Iroquois tribes. By late 1649, the Iroquois had defeated the Tobaccos; from 1650 to 1656, they warred against the Neutrals on the Niagara peninsula and the Eries on southern Lake Erie, devastating them and taking over their hunting territories. They successfully maintained trade with the Dutch under Governor Peter Stuyvesant.

By 1654, the Ottawas had taken over the Hurons' position as middlemen for the French. When the Iroquois attempted to displace them, the Ottawas moved westward to the Straits of Mackinac. For the next thirty years, they supplied two-thirds of the furs sent to France. By 1670, the Iroquois controlled the woodland territory surrounding the eastern Great Lakes, while the French claimed Lakes Huron and Superior.

In 1680, several hundred Iroquois invaded the territory of the Illinois and Miami tribes. In 1684, an unsuccessful attempt to take Fort St. Louis from Illinois marked the end of the nearly century-long Iroquois campaign to overturn the French-Huron trade monopoly.

During the Beaver Wars, the Iroquois had established a political agreement with the English through Governor Edmond Andros. This Covenant Chain was forged for two purposes: safe access to Albany for Iroquois traders and easy entry into the natives' affairs for the English. By 1685, the League of Five Nations had been consolidated to deal with external affairs.

Leagues, alliances, treaties, covenants, and confederacies all worked against the Europeans' establishing a niche in the New World. The powers of France and England had been balanced almost equally for many years, but long-held Iroquois hostility turned the scale against the French, and their magnificent schemes of colonization in the northern part of America were lost. Had it not been for the determination of the Iroquois, the official language throughout North America might have been French.

See also: Fur trade; Indian-white relations: Dutch colonial; Indian-white relations: French colonial; Iroquois Confederacy.

Gale M. Thompson

Sources for Further Study

Brandao, Jose. *Your Fyre Shall Burn No More: Iroquois Policy Toward New France and its Allies to 1701.* Lincoln: University of Nebraska Press, 1997. Offers a revisionist stance toward the Beaver Wars, arguing that the Iroquois were more interested in taking captives to replenish their disease-ravaged populations than in obtaining beaver skins for trade.

Cleland, Charles E. *Rites of Conquest: The History and Culture of Michigan's Native Americans*. Ann Arbor: University of Michigan Press, 1992. A multiethnic, regional approach to the history of the Ojibwa, Ottawa, and Potawatomi, from precontact to the late twentieth century. Maps, photographs, biographical sketches, chapter notes, bibliography, index.

Grinde, Donald A., Jr. *The Iroquois and the Founding of the American Nation*. San Francisco: Indian Historian Press, 1977. Provides cultural and historical background; discusses Iroquois relationships with colonists before and after the American Revolution. Photographs, maps, illustrations, references, sources. Constitution of the Five Nations and Albany Plan of Union are included as appendices.

Harvey, Karen D., and Lisa D. Harjo. *Indian Country: A History of Native People in America*. Golden, Colo.: North American Press, 1994. Written and illustrated by American Indians. Presents ten culture areas, historical perspectives, contemporary issues, major ceremonies, and time lines from 50,000 B.C.E. to the twentieth century. Summaries, lesson plans, resources, and index; appendices include "Threats to Religious Freedom," the text of the Fort Laramie Treaty of 1868, and a list of Indian activist organizations and events.

Steele, Ian K. *Warpaths: Invasions of North America*. New York: Oxford University Press, 1994. Discusses American Indian-European warfare in eastern North America, from the defeat of Juan Ponce de León (1513) to negotiated peace with the British (1765); combines social and military history for a balanced perspective. Maps, illustrations, extensive chapter notes, index.

Bering Strait migrations

Date: Beginning c. 10,000 B.C.E.
Locale: Bering Strait, between Siberia and Alaska
Tribes involved: Paleo-Indians
Categories: Pre-Columbian history
Significance: The first humans arrive in the Western Hemisphere.

About two million years ago, for reasons not entirely understood, Earth's temperature began to fall. In the north, more snow fell in winter than melted in summer, and great sheets of ice formed on the landmasses. These glaciers went through a series of advances and retreats—sliding forward under the influence of gravity and melting back under warmer climatic conditions.

At the same time, a group of primates (monkeys, apes, and their relatives) was evolving in Africa. The group of interest had already developed the ability to walk on their hind limbs rather than on four feet, thus freeing the forelimbs for functions other than locomotion. Climatic change had initiated a drying trend in Africa, replacing rain forests with grasslands and savannas. Several species of the two-legged primate group had successfully invaded the grassland environment and spread throughout Africa. Well into the ice age, late-developing species migrated north into Europe and Asia, using tools, animal skins, and especially fire to cope with the cold. Some members of one species, today called *Homo sapiens* (literally, "wise human"), eventually moved into frigid Siberian environments.

Eastern Siberia and western Alaska were not covered by glaciers, even at the height of glacial advance. Although the climate in these unglaciated regions was cold, a number of large mammal species (mammoths, mastodons, giant bison, and others) had invaded the northern environment ahead of the humans. The newcomers probably used many food sources, but they became especially skilled at hunting the large animals.

Tremendous amounts of water were required to build the continental glaciers. That water came primarily from the most abundant source of water on the planet, the oceans. As a result, each advance and retreat of the glaciers was accompanied by dramatic changes in sea level—the sea rose as glaciers melted, and fell with each glacial advance. Today, only about fifty miles of water separate Siberia from Alaska across the Bering Strait. The Bering Strait is less than two hundred feet deep, and the adjacent parts of the Chukchi and Bering seas are not much deeper. Because of this, a strip of Bering Strait and adjacent sea floor one thousand miles wide became dry land whenever extensive glaciation occurred. Along with adjacent parts of Siberia and Alaska, this region is called Beringia. When the glaciers were in full retreat, the Bering Strait reformed, splitting Beringia and placing a barrier between the two continents.

The sea level rose and fell throughout glacial times, and the connection between Alaska and Siberia was established and broken repeatedly. Various land organisms crossed the bridge when it was available, but exchange between the continents was blocked when it was inundated. Mammoths, mastodons, camels, horses, and many other species of animals and plants

Bering Strait Migrations

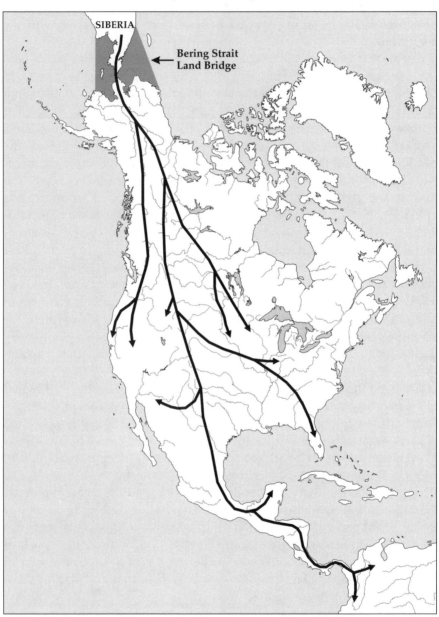

As early as 15,000 B.C.E., during a period when the huge ice sheet covering the top half of North America had retreated, indigenous peoples from Siberia began to make their way across a land bridge that today is the Bering Strait. Eventually, traveling between glaciers, they reached eastern, central, and southern North America and Mesoamerica.

crossed throughout the ice age, but humans probably did not reach northeastern Siberia until the most recent glacial advance.

In North America, the last glacier (the Wisconsin) advanced until approximately sixty thousand years ago, at which time it began a retreat called the "mid-Wisconsin interglacial." Fewer than thirty thousand years ago, it began its final advance (the late Wisconsin glaciation) followed by its most recent retreat, which began eighteen thousand years ago. It was during or after the mid-Wisconsin interglacial that humans from Siberia made their way across Beringia into North America.

The Post-Glacial Period. This migration was not a directed, purposeful movement to a new continent. It is unlikely that the first Americans had any sense of their role in history or the nature of continents. The migration probably was the simple result of growing populations expanding into new regions, perhaps drawn by the presence of herds of the large mammals they were so adept at hunting.

The populations continued to expand throughout Alaska and adjacent Canada but were restricted from much of Canada by two major glacial masses. The Laurentide ice sheet covered most of Canada and much of the northern United States, from the east coast to the Rocky Mountains. The second mass of ice resulted from the coalescence of a number of mountain glaciers into a single glacial complex, the Cordilleran glacier, located between the Rockies and the coastal mountain ranges.

During glacial advance, the two ice masses probably met and blocked the migrants' route south. However, when the glaciers melted, a corridor opened between them. The migrants moved south through Mexico and Central America, and on to the tip of South America. As the most recent glacial retreat continued, the first Americans expanded their range into all parts of Canada as well.

Paleo-Indians. Anthropologists and archaeologists call these first Americans (or their immediate descendants) Paleo-Indians. Many details of relationship and pathways of descent are not known, but the Paleo-Indian culture gave rise to another widespread culture, called the Archaic, around 7000 B.C.E. Approximately two thousand years ago, the Archaic culture began to give way to the mound-building culture of eastern North America (the Adena, Hopewell, and Mississippian), the agricultural groups of the southwestern deserts (the Hohokam, Mogollon, and Anasazi), and other cultures. Some time before 1500 C.E., these prehistoric cultures gave rise to the Native American tribes that were later displaced by European settlement. A similar sequence of cultural replacement took place in Mexico and

Central and South America, culminating in the Inca, Aztec, and Mayan civilizations that were later decimated by the Spanish conquistadores in the 1500's.

One of the most vituperative arguments in the history of science centers on the question of when the first Americans arrived. A few students of the question argue for dates earlier than the mid-Wisconsin interglacial, many argue for entry times more than thirty thousand years ago (during the mid-Wisconsin interglacial), but most favor a time somewhat more than twelve thousand years ago (during the Wisconsin glacier's retreat).

The basis for the most popular position is the absence of strong evidence for earlier human occupation of the continent. The widespread occurrence of a particular type of spear point found at archaeological sites all over North America, sites determined to be between 11,500 and 10,500 years old, is the first irrefutable and extensive evidence of such occupation. These sites constitute the first recognized North American Paleo-Indian culture, now called the Clovis culture because it was established on the basis of finds in Blackwater Draw near Clovis, New Mexico. Because the culture was so widespread, archaeologists assume that Native Americans must have been on the continent some time before the Clovis dates. Some believe that a thousand years is enough time for the first immigrants to have spread from Beringia to Tierra del Fuego and throughout both continents; others think a longer time was required.

Evidence based on Native American languages, tooth anatomy, and genetics suggests that there were at least three migrations of different Siberian peoples into North America. The first group of migrants gave rise to most Native American groups. One of the later migrant groups was ancestral to the Navajo, Apache, and some western Canadian tribes; the Eskimo (Inuit) and Aleut peoples derived from the other group. Each migration probably involved movement of many subgroups through an extended time period. Some archaeologists believe that marine travelers, along the coast or across open seas, may have contributed to the colonization as well.

The timing and details of the colonization of North America are unsettled, but most archaeologists agree on its basic character. Northern Asiatic people crossed Beringia into North America some time before twelve thousand years ago and spread fairly rapidly throughout North and South America. These people, with possible contributions from later (and earlier) immigrants, developed into the multitude of Native American groups present when Europeans "discovered" the continents. Ancestors of the Native Americans who met the European explorers and colonists some five hundred years ago had occupied the Americas for more than twelve thousand years.

See also: Prehistory: Arctic; Prehistory: California; Prehistory: Great Basin; Prehistory: Northeast; Prehistory: Northwest Coast; Prehistory: Plains; Prehistory: Plateau; Prehistory: Southeast; Prehistory: Southwest; Prehistory: Subarctic.

Carl W. Hoagstrom

Sources for Further Study

Dillehay, Thomas D. *The Settlement of the Americas: A New Prehistory.* New York: Basic Books, 2001. Offers the archaeological and anthropological evidence for population of the Americas prior to the glaciation twenty thousand years ago.

Dillehay, Tom D., and David J. Meltzer. *The First Americans: Search and Research.* Boca Raton, Fla.: Chemical Rubber Company Press, 1991. A set of papers written to explore and encourage exploration of the total context of migrations into North America. Illustrations, reference lists.

Dixon, E. James. *Quest for the Origins of the First Americans.* Albuquerque: University of New Mexico Press, 1993. An archaeologist discusses the first Americans in the context of his own research. Illustrations, index, bibliography.

Fagan, Brian M. *Ancient North America: The Archaeology of a Continent.* Rev. ed. New York: Thames and Hudson, 1995. A consideration of the first Americans in the context of North American archaeology. Illustrations, index, bibliography.

Fladmark, Knut R. "Getting One's Berings." *Natural History* 95, no. 11 (November, 1986): 8-19. The first of thirteen articles on the peopling of North America published in *Natural History* between November, 1986, and January, 1988. Illustrations.

Thomas, David Hurst. *Exploring Ancient Native America: An Archaeological Guide.* New York: Macmillan, 1994. An outline of Native American prehistory and a guide to accessible sites. Illustrations, index, appendix of sites to visit, bibliography.

Bison slaughter

Date: Peaked 1872-1874
Locale: Great Plains
Tribes involved: Cheyenne, Crow, Lakota Sioux
Categories: Nineteenth century history

Significance: Mass killings of buffalo lead to the near-extinction of the species and destroy the lifeblood of the Plains Indians.

In 1853, the American bison population was estimated at between sixty and seventy million animals. It was reduced to a few thousand in thirty years. The bison's decline was the result of human greed, uncontrolled exploitation, and United States government policy. Also called the American buffalo, the bison ranged throughout North America from the Rocky Mountains to the Atlantic shoreline and from northern Mexico to southern Canada. Its greatest concentration was on the grasslands of the Great Plains. It was the basis for a total way of life for the Native Americans. The animals provided food, clothing, and shelter. An important part of the nomadic plains tribes' culture was the buffalo-hide tipi, which could be collapsed quickly when the tribe was ready to move on. On the treeless plains, the herds' dried droppings were fuel for the cooking fires.

On the northern Great Plains, where the terrain was rugged, a herd feeding near a cliff would be driven over the precipice by Indian men and boys waving buffalo robes and shouting, an event known as a buffalo jump. The

The bison, which formed the basis for the economy of many Native Americans, once roved the Great Plains in large herds, but during the 1870's the incursion of the railroads hastened their demise as thousands were helplessly slaughtered by white "buffalo hunters," engaging in the activity for sport as well as profit. (Library of Congress)

waiting tribe rushed in to butcher as many of the animals as they could. Frequently, many more animals were left dead or dying than could be handled. Contemporaneous writers described the slaughter of from two hundred to two thousand bison in such hunts. However, because of the relatively small population of Native Americans in North America and their primitive weapons, the impact on the bison was slight.

With the end of the Civil War, in April, 1865, army troops traveled west to battle the Cheyenne, Lakota Sioux, and Crow. The army contracted with local settlers to supply the troops with "buffalo beef." Workers constructing the new transcontinental railroad also had to be fed. Contractors included William F. Cody, better known as Buffalo Bill, probably the best-recognized of all the bison killers. Hunters frequently skinned the bison, cut out the tongue, and took only some of the meat, leaving the remainder to rot on the prairie.

Bison Products. Dressed hides were shipped east as lap robes for winter sleigh and buggy rides or were turned into overcoats. Highly romanticized stories by eastern writers about the exploits of Buffalo Bill and other bison hunters quickly made buffalo robes a status symbol. Demand increased and more bison were slaughtered. Often only the skin was taken, the carcass left to scavengers. Hundreds of thousands of bison were killed each year for food and hides.

Bison also were killed for sport, as it became popular for groups of people to travel to the Great Plains simply to shoot bison. The railroads that linked the East and West cut across the ancient north-south routes of the bison. The seemingly endless herds were an annoyance to the train crews and a temptation to the passengers. When trains were delayed, passengers fired into the massed animals, killing some and wounding many more. The railroads encouraged this, with advertising to induce people to ride their trains.

Extent of Slaughter. It is difficult to obtain accurate data on the number of bison slaughtered. Few records were kept and the killing took place over a wide area. In 1872, in western Kansas, approximately two thousand hide hunters were each bringing down about fifteen bison a day. At that rate, hunters were killing thirty thousand bison per day. As soon as the herds in one area were reduced beyond the point of diminishing returns, the hunters moved elsewhere, seeking larger herds. An 1869 report notes that in a good year, about two hundred fifty thousand hides were shipped to the New York market alone. Railroad shipments between 1872 and 1874 totaled 1,378,359 hides.

A peculiarity in the behavior of the bison made them easy targets for hunters. Although bison could be stampeded, hunters in ambush could pick off the animals one by one, because they simply stood as others were shot and dropped in place. Hide hunters called it "a stand." Some of the herd nosed at their fallen comrades and then calmly joined the rest of the animals in grazing. A good hunter could kill seventy-five to one hundred bison per day. One especially skillful hunter, in a bet with his fellows and shooting at a stand from ambush, killed one hundred twenty bison in forty minutes.

The slaughter of the bison was far from a managed or controlled affair. Hunters indiscriminately shot the adults and subadults. Calves were ignored except, possibly, for camp meat. Unweaned, orphaned calves, not yet able to graze the abundant grasses, were left to starve to death. After one particularly large herd was killed, five hundred to one thousand calves wandered off to starve.

The United States government took the position that the still-warring Native Americans could be subdued if the bison were denied to them. The U.S. Army began a program of interdiction of the herds. General Philip Sheridan spoke out strongly in favor of continuing the slaughter of the buffalo "to settle the Indian question." Sheridan's Civil War comrade, General William Sherman, echoed these sentiments. He stated that the only way to force the Native Americans to reservations and turn them into farmers was to clear the prairies of the bison. The government further supported the bison slaughter by providing free ammunition to any buffalo hunter on request.

As early as 1873, fewer and fewer bison were encountered in western Kansas. Hide hunters moved to the northern Great Plains territories and continued the slaughter. The decline spread throughout the range of the bison, and it soon became obvious to most observers that the great herds were gone.

Aftereffects. The intensive slaughter for hides was brief, occurring mostly from 1872 to 1874, but the activity extended from 1871 through 1883. Most herds were shot out in about four years, and the hunters then moved on to other areas. Although a few bison survived, undoubtedly the species' numbers had slipped below that level ecologists call the minimum viable population size. For many animals, more than one male and one female are required to begin a breeding population. The great slaughter left the prairies littered with bison skeletons. For years, farmers could gather a cartload or two of bones and sell them to processors for fertilizer. One bone buyer estimated that from 1884 to 1891, he bought the bones of approximately six million bison skeletons.

Neither the settlers nor the Native Americans could believe that the bison was no more. The settlers thought that the herds had migrated to Canada and would soon return. The Native Americans, drawing on their mythology, believed the animals had returned to a great cavern in the ground to reappear if the right prayers were said and the right supplications were made. The great herds were, however, gone. The impact of the hide hunters' indiscriminate slaughter and the U.S. government's interdiction policy eliminated not only the bison but also the Native American's traditional nomadic way of life. Reluctantly, but with resignation, they became farmers on reservations as the U.S. government had sought. Perhaps the worst blow to the plains Indians was their loss of the religious and cultural relationship with the bison. Their entire civilization and lifeways had been destroyed along with the animals on which they depended.

Only a few scattered bison and some in private herds escaped the slaughter. Today, brought together in national parks, preserves, and other protected areas, they have survived and multiplied.

Buffalo Depletion from 1850 to 1895

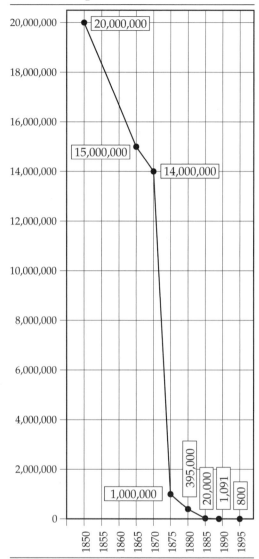

Note: In the twentieth century the buffalo population began to rebound from its 1895 low of about 800; in 1983 it was estimated at 50,000.

Source: Data are from Thornton, Russell, *American Indian Holocaust and Survival: A Population History Since 1492* (Norman: University of Oklahoma Press, 1987); Thornton, Russell, *We Shall Live Again: The 1870 and 1890 Ghost Dance Movements as Demographic Revitalization* (New York: Cambridge University Press, 1986).

See also: Indian-white relations: U.S., 1871-1933; Sioux War.

Albert C. Jensen

Sources for Further Study

Dary, David A. *The Buffalo Book: The Full Saga of the American Animal*. Chicago: Swallow Press, 1974. Detailed account of bison in North America. Black-and-white photos, index, bibliography.

Foster, John, ed. *Buffalo*. Edmonton, Canada: University of Alberta Press, 1992. A short collection of papers by specialists in ecology and sociology detailing the relationship between the plains Indians and the American bison. Illustrations.

Isenberg, Andrew C. *The Destruction of the Bison: An Environmental History, 1750-1920*. New York: Cambridge University Press, 2001. A study of the human and ecological factors leading to the near-extinction of the bison.

McHugh, Tom. *The Time of the Buffalo*. New York: Alfred A. Knopf, 1972. A factual, readable revision of a professional wildlife biologist's dissertation. Illustrations, index, and detailed bibliography.

Matthews, Anne. *Where the Buffalo Roam*. New York: Grove Weidenfeld, 1992. Describes a plan to restore the Great Plains to their natural condition and the bison to their former numbers. Illustrations and index.

Russell, Don. *The Lives and Legends of Buffalo Bill*. Norman: University of Oklahoma Press, 1960. A detailed examination of the Army scout and bison hunter. Footnotes, extensive bibliography, index, illustrations.

Black Hawk War

Date: 1832
Locale: Illinois and Wisconsin
Tribes involved: Fox, Sauk, Winnebago
Categories: Nineteenth century history, Wars and battles
Significance: Defeated by U.S. troops, the Sauks, Fox, and Winnebagos lost most of their land in futile resistance to white settlement.

Into the early nineteenth century, the Sauks, Fox, and Winnebagos were relatively free of white pressure, most warfare being against such enemies as the Sioux or Osage. Their traditional world remained strong until the post-

An engraving of the Battle of Bad Axe, the fight that ended the Black Hawk War on August 2, 1832. (Library of Congress)

revolutionary decades. Yet soon American settlers, migrating west in steady streams, threatened to destroy the old ways.

Historical Background. Fleeing powerful eastern rivals, the Sauks (Black Hawk's people) and their main allies, the Fox (Mesquakies), had migrated into parts of Michigan, Wisconsin, Illinois, and Iowa by the late 1600's. They became farmers and trappers, trading regularly with the French, whose hunger for furs and competition with the British would embroil the tribes in warfare.

By the time of Black Hawk's birth in 1776, the Sauks were settled near present-day Rock Island, Illinois, and in eastern Iowa. His childhood and youth were years of seasonal moves dictated by farming, fishing, and trapping. Frequent warfare gave warriors a high status within the tribe, and Black Hawk joined a war party at fifteen, seeking family and tribal respect. By his thirties, he was a premier war leader and a committed traditionalist who, at a terrible cost to his people, would resist change.

Before 1800, neither the Sauks nor the Mesquakies had signed a peace treaty with the United States, resenting bitterly the seeming American favoritism toward the hated Osages. In 1804, however, the United States, Sauk, and Mesquakie leaders signed a treaty wherein the chiefs ceded fifty million acres of land. Disregarding any Indian rights, white settlers poured into the territory. They burned Indian homes and cornfields while the Indians received neither adequate compensation nor protection from the federal government. Black Hawk protested, claiming that the chiefs had not understood the full implications of the 1804 treaty and that his people were being cheated.

Tribal cohesion was splintering among the Sauks and the Mesquakies. Traditionalists—with Black Hawk as their main spokesman—wanted to retain the old ways and therefore sought to resist the Americans. Nontraditionalists—led by a young Sauk warrior named Keokuk—called for accommodation with the Americans. Keokuk had visited Washington and feared the strength of the government, but Black Hawk and his followers, relatively isolated, refused to compromise.

The rivalry between Black Hawk and Keokuk broke the Sauks into factions; gradually Keokuk's influence grew stronger. In a council held at Prairie du Chien in 1825, Keokuk was a major spokesman for the Sauks and the Mesquakies. Black Hawk refused to attend and brushed aside the council's decisions for peace. He was further enraged when, in 1827, the government began plans to remove all Indians from Illinois as of 1829.

The 1832 War. White squatters moved into Saukenuk, Black Hawk's home and the major Sauk village. In July, 1829, the United States General Land Office announced that the land around Saukenuk would go on sale in October. Black Hawk and his people—some three hundred warriors and their families—vowed to reoccupy their land. General Edmund P. Gaines, commander of the army's Western Department in St. Louis, led troops to the area.

Gaines and Black Hawk confronted each other, the latter insisting that the treaty of 1804 was invalid and that he would not leave Saukenuk. Gaines, in turn, warned that he was there to enforce the treaty, either peacefully or by force. Keokuk persuaded some Indian families to join his peace faction, but Black Hawk resisted removal, counting on aid from nearby Winnebagos and Potawatomis.

On June 25, 1831, soldiers attacked Saukenuk at dawn. Black Hawk and his followers had left during the night, crossing to the west side of the Mississippi. His village in ruins, Black Hawk signed a peace treaty with Gaines on June 30. Gaines then ordered white settlers at Rock River to provide the Indians with corn. Only token amounts were sent, however, and Black Hawk's band faced starvation.

Convinced by his chief lieutenant, Napope, that the British would assist him and that the Potawatomis and Chippewas were also ready to enlist, Black Hawk chose to go to war. By early 1832 he commanded some six hundred warriors and prepared to retake Saukenuk. Hoping to defuse the situation, General Henry Atkinson called on friendly Sauk and Mesquakie chiefs to negotiate and warned that if Black Hawk crossed to the east side of the Mississippi his troops would attack. Neither the Potawatomis nor the Winnebagos gave Black Hawk the help he expected.

General Atkinson had mustered more than 1,700 Illinois militia into federal service in early May, 1832, combining them with his regular army troops, numbering three hundred. By late May he led these forces toward Rock River. The militia was in advance, and, fearing treachery, they killed several of Black Hawk's scouts carrying a flag of truce. The Sauks fought back, defeating the militia in what is called the Battle of Stillman's Run. The Sauks kept on the move, eluding Atkinson and his men.

During the summer, Black Hawk's band raided frontier settlements for food and livestock. Atkinson sent Colonel Henry Dodge to lead a militia against the band. Weakened by malnutrition, Black Hawk and his band were overtaken by the militia in late July, 1832. As the band began crossing the Wisconsin River, the militia attacked. Although most of the band escaped, many lives were lost. The remainder pressed on toward the Mississippi, reaching it on August 1.

The Battles of August 1 and 2. While the Sauks were crossing the river, the steamboat *Warrior* appeared with troops aboard. They opened fire, and a fierce battle ensued. The *Warrior* broke off the fight when it ran low on fuel. The main battle between the Sauks and the army began on the morning of August 2. Atkinson's and Dodge's men, supported by the *Warrior*, trapped the Sauks and began a systematic slaughter. The Battle of Bad Axe, resulting in some 150 to 300 Sauk deaths, ended the Black Hawk War. Black Hawk and perhaps fifty others escaped, heading for LaCrosse, Wisconsin, site of a Winnebago village. There they decided to surrender, traveling to Prairie du Chien, headquarters of the Indian agency. Black Hawk, two of his sons, and eight other ringleaders were imprisoned, but all were released within a year.

A treaty, signed on September 21, 1832, formally ended the war. The Sauks, Mesquakies, and Winnebagos lost approximately six million acres of land—most of eastern Iowa—receiving in return a promise of an annuity of $20,000 for thirty years. Broken in spirit and poverty-stricken, the Sauks and their allies never again attempted armed resistance against the United States.

See also: Fox Wars; Indian-white relations: U.S., 1831-1870; Kickapoo Resistance.

S. Carol Berg

Sources for Further Study

Gurko, Miriam. *Indian America: The Black Hawk War.* New York: Thomas Y. Crowell, 1970.

Jackson, Donald, ed. *Black Hawk.* Urbana: University of Illinois Press, 1964.

Josephy, Alvin M., Jr. *The Patriot Chiefs: A Chronicle of American Indian Resistance.* New York: Viking Press, 1961. Reprint. New York: Penguin Books, 1976.

Nichols, Roger L. *Black Hawk and the Warrior's Path.* Arlington Heights, Ill.: Harlan Davidson, 1992.

Utley, Robert M., and Wilcomb E. Washburn. *The Indian Wars.* Rev. ed. New York: American Heritage, 1985.

Waters, Frank. *Brave Are My People: Indian Heroes Not Forgotten.* Santa Fe, N.Mex.: Clear Light Publishers, 1992.

Boarding and residential schools

Date: 1568-present
Locale: Canada, United States
Tribes involved: Pantribal
Categories: Colonial history, Education, Eighteenth century history, National government and legislation, Nineteenth century history, Religion and missionary activities
Significance: Boarding and residential schools, established for Indian youth by both Canada and the United States, intended to accelerate the assimilation of Indian children into mainstream society.

Treaties concluded with Indians beginning in the colonial era contained provisions for education. Indians sought schools and envisioned them as a means to prepare their children for dealing with the new way of life that lay ahead. Native people expected to retain their own languages and traditions as well as to learn European-American ways. However, from the earliest days, the European (later Canadian and American) goal was to use the schools as instruments of European civilization. Churches and religious institutions took on the task of educating Indian youth. Boarding schools were viewed as the optimum means to accomplish these ends, because they separated Indian children from their families, extinguished tribal knowledge and languages, and imprinted children with Christian teachings. As early as 1568, Indian children from Georgia and Florida were placed in Jesuit schools in Cuba. Commitments to educating Indian children during colonial times were inconsistent due to political rivalries among the various powers.

Girls study shorthand in a classroom c. 1910 at the Haskell Institute, a boarding school established in 1884 in Lawrence, Kansas. In the 1990's it was renamed Haskell Indian Nations University, offering degrees in disciplines such as American Indian studies, environmental science, and business administration. (National Archives)

Government-Sponsored Schools. Prior to 1870, Indian education in the United States was almost exclusively in the hands of religious organizations. Beginning in 1802, Congress appropriated funds to religious groups to establish schools, and in 1819, Congress increased the appropriation with passage of the Indian Civilization Fund Act. Numerous schools, both boarding and day schools, were established for the education of Indian youth. Churches that sponsored schools received access to treaty monies and assumed the federal obligation to educate Indian people. These schools became known as "contract schools." Since Indian children generally were prohibited from attending public schools until the turn of the twentieth century, religious contract schools became primary education institutions until the 1880's.

In Canada, the government also was obliged, through treaty provisions, to develop facilities for the education of Indian youth. The government deemed it more economical to develop and fund existing missionary schools rather than develop its own infrastructure. The government contracted for educational services with the Anglican and Catholic churches. The government financed construction and maintenance of the schools, while the churches provided teachers and staff for day-to-day operations. In Canada there were two types of residential schools: boarding schools were located on reservations and served students between eight and fourteen years old; and industrial schools were located off reservations, close to non-Indian towns, and admitted students up to fourteen years old. The industrial schools sought to prepare students for life off the reserves and vocational education was a mainstay of the curriculum. Boarding schools were favored in the United States and Canada because it was believed they would be the most efficient means to accomplish assimilation.

Squabbling among Protestants and Catholics in the United States led to repeal of the Civilization Fund in 1873, and this marked a transition period when the federal government began to assume a more direct role in operating Indian schools. Religious schools continued to operate, but federal officials were convinced they could run schools more efficiently and accomplish assimilation with greater success. The federal government endorsed education as the quickest way to civilize Indians and stated that the soundest education policies would entail removal of children from their homes. Carlisle Indian School, the first federally operated boarding school, opened in 1879 with the goal of transforming the Indian into a patriotic American citizen. Indian education, whether sponsored by the United States government, sponsored by religious organizations, or in partnership, was intended to strip Indian children of their language and culture and change them into mainstream Americans.

Schools in both Canada and the United States mandated that English be the only language spoken both in and out of the classroom and emphasized the acquisition of basic skills in reading, writing, and arithmetic, along with industrial training. Many of these schools were supported by the manual labor of their students. Girls worked in the laundry, kitchen, dining hall, and sewing rooms; boys worked in fields, dairy barns, carpentry shops, and blacksmith and tinsmith shops. At many schools, students spent more time working than in learning basic skills, and this became an issue in both Canada and the United States. After unfavorable publicity, both governments insisted on greater balance between basic skills and industrial education. Nonetheless, the goal of this education remained the provision of a trade, so the young people would no longer return to the reservation once they completed their education.

Poor health was a continuous problem in boarding schools. Students contracted communicable diseases such as tuberculosis, trachoma, measles, and whooping cough, and some youth died while at school. Because parents were fearful their children would die in the schools, they began to hide the young people from agency officials at the start of the school year. In both Canada and the United States, agents of the federal governments would sweep through Indian camps and literally take children. In the United States, this was known as "kid catching." Discipline was harsh and punitive in the schools and was in stark contrast to the positive reinforcement Indian children were familiar with in their families.

Reforms to Hasten Assimilation. Canadian residential schools came under increasing attack in the early 1900's because they were expensive, inefficient, and rife with health and physical and sexual abuse problems. The Bureau of Indian Affairs assumed greater responsibility for managing the finances of the schools, while the churches continued to provide personnel. In 1927, compulsory attendance was strengthened, and on authority of the Indian agent, children could be committed to boarding schools and kept until age eighteen. Once done with their education, Indian youth were generally told they were not to return to their reserves or reservations.

In the United States, a scathing critique of federal Indian programs, the Meriam Report, was published in 1928. It condemned almost every aspect of Indian education, particularly boarding schools. School reforms were instituted, many boarding schools closed, and children were sent to day schools located on their reservations. Progressive educators stepped forward and stressed the importance of family to children, provided training to teachers, and began to include tribal cultures in school curriculum.

However, school reforms ended with the Great Depression of the 1930's and World War II. After World War II, federal policies in Canada and the United States once again sought to dissolve the trust relationship with tribes. In the 1950's, as a way to accomplish assimilation once and for all, the United States government again reopened many off-reservation boarding schools. Similarly, in Canada, concerns surfaced about how to best accomplish assimilation, and the government's solution was to revise the Indian Act in 1951 and integrate Indian children into public schools.

Indian-Controlled Schools. In the 1960's and 1970's, tribes began to insist on the trust relationship with their governments, and they asserted their rights to set their own direction and especially to manage the education of their children. American and Canadian Indians pressed for self-determination and lobbied intensely to close boarding schools and put education in the hands of Native people. In both Canada and the United States, a series of education acts permitted tribes to have a more active role in directing education, and to enfold tribal languages and cultures into the curriculum.

The last federal residential school closed in Canada in 1988. Many boarding schools in the United States closed during the 1970's and 1980's, and those that remain open provide specialized services such as foster care and developmental education to small numbers of youth. The goal is no longer to assimilate but to educate and instill a sense of pride and self-worth in the students. Boarding schools, once considered by both countries the optimal way to educate Indian children, have given way to innovative tribal-controlled schools that underscore self-determination and sovereignty. Tribal languages, cultures, and histories are vital parts of the curriculum in these schools. In both Canada and the United States, Indian education is a federal responsibility, but budgets are inadequate.

See also: American Indian Higher Education Consortium; Bureau of Indian Affairs; California missions; Carlisle Indian School; Indian Education Acts; Indian Self-Determination and Education Assistance Act; Indian-white relations: Canadian; Indian-white relations: U.S., 1775-1830; Indian-white relations: U.S., 1831-1870; Indian-white relations: U.S., 1871-1933; Kennedy Report; Meriam Report; National Indian Education Association.

Carole A. Barrett

Sources for Further Study

Child, Brenda. *Boarding School Seasons: American Indian Families, 1900-1940.* Lincoln: University of Nebraska Press, 1998. The author uses letters from students at Flandreau Indian School in South Dakota and Haskell Institute in Kansas to chronicle the emotional and cultural impact of boarding schools on students, families, and communities.

Ellis, Clyde. *To Change Them Forever: Indian Education at the Rainy Mountain Boarding School, 1893-1920.* Norman: University of Oklahoma, 1996. A case study of one school, illustrating the forced assimilation policies of the federal government through students' oral accounts and government documents.

Johnston, Basil. *Indian School Days.* Norman: University of Oklahoma Press, 1988. This first-person narrative explores experiences and contains analysis of student life in a Jesuit boarding school in Ontario, Canada.

Lomawaima, K. Tsianina. *They Called It Prairie Light: The Story of Chiloco Indian School.* Lincoln: University of Nebraska Press, 1994. Through oral histories of former students and archival materials, the author examines the effect the boarding school had on its students and provides insight into why the school's assimilation policies never succeeded.

Standing Bear, Luther. *Land of the Spotted Eagle*. Lincoln: University of Nebraska Press, 1978. In this autobiography a young Lakota boy compares and contrasts traditional tribal education with education at Carlisle Indian School.

Bozeman Trail War

Date: June 13, 1866-November 6, 1868
Locale: Powder River country, Dakota Territory, east of the Bighorn Mountains
Tribes involved: Arapaho, Cheyenne, Sioux,
Categories: Nineteenth century history, Reservations and relocation, Wars and battles
Significance: The end of Red Cloud's war opens the door to the U.S. reservation system.

In 1862, John M. Bozeman sought a more direct route connecting the newly discovered gold fields around Virginia City, Montana, to the east. Leaving Virginia City, he located a pass that led him to the headwaters of the Yellowstone River, then southeastward along the eastern flank of the Bighorn Mountains, where he traversed the headwaters of the Bighorn, Tongue, and Powder Rivers. Continuing southeast, he intersected the Oregon Trail along the North Platte River seventy miles west of Fort Laramie. This new Bozeman Trail cut directly through the best hunting grounds of the Teton Dakota Sioux—Red Cloud's people.

The Powder River country was a hunter's paradise, home to the great northern bison herd. It had been guaranteed to the Sioux by the Fort Laramie Treaty of 1851, it was the locus of their free-ranging lifestyle, and they meant to keep it. Responding to growing pressure from miners and settlers, however, the government was keenly interested in securing the Bozeman Trail but was uncertain of the best method. Using force to subjugate or exterminate native peoples was a popular idea in the West. Alternatively, an approach based on peace through justice gained support, especially in the East after the Civil War (1861-1865), when humanitarians who previously had been devoted to emancipation and the abolition of slavery turned their attention to the "Indian problem." This East-West rift led to a schizophrenic policy toward American Indians, in which both approaches were tried, often at the same time.

Forts and Treaties. Pursuing force, a string of three forts was built along the Bozeman Trail. Fort Reno was the first, built seventy miles up the Bozeman Trail in late summer of 1865 by General Patrick E. Connor. Best known for slaughtering 273 Paiutes at Bear Creek in 1863, Connor issued the directive to "accept no peace offers and kill any male over twelve." Red Cloud, with Cheyenne and Arapaho allies, mauled Connor's columns; they withdrew, but the fort remained. On July 10 of the following year, Colonel Henry B. Carrington established Fort Phil Kearny forty miles north of Fort Reno at the fork of the Piney Creeks, and in early August, Fort C. F. Smith ninety miles beyond that.

Red Cloud, leader of the Teton Dakota Sioux, not only led his people to a victorious conclusion of the Bozeman Trail War but also became famous nationwide as a diplomat and negotiator, deeply respected by both his people and white reformers. (National Archives)

The peace process was tried also. On October 28, 1865, a commission under Governor Newton Edmunds of Dakota Territory announced peace with the Sioux, producing a treaty signed by chiefs already friendly to the settlers. None of the Powder River chiefs signed, as they were all fighting Connor. Red Cloud did go to Fort Laramie the next spring to discuss peace, trade, and Fort Reno. In the middle of peace negotiations, Colonel Carrington arrived at Fort Laramie on June 13, 1866, in a masterpiece of bad timing. He had seven hundred troops, more than two hundred wagons, and orders to build his Bozeman forts. Red Cloud excoriated the commissioner, E. B. Edwards, for already stealing what they were negotiating, and his entire camp was gone the next morning.

Edwards collected some signatures and blithely informed Washington that a satisfactory treaty had been concluded with the Sioux. While Colonel Carrington went on to build his forts, Red Cloud was galvanizing opposition with stunning oratory:

> Hear Ye, Dakotas! . . . before the ashes of the council fire are cold, the Great Father is building his forts among us. You have heard the sound of the white soldier's axe upon the Little Piney. His presence here is an insult and a threat. It is an insult to the spirits of our ancestors. Are we then to give up their sacred graves to be plowed for corn? Dakotas, I am for war!

Recruiting a coalition of three thousand warriors, Red Cloud's war against the Thieves' Road began in earnest.

Guerrilla Warfare. Within days of their completion, Carrington's forts were under unrelenting guerrilla warfare. In the first five weeks, the colonel reported thirty-three whites killed. By December, ninety-six soldiers and fifty-eight civilians had been killed, many were wounded, and nearly one thousand oxen, cows, mules, and horses had been lost. There were fifty-one separate attacks on Fort Kearny alone.

The worst loss came on December 21, 1866, when the command of Captain William Fetterman was completely annihilated. Having once boasted that he could ride through the whole Sioux nation with eighty good men, Fetterman led exactly eighty soldiers out of Fort Kearny to relieve an embattled party of woodcutters. Disobeying Carrington's orders not to ride out of view of the fort, Fetterman could not resist chasing Crazy Horse, who, acting as a decoy, lured Fetterman into an ambush by two thousand Sioux, Cheyenne, and Arapaho. In the Battle of One Hundred Slain, Fetterman's arrogance had handed the U.S. Army its worst defeat in the Plains Wars.

On August 1, 1867, the Cheyenne attacked hay cutters at Fort Smith, and the next day at Fort Kearny, Red Cloud's Sioux attacked a woodcutters' camp. Although these Hayfield and Wagon Box fights were standoffs, the government began to realize the speciousness of Edmunds's and Taylor's treaties. John Bozeman himself had been caught in 1867 by Blackfoot warriors and killed on his own road.

Major peace initiatives in 1867 were rebuffed by Red Cloud, who persistently refused to sign anything until the forts were gone. Concerned about the cost of a full military campaign and the safety of the new railroads inching westward, Congress decided to concede the Bozeman overland route. Soldiers left Fort Smith on July 29, 1868, Fort Kearny a month later, and Fort Reno a few days after that. Jubilant warriors burned the three forts to the ground, and the Bozeman Trail was closed. On November 6, 1868, Red

Cloud signed the Sioux Treaty of 1868 at Fort Laramie. Red Cloud had won his war.

Red Cloud Goes to Washington. In 1870, Red Cloud and other Sioux were invited to Washington, D.C., to discuss the treaty. Here Red Cloud heard for the first time of provisions calling for permanent settlements on a reservation. Although deeply upset, he was persuaded to make an address at the Cooper Institute in New York City before an audience of social reformers. At noon on June 16, he began with a prayer to the Almighty Spirit, then recited wrongs done to his people, and asked for justice. Praised for its piety, charisma, and sincerity, the speech was an immense success.

His growing influence with the Eastern peace and reform circles allowed Red Cloud to extract future concessions for his people from the government. The treaty articles that had not been explained to him, however, hastened the pace of the Sioux toward becoming "reservation Indians." Still, the success of his implacable opposition to the Bozeman Trail makes his name an appropriate eponym for "Red Cloud's War."

See also: Bear River Campaign; Fort Laramie Treaty of 1851; Fort Laramie Treaty of 1868; Wolf Mountains, Battle of; Wounded Knee Massacre.

Gary A. Olson

Sources for Further Study

Armstrong, Virginia Irving, comp. *I Have Spoken: American History Through the Voices of the Indians*. Chicago: Swallow Press, 1971. Includes three orations by Red Cloud, including the Powder River exhortation (1866) and the complete Cooper Institute speech (1870).

Brown, Dee. "Red Cloud's War." In *Bury My Heart at Wounded Knee*. New York: Holt, Rinehart and Winston, 1970. A good overview of the nineteenth century wars from the Native American point of view.

Hyde, George E. "Red Cloud's War." In *Red Cloud's Folk: A History of the Oglala Sioux Indians*. Rev. ed. Norman: University of Oklahoma Press, 1976. Originally published in 1937 and revised in 1957, this is considered to be a definitive history of the Oglala Sioux. Includes extensive background for the events on the Bozeman Trail. Thirteen illustrations, two maps.

Keenan, Jerry. *The Wagon Box Fight: An Episode of Red Cloud's War*. Conshohocken, Pa.: Savas, 2000. A thorough account of this encounter, with detailed appendices of the official army reports and results of recent archaeological excavation at the site.

Lazarus, Edward. *Black Hills, White Justice: The Sioux Nation Versus the United States, 1775 to the Present*. New York: HarperCollins, 1991. Includes the full text of the Fort Laramie Treaty of 1868.

McDermott, John D. "Price of Arrogance: The Short and Controversial Life of William Judd Fetterman." *Annals of Wyoming* 63, no. 2 (Spring, 1991): 42-53. A look at Fetterman's character and its fatal consequences.

_____, ed. "Wyoming Scrapbook: Documents Relating to the Fetterman Fight." *Annals of Wyoming* 63, no. 2 (Spring, 1991): 68-72. Gives details of the most significant Army loss in the war.

Bureau of Indian Affairs

Date: Established March 11, 1824
Tribes involved: Pantribal in the United States
Categories: National government and legislation, Nineteenth century history, Reservations and relocation, Twentieth century history
Significance: The Bureau of Indian Affairs (BIA) is the central U.S. federal agency for the management of Indian affairs.

Attempting to centralize Indian administration, previously controlled by a bewildering array of government and military officials, Secretary of War John C. Calhoun in 1824 created the Bureau of Indian Affairs (BIA). Although authority over Indians initially resided in the Secretary of War, the fledgling bureau controlled all annuities and expenditures, managed funds for the civilization of Indians, mediated disputes between Indians under the trade and intercourse laws, and handled all correspondence. In 1832 the president was empowered to appoint a commissioner of Indian affairs.

In 1849, the BIA was transferred to the newly created Department of the Interior. Thereafter authority descended from the president of the United States to the secretary of the interior to the commissioner of Indian affairs. The coordination of field superintendents, agents, missionaries, traders, and local Indians was entrusted to a field superintendent who corresponded directly with the commissioner. The BIA grew rapidly, from its original three members to six thousand employees in 1911. By the late twentieth century it had thirteen thousand employees and controlled a budget of nearly $900 million.

Designed to implement federal policy, the BIA has historically reflected prevailing government attitudes toward Indians. Initially it oversaw funding under the 1819 civilization plan designed to aid assimilation through education. Similarly, under the General Allotment Act, passed in 1887, the

BIA was charged with the mammoth task of preparing a list of members of tribes as well as classifying and appraising Indian lands.

After World War I, responding to government economizing mandates, the BIA decentralized its operations. Regional offices were superimposed over the existing administrative structure, and further reorganization in 1946 provided for separate geographical divisions with regional headquarters.

Surveys and studies during the 1920's, including the scathing Meriam Report, revealed the appalling conditions of Indian life under the allotment plan, thereby giving impetus to fresh reforms. Between 1933 and 1945, during Commissioner John Collier's tenure, the BIA for the first time turned from its assimilationist policy. Because of Collier's influence, the Indian Reorganization Act (IRA) of 1934 provided for a revitalization of tribal government and social customs. The IRA also granted Indians priority hiring within the BIA. Indeed, by 1982, Indians accounted for 78 percent of BIA personnel.

Since the 1960's, the BIA's influence over Indian affairs has eroded, thereby favoring a shift of responsibility to Indians themselves. In 1975, for example, the Indian Self-Determination and Education Assistance Act encouraged Indians to assume control over pertinent government programs. In the 1990's, dispersion of BIA activities to states, to other agencies, and to Indians continued, yet the bureau remained a vast organization supporting twelve regional offices and eighty-two agencies headed by a commissioner. The BIA still oversaw several features of Indian life, including education, law enforcement, and the mobilization of public and private funds for economic development and natural resource management.

See also: Allotment system; American Indian Defense Association; Indian Citizenship Act; Indian New Deal; Indian Offenses Act; Indian preference; Indian Reorganization Act; Indian Self-Determination and Education Assistance Act; Indian-white relations: U.S., 1831-1870; Indian-white relations: U.S., 1934-2002; Keeler Commission; Meriam Report; Navajo-Hopi Land Settlement Act; Oklahoma Indian Welfare Act; Pine Ridge shootout and Peltier killings; Reservation system of the United States; Termination Resolution; Trail of Broken Treaties; Wounded Knee occupation.

Mary E. Virginia

Burke Act

Date: May 8, 1906
Locale: United States
Tribes involved: Pantribal in the United States
Categories: National government and legislation, Reservations and relocation, Twentieth century history
Significance: Passed to improve the process of allotting tribal lands to individual American Indians, the Burke Act contributed to the large-scale loss of Indian land between 1887 and 1934.

In 1887, Congress passed the General Allotment Act (or Dawes Act). This act sought to make small farmers out of American Indians by dividing tribal lands into individual allotments. Indians taking allotments received United States citizenship; the government held the title for the lands in trust for twenty-five years, during which time they could not be sold. At the end of the period, the Indian would receive a fee patent giving him full ownership of the land.

The administration of the General Allotment Act prompted considerable criticism. Many of those sympathetic to the Indians were concerned at the distinction between citizenship, which was taken up at the outset, and ownership, which came at the end of the trust period. The discrepancy became a source of worry in 1905 when the Supreme Court ruled that citizenship exempted an Indian from direct federal supervision, thus invalidating federal restrictions on liquor on allotments. Other people simply thought that the trust period postponed too long the time when an Indian might sell his allotment.

In 1906, Congress passed the Burke Act, named for South Dakota Congressman Charles Henry Burke. The act provided that the trust period could be extended indefinitely on presidential authority, though it also permitted the secretary of the interior to cut the period short if requested, provided an individual Indian could prove that he was competent to manage his own affairs. In either case, there would be no citizenship until the end of the trust period, during which the Indian would remain subject to federal control.

The Burke Act had a major effect on the awarding of allotments, though not the one that some of its supporters had hoped. Though certificates of competency (and fee patents) were awarded cautiously at first, there were clear signs that many allotments quickly passed out of Indian possession once they could be sold or mortgaged. During the act's first decade of operation, roughly ten thousand fee patents were issued, the vast majority of allotments passing out of Indian ownership. When the ardent assimilationist Fred K. Lane became secretary of the interior in 1917, the process speeded up. Competency certificates and fee patents were often given without the requisite individual investigation, sometimes to Indians who had not asked for them. In four years twenty thousand fee patents were issued, again with much of the land quickly alienated.

During the 1920's, when Burke himself was commissioner of Indian affairs, the process slowed, but the overall trend of allotment lands passing into the hands of non-Indians continued. By 1934, when the Indian Reorganization Act finally stopped the allotment process, Indians had lost 86 million of the 138 million acres they had controlled in 1887. In the meantime the citizenship available under the Burke Act had been made redundant by Congress's grant of citizenship to all Indians in 1924.

See also: Allotment system; General Allotment Act; Indian Reorganization Act.

William C. Lowe

California missions

Date: July 17, 1769-1824
Locale: Coastal regions of California, from San Diego to Sonoma
Tribes involved: Achumawi, Atsugewi, Cahuilla, Chemehuevi, Chumash, Costano, Cupeño, Diegueño, Esselen, Fernandeño, Gabrielino, Hupa, Juaneño, Kamia, Karok, Kato, Luiseño, Maidu, Mattole, Miwok, Patwin, Pomo, Quechan, Salinan, Serrano, Shasta, Tolowa, Tubatulabal, Wailaki, Wappo, Wintun, Wiyot, Yahi, Yana, Yokuts, Yuki, Yurok
Categories: Colonial history, Nineteenth century history, Religion and missionary activities
Significance: Twenty-one Catholic missions, four military installations, and several towns established Spain's claim to Alta California and altered the lives of thousands of Native Americans.

The worldwide Spanish Empire had gradually developed a mission system that suited imperial policy in places as distant as the Philippines, Paraguay, and Baja California. With a relatively modest investment, the Crown could extend its frontiers and establish opportunities for further expansion later. Two or three missionaries per location could attract indigenous peoples to a different way of life. The native peoples would learn manual trades, farming, cattle-raising, smithing, tanning, weaving, and other rudimentary skills, so that they could manage the institution on their own. A few soldiers at each mission—never more than ten—would enforce discipline. On occasions of serious trouble, appeal could be made to strategically placed presidios that housed sizable, highly mobile military forces capable of putting down any rebellions. When the missions developed enough, a pueblo might be established nearby, able to make use of the growing mission economy without having to follow the often austere mission routine.

The Spanish missionaries, usually members of religious orders (the regular clergy), expected to complete their work in ten years, after which the establishments were to be secularized: The administration of church affairs would be in the hands of the secular clergy, and all the mission's properties and possessions would be dispersed. Church authorities would receive the church buildings and some surrounding land. Indigenous peoples would receive at least half of all the possessions and land.

For 160 years, missionaries in New Spain sought to evangelize the peoples of the Upper California territories, claimed for Spain by Juan Rodríguez Cabrillo in 1524 and Sebastián Vizcaíno in 1611. Without royal approval, however, ecclesiastical initiatives were not implemented in the Spanish Empire. Even many popes, as well as lowly missionaries, discovered this policy.

In 1741, Captain Vitus Bering had reached Alaska and claimed much of North America's west coast. Carlos Francisco de Croix became the Viceroy of New Spain in 1766. Along with Don José de Gálvez, *visitador general* of King Charles III, Croix laid plans for a series of missions in Alta California to blunt Russian expansionist plans. Galvez's plans called for a mission and fort at Monterey Bay in the north. They chose San Diego in the south as the site of the first mission, because it was about half the distance from the base in Loreto, Baja California. Gálvez selected Don Gaspar de Portolá to be governor of California and Fray Junípero Serra as president of the missions.

The Mission Trail. Four foundation parties, two by land and two by sea, set out from Baja for the arduous journey. Most of the sailors died, as did many of those taking part in the overland trek. On July 17, 1769, Serra dedicated the mission of San Diego de Alcalá on a site five miles west of the present mission. Portola pushed on to Monterey with a small party, but left no permanent settlement. That came about the following year, under Serra.

Between Serra and his immediate successor, Fray Fermín de Lausen, eighteen of the twenty-one missions were built by 1798.

Economics determined the sequence of building the missions. Largely dependent on shipping for supplies in the earliest years, the missions were first clustered in three coastal areas: south (San Diego), central (Santa Barbara Channel), and north (Monterey). Gradually, the gaps between the missions were closed to lessen their reliance on the vagaries of eighteenth century shipping. In 1776, Juan Bautista de Anza led an arduous overland expedition to San Francisco through the southern deserts, demonstrating that New Spain no longer need rely on the sea to supply California. In all, Spain founded twenty of the missions. After independence, Mexican authorities founded the last of the missions at Sonoma, San Francisco Solano, dedicated in 1824.

In late eighteenth century California, there were about 130,000 Native Americans living in many small bands. The land supported them well in a life that was not much different from the one they had lived five thousand years before. Abundant potable water, fish, and game were within easy reach. Of all the indigenous peoples of what would become the United States, they made the swiftest, most seaworthy boats, without knowing metal trades. Their loosely structured societies lacked a central organization. They had no writing system for their six languages and several dialects. There were no organized wars, although occasional raids to steal goods were not unknown. Shelter was modest, at most.

It quickly became clear to the missionaries that they needed more workers if the missions were to become self-sufficient. They stepped up recruitment of the indigenous people as laborers, often luring them with trinkets. The Franciscan missionary plan initially included teaching the native populations in their own languages, but the diversity was so extensive that that plan was abandoned, and Spanish was chosen instead to be the common language of California.

Cultural Effects. The missions attracted people from surrounding areas with the promise of better living conditions and some amenities unavailable to those on the outside. If the natives converted to Christianity—a condition for remaining within the economic ambit of the mission—they were no longer at liberty to return to their previous way of life, although many did, in fact, escape. Native Americans living in the mission were permitted, even encouraged, to visit their families for weeks at a time. This policy proved to be the best recruiting tool the missionaries possessed.

The workers did learn trades and some even learned to read and write. Daily work usually finished by mid-morning, and numerous feast days provided diversion from the normal regimen. By the time of secularization in 1834, approximately thirty thousand natives resided at the missions, with only sixty friars and three hundred soldiers along the 650 miles from San Diego to Sonoma. The missions held 230,000 cattle, 34,000 horses, and 268,000 hogs, sheep, and goats.

The life was far removed from that visited upon the natives' ancestors by the savage conquistadores of the sixteenth century. The process of colonization was relatively peaceful, and on balance the native population fared better under the Spanish friars than people in other colonies and received better treatment than they received subsequently in Mexico or in the United States. However, because the mission system destroyed their previous tranquil existence and failed to prepare them for the promised secularization, it cannot escape historical criticism. The Indians were introduced into an alien culture as little more than slaves; they suffered tragically from European diseases and, in the end, were ill-equipped for any other existence, either that of their own rapidly declining culture or that of the new California.

When Mexico gained independence from Spain, the new government resolved to secularize the missions. When secularization began, Native Americans were either tricked into giving up their rights or their rights simply were ignored in the land grab of what had been the missions. Stranded after secularization, many of the natives at the missions had nowhere else to go, so they stayed on, continuing menial work under new masters. Only in the twentieth century were there some modest advances in their status. The U.S. government gave most of the mission buildings back to the Catholic church after California entered the Union. Many of the missions have been restored to a romantic, tranquil, even charming condition that belies their troubled history.

See also: Boarding and residential schools; Indian-white relations; Spanish colonial.

Daniel A. Brown

Sources for Further Study

Cook, Sherburne Friend. *The Conflict Between the California Indian and White Civilization.* 4 vols. Berkeley: University of California Press, 1943. A scholarly collection that chronicles the troubled history of Native Americans during and after the mission period. Rich bibliographies.

Costo, Rupert, and Jeannette Henry Costo, eds. *The Missions of California: A Legacy of Genocide.* San Francisco: Indian Historian Press, 1987. A collection that vigorously indicts the evils of the mission system.

Englehardt, Zephyrin. *The Missions and Missionaries of California.* 4 vols.

Santa Barbara, Calif.: Mission Santa Barbara, 1929. The monumental standard reference work on the missions, giving an overall positive evaluation of the system.

Font Obrador, Bartolome. *Fr. Junipero Serra: Mallorca, Mexico, Sierra Gorda, Californias.* Palma, Mallorca, Spain: Comissio de Cultura, 1992. A biography of Serra that depends on, but summarizes well, the work of many earlier authors.

Geiger, Maynard J. *The Life and Times of Fray Junipero Serra, OFM.* 2 vols. Washington, D.C.: Academy of American Franciscan History, 1959. A large, sympathetic biography that relies heavily on original sources.

Jackson, Robert H., and Edward Castillo. *Indians, Franciscans, and Spanish Colonization: The Impact of the Mission System on California Indians.* Albuquerque: University of New Mexico Press, 1995. An ethnohistory of Indian life under the mission system.

Johnson, Paul C., et al., eds. *The California Missions: A Pictorial History.* Menlo Park, Calif.: Lane, 1985. A colorful, popular, accessible, and reliable work.

Kroeber, Alfred Louis. *Handbook of the Indians of California.* New York: Dover, 1976. A large anthropological tome.

Carlisle Indian School

Date: 1879-1918
Locale: Carlisle, Pennsylvania
Tribes involved: Pantribal in the United States
Categories: Education, Nineteenth century history, Organizations, Religion and missionary activities, Twentieth century history
Significance: The Carlisle Indian School sought to assimilate Indian children into white society; it served as a model for many other Indian boarding schools.

In 1879, a U.S. military officer, Captain Richard Henry Pratt, opened a school for Indians in a military barracks in Carlisle, Pennsylvania. Pratt belonged to a generation of policy-makers working for what many believed to be a more humane, progressive approach to Indian policy. Unlike many of his predecessors, Pratt believed that Indian people were capable of being transformed into the European American model of the law-abiding, Christian, wage-earning citizen. According to Pratt, this was the only way for Indian people to survive—by leaving behind everything that distinguished Indian people as "Indian," including language and spirituality.

Pratt first experimented with Indian education by training Plains Indian prisoners being held at Fort Marion in Florida. After persuading the federal government to allow eighteen male prisoners to attend Hampton Normal Institute, an all-black school in Virginia, Pratt recruited both male and female students from Indian communities across the country for enrollment in the Carlisle Indian Industrial School. At Carlisle, students were required to speak only English and to adopt middle-class European American ways of living. Students did not, however, follow a middle-class curriculum: In addition to being taught very basic academic skills, girls were trained in domestic skills such as ironing and cooking, while boys learned industrial skills. Such a curriculum did little to prepare students for life in Indian communities.

Students, however, proved much more able to maintain strong Indian identities than Captain Pratt had expected. Pratt was disappointed that so many students left Carlisle to return to their tribal homelands. The Carlisle experience also fostered new forms of Indian identity. Bringing together students from many different Indian communities, Carlisle tended to encourage students to form new bonds with members of other tribes and to work together, not just as members of specific tribes and local communities, but as American Indians with certain interests in common. Although Carlisle required a traumatic isolation from family and community, some students did, nevertheless, emerge from the experience with new skills and a determination to improve political and social conditions for other native people.

A group of Sioux boys being "civilized" at the Carlisle Indian School. (Library of Congress)

See also: American Indian Higher Education Consortium; Indian Education Acts; Indian Self-Determination and Education Assistance Act; Kennedy Report; National Congress of American Indians.

Molly H. Mullin

Cayuse War

Date: 1847-1850
Locale: Southeastern Washington State
Tribes involved: Cayuse, Tenino
Categories: Nineteenth century history, Wars and battles
Significance: The Cayuse War began when the Cayuse attacked a mission because they were angry about the disruption and disease that had come with the whites; the war gained the Cayuse a reputation as a fierce and warlike tribe.

The Waiilatpu Mission was established near Fort Walla Walla in southeastern Washington by a medical doctor, Marcus Whitman. The mission was located on Pasha Creek (called Mill Creek by most European Americans). The land on which the mission was built was actually part of the ancient Cayuse lands, a situation which would later lead to friction between the missionaries and the Cayuse. The Cayuse land was in the center of an area through which many Europeans passed on their way to a number of destinations in the Pacific Northwest, another cause of friction between the two groups.

Whitman's preachings in the mission were designed to persuade the Cayuse to forsake their traditional ways and adopt his version of Christian values. Gradually, the Cayuse became convinced that Whitman was an evil man. To make matters worse, many Cayuse tribal members contracted measles, and some of them blamed Whitman. He returned to his mission during the fall of 1847 after ministering to the sick at Umatilla. His mission complex was attacked by the Cayuse, and the Whitmans and twelve others were killed.

A retaliatory effort was mounted against the small group of Cayuse and the dissidents, but it was repulsed. On January 28, 1848, a group of Cayuse warriors and some recruited Teninos defeated a volunteer party under the command of Major Henry Lee; although the Cayuse tried to persuade other area tribes to join them in the battle, only a few did.

The Cayuse later suffered a defeat during the Sand Hollow battle of 1848, in which Cayuse chief Gray Eagle was killed. A number of other skirmishes ensued during the remainder of 1848 and in 1849. The refusal of other tribes to join the Cayuse would ultimately lead to their downfall.

In a message to the territorial legislature in 1850, Joseph Lane, the new governor of Oregon Territory, declared that the entire Cayuse tribe would be considered responsible for the deaths of the European Americans in the Whitman mission attack until the guilty parties were turned over to the government for trial. An increasing number of Cayuse and other bands attempted to capture the members of the Cayuse tribe who had attacked the missionaries. Finally, five of the attackers were captured after being pursued by members of their own tribe. They were turned over to the Oregon territorial government for trial. It has been speculated that the accused Cayuse had little understanding of the American legal system which would judge their case. They were provided defense council by the Oregon territorial government. On May 24, 1850, the jury pronounced them guilty as charged, and they were hanged on Monday, June 3, 1850.

See also: Walla Walla Council.

Bruce M. Mitchell

Cherokee legal cases

Date: March 18, 1831, and March 3, 1832
Locale: Georgia
Tribes involved: Cherokee
Categories: Court cases, Native government, Nineteenth century history, Religion and missionary activities
Significance: Two decisions rendered by the U.S. Supreme Court limit the sovereignty of Native American tribes by placing them under federal protection.

In 1823, the U.S. Supreme Court, with John Marshall as chief justice, made the first serious judicial effort to define the relationship between the federal government and Native Americans. The case, concerning disputed land titles, was *Johnson v. McIntosh*. The decision was that the federal government was, in effect, the Native Americans' ultimate landlord and they were the government's tenants. Marshall and the Court majority thus judged the federal government to be responsible for Native American affairs, including the protection of Native American peoples against state actions, which materially affected Native American lives and property.

During a period in which the federal government and the states were locked in disputes about where the Constitution intended ultimate sovereignty to reside and federal authority seemed unsure, Georgia contemplated removing Cherokee and Creek peoples from northern and western portions of the state. To legitimate its plans, Georgia charged that when it had agreed, in 1802, to cede its western land claims to the federal government, the latter had agreed to extinguish Native American titles to those lands and then to return them to the state. The federal government had not done so, and Georgia had been obliged to live since with a Native American state within a state. Land-hungry as a result of expansive pressures from the cotton culture, Georgians themselves initiated steps to remove Native Americans, primarily Cherokees. They denied the relevance of federal treaties with the Cherokees and threatened to use force against federal troops if they were dispatched to protect the tribe. Andrew Jackson's election as president in 1828 accelerated Georgia's actions to begin removal, because Jackson, a veteran Indian fighter who deemed Native Americans "savages," was a proponent of removal.

In December, 1828, the Georgia legislature added Cherokee lands to a number of Georgia counties. Far from being savages, the Cherokees who protested this action had become a successful farming people. Thanks to a syllabary produced by their own Sequoyah, they were literate and produced their own newspaper, the *Cherokee Phoenix*. They instantly assembled a distinguished delegation to appeal to Congress for assistance. This course was applauded by a host of congressmen and public officials— including Daniel Webster and William Wirt—who proclaimed Georgia's legislation unjust, on moral as well as legal grounds. Nevertheless, in December, 1829, Georgia's legislature enacted a comprehensive law that essentially nullified all Cherokee laws. Aggravating the Cherokees' plight, gold was discovered in the following year in western Georgia, and a gold rush flooded their lands with gold seekers, in violation of Cherokee treaties. Under great pressure, Governor George Gilmer claimed the gold as state property and threatened to oust the Cherokees forcibly. Having failed in Georgia's courts, the Cherokees, as a last peaceful resort and encouraged by missionaries such as Jeremiah Evarts and public officials such as Webster and Wirt, appealed to the U.S. Supreme Court under Article III, Section 2 of the Constitution, which gave the

Court original jurisdiction in cases brought under treaties or by foreign nations.

Georgia Land Disputes. In *Cherokee Nation v. Georgia*, Chief Justice Marshall, who had been sympathetic to Cherokee claims but also was aware of Jackson's hostility toward both Native Americans and Marshall's court, dismissed the case. Marshall asserted that the Court lacked the jurisdiction to halt Georgia's sequestration of Cherokee lands. In doing so, he defined the relationship of Cherokees (and, by inference, other Native American tribes) to the federal government as that of a "domestic, dependent nation" rather than a sovereign one.

Marshall modified his decision in 1832, however, when deciding *Worcester v. Georgia*. *Worcester* resulted from a Georgia law enacted in 1831. The law forbade whites from residing on Cherokee lands without a state license; it was aimed primarily at white missionaries who were encouraging Cherokee resistance to removal. Georgia arrested, convicted, and sentenced two unlicensed missionaries, Samuel Worcester and Elizur Butler, whom the American Board of Commissioners for Foreign Missions promptly defended, hiring William Wirt as their counsel. Wirt then was running as a vice presidential candidate for the National Republican Party and as a presidential candidate for the Anti-Masonic Party. Therefore, he hoped for a decision that would embarrass Jackson.

Because the plaintiff in *Worcester* was a white missionary and the defendant the State of Georgia, the Court had clear jurisdiction. Without overruling his *Cherokee Nation* decision, Marshall ruled that the Georgia law was unconstitutional and therefore void, because it violated treaties, as well as the commerce and contract clauses of the Constitution. Furthermore, Marshall declared, Georgia's laws violated the sovereignty of the Cherokee nation, and, in this case, the Court was constrained to define relationships between Native Americans and a state.

Competing Concepts of Sovereignty. As historians and legal scholars have observed, the Cherokee cases advanced two contradictory descriptions of Native American sovereignty. In *Cherokee Nation v. Georgia*, Marshall delineated the dependent relationship of Native American tribes to the federal government. In *Worcester*, sympathetically stressing historic aspects of Native American independence, nationhood, and foreignness rather than their domestic dependency, he defined the relationship of Native American tribes to the states. Together, these decisions suggested that although Native American tribes lacked sufficient sovereignty to claim political independence and were therefore wards of the federal government, they nevertheless possessed sufficient sovereignty to guard themselves against intrusions by the states, and that it was a federal responsibility to preserve this sovereignty. In subsequent years, these conflicting interpretations were exploited by both the federal government and Native Americans to serve their own purposes.

Marshall's pronouncements were one thing; making them effective was yet another thing. President Jackson, who as chief executive was the only party capable of enforcing the Court's decision, chose to ignore it. Instead, Jackson threw federal troops into the removal of Cherokees and others of the Five Civilized Tribes to designated Indian Territory beyond the Mississippi. The resulting tragedy became known as the Trail of Tears.

See also: *Cherokee Phoenix*; *Cherokee Tobacco* case; Cherokee War; Indian Removal Act; Indian-white relations: U.S., 1831-1870; Trail of Tears.

Mary E. Virginia

Sources for Further Study

Deloria, Vine, Jr., and Clifford M. Lytle. *American Indians, American Justice.* Austin: University of Texas Press, 1983. A clearly written study focusing on the development of the Native American judicial system as it existed in the early 1980's. Explains the complexities of Native American legal and political rights as they are understood by the tribes and by the federal government.

_____. *The Nations Within.* New York: Pantheon Books, 1984. Traces the past and weighs the future of Native American sovereignty, from the Doctrine of Discovery through the shift from tribal and federal notions of self-government to self-determination.

Prucha, Francis Paul. *American Indian Treaties.* Berkeley: University of California Press, 1994. Unravels the political anomaly of the treaty system, a system devised according to white perspectives that made the relationships between Native Americans and the federal government unlike the legal and political relationships of any other two peoples.

_____. *The Great Father.* Vol. 1. Lincoln: University of Nebraska Press, 1984. A masterful, detailed analysis of historical relationships—political, economic, and social—between the federal government and Native Americans through cultural changes affecting both groups, from the Revolutionary War to 1980. Chapter 2 discusses the Cherokee cases and American Indian removal.

Satz, Ronald N. *American Indian Policy in the Jacksonian Era.* Lincoln: University of Nebraska Press, 1974. Excellent coverage of the Cherokee cases; also clarifies the complex political climate in which the cases developed around conflicts between the Jackson administration, Georgia, and the Cherokees.

Wilkins, David E. *American Indian Sovereignty and the U.S. Supreme Court: The Masking of Justice.* Austin: University of Texas Press, 1997. Close analysis of legal cases that Wilkins argues "mask questionable federal and administrative activities against tribes and individual Indians."

Williams, Robert A. *The American Indian in Western Legal Thought.* New York: Oxford University Press, 1990. Starting with the thirteenth century notion that the West had a mandate to conquer the earth, this intriguing study explores the laws that evolved to legitimate this mandate, specifically as the mandate was interpreted by Spanish, English, and U.S. laws regarding relations with Native Americans.

Cherokee Phoenix

Date: 1828-1839
Locale: New Echota, Cherokee Nation, Georgia
Tribes involved: Cherokee
Categories: Education, Nineteenth century history, Religion and missionary activities
Significance: The *Cherokee Phoenix* was the first Native American newspaper and the first published in a Native American language.

The *Cherokee Phoenix*, the first Native American newspaper, began on February 21, 1828, as the Cherokee nation created institutions and built its new capital at New Echota in Georgia. Cherokees, who had ceded land in several Southeastern states, remained on a reservation in northwestern Georgia. There they created their own governing institutions following the European model: They wrote a constitution, established a legislature, and built schools and churches.

While Georgia passed laws stripping Cherokees of their rights, the Cherokees used every peaceful means of protest, including the printing press. When the *Cherokee Phoenix* wrote editorials against the laws, Georgians stole the printing press and jailed the staff. Cherokees fought against their removal from Georgia through the press, the courts, and Congress.

Editor Elias Boudinot, a college-educated missionary and clerk of the Cherokee National Council, wrote in both Cherokee and English, hoping the newspaper would help Native Americans to improve both their living conditions and their image in the larger white society. In this era, newspaper editors were often advocates, and political parties or other special interests often subsidized their publications. The *Cherokee Phoenix* received its support from the National Council, white Christian missionaries, and the fund-raising efforts of Boudinot and other Cherokee leaders. Improving a people's image through newspapers was another premise of contemporary journalism, especially among political parties and town boosters. As the First Amendment protected the U.S. press, the Native American press was to be free from restraint, despite its subsidy from the National Council.

The *Cherokee Phoenix* also depended upon the Cherokee language, a writing system that had been invented by a young Cherokee genius, Sequoyah, a few years earlier. Sequoyah was born around 1770 of a Cherokee mother and a white drifter. He saw that his people were at a disadvantage compared to the whites, who had a printed and written language. With no formal education, this half-breed child grew up to be the only person in history known to have created a written language single-handedly. His eighty-six-character syllabary, using syllables or sounds instead of letters as a basic form, allowed the easy translation of the traditionally oral Cherokee language into written form. Assembling words from these sounds proved easier than doing it from twenty-six letters. White observers were astonished at the speed with which young people learned the language. Cherokee children learned as much language in a few days as English children learned of their language in one or two years. Most of the nation became literate in a matter of months.

In its prospectus, the *Cherokee Phoenix* said the biweekly newspaper would provide laws and public documents of the Cherokee nation; accounts of manners, customs, and the progress of the nation in education, religion, and "the arts of civilized life"; the interesting news of the day; and miscellaneous articles to promote learning among the Cherokees.

The Reverend Samuel Worcester, a Protestant missionary to the Cherokees, provided essential support for the newspaper. Two white printers also accompanied the press, which had to await the manufacture of special type in New England to accommodate Sequoyah's syllabary. The printers set type on the hand press by taking detailed instructions from Worcester instead of learning the language. The printing office also published translations of the Bible into Cherokee. Trying to build an independent state within Georgia, the Cherokees received support from missionaries, Whig Party leaders, and ultimately the U.S. Supreme Court in *Worcester v. Georgia* (1832).

Worcester had refused to sign the loyalty oath that Georgia required of whites working among Native Americans. President Jackson refused to enforce the Court's decision, and Congress had passed the Indian Removal Act of 1830, setting up the process of forcing the Cherokees to move to Indian Territory, now parts of Oklahoma and Kansas. Reflecting his missionary-school background, Boudinot editorialized that Cherokees could become civilized and showed a condescending attitude toward Native Americans and other ethnic groups that did not accept Christian assumptions of progress. At first, Boudinot strongly editorialized against removal, despite the growth of individual acts of violence against Cherokees. As a relative of the Ridge family that eventually concluded that getting the best terms for removal was better than resistance, Boudinot signed the removal treaty without approval of the National Council.

Boudinot resisted pressure from Georgians, whose legislature in 1829 stripped Cherokees of their civil rights. Under the new laws, whites could commit crimes against Cherokees without punishment, because Cherokees were not allowed to testify against whites in court. Despite a Supreme Court decision supporting them, Jackson refused to intervene. "Full license to our oppressors, and every avenue of justice closed against us," the *Cherokee Phoenix* said. "Yes, this is the bitter cup prepared for us by a republican and religious government—we shall drink it to the very dregs." A year later, the newspaper reported harassment, arrest, and threats of physical harm to its staff members. After the newspaper protested the postmaster's sale of liquor to American Indians to encourage violent incidents, the postmaster retaliated by cutting off the mail.

The move left the *Cherokee Phoenix* without its source of supplies and exchange papers. "This new era," Boudinot wrote, "has not only wrested from us our rights and privileges as a people, but it has closed the channel through which we could formerly obtain our news. By this means the resources of the *Phoenix* are cut off." The newspaper said Native Americans had become more dependent upon sympathetic whites.

The *Cherokee Phoenix* debated basic issues within the Cherokee nation, including acculturation and Christianity. In the paper, national leaders debated how the new government should be organized and how elections should be conducted. While political candidates argued election issues, the newspaper proclaimed the need for national unity. Leaders debated the division of the legislature into two houses and the political system into two parties. The newspaper said all Cherokees must keep "the preservation of ourselves as a free and sovereign people" as their primary goal. The National Council approved a punishment of one hundred lashes against people who formed organizations to foster disunity among the Cherokees.

Violent conflicts between whites and natives became so common that many feared for the safety of Native Americans who remained in the Southeast. Friends seeking to protect Native Americans and enemies seeking to eliminate them came together to remove the Five Civilized Tribes to land west of the Mississippi. Because early voluntary removals had proved so disastrous to the Cherokees and the Choctaws, those remaining in Georgia vowed to remain on their native land. The elected principal chief, John Ross, ordered Boudinot to suppress news of dissention within the National Council over the removal issue; instead, the editor was to present a united front of Cherokee resistance against white encroachment.

The editor resigned in 1832, revealing that he could not manage the paper without a free discussion of such important issues. "I should think it my duty to tell them the whole truth. I cannot tell them that we shall be reinstated in our rights when I have no such hope." Ross appointed his brother-in-law, Elijah Hicks, but Hicks lacked Boudinot's journalistic experience and rhetorical power.

Outside pressure continued. In 1833, the postmaster sent letters to the *Cherokee Phoenix*'s exchanges, stating that the newspaper had been discontinued. The paper's publication became erratic, and in 1834, Hicks suspended publication. His parting editorial asked readers not to give up the fight. "Although our enemies are numerous we are still in the land of the living and the JUDGE of all the earth will impart the means for the salvation of our suffering Nation."

In the fall of 1838, Cherokee men, women, and children were rounded up and forced by the U.S. Cavalry to march from their Georgia home to Indian Territory. Thousands of people suffered and died on the walk that became known as the Trail of Tears. One morning in June, 1839, a band awaited Boudinot in trees near his new home, under construction. Two men approached him and asked him, as keeper of public medicine, for help. While they walked together, two others joined them. The group then stabbed Boudinot and smashed the former editor's head with a tomahawk six or seven times. They were part of a vigilante organization that held Boudinot and two other members of the Ridge faction responsible for selling Cherokee land, and in revenge carried out their capital punishment. Worcester, with whom Boudinot and his family had been staying, said the killers had cut off his right hand. Boudinot left a wife and six children. Worcester and printer John F. Wheeler, both of whom served prison time in Georgia for their work on the *Cherokee Phoenix*, helped the Cherokees start the *Cherokee Advocate* in 1844 with William P. Ross, the chief's nephew, as editor. It continued free distribution and publication in both Cherokee and English.

See also: Cherokee legal cases; *Cherokee Tobacco* case; Cherokee War; Indian Removal Act; Indian-white relations: U.S., 1831-1870; Trail of Tears.

William E. Huntzicker

Sources for Further Study

Boudinet, Elias. *Cherokee Editor: The Writings of Elias Boudinet.* Edited by Theda Perdue. Athens: University of Georgia Press, 1996. Collects nearly all of Boudinet's writings, with a biographical introduction and thorough annotations.

Danky, James P., ed. *Native American Periodicals and Newspapers, 1828-1982.* Westport, Conn.: Greenwood Press, 1984. Overview of the history of Native American newspapers.

Luebke, Barbara P. "Elias Boudinot, Indian Editor: Editorial Columns from the *Cherokee Phoenix.*" *Journalism History* 6 (1979): 48-51. Discusses Boudinot's conflicts as editor of the *Cherokee Phoenix.*

McLoughlin, William G. *Cherokees and Missionaries, 1789-1839.* New Haven, Conn.: Yale University Press, 1984. Discusses missionary support for the Cherokees.

Mooney, James. *Historical Sketch of the Cherokee.* Chicago: Aldine, 1975. Valuable study by a contemporary who interviewed people involved.

Murphy, James E., and Sharon M. Murphy. *Let My People Know: American Indian Journalism, 1828-1978.* Norman: University of Oklahoma Press, 1981. A history of Native American journalism, with some discussion of the *Cherokee Phoenix.*

Perdue, Theda, ed. *Cherokee Editor: The Writings of Elias Boudinot.* Knoxville: University of Tennessee Press, 1983. Brief biographical introduction to Boudinot, with reproductions of important documents in the history of the *Cherokee Phoenix* and Boudinot's fund-raising.

Riley, Sam G. "The *Cherokee Phoenix:* The Short, Unhappy Life of the First American Indian Newspaper." *Journalism Quarterly* 53, no. 4 (Winter, 1976): 666-671. Discusses Boudinot's editorial dilemmas and political pressure.

Cherokee Tobacco case

Date: Argued April 11, 1871; decided May 1, 1871
Locale: United States
Tribes involved: Cherokee, pantribal
Categories: Court cases, Nineteenth century history
Significance: This case, also known as *Boudinot v. United States*, established the "last-in-time" precedent—the concept that later statutes overrode earlier treaties—and the rule that tribes are "included" in congressional acts unless they are specifically "excluded."

In the *Cherokee Tobacco* suit, two Cherokee nationals, Elias Cornelius Boudinot and Stand Watie, challenged the imposition of an 1868 federal tax law on their tobacco factory, which had been established in the Cherokee Nation under provisions of the Cherokee/U.S. Treaty of 1866. (Although the year 1870 is often given for this case, it was actually argued in 1871; it was received by the Court in 1870.)

Article 10 of the 1866 treaty stated that Cherokee citizens had the right to sell any product or merchandise without having to pay "any tax thereon which is now or may be levied by the U.S." Two years later, Congress enacted a general revenue law which imposed taxes on liquor and tobacco products "produced anywhere within the exterior boundaries of the U.S." Justice Noah Swayne, speaking for a deeply fractured court (three justices concurred with Swayne, two dissented, and three did not participate), said that the case boiled down to which of the two laws—treaty or general domestic—was superior. (Swayne created this scenario even though there was no evidence that Congress in enacting the 1868 revenue law intended to abrogate Article 10 of the treaty.)

"Undoubtedly," said Swayne, "one or the other must yield. The repugnancy is clear and they cannot stand together." Swayne then developed what has been termed the "last-in-time" rule. In effect, whichever is latest in time, be it treaty or statute, stands.

This was a catastrophic precedent for tribes, since the treaty termination law, which had been attached as a rider to the March 3, 1871, Indian Appropriation Act, had closed the door on Indian treaties, although preexisting ratified treaties were still to be honored by the U.S. This law effectively froze tribes in political limbo: They were no longer recognized as nations capable of treating with the federal government, yet they remained separate sovereignties outside the pale of the federal Constitution.

Tribes, as a result of this decision, were virtually bereft of legal or political protection. The federal government could hereafter explicitly or implicitly abrogate treaty provisions and tribes had little recourse, save returning to the corridors of the very Congress that had enacted the abrogating legislation. The Supreme Court generally deferred to the political branches on Indian matters, going so far as to say that "the act of Congress must prevail as if the treaty were not an element to be considered."

This opinion ignored the historical and political reality that the Cherokee Nation was a separate and autonomous political entity not subject to general domestic laws unless they had given their express consent; it denied the fact that Congress itself had not explicitly stated in the 1868 law that the revenue act applied to Indian Territory. Moreover, it disavowed the general principle that specific laws, such as treaties, which create special rights are not to be held "repealed by implication by any subsequent law couched in general terms."

Notwithstanding earlier U.S. guarantees of the sanctity of treaty rights, *Cherokee Tobacco* announced that those hard-fought-for rights, often secured at the cost of great amounts of tribal land and the loss of other rights, could be destroyed by mere implication.

This cartoon in Puck *magazine satirizes the confused and inconsistent nature of U.S. Indian policy in the late nineteenth century; among the problems here are the "Boston sentimentalist," the weapons trader, and the government Indian agent.* (Library of Congress)

See also: Cherokee legal cases; *Cherokee Phoenix*; Cherokee War; Indian Appropriation Act; Indian Removal Act; Indian-white relations: U.S., 1831-1870; Trail of Tears.

David E. Wilkins

Cherokee War

Date: October 5, 1759-November 19, 1761
Locale: Charles Town, South Carolina, and several Cherokee territories
Tribes involved: Cherokee
Categories: Colonial history, Wars and battles
Significance: Total destruction of several Cherokee communities presages the Cherokee alliance with the British in the Revolutionary War.

The Cherokees, a Native American people inhabiting the southern Appalachian highlands, first encountered visitors from the Old World on May 30, 1540, during the wanderings of the Spanish explorer Hernando de Soto. For more than a century after this first meeting, the Cherokees had little direct contact with European colonists. During the late seventeenth century and early eighteenth century, trade began to develop between the Cherokees and the English colonies of Virginia, North Carolina, and South Carolina. This relationship was strengthened during the Yamasee War (1715-1728), when the Cherokees were allied with the colonists against other Native American peoples. The relationship was enhanced in 1730, when Scottish aristocrat Alexander Cumming visited the Cherokees and took seven of them to England, where they met King George II and signed a trade agreement. One of the seven was the young Attakullakulla, who would turn out to be the strongest advocate for peace with the English colonists.

The 1750's saw increasing rivalry between France and England, which evolved into the Seven Years' War (1756-1763), a conflict that had already begun to manifest itself in North America as the French and Indian War (1754-1763). Because of the threat of the French and their Native American allies, the South Carolinians built Fort Prince George near the Cherokee town of Keowee in 1753 and Fort Loudoun near the town of Chota in 1756. These forts were designed to offer protection to the Cherokees in exchange for their aid to the English in the war with the French.

From 1756 to 1759, even as the forts were being built, several violent incidents between Cherokees and colonists led the way to war. The most critical of these occurred when a group of Cherokees making their way home from an abortive battle with the French-allied Shawnee through the back-country of Virginia were attacked by settlers, who killed twenty-four of them. The settlers defended their action by accusing the Cherokees of stealing their horses and food. The governor of Virginia, Robert Dinwiddie, offered gifts and apologies to the relatives of the victims, but many Cherokees demanded retribution. Cherokee warriors killed twenty-four settlers in South Carolina in revenge.

Lyttleton Plans an Invasion. The Cherokee War can be thought of as officially beginning on October 5, 1759, when William Henry Lyttelton, governor of South Carolina, announced his intention to lead an army into Cherokee territory. On October 20, a peace delegation led by Oconostota, the head warrior of the Cherokees, arrived in Charles Town in an attempt to prevent further hostilities. They were placed under arrest and forced to march with the troops. When Lyttelton arrived at Fort Prince George on December 10, the prisoners were held captive inside the fort. Attakulla-kulla, the most important negotiator for the Cherokees, arrived on December 17 and managed to secure the release of Oconostota and several other prisoners, but twenty-two remained hostages. Lyttelton refused to release them until twenty-four Cherokees were executed for the killing of the settlers. He was forced to retreat on December 28, when symptoms of smallpox, which had been raging in the town of Keowee, began to appear among his troops.

Cherokee warriors led by Oconostota surrounded the fort as soon as Lyttelton left. On February 16, 1760, the commander of the fort was lured out with the promise of negotiation and shot by concealed warriors. In retaliation, the soldiers at the fort killed the hostages. This ended any possibility of preventing a full-scale war and led to attacks on settlers.

William Bull, lieutenant governor and Lyttleton's successor, appealed to General Jeffrey Amherst, supreme commander of British forces in North America, for help. On April 1, twelve hundred soldiers commanded by Colonel Archibald Montgomery arrived in Charles Town. On June 1, they reached Keowee, which they burned to the ground. Other towns in the area, known to the colonists as the Lower Towns, were also destroyed, along with all the crops being grown there.

During these attacks, Montgomery's troops killed sixty Cherokees and took forty prisoners, while facing little opposition. Montgomery relieved the garrison at Fort Prince George and marched toward the area known as the Middle Towns. On June 27, near the town of Echoe, Cherokee warriors launched a surprise attack on the British troops, killing twenty of them and wounding seventy. Although the Cherokees withdrew, the British were forced to retreat. A month later, they left South Carolina to rejoin the war against the French in Canada.

Meanwhile, Oconostota's warriors had surrounded Fort Loudoun. Deprived of the relief given to Fort Prince George, Captain Paul Demere, commander of the fort, surrendered on August 8 rather than face starvation. The surrendering garrison was to turn over all its munitions and be escorted safely out of Cherokee territory. Because Demere attempted to conceal some of the fort's munitions, he and thirty-two of his soldiers were killed and the rest taken prisoner.

Amherst sent two thousand troops under the command of Colonel James Grant to avenge the loss of the fort. On March 20, 1761, Grant left Charles Town, arriving at Fort Prince George on May 27. There he met with Attakullakulla, but Grant refused the Cherokee's offer to intercede with the warriors. On June 7, Grant left the fort and headed for the Middle Towns. On June 10, within two miles of the place where Montgomery's troops were attacked, Grant fought a battle with the Cherokees, leaving ten British soldiers killed and fifty wounded. The Cherokees withdrew because of a lack of ammunition. Grant spent the next month destroying fifteen Middle Towns and fifteen hundred acres of crops. Approximately five thousand Cherokees were forced to flee into the forest to survive on whatever food they could find in the wild.

Peace Negotiations. After this devastating attack, Attakullakulla and several other Cherokee leaders met with Grant at Fort Prince George to ask for peace. A treaty was prepared demanding the execution of four Cherokee leaders, the elimination of all relations between the Cherokees and the French, the sovereignty of the British courts over all offenders within Cherokee territory, and the establishment of a line twenty-six miles east of Keowee as the border of South Carolina. The Cherokees could not accept the demand for executions. Attakullakulla asked to speak to Bull directly. He was allowed to travel to Charles Town and was welcomed by the governor as a loyal friend of the English. The demand for executions was dropped, and the treaty was signed on September 23. A separate treaty was signed with Virginia on November 19, officially ending the Cherokee War.

Conflicts between the Cherokees and the colonists continued until well after the end of the American Revolution (1783), during which the Cherokees were allied with the British. A series of land cessions to the newly independent United States during the late eighteenth and early nineteenth centuries left the Cherokees with only a small portion of their land. In a final attempt to survive as an independent people, the Cherokees adopted the ways of the Americans, even going so far as to set up a government modeled after that of the United States. Despite this effort, the Cherokees were finally forced to leave their native land for Oklahoma during the infamous Trail of Tears removals in the 1830's.

See also: Cherokee legal cases; *Cherokee Phoenix; Cherokee Tobacco* case; Indian Removal Act; Indian-white relations: U.S., 1831-1870; Trail of Tears; Yamasee War.

Rose Secrest

Sources for Further Study

Corkran, David H. *The Cherokee Frontier: Conflict and Survival 1740-1762.* Norman: University of Oklahoma Press, 1962. A detailed account of the complex relations between the Cherokees and English colonists during the mid-1700's.

Hatley, Tom. *The Dividing Paths: Cherokees and South Carolinians Through the Era of Revolution.* New York: Oxford University Press, 1993. Focuses on the multicultural aspects of the Cherokee War, including a discussion of the roles of women and African slaves.

Mails, Thomas E. "Transformation of a Culture." In *The Cherokee People: The Story of the Cherokees from Earliest Origins to Contemporary Times.* Tulsa, Okla.: Council Oak Books, 1992. Describes the history of relations between Cherokees and Europeans up to the Trail of Tears.

Milling, Chapman J. "The Cherokee War." In *Red Carolinians.* Chapel Hill: University of North Carolina Press, 1940. A detailed, carefully documented account of the war. An important reference despite its age.

Oliphant, John. *Peace and War on the Anglo-Cherokee Frontier, 1976-1763.* Baton Rouge: Louisiana State University Press, 2001. Focuses on the clashes of individual personalities that fomented the war.

Woodward, Grace Steele. "'The King, Our Father.'" In *The Cherokees.* Norman: University of Oklahoma Press, 1963. A history of the Cherokee people from the start of the Yamasee War until the end of the Cherokee War.

Civil War

Date: 1861-1865
Locale: Indian Territory, southwest Missouri, western Arkansas
Tribes involved: Cherokee, Chickasaw, Choctaw, Creek, Seminole

Categories: Nineteenth century history, Wars and battles
Significance: A great Native American leads an Indian regiment for the Confederacy and is the last to surrender.

With the outbreak of the Civil War in 1861, both the Union and the Confederacy looked toward the Indian Territory for support. American Indians there, mostly members of the famed Five Civilized Tribes (the Cherokee, Chickasaw, Choctaw, Creek, and Seminole), had connections with the federal government through various agencies, but most also had Southern roots in the Carolinas, Alabama, Kentucky, Georgia, and Tennessee. In March, 1861, Confederate president Jefferson Davis commissioned Albert Pike to visit Indian Territory to seek treaties with the Five Civilized Tribes. It was hoped that a strong Confederate force in Indian Territory would prevent Union sympathizers in Kansas from raiding Texas. Pike's visit with all the tribes in Indian Territory was largely successful. Shortly afterward, General Ben McCulloch raised two American Indian regiments: one led by Colonel John Drew and the other by Colonel Stand Watie. Drew and Watie were bitter enemies, and during much of the war commanders on the western front kept the two Cherokee regiments separated as much as possible. Watie, a mixed-blood Cherokee, had been born in Georgia and was one of the signers of the New Echota Treaty, which sold Cherokee lands in Georgia to the United States government. He was also a prosperous Cherokee landowner and businessman, a brilliant warrior, and a member of an opposition faction within the Cherokee tribe. His signature on the new Echota Treaty put him at odds with the more dominant faction of the Cherokee Nation, led by John Ross.

Stand Watie was one of the Cherokee signers of the Treaty of New Echota; he later raised a Cherokee regiment for the Confederacy. (Library of Congress)

Watie Joins the Confederacy. Watie was a great leader, and even in the face of extreme hardships, especially during the winter months, he kept his regiment together and participated in numerous battles. Although the treaties that had been signed with the Confederacy promised that Indian regiments would not be required to fight outside Indian Territory, Watie's troops also were called to duty in Missouri and Arkansas. Over a four-year span, the old Cherokee warrior and his forces fought at Wilson's Creek, Newtonia, Bird Creek, Pea Ridge, Spavinaw, Fort Wayne, Fort Gibson, Honey Springs, Webber's Falls, Poison Spring, Massard Prairie, and Cabin Creek. Watie's abilities on the battlefield were widely recognized and greatly heralded by both his contemporaries and historians. His greatest skills were gaining and keeping the confidence of his troops and his wily guerrilla tactics. Watie's regiment, without his presence on the field, also fought the Second Battle at Newtonia in Southwest Missouri in 1864. The first Newtonia battle, fought in 1862, is of major historic significance, because it was the only Civil War battle in which American Indians fought on both sides. In most battles, Watie's Confederate Cherokees fought admirably. In a losing cause at the Battle of Pea Ridge in Arkansas, however, they and Colonel Drew's troops were accused of bad conduct because they were too easily routed during the battle and because they allegedly scalped some of the federal casualties. This act, when reported to the upper command of the Confederate Army, created a great embarrassment among officers, most of whom had been trained at such prestigious military academies as West Point, where cadets were taught to be gentlemen as well as warriors. The loss at Pea Ridge was made even greater by the death of General McCulloch, who had organized and fought with the Cherokees from the beginning.

Despite the overwhelming support given the Confederacy in 1861, when the tide of war turned in favor of the Union and the Confederacy became unable to supply its forces on the frontier, disenchantment took hold of the leaders of the various tribes. In February, 1863, the Cherokee Council met on Cowskin Prairie in Indian Territory and voted to end its alliance with the Confederacy. Colonel Watie refused to accept the vote and vowed to continue his fight. This created an even deeper split in the Cherokee tribe. Watie's forces and Cherokee civilians with attachments in the South remained loyal to Watie, even establishing a government that they claimed was the legitimate government of the Cherokee Nation. These Southern sympathizers elected Watie as the principal chief. Those now aligned with Union forces recognized John Ross as their chief, although he left Indian Territory and returned to his wife's family in Pennsylvania. At the time of this deepening split, there were about ten thousand Cherokees with Union sympathies and seven thousand supporters of the Confederacy. This situation actually created a civil war within a civil war.

On May 10, 1864, Watie was promoted to the rank of brigadier general, the only American Indian to attain this rank in the Civil War. In the remaining months of the conflict, General Watie fought without reservations for his beloved Confederacy. One of his most spectacular successes was the sinking of the steam-driven ferry *J. R. Williams* on the Arkansas River at Pleasant Bluff and making off with food and clothing for his Cherokee and Creek troopers, breaking a major supply route for Union forces at Fort Gibson. Successful raids on Union supplies kept Watie's forces busy, supplied, and inspired to stay in the fight.

The Battle of Cabin Creek. Because the battlefield situation for the Confederacy was growing worse, Watie called all the Cherokee units to his camp on June 24, 1864. At that meeting, the Cherokee Troops, Confederate States of America, resolved to "unanimously re-enlist as soldiers for the war, be it long or short." In September of 1864, Watie masterminded a plan to attack and steal a Union supply-wagon train worth one million dollars. This battle was fought at Cabin Creek in Indian Territory and is said to have been Watie's greatest success. His brilliance and bravery were not enough, however, as the Confederacy was losing battle after battle. On April 9, 1865, General Robert E. Lee surrendered for the Confederacy at Appomattox Courthouse in Virginia. General Watie fought on, hoping to win the battle for the West, but it was not to be. On June 23, 1865, Brigadier General Stand Watie surrendered at Doakesville in Indian Territory, the last Confederate general to lay down his sword.

The contribution made by American Indians in the Civil War was enormous. An estimated 3,500 fought for the Union and 1,018, or more than 28 percent, died while in service to their country. Census figures in the Cherokee Nation showed a population of 21,000 in 1860. By 1867, that number had dropped to 13,566. Approximately one-third of the nation had been lost, either in battle or to hunger and exposure, which were suffered by soldiers and civilians alike. After the war, General Watie became more involved in the political activities of the Cherokee Nation and in resettling his people in the aftermath of the conflict. On September 7, 1871, the great general became ill and was taken to his old home at Honey Creek, where he died on September 9.

See also: *Cherokee Tobacco* case; Indian-white relations: U.S., 1831-1870.

Kay Hively

Sources for Further Study

Cunningham, Frank. *General Stand Watie's Confederate Indians*. 1959. Reprint. Norman: University of Oklahoma Press, 1998. A full account of Stand Watie's efforts during the Civil War and his political life within the Cherokee Nation. Many photographs of that era.

Dale, Edward Everett, and Morris L. Wardell. *History of Oklahoma*. New York: Prentice-Hall, 1948. Contains a thorough chapter on the Civil War in Oklahoma by two outstanding Oklahoma historians.

Gaines, W. Craig. *The Confederate Cherokees: John Drew's Regiment of Mounted Rifles*. Baton Rouge: Louisiana State University Press, 1989. Concentrates on Colonel John Drew's regiment and contrasts it with Stand Watie's more successful regiment.

Josephy, Alvin M., Jr. *Civil War in the American West*. New York: Alfred A. Knopf, 1991. Discusses the Civil War battles that were fought west of the Mississippi River.

Woodworth, S. E. *Jefferson Davis and His Generals: The Failure of Confederate Command in the West*. Lawrence: University Press of Kansas, 1990. Discusses Jefferson's top military men and their leadership on the Western front during the Civil War.

Code of Handsome Lake

Date: 1799
Locale: Western New York State
Tribes involved: Iroquois Confederacy
Categories: Eighteenth century history, Nineteenth century history, Religion and missionary activities
Significance: Native American and Christian traditions merge to create the Longhouse religion, aimed at reviving indigenous cultures.

The Code of Handsome Lake was one of several Native American religions that evolved in reaction to European colonization. These religions often combined traditional Native American beliefs and rituals with the introduction of a Christian-style savior who was said to be able to recapture for Native Americans the better days they had known before colonization. One well-known example of this fusion was the Ghost Dance religion, which was begun by the prophet Wovoka, who had been raised with both Native American and Christian influences. Tenskwatawa (also known as the Delaware Prophet) also formulated a religion that combined both traditions during the eighteenth century.

Handsome Lake. Handsome Lake was born at Conawagus, a Seneca village near contemporary Avon, New York, on the Genesee River. He was a member of the Seneca nation, one of the five nations that had joined together as the Iroquois Confederacy. His personal name was Ganeodiyo; Handsome Lake, a reference to Lake Ontario, is one of the fifty chieftainship lines of the Iroquois Confederacy, a title bestowed on him by clan mothers. He was a half brother of the Seneca chief Cornplanter and an uncle of Red Jacket. Handsome Lake and many other Senecas sided with the British in the French and Indian War and the American Revolution. George Washington and his subcommanders, principally General John Sullivan, were merciless with Native Americans who supported the British. During the late stages of the revolution, many Seneca communities were laid waste by scorched-earth marches that destroyed crops, livestock, and homes.

After that war, many Iroquois and other Native Americans who had supported the British were forced into Canada, principally to lands secured by Joseph Brant at Grand River. Others fled westward to join other Native Americans who were still free. Those who remained in their homelands were forced onto small, impoverished reservations, and repeated attempts were made to force them out. It is estimated that by 1794, the Iroquois population had shrunk to approximately four thousand people.

Handsome Lake's revival occurred in an atmosphere of dissension within a fractured Iroquois Confederacy. The course of his life reflected the devastation of his people. Born into a prominent family of the Turtle clan, Handsome Lake distinguished himself as a leader as a young man, before the American Revolution, when Iroquois society was still largely intact. Handsome Lake's decline began after his birthplace was taken by whites, and he was forced to move to the Allegheny Seneca reservation. The Seneca ethnologist Arthur Parker characterized Handsome Lake as a middle-sized man, unhealthy looking, dissolute, and an alcoholic. After four years lying ill in a small cabin under the care of a daughter, Handsome Lake began having a series of visions. Later, he used these visions to rally the Iroquois at a time when some of them were selling their entire winter harvest of furs for hard liquor, turning traditional ceremonies into drunken brawls, and in winter, often dying of exposure in drunken stupors.

Visions and Spiritual Rebirth. Handsome Lake experienced considerable remorse over his alcoholism, but he did not stop drinking until he was nearly dead. In 1799, Handsome Lake experienced a number of visions in which he was taken on a great journey to the sky. During this journey, he was shown a number of personages and events from the past, present, and future. In one of his visions, Handsome Lake met George Washington, who had died that year, and heard him confirm the sovereignty of the Iroquois.

After this series of visions, Handsome Lake stopped his heavy drinking and later committed his code to writing. He persuaded many other Iroquois to stop drinking and to reconstruct their lives. During his own lifetime, Handsome Lake achieved some political influence among the Senecas, but his popularity was limited because of his ideological rigidity. In 1801 and 1802, he traveled to Washington, D.C., with a delegation of Senecas to meet with President Thomas Jefferson and resist the reduction of Iroquois landholdings.

The Code of Handsome Lake combines European religious influences (especially those practiced by the Quakers, which Handsome Lake had studied) with a traditional Iroquois emphasis on family, community, and the centrality of the land to the maintenance of culture. Handsome Lake's largest following came after his death. Adherents to his code rejected alcohol and accepted his concepts of social relationships, good, and evil, which closely resemble Quakerism. The Quaker creed appealed to many Iroquois because the Quakers had been persecuted before coming to America, they had no ornate temples, and they lived frugally and communally, doing their best to respect their Native American neighbors.

Syncretistic Religion. A nationalistic figure in a religious context, Handsome Lake also borrowed heavily from the Iroquois Great Law of Peace, popularizing concepts such as looking into the future for seven generations and regarding the earth as mother, ideas that became part of pan-Indian thought across North America and were incorporated into late twentieth century popular environmental symbolism. With its combination of Old and New World theologies, the Code of Handsome Lake sought to reconcile the gods of Europe and America. It was to be so successful that it both subsumed the ancient religion and halted the spread of Christianity among the Iroquois. The Code of Handsome Lake has continued to be widely followed in Iroquois country as the Longhouse religion. In the late twentieth century, roughly a third of the thirty thousand Iroquois in New York State attended Longhouse rites.

Although his code remained popular among many Iroquois, others accused Handsome Lake of having sold out to the Quakers and white religious interests in general. Louis Hall, ideological founder of the Warrior

Society in Iroquois country, regarded the religion of Handsome Lake as a bastardized form of Christianity grafted onto native traditions. Hall called Handsome Lake's visions "the hallucinations of a drunk." Opposition to these teachings is one plank in an intellectual platform that allows the Warriors to brand both the Mohawk Nation Council at Akwesasne and the Iroquois Confederacy Council as enemies of the people, and to claim that the Warriors are the true protectors of "Mohawk sovereignty." Hall, who died in 1993, regarded Handsome Lake's followers as traitors or "Tontos." Hall's Warriors split bitterly with followers of Handsome Lake over gambling and other issues, leading to violence at Akwesasne, which peaked in 1990 with the deaths of two Mohawks.

See also: Iroquois Confederacy; Iroquois Confederacy-U.S. Congress meeting.

Bruce E. Johansen

Sources for Further Study

Deardorff, Merle H. *The Religion of Handsome Lake: Its Origins and Development*. American Bureau of Ethnology Bulletin 149. Washington, D.C.: Smithsonian Institution Press, 1951. Presents a detailed analysis of the Handsome Lake religion from an ethnographic perspective.

Handsome Lake. *The Code of Handsome Lake, the Seneca Prophet*. New York State Museum Bulletin 163. Albany: University of the State of New York, 1913. Outlines the Handsome Lake religion and discusses the historical circumstances of its creation.

Johansen, Bruce E. *Life and Death in Mohawk Country*. Golden, Colo.: North American Press, 1993. Details conflicts involving followers of Handsome Lake's code and Louis Hall's Warriors at Akwesasne in the late twentieth century.

Parker, Arthur. *Parker on the Iroquois*. Edited by William Fenton. Syracuse, N.Y.: Syracuse University Press, 1968. A detailed description of the Handsome Lake religion by a noted Seneca ethnologist.

Wallace, Anthony F. C. *The Death and Rebirth of the Seneca*. New York: Alfred A. Knopf, 1970. A classic work on the history of the Seneca at the time of Handsome Lake.

Wright, Ronald. *Stolen Continents*. Boston: Houghton Mifflin, 1992. A wide-ranging study of North America since the voyages of Columbus. Contains extensive treatment of the Iroquois Confederacy; describes Handsome Lake and his religion in the general context of the subjugation of the confederacy after the Revolutionary War.

Code talkers

Date: 1942-1945
Locale: United States, Pacific theater of World War II
Tribes involved: Navajo
Categories: Twentieth century history
Significance: Navajo code talkers provided a secure communications system that helped significantly in the United States' defeat of Japan in World War II.

By the late nineteenth and early twentieth centuries, industrialization had progressed to such a point that every area of American life was impacted. Communications particularly was affected by the invention and widespread adoption of the telephone, telegraph, and radio. When applied to military operations and strategy, the impact of such devices was readily apparent. As military operations reached large-scale operations, as field commanders' need to keep in touch with ground and air forces intensified, and as the avoidance of "friendly fire" casualties became a serious concern, the armed services searched for ways to communicate with each sector of their organizations without having the enemy eavesdrop or decipher what was being said. Early examples of these efforts to secure an effective encrypted communications network included the British reliance on Latin in the Boer War; the United States' reliance on the Choctaw language in October, 1918, against the German army in field operations; and American army efforts, through the Bureau of Indian Affairs early in World War II, to use the Comanche language. Although each of these attempts had limited success, it was the Navajo code talkers who would be the most important of all.

Given the lack of knowledge of Native American languages by America's enemies in World War II, as well as the reliance of these languages on oral, not written, tradition, the American military command, especially Major General Clayton Vogel (Army) and General Thomas Holcomb (Marines), investigated the possibilities of using these languages. What made the Navajo language so attractive was that fact that it is primarily verbal, relies heavily on intonation, and includes words with multiple meanings and highly complex verbs. Once the logistical problems were resolved, the Navajo language would prove to be an almost perfectly encrypted tool for military communications in the Pacific theater of the American war.

Adoption and Recruitment of Code Talkers. The individual most responsible for the Marines' use of the Navajo language in World War II was

Philip Johnston. The son of missionaries, he was familiar with the Navajo's culture and language. He contacted the Marine Corps' Signal Corps and explained his ideas to the officers in charge. Arguing that the Navajo language was not well known and relied heavily on verbal intonations, Johnston persuaded the Marines to give it a test. On February 28, 1942, the test was conducted at Camp Elliot in California. In every test situation, the Navajos successfully sent and received messages. Within three months of the successful test, twenty-nine Navajos (the First 29) were recruited and sent to San Diego, California, for training. Recruit Platoon 382 was in boot camp for eight weeks and then shipped out. This original group of the First 29 developed the code that would be used throughout the war. Working together, First 29 established a code of 211 words and phrases. After field experience and experimentation, the code increased to 619 words and phrases by the end of 1945. Given the fact that the Navajo language did not contain words for military names or operations, the code talkers devised their own code for identifying what was lacking in the language itself. For instance, Adolf Hitler was *Daghailchiih* (Mustard Smeller), "bat-

Navajo communications men known as "code talkers" with the U.S. Marines on Saipan c. June, 1944. (National Archives)

tleship" was *lotso* (whale), and "torpedo plane" became *taschizzie* (swallow). Many other name changes, vowel inversions, and specific intonations were incorporated into the code, making it even more difficult to unravel—so much so that even native Navajos had a difficult time in understanding everything that was being said unless they had been trained in the code itself.

World War II. Given the government's policy of assimilation and all it entailed for Native Americans, it is surprising that the Navajo were interested in helping the American war effort. If nothing else, the Meriam Report (1928) demonstrated just how terrible conditions were on the reservations throughout the country. Fortunately, enough attention was drawn to these problems that President Franklin D. Roosevelt signed into law the Wheeler-Howard Act (the Indian New Deal) in 1934. Under the guidance of John Collier at the Bureau of Indian Affairs, the dismemberment of general allotment took place and Native Americans were at least accorded their rights to communal land ownership and tribal identity. What made the Navajos join in the war effort depended on each individual. Essentially, however, it seems that the New Deal effort had its effect, because those Navajos who did sign up did so for patriotic reasons, to defend their country. Some Navajos also openly admitted that the Marines were very attractive to them because of their dress uniforms.

Due to the efforts of John Benally and John Manuelito, two hundred Navajos were recruited for the code talking sector of the Corps. Recruiting was a difficult task, in that the Navajos recruited had to speak both Navajo and English proficiently. Also, the problems associated with the code and its importance had to be overcome. For example, since the code was so important to military operations, the Marines literally kept it secret, thereby preventing the Navajos from keeping in touch with relatives and friends. Even in field operations, not all officers and men were informed of the purpose of the Navajos. To make matters worse, the Navajos, who in many ways physically looked like the enemy, were sometimes mistaken for Japanese. The Marines overcame these problems quickly by assigning bodyguards to each code talker, as well as allowing the tribal members to continue cultural practices whenever feasible. Despite the fact that they were often referred to as "Chief" or "Geronimo," the Navajos got along well with their compatriots in the Corps.

Thirty-six hundred Navajos served in World War II, but only 420 were code talkers. The list of battles in which the code talkers participated was impressive: Saipan, Tinian, Bougainville, Okinawa, Tarawa, Guadalcanal, Iwo Jima, the Solomon Islands (on loan to the American Navy). The code talkers were also used to report on the effects of the atomic bombs at Hiroshima and Nagasaki.

Despite all their efforts, the Japanese could never successfully break the Navajo code. At one point, the Japanese captured a code talker and tortured him to get the secrets of encryption. However, what the Japanese did not realize was that even the captured Navajo could not completely unravel the language and codes developed by the First 29.

Postwar Recognition. The Marines were so concerned with protecting the secrecy of the code talkers that anyone who gave the information out was dealt with immediately. One good example was Philip Johnston himself, who had approached the Army with the possibility of using the code talkers. The Marines actually reprimanded Johnston for doing so. Such secrecy also meant that the code talkers could not tell their relatives and friends what they had done during the war. This often led to psychological problems for the code talkers themselves. It was not until much later that official recognition was finally accorded to the Navajo code talkers.

The Navajo code talkers had their first reunion in 1969, thereby drawing national attention to what they had done. In 1982, President Ronald Reagan pronounced August 14 as "National Navajo Code Talkers Day." Ten years later, the Pentagon officially recognized the code talkers in ceremonies performed there when an historical exhibit was opened to the public. Today, the remaining code talkers still maintain contact through their organization, the Navajo Code Talkers Association (formed in July, 1971). Fortunately for posterity, the significant contributions of the Navajo code talkers in World War II will not be forgotten.

Michael V. Namorato

See also: World wars.

Sources for Further Study

Adkins, Adam. "The Navajo Code Talkers in World War II." *New Mexico Historical Review* (October, 1997): 319-347. Good overview of the literature, founding, and problems of the code talkers in World War II.

McClain, Sally. *Navajo Weapon*. Boulder, Colo.: Books Beyond Borders, 1994. Provides an overview of the code talkers.

Paul, Doris. *The Navajo Code Talkers*. Pittsburgh, Pa.: Dorrance, 1973. Gives a good overview of the Navajo code talkers and their contributions during World War II.

Watson, Bruce. "Navajo Code Talkers: A Few Good Men." *Smithsonian* (August, 1993): 34-43. A personal account of some of the code talkers themselves.

Colliflower v. Garland

Date: 1964
Locale: Fort Belknap, Montana
Tribes involved: Pantribal in the United States
Categories: Civil rights, Court cases, Twentieth century history
Significance: The U.S. Court of Appeals decision that federal courts do have the right to determine the legality of tribal court orders of detention influenced the U.S. Congress to pass the Indian Civil Rights Act in 1968.

In 1964, Madeline Colliflower was arrested and held in jail over a minor dispute with the Fort Belknap (Montana) tribal council and tribal court about renewal of a land lease. She was an enrolled member of the tribe. She objected to being jailed and sued the tribe in federal court on a writ of *habeas corpus*, claiming she was illegally imprisoned, was denied the right to counsel, was denied a trial, and was never confronted with witnesses against her. She charged that her constitutional rights had been violated.

The federal district court denied Colliflower's petition, stating that tribal governments were not bound to protect constitutional rights of enrolled members living on the reservation. The U.S. Court of Appeals overturned that decision and ruled in Colliflower's favor. It ruled that federal courts do have the right to determine the validity and legality of tribal court orders of detention. This decision was a blow to tribal sovereignty and brought forth issues of civil rights in Indian country. Among others, this case influenced the U.S. Congress to pass the Indian Civil Rights Act (1968), which extends certain protections to individuals living under tribal government.

See also: Indian Civil Rights Act;

Carole A. Barrett

Council of Energy Resource Tribes

Date: Established 1975
Locale: United States
Tribes involved: Pantribal in the United States

Categories: Organizations, Twentieth century history
Significance: The Council of Energy Resource Tribes (CERT), founded by a group of tribal leaders, provides tribes with advice on developing and marketing the mineral and energy resources on their lands in ways that will maximize profit for, and control by, the tribes themselves.

The Council of Energy Resource Tribes (CERT), with offices in Denver, Colorado, was organized in 1975 to gain an understanding of the natural resources controlled by the Native American tribes within the United States. Peter MacDonald, then chairperson of the Navajo Nation, was the first elected chair of the organization. It initially set out to inventory the natural resources of the various tribes in the western United States. It found that the tribes controlled one-third of the energy sources in coal and uranium as well as large supplies of petroleum, natural gas, and other essential resources. The next step was to integrate all aspects of reservation development.

The Council of Energy Resource Tribes undertook a series of studies that indicated that the U.S. Bureau of Indian Affairs (BIA) had based its development efforts on irrelevant and inaccurate assumptions. CERT indicated that it was imperative that American Indian tribes work harder to provide employment. Tribes and CERT had to leverage funds and services to obtain the financial resources necessary for balanced development. CERT recognized the desire to advance on the part of the tribes, whereas the BIA could not recognize this in tribal actions. CERT also saw that prosperity and the Indian ways of doing things were not mutually exclusive.

See also: Alaska Native Brotherhood and Alaska Native Sisterhood; Bureau of Indian Affairs.

Howard Meredith

Creek War

Date: July 27, 1813-August 9, 1814
Locale: Alabama
Tribes involved: Muscogee (Creek)
Categories: Nineteenth century history, Wars and battles
Significance: The destruction of the Creek nation opens Alabama to settlement and positions Andrew Jackson to win the War of 1812.

Of all American Indian cultures, the Muscogee (called "Creeks" by the white populace) seemed the most likely to assimilate into the advancing white culture of the 1700's and early 1800's. Colonial deerskin traders from Charleston, South Carolina, married into this matrilineal native culture, establishing kinship ties with their wives' families throughout the nation of Muscogee and siring mixed-blood children who became the nation's cultural and political elite. Alexander McGillivray—of Scottish, French, and Muscogee background—was educated in Charleston and became one of the most powerful and influential micos (chiefs) in the culture's history. William Weatherford, William McIntosh, and others born to both cultures remained influential in the tribe through and beyond the coming Creek War.

President George Washington appointed Revolutionary War veteran Benjamin Hawkins as Indian Agent to the Muscogee, and Hawkins attempted to teach the Muscogee modern, European-derived farming techniques. With well-established agricultural traditions of their own, the Muscogee took easily to the teachings of both Hawkins and their own mixed-blood people. The Muscogees established within their nation a subculture that featured frame houses, fenced fields, domesticated animals, the adoption of Anglo clothing and technology, and all the other vestments of the traditional frontier South, including cotton production with African American slave labor for the wealthy.

The transition was not smooth, however. One problem was the continued encroachment of white civilization. So relentless were the demands of state governments for cessions of Muscogee lands that the natives named one Tennessee governor the Dirt King and gave a Georgia governor the name Always Asking for Land.

Land Hunger and Genocide. As buckskin breeches went out of fashion in Europe, the market for American deerskins evaporated. The Muscogee now found themselves with nothing to trade for the white man's clothing, weapons, household utensils, and other goods to which they had become accustomed. Continuing to buy these goods on credit, they fell deeply into debt to U.S. and British trading houses. The Jefferson administration, through Hawkins, encouraged the paying off of these debts through cessions of land. The Muscogee strenuously objected to this plan, even when the U.S. government offered perpetual annuities to the tribe and bonuses to local micos who signed land treaties. The pressure on Muscogee hunting grounds intensified, and those micos who ceded land became enemies in the eyes of many of their kinsmen.

More sinister than the United States' insatiable land hunger was its innate distrust of American Indians and its general desire to eliminate rather than assimilate them. Some segments of the native population—Iroquois, Shawnee, Cherokee, Muscogee— seemed to be constantly at war with the frontiersmen. For whites, these violent clashes supported their belief that American Indians were dangerous savages in need of extermination. Another problem was the strength and depth of the Muscogees' own native culture. Their relationship to their environment and their tribal traditions had been deeply satisfying. Although white culture made life more comfortable, it did not resolve any life-threatening problem for the Muscogee. Thus, it was a luxury, not a necessity.

Choctaw leader Pushmataha was made a brigadier general in the U.S. Army for his service in the Creek War and the War of 1812. (Library of Congress)

The pressure of encroaching white settlement continued to increase all along the U.S. frontier in the early 1800's, prompting the Shawnee chief Tecumseh to attempt an alliance of all Native American tribes so that, together, they might resist further white advances and save American Indian lands and culture. When Tecumseh and his brother, Tenskwatawa, known as the Prophet, visited the Muscogee tribal council to urge an alliance with the Shawnee, head mico Big Warrior rejected the idea and called for continued peace with white Americans. A movement—part spiritual, part political—was already growing among the Muscogee, however, calling for a return to the roots of Muscogee tradition and a rejection of the values and artifacts of white society.

The traditionalists were primarily young. Among their leaders were men who had successfully assimilated white culture—half-white cotton planters such as Peter McQueen, and such white traders' sons as William Weatherford and Josiah Francis. The leaders of the progressive, assimilationist wing were often older. Some, like William McIntosh, lived like white men. Others, like Big Warrior, maintained a traditional Muscogee lifestyle yet accepted the reality of progress.

Indian Civil War. On July 27, 1813, this cultural and political dispute broke into open warfare, a civil war within the nation over the direction the culture should take: toward the white man's style of life or back to the purity and spirituality of Muscogee life. The reactionary wing, led by a reluctant Weatherford, a vengeful Francis, and McQueen, became known, from the red color symbolic of war, as Red Sticks.

The war spilled over into white society with the killing of isolated settlers in southern Tennessee and the massacre of two large populations of whites, blacks, and Creeks at Forts Sinquefield and Mims in lower Alabama. These killings brought Major General Andrew Jackson into the conflict with an army of Mississippi, Georgia, and Tennessee militia, joined by progressive Muscogee, Choctaw, and Cherokee allies.

The early campaign was tedious and unsuccessful. With winter approaching, pay in arrears, little to eat, and enlistments expiring, many militiamen prepared to go home. Jackson branded them all mutineers and arrested and executed six leaders, cowing the frontiersmen into remaining to continue the fight. Through hard marching and sporadic fighting, the allied force of frontiersmen and progressive Native Americans chased and battled the Red Sticks across Alabama, finally cornering a large contingent at Tohopeka (Horseshoe Bend) on the Tallapoosa River. In this battle, more than five hundred Red Sticks were killed, destroying Red Stick resistance.

In the ensuing Treaty of Horseshoe Bend (August 9, 1814), Jackson took approximately twenty-five million acres of land from both Red Stick insurgents and his Muscogee, Choctaw, and Cherokee allies. The cession opened the land to immediate white and African American settlement and created the heart of the cotton South. The Creek Indian War left Andrew Jackson with a veteran and victorious army well-positioned to block the British invasion of New Orleans, giving the United States its most impressive land victory in the War of 1812 and opening the path to the White House for Andrew Jackson.

For the Muscogee, the defeat spelled the beginning of the end of their existence in their homeland. Within two decades, they and most other surviving members of the South's Five Civilized Tribes were banished to the Indian Territory, Oklahoma.

See also: Horseshoe Bend Treaty; Indian-white relations: U.S., 1775-1830.

Maurice Melton

Sources for Further Study

Braund, Kathryn E. Holland. *Deerskins and Duffels: The Creek Indian Trade with Anglo-America, 1685-1815.* Lincoln: University of Nebraska Press,

1993. Describes the competitors, pricing, credit policies, markets, and distribution of the Muscogee deerskin trade; provides a detailed look at Muscogee life.

George, Noah Jackson. *A Memorandum of the Creek Indian War.* Meredith, N.H.: R. Lothrop, 1815. 2d ed. Edited by W. Stanley Hoole. University, Ala: Confederate Publishing Company, 1986. Based on General Jackson's reports and correspondence, this pamphlet gives a battle-by-battle account of the campaign from the U.S. perspective. Written amid the passions of the War of 1812, it asserts that the Red Sticks were tools of the British.

Griffith, Benjamin W., Jr. *McIntosh and Weatherford, Creek Indian Leaders.* Tuscaloosa: University of Alabama Press, 1988. A highly readable account of the war. Argues that Weatherford was a most reluctant Red Stick, knowing from the outset that the movement was doomed.

Halbert, Henry Sale, and T. H. Ball. *The Creek War of 1813 and 1814.* Chicago: Donohue and Henneberry, 1895. Reprint with introduction and annotation by Frank L. Owsley, Jr. University: University of Alabama Press, 1969. Provides a lengthy discussion of the causes of the war, presenting it as an intertribal difference that would have been resolved had whites not interfered.

Hudson, Charles M. *The Southeastern Indians.* Knoxville: University of Tennessee Press, 1976. Places the Muscogee within the larger framework of the native population of the area. One of several excellent volumes on Southeastern American Indians by ethnologist Hudson.

Martin, Joel. *Sacred Revolt: The Muscogees' Struggle for a New World.* Boston: Beacon Press, 1991. Emphasizes the importance of spirituality in Muscogee life, in the evolution of the Red Sticks' back-to-our-culture campaign, and in their war making.

Owsley, Frank Lawrence, Jr. *Struggle for the Borderlands: The Creek War and the Battle of New Orleans, 1812-1815.* Tuscaloosa: University of Alabama Press, 2000. Considers the Creek War in the larger context of the War of 1812.

Woodward, Thomas S. *Woodward's Reminiscences of the Creek, or Muscogee Indians, Contained in Letters to Friends in Georgia and Alabama.* Tuscaloosa: Alabama Book Store, 1859. Reprint. Mobile, Ala.: Southern University Press, 1965. A veteran of the war, Woodward knew many Muscogee leaders and their culture. Although written with the wisdom and common sense of later years, this entertaining little volume has its errors and must be read with a critical eye.

Dancing Rabbit Creek, Treaty of

Date: September 27, 1830
Locale: Mississippi
Tribes involved: Choctaw
Categories: Nineteenth century history, Reservations and relocation, Treaties
Significance: In the first treaty signed after passage of the Indian Removal Act of 1830, the experience of the Choctaws foreshadowed that of many tribes as they sold their lands in Mississippi and agreed to move west.

The Choctaws originally occupied much of present-day Mississippi. The tribe prided itself on good relations with the United States and the fact that it had never fought against the United States. Instead Choctaws had fought as American allies in the Creek War (1813-1814) and War of 1812.

Nevertheless the Choctaws came under increasing pressure from American settlers as the area filled rapidly after the War of 1812. In treaties going back to 1801, the Choctaws had ceded land to facilitate settlement. Pressed by General Andrew Jackson, in 1820 the tribe agreed to the Treaty of Doak's Stand. Five million acres of land in western and west-central Mississippi were sold to the United States; in return, the Choctaws acquired thirteen million acres west of the Mississippi. The acquisition of western land clearly raised the prospect of removal, though few Choctaws chose to emigrate.

American pressure mounted, however, especially after Jackson's election to the presidency in 1828. Encouraged by his administration's stated goal of removing the tribes east of the Mississippi, in January, 1830, the Mississippi legislature voted to extend state jurisdiction over Choctaw lands, effectively ignoring tribal claims to the land. Feeling pressured and believing that American power was irresistible, Choctaw leaders agreed to negotiate. Terms proposed by Greenwood LeFlore, recently elected principal chief of the tribe, were rejected as too expensive. The Choctaws then agreed to a new round of negotiations at Dancing Rabbit Creek.

There in September, 1813, chiefs LeFlore, Mushulatubbee, and Nitekechi and six thousand Choctaws met American commissioners John Eaton and John Coffee. The Americans had made elaborate preparations to feed and entertain the Choctaws and to create a festive air for the negotiations. Reluctantly, the chiefs agreed to the terms requested: In return for a $20,000, twenty-year annuity and other financial considerations, the Choctaws would give up the remaining ten million acres of their land in Mississippi and move to their lands in present-day southeastern Oklahoma. Choctaws who wished to stay in Mississippi would receive one-square-mile allotments and U.S. citizenship, provided they registered within six months of the treaty's ratification and lived on their lands for five years. (Federal officials saw to it that relatively few Choctaws remained under this provision.)

Though a few hundred Choctaws had departed for Indian Territory in 1830 in hopes of locating the best land, removal of the bulk of the tribe began in 1831 and extended over a three-year period. Much hardship accompanied the Choctaw Trail of Tears, especially in 1831, and about 15 percent of the tribe died during removal. The Choctaws were the first major tribe to be moved under the Indian Removal Act, and their experience established an important precedent that would be followed with other eastern tribes.

See also: Creek War; Indian Removal Act; Indian-white relations: U.S., 1831-1870; Trail of Tears.

William C. Lowe

Declaration of First Nations

Date: 1981
Locale: Canada
Tribes involved: Pantribal in Canada
Categories: National government and legislation, Native government, Twentieth century history
Significance: Increased activism beginning in the 1960's resulted in a statement of principles that has guided subsequent native political activities and land-claims negotiations in Canada.

Though not without strains, Canadians generally regard their country's multiethnic heritage with pride. Diversity is applauded in a variety of ways, but special recognition is accorded to the "founding nations" of Canada. Unfortunately for Native Canadians, the term "founding nation" is usually reserved for only two groups—the French and the English.

Public and government recognition that Canadian Indians as a group had suffered economically, socially, and educationally became widespread in the 1960's. In order to engage natives in a dialogue regarding the issues that most affected them, the federal government encouraged the development of both regional and national native political organizations. The National Indian Council, which was formed in 1961, represented treaty Indians, nontreaty Indians, nonstatus Indians, and Metis. In 1968 this group divided into the Canadian Metis Society, representing Metis and nonstatus Indians, and the National Indian Brotherhood as the organization of status Indians (both treaty and nontreaty).

Politicization grew, particularly following introduction by the government of its White Paper on Indian Affairs in 1969. In 1975, the various Dene bands sought Canadian recognition of the Subarctic Athapaskans as a distinct nation. The National Indian Brotherhood became highly involved in Canadian constitutional reform. The Declaration of First Nations, issued in 1981, was a concise statement of native sovereignty meant to influence the constitutional reform process. Following the Declaration of First Nations, the National Indian Brotherhood was dissolved and reconstituted as the Assembly of First Nations. They were ultimately successful in inserting language that affirmed "existing aboriginal and treaty rights," though not explicitly defined, into the Constitution Act of 1982.

Natives continued to pursue the recognition of their cultures as distinct societies and as "founding nations" of Canada by defeating the Meech Lake Accord and by working for a form of native self-government apart from the provinces and the federal government.

See also: Fifteen Principles; Indian Act of 1989; Indian-white relations: Canadian; Meech Lake Accord.

Pamela R. Stern

Delgamuukw v. British Columbia

Date: December, 1997
Locale: British Columbia and Canada
Tribes involved: Pantribal in Canada
Categories: Court cases, Twentieth century history
Significance: A landmark Canadian Supreme Court decision on land claims proclaimed the acceptability of oral tradition as legal evidence and outlined eight core components and a threefold test of aboriginal title to land.

This landmark case involving the Supreme Court of Canada, decided in December, 1997, conceivably revolutionized aboriginal affairs in Canada—particularly land claims—as well as jurisprudence in some fundamental ways. The high court overturned the decision of the British Columbia Court of Appeal in the matter of land claims by the House of Delgamuukw. The House, speaking on behalf of fifty-one hereditary chiefs, claimed ownership and jurisdiction over fifty-eight thousand square kilometers of land in northwestern British Columbia as native lands whose title dated back before confederation. The group further argued that aboriginal title had not been extinguished when British Columbia entered the confederation. The group attempted to use oral tradition to argue the first claim and section 35 of the 1982 Constitution Act to argue the latter point. Justice Alan McEachern of the British Columbia Supreme Court threw out the aboriginal case after one of the longest trials in Canadian history, rejecting the use of oral evidence and agreeing with the British Columbia government's position that title had been extinguished with entrance into the confederation.

The case then went to the British Columbia Court of Appeal, which, by a three-to-two decision, overruled Judge McEachern on the question of extinguishment. The court did, however, agree with him on rejecting claims of ownership although it did not entertain questions of the fiduciary duties of the Crown in relation to lands claimed. The case then went before the Supreme Court of Canada, which issued a unanimous landmark decision in December, 1997. The Court ordered a new trial, largely for two reasons. First, it ruled that Judge McEachern had erred in rejecting oral tradition as evidence. Noting that the laws of evidence typically work against the rights and customs of aboriginal people, the Court argued that, notwithstanding the challenges created by the use of oral histories as proof of historical facts, the laws of evidence must be adapted in order that this type of evidence can be accommodated and placed on an equal footing with the type of historical evidence that courts are familiar with, which largely consists of documentary evidence.

Second, it ruled that the question of aboriginal title had to be dealt with more closely and clearly. The court therefore spelled out eight core components of aboriginal title. Title is a collective right, it is inalienable, it is a legal right to the land itself, it arises from aboriginal occupation of the land before colonial assertion, it is an exclusive right to use the land for a variety of purposes, it includes mineral rights, it is to protect aboriginal relationship to the land, and lastly it is a right but not an absolute right.

To prove aboriginal title, the Supreme Court set out a threefold test. First, the land must have been occupied by aboriginal peoples before

Crown assertion of sovereignty (for British Columbia, that means before 1846); second, there must be continuity between present occupancy of the land extending back prior to 1846 (that is, occupancy must not have been interrupted or given up); and third, at the date of Crown assertion of sovereignty, the occupation of the land by aboriginals must have been exclusive.

The case presented many issues unaddressed by the Canadian Supreme Court, issues largely outside its competency, so it ordered a new trial in which the foregoing principles were to have been taken into account. The high court thus urged all parties to serious negotiations in "good faith," which it hoped would result in compromises but ultimately a settlement because, as the majority decision concluded, "let us face it, we are all here to stay."

See also: Fifteen Principles; Indian Act of 1989; Indian-white relations: Canadian; Meech Lake Accord; Nisga'a Agreement in Principle; Nunavut Territory; Reserve system of Canada; Royal Commission on Aboriginal Peoples.

Gregory Walters

Department of Indian Affairs and Northern Development

Date: Established 1967
Locale: Canada
Tribes involved: Pantribal in Canada
Categories: National government and legislation, Twentieth century history
Significance: Since the Indian Act of 1868, Indian affairs have been handled by various Canadian government departments; DIAND officially took over this function in 1967.

The Department of Indian Affairs and Northern Development in its present form was created as a separate entity within the Canadian government in 1967 by an act of Parliament. Before that time, Indian affairs and policy were overseen by a Department of Indian Affairs that was often part of a larger governmental unit with other responsibilities. The Indian Act of 1868 gave responsibility for Indian affairs to the secretary of state. In 1880, a revision of the 1876 Indian Act created a separate Department of

Indian Affairs. The department was given the power to "depose" western Indian leaders in 1894; in 1895 it was given the power to rent out reserve lands to individual Indians regardless of whether the band approved. In 1936, Indian affairs became the responsibility of a branch of the Department of Mines and Resources. In 1959 the Indian Affairs branch was transferred to the Minister of Citizenship and Immigration. In 1965 the Department of Northern Affairs and Natural Resources took charge of Indian affairs.

As its name implies, the Department of Indian Affairs and Northern Development was established with a twofold purpose: to administer the Indian Act, including the provision of funds and services to the eligible Indian and Inuit populations, and to promote and manage development of the northern territories. DIAND is involved in providing or assisting with Indian education, housing, medical care, and economic assistance. DIAND generally is concerned with those bands recognized under the Indian Act; therefore, many thousands of Indian, Inuit, and Metis people—perhaps 75 percent of the population of these groups—receive no services from DIAND. The Indian and Inuit services section of DIAND is composed of a number of branches that report to a deputy minister and to the minister, who is a member of Parliament. There are also a number of regional and district offices; since 1988, the structure has been changing (many district offices have been closed) as First Nations themselves have assumed responsibility for delivering programs, with DIAND acting in an advisory capacity and providing technical support.

Under Canada's Department of Indian Affairs and Northern Development, eligible indigenous Indian and Inuit populations receive education, housing, medical care, and economic assistance, but because DIAND generally is concerned with those bands recognized under the Indian Act thousands of Indian, Inuit, and Metis receive no services. (National Archives)

Historically, the Department of Indian Affairs long continued the paternalistic attitude established by the British; this began to change significantly only in the late 1960's. One controversy involved the Canadian government's proposed "White Paper," released in 1969, intended to provide a new framework for Indian-government relations. Many bands strongly opposed the White Paper's proposals, and the government withdrew it two years later. In 1973, the Office of Native Claims was established as a branch of DIAND to consider and negotiate native land claims. Since the 1970's, DIAND has been dealing with Indian concerns about environmental damage to their land base. DIAND has also been involved in negotiations concerning the establishment of a new native territory in the north, to be known as Nunavut. Nunavut will comprise most of the eastern Northwest Territories.

See also: Indian Act of 1876; Indian Act of 1951; Indian-white relations: Canadian; Royal Commission on Aboriginal Peoples.

Gregory Walters

Determined Residents United for Mohawk Sovereignty

Date: Established 1974
Locale: U.S.-Canadian border of New York State and Ontario
Tribes involved: Mohawk
Categories: Organizations, Protest movements, Reservations and relocation, Twentieth century history
Significance: DRUMS opposed speakeasies and casinos on Mohawk reservations.

Determined Residents United for Mohawk Sovereignty (DRUMS) was established at the Akwesasne Mohawk reservation in 1974. The Akwesasne Mohawk reservation (also called the Saint Regis Mohawk reserve) straddles the United States-Canadian border near Massena, New York, and Cornwall, Ontario. Beginning in the early 1970's, Akwesasne residents established DRUMS to combat increasing smuggling across the border. In the late 1970's and early 1980's, DRUMS's main focus turned to "speakeasies"—small, illegal drinking establishments that were contributing to an increasing number of traffic accidents on the reservation.

By June, 1989, DRUMS members were beginning to talk of blockading Route 37, the reservation's main highway, to keep away the clientele of several illegal casinos that had been constructed with smuggling profits.

Many people believed that, if the New York state police refused to close the gaming houses, civil disobedience was their only option. DRUMS planned a blockade for June 9 but abandoned it in favor of a peaceful march. On July 20, two hundred Federal Bureau of Investigation (FBI) agents and New York state troopers raided seven casinos on the reservation, arresting thirteen people and seizing cash and financial records. DRUMS continued to oppose the casinos until May 1, 1990, when two Mohawk men, Mathew Pyke and "Junior" Edwards, were shot to death in firefights. After that, New York, Ontario, and Quebec police occupied the reservation, and the gaming houses were closed.

See also: Indian Gaming Regulatory Act.

Bruce E. Johansen

Duro v. Reina

Date: 1984-1990
Locale: Arizona
Tribes involved: Pima-Maricopa
Categories: Court cases, Native government, Twentieth century history
Significance: A U.S. Supreme Court decision on tribal sovereignty limited the legal jurisdiction of a tribe to its members only.

In 1984, while living on the Salt River Pima-Maricopa Reservation in Arizona, Albert Duro, an enrolled member of another tribe, shot and killed an Indian youth within reservation boundaries. Under the Major Crimes Act (1885 and amended), Duro was charged with murder, but eventually federal charges were dismissed. Duro then was placed in the custody of the Pima-Maricopa police and was charged in tribal court with illegally firing a weapon on the reservation. Tribal courts' powers are regulated by a federal statute that limits tribal criminal penalties to misdemeanors.

After the tribal court denied Duro's motion to dismiss his case for lack of jurisdiction, he brought a petition before the federal court to dismiss. Duro's case was accepted on the basis that the Pima-Maricopa tribe's attempt to assert jurisdiction over a nonmember Indian would constitute discrimination based on race, a violation of equal protection guarantees of the Indian Civil Rights Act (1968). Ultimately, in 1990, the U.S. Supreme Court determined that Indian tribes lack jurisdiction over persons who are not tribal members. Therefore, the Pima-Maricopa tribe had no criminal jurisdiction over Duro, a nonmember. The Court's decision set boundaries on the concept of tribal sovereignty in criminal cases and limited tribes to controlling internal relations among their own tribal members.

See also: Indian Civil Rights Act; Major Crimes Act.

Carole A. Barrett

Elk v. Wilkins

Date: 1884
Locale: Nebraska
Tribes involved: Pantribal in the United States
Categories: Court cases, Nineteenth century history
Significance: A U.S. Supreme Court decision found that Native Americans are not citizens of the United States and therefore not entitled to vote in U.S. elections.

In 1884, John Elk, an American Indian, was refused permission to register to vote in a local election in Omaha, Nebraska. When he later appeared at the polls, he was again refused the right to vote. Elk lived apart from his tribe and met all residence and other requirements of the city of Omaha and the state of Nebraska but was turned away on the basis that he was an Indian and, therefore, not a United States citizen. Elk filed a lawsuit charging the state of Nebraska with violation of his Fourteenth Amendment rights by denying his right to vote.

As an Indian born in the United States, Elk argued he was a United States citizen as well as a state citizen. Nebraska courts ruled Elk ineligible to vote, and on November 3, 1884, the U.S. Supreme Court found Nebraska correct in denying Elk's right to vote. The majority of the Court determined that an Indian who was born a member of a tribe was not a United States citizen but a member of a distinct nation that was separate and apart from the United States. Therefore, the Court determined, a specific act of Congress would be required to make Indian people citizens of the United States.

See also: Indian Citizenship Act; Indian-white relations: U.S., 1871-1933.

Carole A. Barrett

Employment Division, Department of Human Resources of the State of Oregon et al. v. Smith

Date: 1990
Locale: Oregon
Tribes involved: Pantribal in the United States
Categories: Court cases, Religion and missionary activities, Twentieth century history
Significance: A U.S. Supreme Court decision allows states to apply drug laws to Native American employees who use peyote as a religious sacrament.

In this April 17, 1990, decision, the U.S. Supreme Court adopted a narrow interpretation of the free exercise clause, allowing Oregon to apply its drug laws to prohibit Native Americans from using peyote in religious ceremonies. Alfred Smith and Galen Black, two members of the Native American Church, were fired from their jobs in a drug rehabilitation clinic after their employer discovered that they used the hallucinogenic drug peyote during religious rituals. They applied for unemployment compensation, but Oregon's Department of Human Resources denied their claims based on a state law that disqualified employees who were discharged for work-related "misconduct." A state appellate court and the Oregon Supreme Court ruled that the denial of benefits was a violation of the free exercise clause of the First Amendment. Oregon appealed to the U.S. Supreme Court, contending that Smith's free exercise of religion had to be balanced by the state's interest in preventing the use of harmful drugs. The Supreme Court's first judgment was to remand the case to the Oregon Supreme Court to decide whether state law made an exception for the religious use of peyote. Oregon's court responded that state law provided no exception and that the only issue was the religious freedom of the First Amendment. The Supreme Court accepted the case for a second time.

The Supreme Court's major precedent, *Sherbert v. Verner* (1963), suggested that Oregon could prevail only if it could defend its policy with the "compelling state interest" test combined with the "least restrictive alternative" test. From this perspective, it appeared difficult for Oregon to justify the refusal of unemployment benefits to Smith and Black. The Court had upheld the *Sherbert* tests in at least seven cases since 1963.

In the *Smith* case, however, the Court voted six to three that Oregon had no constitutional obligation to make a religious exception for illegal drugs, provided that the law was reasonable, neutral, and generally applicable to all persons. Writing for the majority, Justice Antonin Scalia argued that in enforcing valid criminal laws not specifically directed at religious acts, government had no obligation to make a religious exemption. Such matters were generally left to the legislature's discretion, even if an "unfortunate consequence" was an incidental burden on unpopular religious practices. The three dissenting justices maintained that Oregon had not shown a compelling state interest to refuse to allow peyote for religious usage.

The *Smith* decision appeared to limit the extent to which religious minorities might claim constitutional protection for unpopular practices. Religious leaders and civil libertarians were outraged at the ruling, and Congress responded to the anti-*Smith* movement by passing the Religious Freedom Restoration Act (RFRA) of 1993, which was designed to restore both the compelling state interest test and the least restrictive means test against any incidental burden on religious practice.

See also: American Indian Religious Freedom Act; *Lyng v. Northwest Indian Cemetery Protective Association*; National Council of American Indians; *Native American Church v. Navajo Tribal Council*; Society of American Indians.

Thomas T. Lewis

Epidemics and diseases

Date: Colonial times-present
Locale: North America
Tribes involved: Pantribal
Categories: Colonial history, Eighteenth century history, Nineteenth century history, Twentieth century history
Significance: Within decades after contact with Europeans, Native American societies experienced rapid population declines; although the reasons for the demographic collapse of native North America are complex, a prominent factor in that decline was Old World infectious diseases, introduced by European explorers and settlers.

After the arrival of Europeans, the estimated aboriginal population of native North America began to decline. The Spanish intrusion into the Southwest and Southeast (c. 1520) launched a series of lethal epidemics that infected various Native American people. The epidemiological conquest of native North America accelerated after the early seventeenth century with English and French colonization along the Atlantic seaboard. The dramatic population decline of indigenous people continued until the early twentieth century. By 1920, only 270,995 Native Americans remained after the epidemiological onslaught of European colonization. They were the survivors of perhaps 1.2 million to 18 million Native Americans who inhabited North America at the time of the arrival of Europeans.

Increased mortality among Native Americans as a result of introduced European diseases is not attributable to a lack of sufficient immunological response to infections in general but to the fact that Native Americans had no prior exposure to these pathogens. The "new" pathogens therefore not only created a high degree of physiological stress but also engendered cultural stress. Epidemic episodes often resulted in a breakdown in the social system, elevating mortality levels.

Although it is recognized that European infectious diseases devastated many Native American societies, it also must be acknowledged that pre-contact native North America was not a disease-free paradise. Biological and archaeological evidence documents the fact that pre-contact Native American populations suffered from a number of afflictions. Malnutrition, anemia, and a variety of tuberculoid, trepanematoid, and other degenerative, chronic, and congenital conditions plagued indigenous populations. The general state of health, in combination with ecological and cultural factors, therefore, greatly affected the post-contact disease experience of Native American societies.

Sixteenth and Seventeenth Centuries. No Old World pathogen was more lethal than smallpox, which was unleashed in the Americas during the Spanish conquest. For four years, 1520-1524, the disease diffused across Central and North America. Whether smallpox reached pandemic proportions is debatable, but in populations with no prior exposure, mortality could be as high as 60 percent. The infected native populations experienced high death rates. Florida's Timucua population may have once had 772,000 people, but by 1524 the group was reduced to 361,000. Today the timucua are no longer a distinct ethnic group.

Throughout the 1500's and into the next century, twenty-three European infectious diseases appeared in native North America. In these various regions, Native American populations contracted diseases on the average of every 7.3 years. Smallpox, measles, influenza, and the bubonic plague affected Native American populations largely east of the Mississippi and in

North American Epidemics and Regions Affected, 1520-1696

Date of Onset	Epidemic	Regions Affected
1520	Smallpox	All regions
1531	Measles	Southwest
1545	Bubonic plague	Southwest
1559	Influenza	South Atlantic states, Gulf area, Southwest
1586	Typhus	South Atlantic states, Gulf area
1592	Smallpox	North Atlantic states, South Atlantic states, Old Northwest, Great Lakes states, Midwest east of Mississippi River, Southwest
1602	Smallpox	Southwest
1612	Bubonic plague	North Atlantic states, South Atlantic states, Gulf area, Southwest
1633	Measles	North Atlantic states
1637	Scarlet fever	North Atlantic states
1639	Smallpox	North Atlantic states, South Atlantic states, Old Northwest, Great Lakes states, Midwest east of Mississippi River
1646	Smallpox	Gulf area, Southwest
1647	Influenza	North Atlantic states
1649	Smallpox	North Atlantic states, South Atlantic states, Gulf area
1655	Smallpox	Gulf area
1658	Measles, diphtheria	North Atlantic states, Gulf area, Old Northwest, Great Lakes states, Midwest east of Mississippi River, Southwest
1662	Smallpox	North Atlantic states, Old Northwest, Great Lakes states, Midwest east of Mississippi River
1665	Smallpox	South Atlantic states, Old Northwest, Great Lakes states, Midwest east of Mississippi River
1669	Smallpox	North Atlantic states
1674	Smallpox	Gulf area, southern Plains
1675	Influenza	North Atlantic states
1677	Smallpox	North Atlantic states
1687	Smallpox	North Atlantic states
1692	Measles	North Atlantic states, Old Northwest, Great Lakes states, Midwest east of Mississippi River
1696	Smallpox, Influenza	South Atlantic states, Gulf area

Sources: Data are from Dobyns, Henry, F., *Their Number Became Thinned* (Knoxville, University of Tennessee Press, 1983); Thornton, Russell, *American Indian Holocaust and Survival: A Population History Since 1492* (Norman: University of Oklahoma Press, 1987).

the Southwest. The Huron tribe, which possibly numbered up to thirty-five thousand people in the early 1600's, was reduced by 1640 to an estimated ten thousand people.

Seventeenth century Europeans generally viewed the decline of surrounding Native American populations as evidence of divine intervention. God would destroy "Godless savages," they thought, so that Christian civilization could prosper. Demographically, European populations grew and expanded geographically as declining indigenous populations relinquished their lands and resources. Those Native Americans that resisted white encroachment were vanquished through genocidal warfare or reduced to mission life.

Eighteenth Century. By the eighteenth century, the European population had reached an estimated 223,000 people. Although Europeans were not the demographic majority, epidemics continued to pave the way for further colonization. Throughout the Atlantic coastal region and into the interior westward, native populations were decimated through genocidal warfare and diseases. In the southeastern region of North America, for example, the estimated Native American population in 1685 was 199,400. By 1970, the population was reduced to approximately 55,900—a decline of 71.9 percent. By contrast, Europeans and African Americans in the region increased their population to 1,630,100 or 31.4 percent.

In sum, European expansion during the three first centuries of colonization produced a demographic collapse of Native American populations. Introduced European infectious diseases, combined with periodic genocidal warfare and the destruction of indigenous lifeways, reduced Native Americans to approximately 600,000. By contrast, the European population grew to 5,308,483.

Nineteenth and Twentieth Centuries. The nineteenth century represents the final century of Native American population decline as a result of epidemics. During this century, twenty-four epidemics affected Native American populations. Smallpox continued to appear every 7.9 years among some segment of the Native American population. Between the smallpox episodes, Native Americans contracted measles and cholera every 22.5 years. According to Henry Dobyns, an anthropologist and authority on Native American historical demography, more epidemics occurred during this century, with more frequency, than during any other.

One of the most devastating epidemics during this century was the 1837-1838 smallpox epidemic. The disease diffused across most of native North America, but the Northern Plains region was hit especially hard. It is estimated that seventeen thousand Native Americans on the northern Plains died before the epidemic subsided. Such acute infectious diseases continued to plague Native American communities into the early reservation period. Only then did these infections give way to the twentieth century epidemics of influenza, tuberculosis, and trachoma—chronic conditions that would infect Native Americans until the 1950's.

The post-contact epidemic history of Native North America can be described as one of continual population decline coupled with the destruction of numerous unique lifeways. Native Americans, however, during these tragic times, did not remain passive actors. Native American societies employed a number of cultural adaptations to respond to the onslaught of infectious diseases. Some societies modified their kin systems, fused with other tribal nations, or created new nations from various remnant tribes. Diseases were powerful agents of cultural and biological change.

The placement of Native Americans on reservations or in rural communities did not mark the end of epidemics. Acute infectious diseases have been replaced by "diseases of poverty." Many of these afflictions reach epidemic proportions in some Native American communities. Deaths from tuberculosis, type II diabetes mellitus, violence, suicide, accidents, and alcoholism exceed the national average. In addition, Native Americans now have to contend with another epidemic—the threat of human immunodeficiency virus (HIV) infection—a disease that has made its presence felt in some Native American communities.

See also: Beaver Wars; Indian-white relations: Canadian; Indian-white relations: Dutch colonial; Indian-white relations: English colonial; Indian-white relations: French colonial; Indian-white relations: Norse; Indian-white relations: Russian colonial; Indian-white relations: Spanish colonial; Indian-white relations: Swedish colonial.

Gregory R. Campbell

Sources for Further Study

American Indian Culture and Research Journal 13 (1989). Special issue on contemporary issues in Native American health, edited by Gregory R. Campbell. A collection of articles that focus on issues revolving around American Indians' health in the later 1980's.

Campbell, Gregory R. "The Politics of Counting: Critical Reflections About the Depopulation Question of Native North America." In *Native Voices on the Columbian Quincentenary*, edited by Donald A. Grinde. Los Angeles: American Indian Studies Center, University of California, 1994. An examination of the European manipulation of Native American population counts as justification for continued colonial expansion.

Cook, Noble David. *Born to Die: Disease and New World Conquest, 1492-1650*. New York: Cambridge University Press, 1998. Sweeping yet detailed look at the effect of disease in the European colonization of the Americas.

Cook, Noble David, and W. George Lovell, eds. *Secret Judgments of God: Old World Disease in Colonial Spanish America*. Norman: University of Oklahoma Press, 2001. A collection of symposium papers, presented from a wide range of disciplines, assessing the impact of European diseases and epidemics on the Native American population.

Dobyns, Henry F. *Their Number Became Thinned*. Knoxville: University of Tennessee Press, 1983. A comprehensive volume addressing the population dynamics of eastern North America.

Stannard, David E. *American Holocaust*. New York: Oxford University Press, 1992. A discussion of Native American population decline in relation to European conquest and colonization.

Thornton, Russell. *American Indian Holocaust and Survival: A Population History Since 1492*. Norman: University of Oklahoma Press, 1987. Provides an overview of Native American population and recovery from European contact to 1980.

Verano, John W., and Douglas H. Ubelaker, eds. *Disease and Demography in the Americas*. Washington, D.C.: Smithsonian Institution Press, 1992. A collection of articles assessing the health and demography of pre-contact and post-contact Native American populations.

Ex parte Crow Dog

Date: 1883
Locale: Dakota Territory
Tribes involved: Lakota
Categories: Court cases, Native government, Nineteenth century history
Significance: A U.S. Supreme Court decision found that the United States had no jurisdiction in cases between two Indians concerning events on Indian land.

Crow Dog, a well-known Lakotan, killed Spotted Tail, another popular tribal leader, at the Rosebud Agency in Dakota Territory in 1883. Crow Dog was arrested, removed from the reservation, and tried in the territorial court of Dakota, where he was convicted and sentenced to death. In killing

Brule Sioux war chief Crow Dog, pictured circa 1900. (Library of Congress)

Spotted Tail, Crow Dog admitted he had broken Lakota law, but he maintained he should be punished according to Lakota customs, not by United States law. Under tribal law, Crow Dog would be shunned by his own family and would become responsible for care and protection of Spotted Tail's family.

The U.S. Supreme Court sided with Crow Dog and declared the United States had no jurisdiction over the crime of one Indian against another on Indian land. Because Congress provided no federal jurisdiction over Indian crimes on reservations, even a murderer could not be punished. Therefore, Crow Dog returned to his people.

This decision proved to be a major step in relations between Native Americans and the U.S. government, in that it encouraged Congress to enact legislation to give federal jurisdiction over Indians in certain legal matters. One key piece of legislation, the Major Crimes Act (1885), directed federal courts to assume jurisdiction over seven crimes committed on Indian land: murder, manslaughter, rape, assault with intent to kill, arson, burglary, and larceny.

See also: Major Crimes Act.

Carole A. Barrett

Fallen Timbers, Battle of

Date: August 20, 1794
Locale: South of present-day Toledo, Ohio
Tribes involved: Chickasaw, Choctaw, Miami, Shawnee

Categories: Colonial history, Wars and battles
Significance: The resulting Treaty of Greenville secures U.S. control over much of Ohio and ousts its resident Native Americans.

In the 1783 Treaty of Paris, which ended the Revolutionary War, the British acknowledged the United States' claims to territory west of the Appalachians and made no effort to protect American Indian lands in the Ohio Valley. Incursions by settlers there led to serious problems, because American Indian leaders refused to acknowledge U.S. authority north of the Ohio River. Between 1784 and 1789, U.S. government officials persuaded some chiefs to relinquish lands in southern and eastern Ohio, but most American Indians refused to acknowledge the validity of these treaties.

Encouraged by the British, the Miami and Shawnee tribes insisted that the Americans fall back to the Ohio River. When the settlers refused, the Miami attacked them. In 1790 and again in 1791, U.S. troops and militia were sent against American Indians along the Maumee River.

The 1790 expedition, the first for the U.S. Army, ended in disaster. In October, Brigadier General Josiah Harmar set out with a poorly trained force of some 1,200 men. Harmar divided his troops into three separate columns, enabling the Miami and Shawnee, led by Miami chief Little Turtle, to win the battle, inflicting three hundred casualties on U.S. troops.

In November, 1791, Arthur St. Clair, governor of the Northwest Territory and a commissioned major general, led a second expedition, which included the entire six-hundred-man regular army and fifteen hundred militiamen. At present-day Fort Recovery, Ohio, Little Turtle and his warriors administered the most overwhelming defeat ever by American Indians on the British or Americans. Some 650 U.S. troops and 250 civilians died; another 300 were wounded. American Indian losses were reported as twenty-one killed and forty wounded.

Mad Anthony Wayne. In December, 1792, Congress authorized establishment of a five-hundred-man Legion of the United States. Despite misgivings, Washington recalled General "Mad" Anthony Wayne from retirement to command the legion. Wayne found his first training camp, near Pittsburgh, too distracting and marched his men twenty-five miles downriver to a site he named Legionville. Utilizing Baron Friedrich von Steuben's Revolutionary War drill manual, Wayne carried out rigorous training. In May, Wayne moved the legion to Cincinnati and then a few miles north to a new camp, Hobson's Choice.

Wayne issued a call for Kentucky mounted militia and in early October, moved north to Fort Jefferson with two thousand regulars. When Kentucky militiamen arrived, Wayne moved a few miles farther north and began a camp to accommodate his larger force. He named it Fort Greenville (now Greenville, Ohio) in memory of his Revolutionary War commander, Nathaniel Greene. In December, 1793, Wayne ordered a detachment to the site of the previous massacre. On Christmas Day, 1793, U.S. troops reoccupied the battlefield. After burying human remains still in evidence, they constructed a fort on high ground overlooking the Wabash.

Wayne's timetable for the campaign was delayed because of unreliable civilian contractors, attacks on his supply trains, the loss of some of his men to other campaigns, and a cease-fire that led him to believe peace might be at hand. Little Turtle, Blue Jacket, and other tribal chiefs rejected peace negotiations, however.

In February, the British commander ordered construction of Fort Miamis, a post on the Maumee River, to mount cannons larger than those that Wayne might be able to bring against it. By mid-April, work on the fort was well along. This further delayed Wayne's advance, then rescheduled for June.

Little Turtle Strikes. On June 29, Little Turtle struck first, at Fort Recovery, Wayne's staging point for the invasion. A supply train had just arrived and was bivouacked outside the walls when two thousand warriors attacked. They hoped to take both the supplies and fort in one bold stroke, but Fort Recovery's commander, Captain Alexander Gibson, was ready. Although many soldiers were killed outside the walls, the attackers were beaten back with heavy casualties. After two days with no success, the tribal warriors withdrew. The attack was the high-water mark of their cause; never again would they be able to assemble that many warriors. Defeat at Fort Recovery led some of the smaller tribes to quit the coalition and also caused the eclipse of Little Turtle, who was replaced as principal war leader by the less effective Blue Jacket.

Wayne now had two thousand men. In mid-July, the Kentucky militia, ultimately sixteen hundred men, began to arrive. Wayne also had a hundred American Indians, mostly Choctaws and Chickasaws. On July 28, the men left Fort Greenville for Fort Recovery. Much was at stake, and Washington had warned that a third straight defeat would be ruinous to the reputation of the government.

The two principal American Indian concentrations were Miami Town, the objective of previous offensives, and the rapids of the Maumee River around Fort Miamis. The two were connected by a hundred-mile Maumee River Valley road. Wayne vowed to cut it at midpoint, forcing his enemy to split his forces and defend both possible objectives. By August 3, he had established both Fort Adams and Fort Defiance. Wayne then sent the chiefs a final offer for peace. Little Turtle urged its acceptance, pointing out the great numbers of the enemy and expressing doubts about British support. Blue Jacket and British agents urged war, however, which a majority of the chiefs approved.

Wayne Strikes Back. Having learned that the American Indians were congregating near Fort Miamis, Wayne decided to move there first. On August 15, Wayne's men still were ten miles from the British fort. Sensing an impending fight, Wayne detached unnecessary elements from his column at a hastily constructed position, Fort Deposit. Manned by Captain Zebulon Pike and two hundred men, it would serve as a refuge in case things did not go well.

On August 20, Wayne again put his column in motion. More than a thousand American Indian warriors, along with some sixty Canadian militiamen, were lying in wait. They hoped to ambush the U.S. troops from the natural defenses of what had been a forest before it had been uprooted by a tornado. The attack plan was sound but based on the assumption that their enemy would either remain in place or run away. Not expecting the daylong delay to build Fort Deposit, Blue Jacket had thought that Wayne would arrive on August 19. The natives had begun a strict fast on August 18 and continued it the next day. When the Americans did not arrive, many of the natives, tired and half-starved, left for Fort Miamis.

Wayne marched his men so as to be ready to meet an attack from any quarter. His infantry were in two wings; well out in front was a select battalion, led by Major William Price, to trigger the enemy attack and allow Wayne time to deploy the main body. When the American Indians opened fire, Price's men fell back into Wilkinson's line. Wayne's troops shattered the ambush with an infantry frontal attack driven home with the bayonet, while cavalry closed in on the flanks. The killing went on to the very gates of the fort, while the British looked on. Of Wayne's troops, only thirty-three were killed and one hundred wounded (eleven of whom later died of their wounds); tribal losses were in the hundreds.

Wayne disregarded Fort Miamis but destroyed American Indian communities and British storehouses in its vicinity. His troops then marched to Miami Town, occupied it without opposition on September 17, and razed it. They then built a fort on the site of Harmar's 1790 defeat, naming it Fort Wayne.

Treaty of Fort Greenville. On August 3, 1795, after six weeks of discussions, chiefs representing twelve tribes signed the Treaty of Fort Greenville. The treaty set a definite boundary in the Northwest Territory, forcing the American Indians to give up most of the present state of Ohio and part of Indiana. All hostilities were to cease, prisoners were to be exchanged, and the United States agreed to pay an eight-thousand-dollar-per-year annuity for the loss of hunting lands and twenty thousand dollars in commodities.

The brief Battle of Fallen Timbers broke forever the power of the American Indians in the eastern region of the Northwest Territory. It also led the British to evacuate their garrisons below the Great Lakes. The victory did much to restore the prestige of the U.S. Army; Wayne, justifiably, is known as its father.

See also: Fort Greenville Treaty; Little Turtle's War.

Spencer C. Tucker

Sources for Further Study

Dowd, Gregory Evans. *A Spirited Resistance. The North American Indian Struggle for Unity, 1745-1815*. Baltimore: The Johns Hopkins University Press, 1991. A useful short survey of American Indian affairs.

Nelson, Paul D. *Anthony Wayne: Soldier of the Early Republic*. Bloomington: Indiana University Press, 1985. The best biography of Wayne to date.

_____. "Anthony Wayne's Indian War in the Old Northwest, 1792-1795." *Northwest Ohio Quarterly* 56 (1984): 115-140. An excellent short account of this war.

Palmer, Dave R. *1794: America, Its Army, and the Birth of the Nation*. Novato, Calif.: Presidio Press, 1994. A helpful study of early U.S. military policy.

Smith, Dwight L. "Wayne and the Treaty of Green Ville." *Ohio State Archaeological and Historical Quarterly* 63 (January, 1954): 1-7. Careful analysis of the treaty.

Sugden, John. *Blue Jacket: Warrior of the Shawnees*. Lincoln: University of Nebraska Press, 1997. A biography of one of the main Indian leaders in the conflict.

Sword, Wiley. *President Washington's Indian War: The Struggle for the Old Northwest, 1790-1795*. Norman: University of Oklahoma Press, 1985. Discusses the struggle for the northwest frontier.

Tebbel, John W. *The Battle of Fallen Timbers, August 20, 1794*. New York: Franklin Watts, 1972. Useful history of the battle.

Wilson, Frazer. *The Treaty of Greenville*. Pigua, Ohio: Correspondent Press, 1894. The only work specifically devoted to the treaty ending the campaign.

Federally recognized tribes

Date: Established 1978
Locale: United States
Tribes involved: Pantribal in the United States
Categories: National government and legislation, Terminology, Twentieth century history
Significance: Federal recognition of tribes is an issue with both political and economic ramifications.

The term "federally recognized tribe" is a U.S. government designation for an American Indian tribe that has official relations with the United States. These relations have been established in various ways through the years—through treaties (treaty making ended in the late nineteenth century), executive orders, court decrees, and acts of Congress, and through meeting the requirements set forth by the Federal Acknowledgment Program. Federal recognition is both a political and an economic issue, as recognized tribes are eligible for federal services that unrecognized tribes cannot receive, such as education, housing, and health benefits.

The Federal Acknowledgment Program (a Bureau of Indian Affairs program) was created in 1978. The Federal Acknowledgment Program established criteria and procedures through which unrecognized tribes could attempt to attain recognized status. The creation of a federal recognition process was hailed a victory by some American Indians, but others countered that the requirements are unnecessarily complex, even unfulfillable. Among the criteria is proof of continuous existence as a tribe; the tribe also must have a governing body, be governed by a constitution or similar document, and have membership criteria and a roll of current members.

In the 1950's a government policy known as termination successfully urged many tribes to disband; subsequently, some terminated tribes have attempted to regain recognized tribal status; the regaining of tribal status by the Menominees was the first major success. (Terminated tribes are not eligible for recognition through the Federal Acknowledgment Program.) In 1991 there were 510 federally recognized tribes; in mid-1994 the number had grown to 543. Some of these groups are very small; for example, there are some two hundred Alaskan village groups.

See also: American Indian; Amerind; Indian; Native American; Termination Resolution; Tribe.

McCrea Adams

Fifteen Principles

Date: 1983; reaffirmed in 1985
Locale: Quebec
Tribes involved: Abenaki, Algonquian, Cree, Huron, Inuit, Micmac, Mohawk, Montagnais, Naskapi
Categories: National government and legislation, Native government, Twentieth century history
Significance: Efforts toward Canadian federal constitutional reform prompted the Quebec provincial government to formulate an administrative and legal policy regarding the Indian and Inuit residents of the province.

In the midst of federal constitutional negotiations, the province of Quebec established a legal framework to guide its relationships with the Inuit and Indian residents of Quebec. Known as the Fifteen Principles, the policy statement affirmed that the province of Quebec accepted native claims to self-determination with respect to culture, education, language, and economic development. It further acknowledged that natives are entitled to certain aboriginal rights and land claims (left to be determined by future negotiations). Finally, the Fifteen Principles recognized that those aboriginal rights applied equally to men and women.

The Fifteen Principles were adopted, in large part, to bolster the claim by the ruling Parti Québécois that Quebec is a distinct and sovereign nation either within or apart from Canada. If this was to be the case, Quebec could not argue, as it had previously, that the federal government bore sole responsibility for natives living within the borders of Quebec. In fact, it was Quebec's earlier insistence that the federal government must absorb all the costs of native administration that led to the 1939 Supreme Court decision that for legal purposes Inuit were to be regarded as Indians as specified in the British North America Act. By adopting the Fifteen Principles, Quebec attempted to place itself on equal footing with the Canadian government.

See also: Declaration of First Nations; Meech Lake Accord.

Pamela R. Stern

Fish-ins

Date: 1960's

Locale: Pacific Northwest

Tribes involved: Alsea, Bella Bella, Bella Coola, Chehalis, Chinook, Coast Salish, Coos, Eyak, Gitksan, Haida, Klamath, Klikitat, Kwaki-utl, Nootka (Nuu-Chah-Nulth), Quileute, Quinault, Siuslaw, Takelma, Tillamook, Tlingit, Tsimshian, Umpqua

Categories: Protest movements, Twentieth century history

Significance: Native tribes protest the restriction of their fishing rights in an attempt to regain economic self-sufficiency.

During the 1960's, American Indians in the Pacific Northwest began to stage fish-ins to protest restrictions on their fishing rights, especially within the states of Washington, Oregon, and Idaho. In turn, sports fishers' groups, commercial fishing operations, and canneries pressured the state governments to get American Indians off the rivers. Controversies over fishing rights stemmed from treaties negotiated with various Pacific Northwest tribes in 1854 and 1855. In those treaties, tribes gave up claim to vast areas of land but specifically preserved fishing rights along waterways ceded to the federal government. Those treaties guaranteed to Indians "the right of taking fish, at all usual and accustomed grounds and stations . . . in common with all citizens of the Territory."

Almost from the start, the states ignored the treaty provisions, and by the 1930's, the

Johnnie Saux, of the Quinaielts, displays a dog salmon in Taholah, Washington, 1936. Fishing has always been a major part of the Native American way of life in the Northwest. (National Archives)

states openly restricted Indian subsistence and commercial fishing. Some tribes challenged the states; however, they had no legal success. During the next two decades, state restrictions increased, particularly in the state of Washington, and although some cases went to court, restrictions on Indian fishing were upheld.

Finally, in the 1960's, Indian nations began to push for economic development, and tribes began to demand their treaty rights. In the Pacific Northwest, the tribes openly challenged the states' ability to exert regulatory authority over matters negotiated in treaties between the federal government and tribal nations. The state of Washington responded by issuing a series of orders forbidding Indian fishing, and in 1964, Washington set aside the treaty guarantees.

Indians from various affected tribes attempted to channel their energies in a unified front and formed the Survival of American Indians Association in 1964. This organization began a series of actions designed to assert their rights. One important strategy was to engage in night fishing in restricted areas. Washington aggressively policed night fishing, and it confiscated boats, nets, and motors, rammed fishing boats, and prosecuted lawbreakers.

The most dramatic and effective protests sponsored by the Indian association were fish-ins. These were highly publicized events, well attended by media, in which Indian people, including many women and children, would assert their treaty rights and fish, despite state restrictions. The state response was aggressive: Often large numbers of game wardens and police swarmed over the protesters and made many arrests. The media documented these incidents, and the fish-ins attracted national attention and even celebrity participants, including actors and entertainers such as Marlon Brando, Jane Fonda, and Dick Gregory. As more Indians were arrested, various church organizations, the American Civil Liberties Union, and prominent lawyers began to provide legal assistance, and this, in turn, increased media coverage.

In 1970, the federal government brought suit to ensure that the states honored the treaties and allowed American Indians a fair harvest of fish. U.S. District Court judge George Boldt sent shockwaves through the Pacific Northwest when he ruled in favor of Indian fishing rights in *United States v. Washington* (1974) and determined that the treaties entitled the Indians to half the fish passing through the waters.

This decision was challenged but remained in force and ultimately allowed many tribes to develop successful economic ventures such as canneries, fish hatcheries, and aquaculture programs. The fish-ins also produced a number of Indian activists who went on to participate in the early years of the American Indian Movement, including Dino Butler, Sid Mills, Janet McCloud, Joseph Stuntz Killsright, and Leonard Peltier.

See also: American Indian Movement; *United States v. Washington*.

Carole A. Barrett

Fort Atkinson Treaty

Date: 1853
Locale: Southwestern Kansas
Tribes involved: Apache, Comanche, Kiowa
Categories: Nineteenth century history, Treaties
Significance: This treaty was an attempt to establish peace among southern Plains tribes in order to ease white passage westward and facilitate the building of a transcontinental railroad through Indian lands.

Personally negotiated by Thomas Fitzpatrick, a white trader and Indian agent of the Upper Platte Agency, the Treaty of Fort Atkinson was one of a series of U.S.-Indian treaties signed during the 1850's to open passage to America's Far West while promoting the Christianization and civilization of the Plains Indians. Fitzpatrick previously had helped to bring the Sioux and seven other Plains tribes together to sign the Treaty of Fort Laramie with the United States in 1851. The signatories to the Fort Atkinson Treaty agreed to establish peace among the affected Indian tribes, as well as between Indians and whites. It sanctioned the passage of whites through Indian lands, and acknowledged U.S. rights to establish military roads and posts thereon. It also provided for annuities to be paid by the United States (for a ten-year term) to the affected Indians.

See also: Apache Wars; Fort Laramie Treaty of 1851.

Clifton K. Yearley

Fort Greenville Treaty

Date: 1795
Locale: Between the Great Lakes and the Ohio River
Tribes involved: Chippewa, Iroquois, Lenni Lenape, Miami, Ottawa, Potawatomi, Shawnee, Wyandot (Huron)

Categories: Colonial history, Treaties
Significance: The Treaty of Fort Greenville, combined with Jay's Treaty, served as an important benchmark in the tripartite Anglo-American-Indian struggle for control of the region between the Great Lakes and the Ohio River.

During the twenty years following the end of the American Revolution in 1783, the question of which power—American Indians, the United States, or England—would control the region between the Ohio River and the Great Lakes constituted one of the greatest challenges confronting the new government of the United States.

Historical Background. According to the terms of the Treaty of Paris (signed on September 3, 1783), Great Britain agreed to remove its commercial and military presence from the region between the Great Lakes and the Ohio River, a region then called the Old Northwest. Notwithstanding this commitment, however, the British delayed in implementing this treaty provision. Several factors accounted for this delay, but one of the most significant was the conviction of many influential Britons that the region north of the Ohio was too strategic to surrender to the Americans. Instead, they believed that Britain should attempt to maintain at least an indirect presence in the area, thereby placing Great Britain in an advantageous position should the loosely confederated United States politically disintegrate. It was in this context that the British considered the possibility of sponsoring the creation of a British satellite or buffer state spanning the territory between the Ohio River and the Great Lakes and consisting of a confederation of Indian tribes. Thus, in the hope of promoting such an entity (there were also other reasons), London opted to maintain its commercial and military presence south of the Great Lakes. Indeed, not only did the British continue their presence at Michilimackinac, Detroit, Fort Niagara, Oswego, and other locations on American soil, but also, in 1786, British authorities issued a directive to hold or, if necessary, recapture these sites should the United States attempt to seize them.

Simultaneously, beginning in 1785, British agents actively attempted to promote the establishment of a pro-British confederation among the tribes. For their part, the Indians were extremely dissatisfied with Congress's policy toward the tribes and the northwest region generally. The Indians thought that the treaties of Forts Stanwix, McIntosh, and Finney, which had been concluded between several of the tribes and the United States government, were unfair to Indian interests. Indeed, many of the original signatory tribes had subsequently repudiated these treaties. Those tribes that had not been parties to these treaties naturally refused to abide by their terms. The treaties, however, provided the context for an infusion of American frontiersmen into the lands north of the Ohio River. The small military force that Congress had raised from the states was clearly insufficient either to prevent the frontiersmen from intruding into Indian territory or to overawe the tribes into abiding by the treaties—to say nothing about convincing them to make additional territorial concessions. Consequently, the British agents sent to promote the establishment of the Indian confederation north of the Ohio under British protection met with a receptive audience.

Finally, in 1788, the Chippewa, Delaware (Lenni Lenape), Iroquois, Miami, Ottawa, Potawatomi, Shawnee, and Wyandot (Huron) tribes formed a confederation and repudiated the treaties of Forts Stanwix, McIntosh, and Finney, agreed not to cede any additional land to the United States without the consent of the entire confederation, and demanded U.S. recognition of an Indian state between the Ohio River and the Great Lakes. This development, combined with the continued British military and commercial presence on U.S. territory south of the Great Lakes, provided London with a strong bargaining position as the United States and Great Britain opened regular diplomatic relations. Great Britain's new ambassador to the United States arrived in Philadelphia in October, 1791, with instructions from his government to agree to the evacuation of the British presence south of the Great Lakes only if the United States agreed to abide by the British interpretation of the terms of the Treaty of Paris and accepted the establishment of the Indian state, de facto under British protection, between the Ohio River and the Great Lakes.

The Washington administration totally rejected the British stance as a violation of U.S. territorial integrity and sovereignty. With only a small military force, the administration attempted to negotiate a new treaty with the Indians. In the negotiations, held at Fort Harmar in January, 1789, the territorial governor, Arthur St. Clair, capitalized on dissension among the tribes and succeeded in concluding a treaty that, while providing some compensation to the Indians, reaffirmed the boundaries established under the terms of the treaties of Forts McIntosh and Finney. By the autumn of 1789, however, war had erupted along the frontier as a result of continued Indian resentment of U.S. policy generally and the Treaty of Fort Harmar specifically, as well as the continued provocations from the American frontiersmen in Indian country.

Military Operations, 1790-1794. Yielding to pressure from the westerners, the Washington administration dispatched a series of military expeditions into the wilderness north of the Ohio River. The first two of these expeditions, in October, 1790, and August-November, 1791, under the successive leadership of Josiah Harmar and Arthur St. Clair, designed to overawe the Indians and assert U.S. control over the region, yielded disastrous results. Harmar's October, 1790, expedition resulted only in the destruction of a few Miami villages along the Maumee River and the death of a small number of Indians at the cost of 75 regulars and 108 militiamen killed and another 31 wounded. Similarly, St. Clair's late summer and autumn 1791 expedition resulted in a second disastrous defeat with 623 soldiers killed and 258 wounded. Indeed, St. Clair's defeat was considered an especially significant setback in asserting U.S. sovereignty over the region north of the Ohio. Conversely, the Indians were euphoric with success and, encouraged by British expression of support for the Indian Confederation, intensified warfare against the American frontiersmen while demanding U.S. recognition of their confederation.

In the autumn of 1793, the new U.S. military commander in the Ohio Valley, Major General Anthony Wayne, initiated a new offensive against the Indians. Throughout the winter and spring of 1794, Wayne carefully launched a limited operation into Indian country. He methodically constructed a series of forts to serve both as a line of defense and as a base for a new offensive against the tribes. Moreover, his emphasis on training and his focus on troop discipline, combined with his perseverance during the harsh winter, impressed the Indians.

Meanwhile, throughout the winter, as Wayne consolidated his position, the British reinforced their policy in the Northwest. In February, 1794, the British governor in Canada told the Indians that when war between the United States and the tribes came, Britain would support the Indian attempt to regain full control over their lands. Simultaneously, the British began construction of a new post, Fort Miami, on U.S. soil along the Maumee River. The new fort was intended to further solidify the British position in Indian country as well as to provide an advance defense for the British presence at Detroit. These developments convinced the Indians that London would support them against General Wayne's army. Hence, confident of future success, the tribes assembled approximately two thousand warriors outside Fort Miami.

On June 30 and July 1, 1794, the Indians attacked Wayne's forces but were repulsed and withdrew into the wilderness along the Maumee River. On July 28, Wayne, now reinforced (bringing his total force to about thirty-five hundred men), advanced into Indian country. Although he reached the Maumee River on August 8, he delayed in assaulting the Indians until he had secured his lines of communications and established a forward base

(Fort Defiance). Finally, on August 20, after a series of deceptive initiatives, Wayne surprised and defeated the Indians at the Battle of Fallen Timbers. Following the battle, the defeated Indians retreated to Fort Miami, whereupon the British refused to provide any refuge or assistance. Realizing that they had been betrayed by the British, the disillusioned Indians retired to the forest.

The Treaties. The dramatic change in the British policy toward the Indians reflected a larger transformation in British policy toward the United States. During the spring of 1794, the British government moved toward a rapprochement with the Americans; during the summer of 1794, negotiations were opened in Britain between the U.S. representative, John Jay, and British officials. It was in the context of this change in the complexion of Anglo-American relations that the British decided to abandon the Indians rather then precipitate a crisis on the Maumee River that could, in turn, lead to the collapse of Anglo-American negotiations before they had begun and possibly provoke a war between the two powers. Eventually, on November 19, 1794, the negotiators concluded a new treaty, Jay's Treaty, which resolved the outstanding Anglo-American disputes stemming from the 1783 Treaty of Paris. Under the terms of Jay's Treaty, London, among other things, agreed finally to evacuate the British posts on U.S. soil.

Deprived of British support, the demoralized Indians entered into new negotiations with General Wayne from a position of weakness. On August 3, 1795, Wayne and chiefs representing the Delaware, Miami, Shawnee, and Wyandot Indians and the United States delineated a demarcation separating Indian lands from those open to settlement. The line ran along the Cuyahoga River, across the portage to the Tuscarawas River, westward to Fort Recovery, and finally southward to the Ohio River across from its confluence with the Kentucky River. Hence, the U.S. government opened for settlement all of the future state of Ohio, except the north-central and northwest portions of the state, as well as opening the extreme southeastern corner of the present-day state of Indiana. In addition, the U.S. government reserved a series of specific sites within Indian country primarily for commercial and/or military purposes. Thus, as a result of the Treaty of Fort Greenville and Jay's Treaty, a new balance between the Americans and the Indians was struck along the northwestern frontier. Almost immediately, however, pressure began to mount which soon challenged the supposed permanence of the Fort Greenville Treaty line, and the stage was set for the next phase in American westward expansion at the expense of the Indians.

See also: Fallen Timbers, Battle of; Fort Stanwix Treaty; Jay's Treaty.

Howard M. Hensel

Sources for Further Study

Bemis, Samuel Flagg. *Jay's Treaty*. Rev. ed. New Haven, Conn.: Yale University Press, 1962.
Billington, Ray Allen. *Westward Expansion*. New York: Macmillan, 1949.
Kohn, Richard H. *Eagle and Sword*. New York: Free Press, 1975.
Philbrick, Francis S. *The Rise of the West, 1754-1830*. New York: Harper & Row, 1965.
Prucha, Francis Paul. *The Sword of the Republic*. New York: Macmillan, 1969.

Fort Laramie Treaty of 1851

Date: September 1-20, 1851
Locale: Fort Laramie, Wyoming
Tribes involved: Arapaho, Cheyenne, Crow, Shoshone, Sioux
Categories: Nineteenth century history, Treaties
Significance: In an unprecedented effort to promote peace during early western expansion, a treaty council was convened at Fort Laramie whereby ten thousand Indians of various nations gathered at one time to sign a peace treaty with representatives of the U.S. government.

During the mid-nineteenth century the continuing rush of covered wagon immigrants across the Plains of the United States began to have an unsettling effect on American Indian tribes living there. Wild game was driven out and grasslands were being cropped close by the immigrants' cattle and horses. U.S. government policy provided some reimbursement to Indians for losses of game, grass, and land caused by the continuing influx of white settlers. In 1847, Thomas Fitzpatrick was appointed the first U.S. government representative to the various nomad tribes of the High Plains. Aware of the mounting losses and the potential for Indian uprisings against the settlers, Fitzpatrick campaigned long and hard for congressional funding to help alleviate growing tensions.

In February, 1851, Congress appropriated $100,000 for the purpose of holding a treaty council with the tribes of the High Plains. D. D. Mitchell, superintendent of Indian affairs at St. Louis, and Fitzpatrick were designated commissioners for the government. They selected Fort Laramie as the meeting location and September 1, 1851, as the meeting date. Word was sent throughout the Plains of the impending treaty council. By September 1, the first arrivals included the Sioux, Cheyennes, and Arapahos. Later arriving participants included the Snakes (Shoshones), and Crows.

Because of the vast number of participants—more than ten thousand Indians and 270 soldiers—it became apparent that the forage available for Indian and soldier ponies and horses was insufficient. The council grounds were therefore moved about thirty-six miles south, to Horse Creek.

On September 8, the treaty council officially began. The assembly was unprecedented. Each Indian nation approached the council with its own unique song or demonstration, dress, equipment, and mannerisms. Superintendent Mitchell proclaimed that all nations would smoke the pipe of peace together. The proposed treaty asked for unmolested passage for settlers over the roads leading to the West. It included rights for the government to build military posts for immigrants' protection. The treaty also defined the limits of territory for each tribe and asked for a lasting peace between the various nations. Each nation was to select a representative, a chief who would have control over and be responsible for his nation. In return, the government would provide each Indian nation an annuity of $50,000 for fifty years, the sum to be expended for goods, merchandise, and provisions.

After much discussion and conferencing, the treaty was signed on September 17 by the U.S. commissioners and all the attending chiefs. Adding to the festivities, on September 20, a delayed caravan of wagons arrived at the treaty council with $50,000 worth of goods and merchandise. These goods were summarily distributed to all the nations represented, and feelings of good will permeated the gathering. To further the sense of lasting peace, Fitzpatrick later took a delegation of eleven chiefs with him to Washington, D.C., where they visited with President Millard Fillmore in the White House.

See also: Fort Laramie Treaty of 1868.

John L. Farbo

Sources for Further Study

Ellis, Richard N. *The Western American Indian*. Lincoln: University of Nebraska Press, 1972.

Hafen, LeRoy, and Francis Young. *Fort Laramie and the Pageant of the West, 1834-1890*. Glendale, Calif.: Arthur H. Clark, 1938.

Hedren, Paul L. *Fort Laramie in 1876*. Lincoln: University of Nebraska Press, 1988.

Fort Laramie Treaty of 1868

Date: April 29-November 5, 1868
Locale: Laramie fork of the North Platte River in modern Wyoming
Tribes involved: Sioux
Categories: Nineteenth century history, Treaties
Significance: This treaty was meant to provide a lasting peace through mutual concessions involving territorial rights and peaceful behavior; the treaty ultimately failed.

By the mid-1800's, the vast area of land claimed by the Sioux Nation was subjected to inexorable pressures from America's westward expansion, which accelerated after the end of the Civil War in 1865. Pioneers, settlers, farmers, gold prospectors, railroads, and the army all encroached on Sioux territory. Inevitably, armed conflict between whites and Indians occurred. Attempts to arrive at a peaceful solution and compromise, such as the treaties of 1851, 1865, and 1866, provided only short-lived respites.

On July 20, 1867, after vigorous debate over whether to subdue the Indians militarily and punish them or reach a peaceful accord with them, both houses of Congress approved a bill which authorized a government commission to make peace with the Plains tribes. The commission was directed by Congress to establish peace, remove if possible the causes of war, safeguard frontier settlements and the rights-of-way for the transcontinental railroads, and establish reservations for the Plains Indians with adequate arable land so they could become self-sufficient farmers.

Terms of the Treaty. The peace commission, headed by Commissioner of Indian Affairs Nathaniel Taylor, worked its way west, meeting various tribes of Sioux and listening to their demands. In April, 1868, the commission convened at Fort Laramie with a draft treaty that met many of these demands. Article 2 established the Great Sioux Reservation, which gave to the Sioux all of present-day South Dakota west of the Missouri River, including the sacred Black Hills, "for the absolute and undisturbed use and occupancy of the Sioux." Article 16 established the Powder River Country to the north and west of the Great Sioux Reservation as "unceded Indian territory," where whites were not permitted to go unless given permission by the Sioux. Article 11 gave the Sioux hunting rights along the Republican River and above the Platte River in Nebraska and Wyoming for "so long as the buffalo may range thereon in such numbers as to justify the chase." Other articles promised that all Sioux who resided within the Great Sioux

Signing of the Treaty of 1868 by General William Tecumseh Sherman and the Indian delegation at Fort Laramie, Wyoming. (National Archives)

Reservation would be provided with food for the next four years (until they learned to become farmers). The reservation was promised schools, mills, blacksmiths, doctors, and teachers and an agent to administer the various programs and maintain order. Additionally, no chief could unilaterally sign away treaty rights, as any sale of land had to be approved by three-fourths of all adult Sioux males.

In return, the United States asked for peace and asked that the Sioux make their permanent residence within the boundaries of the reservation. The Sioux relinquished the right to occupy any lands outside the reservation permanently, including the unceded territory. The Sioux were not to oppose the building of railroads on the plains and were not to attack settlers and their wagon trains or take white prisoners. Additionally, provisions would be distributed by the government not at the western end of the reservation, near traditional hunting grounds and where the Sioux customarily traded with whites, but at agencies established along the Missouri River in the eastern part of the reservation, in order to reorient Sioux life to these agencies.

Failure of the Treaty. Red Cloud was the final Sioux chief to sign the treaty, on November 5, 1868, only after the government abandoned its forts along the Bozeman Trail in Sioux territory. The treaty was rejected, however, by the influential and powerful Sioux chiefs Crazy Horse and Sitting Bull, who remained in the unceded territory and refused to live on the reservation.

In the end, this treaty proved no more effective in maintaining the peace and Sioux way of life than previous ones had been. Violations of Sioux territory by white emigrants and the army, the discovery of gold in the Black Hills (and the taking of the Black Hills by the government in 1877 without compensation), problems administering the reservation, and the refusal of Crazy Horse and Sitting Bull to live on the reservation despite government threats of war undermined any hope that the treaty's terms would be honored and observed. By 1880 the Sioux had been either killed or defeated and were confined to the reservation.

See also: Bozeman Trail War; Fort Laramie Treaty of 1851.

Laurence Miller

Fort Mims, Battle of

Date: August 30, 1813
Locale: Alabama
Tribes involved: Creek
Categories: Nineteenth century history, Wars and battles
Significance: Though William Weatherford's Creeks won a major victory at Fort Mims, reports of a massacre there led to a rapid mobilization of state and federal forces that eventually overwhelmed the Creeks.

Tensions within the Creek (Muskogee) Nation and between some Creeks and European Americans reached the boiling point in 1813. Fighting was already raging between the Creek Red Sticks, who favored maintaining the traditional Creek values and lifestyle and who opposed further encroachments on Creek land, and friendly Creeks, who were more receptive to the assimilationist policies being pushed by the United States government and whose leaders had adopted many aspects of American life, including plantation slavery.

On July 27, 1813, a force of territorial militia unsuccessfully attacked a band of Red Sticks at Burnt Corn Creek, a tributary of the Alabama River. The Creek War now began, though it was only the Red Stick faction of Creeks that waged war with the United States. Encouraged by their initial success, the Red Sticks determined to attack Fort Mims. William Weatherford (Red Eagle), a mixed-blood traditionalist of considerable ability, gathered a force of about 750 warriors and moved toward the fort.

Fort Mims was located near the Alabama River about forty miles north of Mobile and was defended by a garrison of about 120 militia commanded by Major Daniel Beasley. The fort also became a haven for approximately 275 to 300 whites and friendly Creeks plus about a hundred slaves.

Doubting that the Red Sticks would attack a fort, Beasley was lax in maintaining security. On August 29, two slaves reported a large number of hostile Indians nearby. When scouts failed to find any, Beasley ordered the slaves whipped for giving a false alarm. The fort's defenses were unmanned the next day when Weatherford launched his attack at noon, catching the fort's garrison and inhabitants at lunch. Red Sticks rushed into the fort's open entrance. Others began firing into the fort through rifle ports in the walls. The battle raged for several hours before the buildings inside the walls were set on fire. A few militiamen and others managed to escape into the surrounding woods. Most of the whites and friendly Creeks who sur-

The 1813 victory of Creek Red Sticks at Fort Mims, reported by whites as a massacre, soon brought white revenge against the Creeks. (Library of Congress)

vived the battle were killed, some by torture. Most of the slaves who survived the battle were taken away as prisoners.

Whites regarded the Fort Mims fight as a massacre, and the numbers reported to have been killed rapidly swelled. No fort of its size had ever been taken by Indians, and something akin to panic seized the southern frontier.

Fort Mims proved to be a costly victory for the Creeks, however; around a hundred Red Sticks were killed, and the reports of a massacre roused neighboring white settlers to seek revenge. Georgia and Tennessee mobilized their militias for service against the Creeks, and the federal government diverted some of its scarce military resources from the war it was fighting against England for service against the Creeks. The tide soon turned against the Red Sticks, and all Creeks suffered as a result of their eventual defeat.

See also: Creek War; Horseshoe Bend Treaty.

William C. Lowe

Fort Stanwix Treaty

Date: October 22, 1784
Locale: Fort Stanwix, New York
Tribes involved: Iroquois Confederacy
Categories: Eighteenth century history, Reservations and relocation, Treaties
Significance: Iroquois tribes cede lands to the United States and are forced to move westward.

The Treaty of Fort Stanwix, signed in 1784, was a product of the American Revolution that involved colonists and the Iroquois nations. Because several Iroquois tribes had fought alongside the British during the war, victorious Americans maintained that they had won lands occupied by "defeated" Iroquois. The Treaty of Fort Stanwix marked the beginning of negotiations with Native Americans that dealt with them as a conquered people rather than as equals. The Revolutionary War and resulting treaty negotiations irreparably split the Iroquois Confederacy.

At the outbreak of the American Revolution, the Six Nations of the powerful Iroquois Confederacy were divided over whether to support the English, to side with the American rebels, or to remain neutral. The confederation had traded and fought alongside the English for many years and considered the English and colonists as the same. Both British and American Indian agents encouraged Native Americans throughout the colonies to remain neutral. Initially, the Iroquois remained nonpartisan. This allowed the Iroquois to deal with both the British in Canada and the Americans in the colonies, playing one against another as they had the French and British prior to the French and Indian War.

As the Revolutionary War progressed, however, both the British and the Americans saw the advantages of including American Indians in their ranks and urged Native Americans to ally themselves. The pressure to choose sides exerted by British and American agents split the six-nation Iroquois Confederacy into two groups. Unable to agree on which side to support, the confederation decided to allow each nation to choose which side, if either, to endorse. The Oneidas and Tuscaroras fought for the rebels. American attacks on Mohawk settlements encouraged the Mohawks to support the British; they were joined by the Onondagas, Cayugas, and Senecas. These tribes were effective in British attacks on frontier locations, especially in the Mohawk Valley around Fort Stanwix.

Competing Promises. During the war, British officers had made promises of land to Native Americans who fought with them, but during the peace negotiations in Paris, the defeated British ignored the interests of their Native American allies. In 1783, the Treaty of Paris surrendered all the land east of the Mississippi River to the former colonists. Some of this land belonged to various Native American tribes and was not England's to grant.

New York State granted Iroquois lands to Revolutionary War soldiers as compensation for services during the war. New York tried to negotiate land sales with the Iroquois that would directly benefit the state. The United States Congress, under the Articles of Confederation, admonished New York officials and appointed Indian commissioners Oliver Wolcott, Richard Butler, and Arthur Lee to negotiate peace and land cessions for the United States with the Mohawks, Onondagas, Cayugas, and Senecas. A peace conference was called and held in New York at Fort Stanwix near Oneida Lake. A number of Iroquois could not attend because of illness and other factors, and only a quickly formed irregular group of Iroquois representatives was present. The commissioners arrived at Fort Stanwix with an intimidating military escort. Rather than negotiating with the Iroquois as equals, as the English had done previously, American commissioners asserted political sovereignty over all tribal natives on American soil. Iroquois speeches were cut short and credentials challenged.

The commissioners insisted that the Iroquois tribes that fought on the side of the British were a conquered people. All lands held by those tribes, therefore, were forfeit to the United States as spoils of war. The U.S. government would allow them to retain some of their lands but demanded land cessions in reparation for injuries inflicted on Americans during the war. The Iroquois contended (1) that England had had no right to cede tribal lands to the United States (2) that if the Iroquois were to surrender their lands to Americans, they expected something in return, and (3) that they had not, in any event, been defeated in battle and therefore were not party to peace negotiations.

Mutual Concessions. As part of the resulting Treaty of Fort Stanwix, the attending Iroquois ceded a strip of land that began at the mouth of Oyonwaye Creek on Lake Ontario four miles south of the Niagara portage path. The boundary line ran south to the mouth of the Tehosaroro, or Buffalo Creek, to the Pennsylvania line, and along its north-south boundary to the Ohio River. In effect, the treaty took all Iroquois lands west of New York and Pennsylvania and all of Ohio.

The United States released any claim it may have had by right of conquest to tribal lands west of that boundary. Iroquois property in the western region of New York State east of the Oyonwaye remained unaffected. The treaty assured the Oneida and Tuscarora who had fought on the side of the Americans continued peaceful possession of their lands. The United States agreed to protect the remaining Iroquois territories against encroachments, seizures, and other possible violations, and guaranteed the right of the Six Nations of the Iroquois Confederacy to independence.

Representatives for the Iroquois Confederacy agreed to peaceful relations with the United States. The tribes who had fought against the colonies promised to deliver up all prisoners, black and white, whom they had taken during the war. As guarantee of that promise, six Iroquois would be taken as hostages to Fort Harmar by General Arthur St. Clair, governor of the Northwest Territory.

Immediately after the congressional commissioners concluded their negotiations, commissioners from Pennsylvania negotiated for large land grants in their state. In return, the Iroquois received five thousand dollars in goods and supplies. Soon after, New York State, in defiance of Congress, negotiated land sales with the Oneida and Tuscarora. Additional land treaties quickly ensued. Congress's inability to prevent New York State from negotiating separate land sales and to uphold other aspects of the Treaty of Fort Stanwix highlighted the weaknesses in central government under the Articles of Confederation and served as a reminder that each state considered itself a sovereign nation.

In 1786, the Iroquois Confederacy held a council meeting at Buffalo Creek, New York. Disappointed and upset with their delegates, they refused to ratify the Treaty of Fort Stanwix and offered to return gifts presented to the delegates at the negotiations. Congress, however, considered the terms of the treaty to be valid and acted on them accordingly.

British Interference. After the American Revolution, British officials did little to discourage continued relations with northern Native American tribes. The English traded with and provided goods to local tribes and allowed large councils to convene at British-held forts. After the council of Buffalo Creek, the Iroquois sought support from the British in their effort to denounce the treaty and continue their war against the United States. The Iroquois Confederacy soon discovered that the British had no intention of militarily supporting their former allies in defense of their land rights. Lacking the desire to go to war against the Americans alone, the Iroquois let the treaty stand.

On January 9, 1789, St. Clair negotiated the Treaty of Fort Harmar with a group of Senecas. The treaty reaffirmed the terms and boundaries set forth in the Treaty of Fort Stanwix. The Iroquois were given permission to hunt on their old lands "as long as they were peaceful about it."

The treaties of Fort Stanwix and Fort Harmar further fractionalized the confederation's six tribes, a process that had begun in 1777, when the Six Nations had split in choosing sides during the Revolutionary War. Joseph Brant led a group of Mohawk, Cayuga, and other tribe members out of the country and into Ontario, Canada, thereby splitting the confederacy in half. Those who remained in the United States were divided over other issues between the American Indians and the settlers. There was no single chief or council that could speak for the entire Iroquois Confederacy, and the Iroquois Confederacy was never again united.

See also: Fort Greenville Treaty; Iroquois Confederacy.

Leslie Stricker

Sources for Further Study
Downes, Randolph C. *Council Fires on the Upper Ohio: A Narrative of Indian Affairs in the Upper Ohio Valley Until 1795*. Pittsburgh: University of Pittsburgh Press, 1940. Discusses the relations between settlers and various tribes in the Ohio Valley, including those at Fort Stanwix.

Graymont, Barbara. *The Iroquois in the American Revolution*. Syracuse, N.Y.: Syracuse University Press, 1972. Chapters 6 and 7 describe Iroquois warfare, diplomacy, decline, and removal.

Jennings, Francis, ed. *The History and Culture of Iroquois Diplomacy: An Interdisciplinary Guide to the Treaties of the Six Nations and Their League*. Syracuse, N.Y.: Syracuse University Press, 1985. Extensive discussion of treaty negotiations, terms, and results.

Trigger, Bruce G., ed. *Northeast*. Vol. 15 in *Handbook of North American Indians*, edited by William C. Sturtevant. Washington, D.C.: Smithsonian Institution, 1978. Discusses Native Americans from the Northeast in considerable detail, including language, history, customs, culture, and religion.

Washburn, Wilcomb E., ed. *History of Indian-White Relations*. Vol. 4 in *Handbook of North American Indians*, edited by William C. Sturtevant. Washington, D.C.: Smithsonian Institution Press, 1988. Extensive coverage of relations between American Indians and whites across the United States, from first contact to 1987.

Fort Wayne Treaty

Date: September 30, 1809
Locale: Indiana
Tribes involved: Lenni Lenape, Miami, Potawatomi
Categories: Nineteenth century history, Treaties
Significance: Negotiated by William Henry Harrison and repudiated by Tecumseh, the leader of a pan-Indian movement, this treaty precipitated a chain of events that culminated in the Battle of Tippecanoe.

On September 30, 1809, the governor of the Indiana Territory, William Henry Harrison, met with leaders of the Delaware (Lenni Lenape), Miami, and Potawatomi tribes in the fort built by General "Mad" Anthony Wayne. They signed the Treaty of Fort Wayne, which exchanged 2.5 million acres of Indian land southeast of the Wabash River for goods worth about $7,000 and an annuity of $1,750. Later that year, a separate treaty with the Kickapoo and Wea added a half million acres. While the exchange rate of two cents per acre was higher than usual for such treaties, it was still an unfair exchange. The treaty culminated a process begun in 1795 with the Treaty of Fort Greenville, which had ceded a meager six square miles of Miami land to the United States government. In the ensuing period, more than fifteen treaties had been signed, most of them negotiated by Harrison, relinquishing control of Indian lands. While Harrison was able to maintain friendly relations with the major tribal leaders, the loss of native lands had started a countermovement.

Led by the Shawnee prophet Tenskwatawa, a pan-Indian movement developed based on opposition to the cession of Indian lands and to the tribal leaders who had negotiated the treaties. Tenskwatawa, his brother Tecumseh, and their followers refused to recognize the validity of the treaties on the ground that the land belonged to all Indian peoples so the chiefs had no authority to sign the lands away. To show defiance of the treaties, Tenskwatawa established new Indian towns at Greenville from 1806 to 1808 in defiance of the Treaty of Greenville. From 1808 to 1811, he established Prophetstown at Tippecanoe to show that his movement did not honor the Treaty of Fort Wayne.

As Harrison continued his plans to open the recently acquired lands, Tecumseh assumed the role of war chief and took command of the nativist movement. He warned Harrison to keep surveyors and settlers out of the territory. So threatening was his presence that, for two years, virtually no settlement occurred. In order to break the stalemate, Harrison led troops in an attack on Prophetstown in 1811 while Tecumseh was farther south trying to gain allies among the Creek, Choctaw, and Cherokee. The ensuing Battle of Tippecanoe efficiently removed Tecumseh's followers from the immediate area. It was also, however, the opening action of a war that would last until 1815 and would see Tecumseh ally his forces with the British in the War of 1812.

See also: Fort Greenville Treaty; Tippecanoe, Battle of.

Charles L. Kammer III

Fox Wars

Date: Summer, 1714-1741
Locale: West and southwest of Lake Michigan
Tribes involved: Chippewa, Fox, Huron, Kickapoo, Mascouten, Menominee, Potawatomi, Sac, Seneca, Sioux, Winnebago
Categories: Colonial history, Wars and battles
Significance: Generations of intertribal warfare and French attempts to obtain peace.

Although the Fox people trace their own origins to the northeastern seaboard, they clearly emerged in Native American history in the late seventeenth century in the western Great Lakes region. First known under their Algonquian name, Mesquakies (People of the Red Earth), they were later referred to in early French explorers' journals as *renards*, or Foxes, a name that persists in the literature. Most of what is known about the Fox tribe and their often hostile relations with a number of their neighboring tribes comes from the eighteenth century Québécois (New France colonial) archives. Hardly a year passed between 1699 and 1742 without some reference to relations between the Foxes and representatives of Onontia, the natives' name for the French governor general of New France.

In 1699, Governor General Louis-Hector de Callières tried to obtain a peace treaty, not only between France and the tribes of the western Great Lakes region but also among the tribes themselves. His goal was to increase profitable trade in a vast region that remained unpredictable because of recurring intertribal strife. The natives invited to Montreal were well-known tribes associated with the Iroquois Five Nations (including the Senecas) and less well-known tribes along the western shore of Lake Michigan, including the Sacs, Winnebagos, Kickapoos, Menominees, and Foxes. In September, 1700, peace was signed by several important tribes, but many, including the Foxes, held back. Although the Foxes and Chippewas agreed to cease fighting each other in the Wisconsin area, Fox hostilities with neighboring Sioux still raged, disrupting fur trading as far as Sioux territory in Minnesota. In their attempt to stop these conflicts, the French invited Fox chieftains Noro and Miskousouath to Montreal. There the chiefs were assured that, if they remained peaceful in their newly fortified villages at the portage point between the Fox and Wisconsin Rivers, they would have their share of French fur trade in Sioux territory.

The shortcomings of these agreements were particularly evident to Antoine de La Mothe, sieur de Cadillac, commander of the strategic post at Michilimackinac on the straits between Lakes Michigan and Huron. Cadillac's goal was to develop another, eventually much better known, post at Detroit into a major trading center for various tribes. In 1710, he invited a number of Algonquian tribes located in the area from the Green Bay to the Wisconsin River, including Sacs, Foxes, Mascoutens, and Kickapoos, to move to eastern Michigan.

First Stage. Some Foxes, together with other Wisconsin tribes, did go to the Detroit area, but the venture soon was reversed by Montreal's governor general, the marquis de Vaudreuil. Not only did the Foxes expect that their cooperation with the resettlement scheme should be rewarded, but they also became entangled in skirmishes with other tribes, especially Hurons and members of the Illinois Confederacy. They even raided French colonial farms, stealing food and livestock. Instead of heeding French orders in 1711 to return to Wisconsin, the Foxes became even more belligerent, proceeding to build a fort near Fort Pontchartrain on the Detroit River. It took more than a year for the French, taking advantage of alliances with Huron and Illinois Confederacy tribes, to expel the Foxes by force. Most of the besieged Foxes were massacred brutally by French-allied American Indians, despite the French commander's assurance of safe passage upon surrender. Those who escaped sought refuge among the Seneca Iroquois. These violent events on the Detroit River were bound to have repercussions among the Fox tribes that had stayed behind in Wisconsin alongside their allies, the Sacs and Winnebagos. When the defeated Foxes returned to Wisconsin, new alliances were built; by the summer of 1714, they had begun attacks on French traders passing from Detroit to Michilimackinac.

In this first stage of the Fox Wars, some Wisconsin natives hoped that the French would seek an accommodation with the Foxes. As the situation deteriorated and trade became paralyzed, many American Indians began to call for a strong French military campaign against the Foxes. Before long, it appeared that the Foxes had long-distance ties with other allies in British territory, especially the Senecas. This complicated the French strategy considerably, forcing the French to try diplomatic intervention far to the east of Wisconsin. Vaudreuil was unable to report any progress for at least three years.

Although Fox chieftains Okimaoussen and Ouchala agreed to de-escalate the conflict, warfare against the Foxes by their inveterate enemies, the Chippewas and Potawatomis, caused strife to spread into Illinois tribal areas in 1719. By 1721, the Foxes had even sealed peace with their former enemies, the Sioux, to have an ally against the Illinois tribes. In 1725, the French reported that their own hopes to tap the Sioux fur market were seriously hampered by the Sioux-Fox alliance.

By the time of Vaudreuil's death in October, 1725, King Louis XV himself sent orders to replace the French commander at Green Bay, François Amariton, who was suspected of encouraging Fox raids into Illinois territory, and to step up activities against the Foxes. This task, which would lead to disastrous consequences for the Fox tribe, fell to Charles de Beauharnais, governor general of New France from 1726 to 1747.

A major campaign was set for 1728. French forces of four hundred soldiers were joined by *coureurs de bois* (freelance French fur trappers and traders) and hundreds of western natives. The French claimed success, but in reality the Foxes had withdrawn into Iowa rather than risk a battle.

Kickapoo Involvement. The next stage of conflict came when Fox chief Kansekoe tried to force his Kickapoo allies to hand over a dozen French traders who were being held as hostages. Kickapoo refusals incited younger Fox warriors to break away from Kansekoe and attack both Kickapoo and Mascouten hunters. Both tribes soon asked for French alliance status. Then, some Winnebagos and Menominees also joined attacks against the Foxes. Declining chances for a victory again divided the Foxes. Some factions favored a peace, while more hostile tribesmen decided to leave Wisconsin and seek asylum, preferably among the Senecas. The attempted migration left them open to reprisal attacks, especially by members of the Illinois Confederacy, supported by the Foxes' former neighbors, the Potawatomis, Kickapoos, and Mascoutens. A major siege of Fox fortifications on the Illinois prairie in 1730 involved French relief forces, who joined in a general massacre of more than five hundred Foxes, including women and children.

Governor General Beauharnais reported that the remaining Foxes no longer could consider resistance. Continuing reprisals caused Foxes under Chief Kiala to try to resettle peacefully on the north bank of the Wisconsin River and to send emissaries to Montreal. Kiala's apparent failure to meet French terms tempted Beauharnais to allow the Iroquois "volunteers" to pursue the refugee Foxes spread out in areas of Iowa and Illinois. Intertribal fighting continued until 1735, when two refugee groups separated, one to the Rock River in Illinois and the other to the mouth of the Wisconsin. In 1736, White Cat, a friendly Sac chief, asked Beauharnais to grant a pardon. Beauharnais tried unsuccessfully to persuade the Sacs to gain peace by allowing the French to disperse the Foxes among other American Indian nations.

Finally, unable to hold out in the Rock River Valley against other Indians' attacks, and fearful of massive French reprisals for Fox assistance to Sioux warriors near Lake Peoria who had killed French travelers in the area, Fox chief Mekaga agreed to accept French terms of forced relocation. By the fall of 1741, the Foxes and Sacs were trekking to new settlements: ten lodges to the Chicago River, three to Milwaukee, and the rest to their old homeland village on the Fox River in Wisconsin. Although the formal Fox War was over in 1741, these settlements still suffered from attacks by their Chippewa, Menominee, and Ottawa neighbors. In 1743, Beauharnais himself had to intercede to gain another joint pledge of peace.

See also: Fur trade; Indian-white relations: French colonial; Iroquois Confederacy.

Byron D. Cannon

Sources for Further Study

Edmunds, R. David, and Joseph L. Peyser. *The Fox Wars: The Mesquaki Challenge to New France*. Norman: University of Oklahoma Press, 1993. The most complete study to date of the specific events of the Fox Wars.

Hagen, William T. *The Sac and Fox Indians*. 2d ed. Norman: University of Oklahoma Press, 1980. A general history, including cultural and religious topics.

Parkman, Francis. *Count Frontenac and New France Under Louis XIV.* 1877. Reprint. New York: Library of America, 1983. A pioneering work providing background on French interests in the Great Lakes area just before dealings with the Foxes became a focal point.

White, Richard. *The Middle Ground: Indians, Empires and Republics in the Great Lakes Region, 1650-1815.* Cambridge, England: Cambridge University Press, 1991. Places the Fox Wars in a wider chronological and geographical context of French, British, and American Indian relations.

French and Indian War

Date: May 28, 1754-February 10, 1763
Locale: North America
Tribes involved: Algonquian, Huron, Iroquois Confederacy (Mohawk, Oneida, Onondaga, Cayuga, Seneca, Tuscarora)
Categories: Colonial history, Wars and battles
Significance: Defeat of French and Native American forces establishes British dominance in North America but increases the mother country's dependence on colonial resources.

The French and Indian War was the North American part of a larger conflict called the Seven Years' War, fought between France and Great Britain for control of colonies in North America and India and for hegemony in Europe. Both Great Britain and France claimed large territories in North America. In addition to the thirteen colonies spread out along the Atlantic coast, the British claimed what is now northern Canada. The French claimed a huge section of the inner continent, stretching from New Orleans in the

The taking of Quebec, September 13, 1759, during the Battle of the Plains of Abraham proved to be the decisive battle in the French and Indian War. Effectively, the French stronghold east of the Mississippi River was ceded to the British in the 1763 treaty that ended the war. The rights of the indigenous nations that had prior claim to all of this land were not considered. (Library of Congress)

south to what is now Montana in the northwest and Quebec in the northeast. The French built a series of forts along the Mississippi River and its tributaries to defend their claims. One of these tributaries, the Ohio River, flows southwest along the western frontier of Pennsylvania and Virginia. Both French and British claimed this land. British colonists worried about a French invasion and resented the French presence, which limited western expansion.

In 1754, 150 soldiers from Virginia, led by the twenty-two-year-old officer George Washington, headed west to secure British claims by building a fort at the fork where the Monongahela and Allegheny Rivers meet to form the Ohio River. When they arrived, they discovered that the French had built a fort there already, Fort Duquesne. Washington's troops lost the ensuing battle (May 28), which marked the beginning of the war.

As they struggled to expand their North American empires, the British and French did not consider the rights or needs of the people who had been living on the land for thousands of years before Europeans arrived. The only time Europeans took serious notice of the First Americans was when they needed allies in wartime. Both the French and the British sought and received support from some native peoples. For their part, Native Americans, by siding with one party or the other, could get access to European weapons and perhaps succeed in driving at least one group of invading Europeans from the land. Algonquians and Hurons allied themselves with the French, whom they had known mainly as fur traders over the past century and a half. The French seemed less intrusive and permanent than the British, who cleared the land for farming. The Algonquians were, moreover, traditional rivals of those tribes allied with the Iroquois Confederacy. By selling goods at low prices and exploiting traditional enmities, the British also were able to find native allies, including the Mohawks, one of the most powerful Iroquois nations, who agreed to help the British against the French and Algonquians.

The Tide Turns for the British. The war went poorly for the British at first. With thirteen separate colonial governments involved, decisions were difficult to make. Nor were British soldiers accustomed to the American landscape. In 1755, the British general Edward Braddock was badly defeated when he attacked the French at Fort Duquesne. The French and their Native American allies easily scouted out and ambushed Braddock's troops, shooting from behind trees at the British soldiers, whose red coats made good targets. The French won a series of battles until 1757, when the tide changed.

The British had had some advantages from the beginning. There were twenty times as many British in North America as French, and the British had the most powerful navy in the world. Then, in 1757, a dynamic new leader, William Pitt, took over the British government. Pitt sent Britain's best generals to lead the war against the French and motivated British colonists to support the war effort by offering high prices for supplies purchased in America.

A year later, the Lenni Lenape (Delawares), an Algonquian people living in Pennsylvania, withdrew their support from the French, leaving Fort Duquesne vulnerable to attack. The British attacked successfully and renamed the fort to honor their new leader. The city that grew on the site of the fort, Pittsburgh, still contains William Pitt's name.

Battle of the Plains of Abraham. The decisive battle came in 1759, when Pitt sent General James Wolfe to attack the city of Quebec, the French capital. If the British could take this city, they would win the war. Quebec, located at the top of a high cliff that rose steeply from the banks of the St. Lawrence River, was easier to defend than to attack. The French general in charge, the marquis de Montcalm, was an experienced leader, but even he was taken by surprise when Wolfe moved four thousand troops across the St. Lawrence River in small boats, found ways to scale the cliffs, and attacked in the early hours of the morning. Both generals were killed in the battle, but news of the British victory reached Wolfe before he died. This Battle of the Plains of Abraham was the turning point for the French, effectively ending their stronghold in North America.

When the British took Montreal in 1760, fighting ended in North America. There was no formal peace treaty until the war between France and Prussia, Great Britain's ally in central Europe, finally ground to a halt three years later.

Then, in the Treaty of Paris (February 10, 1763), the French ceded Canada and all French lands east of the Mississippi to Great Britain. France retained the land it claimed west of the Mississippi, including the key port of New Orleans. Spain, which had allied itself with France against Great Britain, was forced to give up Florida. The rights of the indigenous nations that had prior claim to all of this land were not considered.

Consequences. The French and Indian War had important consequences for the early development of American history. It increased Great Britain's needs for its North American colonies but had the opposite effect on the colonists' needs for Great Britain. With the French gone, the need for the protection of the British military began to disappear as well. To some colonists, it seemed that the redcoats were starting to get in the way. The British Proclamation of 1763 forbade colonists from settling land west of a line drawn along the Appalachian Mountains. Welcomed by the followers of the Ottawa chief Pontiac, who earlier that year had brought many American Indian nations together to defend their lands against European invasion, the proclamation disappointed those colonists who had expected to benefit from land opened up by the French defeat. In effect, the Proclamation of 1763 had little effect in preserving western lands for their Indian inhabitants as colonists began to push west anyway.

The war brought the colonies closer together. There had been a first effort, called the Albany Plan of Union, to unite the colonies under one government. Although the Albany Plan, discussed by representatives of several colonies in Albany, New York, in 1754, was unsuccessful—the individual colonial governments being hesitant to give up any power—the fact that some sort of union was even discussed reflected a growing tendency to see the colonies as a unified entity distinct from the mother country, England.

Seven years of fighting on three continents and all the world's oceans had exhausted British resources as well. War debts forced the British government to increase tax rates drastically. These rates, however, only applied to British citizens in Great Britain. British citizens in North America continued to pay relatively low taxes. To many British, it seemed only fair that the British in the colonies pay their share for the war that had made their homes safe from invasion.

The self-confidence of the colonists had grown as they helped fight a successful war. They believed they had the same rights to representative government as British citizens in Great Britain. One of these was the right to send representatives to the body of government that levies taxes. Colonists accepted taxes levied by colonial governments, where they were represented, but rejected taxes levied by the British parliament, to which they were not allowed to send representatives. British efforts to tax the colonies, despite colonial protest, thus became one of the causes for the outbreak of the American Revolution.

See also: Albany Congress; Indian-white relations: English colonial; Indian-white relations: French colonial; Proclamation of 1763.

T. W. Dreier

Sources for Further Study

Anderson, Fred. *Crucible of War: The Seven Years' War and the Fate of Empire in British North America, 1754-1766*. New York: Alfred A. Knopf, 2000. Presents the French and Indian War as a conflict in and of itself, rather than merely as a prelude to the Revolutionary War.

_____. *A People's Army: Massachusetts Soldiers and Society in the Seven Years' War*. Chapel Hill: University of North Carolina Press, 1984. This illustrated regional study reveals how average colonists experienced and affected the war.

Auth, Stephen F. *The Ten Years War: Indian-White Relations in Pennsylvania, 1755-1765*. New York: Garland, 1989. Includes Native American perspectives missing in many studies. Final chapter shows the war's implications for later treatment of Native Americans.

Hamilton, Edward P. *The French and Indian Wars: The Story of Battles and Forts in the Wilderness*. Garden City, N.Y.: Doubleday, 1962. The first chapters of this narrative history discuss the role played by George Washington.

Jennings, Francis. *Empire of Fortune: Crowns, Colonies, and Tribes in the Seven Years War in America*. New York: W. W. Norton, 1988. A comprehensive study by a major scholar; offers easily accessible information on all aspects of the war. Illustrations, maps, and indices.

Schwartz, Seymour. *The French and Indian War, 1754-1763: The Imperial Struggle for North America*. New York: Simon & Schuster, 1994. A concise, well-illustrated study that provides a thoughtful, readable overview.

Friends of the Indian organizations

Date: 1879-1900's
Locale: United States
Tribes involved: Pantribal in the United States
Categories: Nineteenth century history, Organizations, Religion and missionary activities, Twentieth century history
Significance: A variety of humanitarian Christian associations sought to reform federal Indian policy by supporting legislation aimed at abolishing "Indianness" and substituting American ideals of individualism, ownership, and Christianity.

Friends of the Indian organizations were formed in the last two decades of the nineteenth century by mainly eastern Christian humanitarians who were determined to influence federal Indian policy. Members of these organizations were convinced of the superiority of Christian civilization and were determined to do away with Indianness and tribal traditions; their goal was to turn individual Indians into patriotic American citizens.

The friends of the Indian groups supported allotment in order to break up tribal land ownership and force individual ownership; they sought to end tribal jurisdiction and bring Indians as individual citizens before the law. They supported vocational education for Indian children, particularly boarding schools, and they were generally intolerant of Indian culture or spiritual expression and worked to outlaw Sun Dances, vision questing, giveaways, plural marriages, and so on. These well-intentioned Christian men and women sought to influence and direct Indian policy by engaging in intense lobbying efforts with federal officials and by educating the general public through newsletters, pamphlets, and speakers. These reformers and their supporters were convinced of the righteousness of their cause and greatly affected federal Indian policy well into the twentieth century.

Beginning in 1883, these groups came together annually for the Lake Mohonk Conference of the Friends of the Indian in New Paltz, New York, to coordinate their efforts. General harmony and a good working relationship existed among the various groups because they shared a common religious outlook that they were doing God's will by guiding Indians from savagery to civilization. The most significant and far-reaching areas affected by these organizations were the federal Indian education system and the General Allotment Act (Dawes Act) of 1887. One of the most prominent groups, the Indian Rights Association, continues to exist; however, it now supports tribalism and tribal self-determination.

See also: Carlisle Indian School; General Allotment Act; Indian Rights Association.

Carole A. Barrett

Fur trade

Date: Early to mid-seventeenth century
Locale: St. Lawrence River and Great Lakes region
Tribes involved: Algonquian peoples, Huron, Iroquois Confederacy
Categories: Colonial history
Significance: The fur trade involved not only material, but also major social and policy exchanges between Indians and whites.

During the early years of fur trading, Europeans and Native Americans met on very widely extended ground. The most concentrated contacts came between the Hudson Bay and the Great Lakes area, down to the Hudson River Valley and westward to Lake Winnipeg. Although forms of interaction varied between regions, two general patterns characterized the impact of the fur trade on Native Americans. One was essentially political (and military) in nature; the other combined commercial considerations with cultural questions.

The earliest reports of plentiful furs came from Stephan Gomez, sailing along the northeastern coast of America on a Spanish expedition in 1524. Ten years later, the attraction of luxury furs such as marten and sable, plus the wider commercial possibilities of beaver furs, brought the French explorer Jacques Cartier to the Atlantic coastal lands of the Micmacs. These tribes had already seen European iron implements and eagerly traded furs for axes and knives. Cartier proceeded to explore inland via the St. Lawrence River. It was during the active years of Samuel de Champlain, after he began to serve in 1608 as an explorer for the French fur trade monopolists Francis Pontgravé and Pierre de Guast Sieur de Monts in New France, that prototypic forms of the fur trade emerged. Extension of the fur trade took many generations. It was Champlain who urged establishment of a trading outpost at the Lachine rapids (near the future site of Montreal) to make it easier for Hurons and Algonquians to reach French traders without risking clashes with their enemies, the Iroquois. The latter controlled zones south of the St. Lawrence and Lake Ontario. Although the territory of the Hurons, along the Ottawa River (which drains into the St. Lawrence near Montreal), was not very rich in furs, they brought goods obtained from tribes farther inland to the Ottawa River. To do this, the Hurons needed quite crude European trade items to exchange for valuable furs; they used the furs to obtain for themselves higher quality goods, mainly French tools and firearms.

In contrast to early and eager French interest in exporting American furs, the British at first lagged behind in taking major trading initiatives. In fact, until fur prices in England began to rise in the early eighteenth century, Atlantic colonists were much more interested in the export of medicinal roots such as sassafras than in beaver or more exquisite pelts. However, this did not keep them from supporting the Iroquois' hostile challenges to French fur trading practices.

Much of the real work in extending fur trading in the early years was done by what the French called *coureurs de bois*, or "woods runners." These were individuals who were able to undergo the rigors of trekking inland, meeting personally with tribal representatives (many learned Indian dialects), and sealing agreements for delivery of furs. The woods runners became the most knowledgeable European intermediaries in dealings with Indians, and they often retained deep respect for Indian cultural traditions.

Various Indian groupings competed for favored positions in dealing with European fur traders. Open competition between tribes led to serious conflicts. The most important of these involved the Hurons and Algonquians. For many years until their 1648 defeat by the Iroquois, the Hurons struggled against Algonquian insistence that Huron canoes could not proceed directly to Quebec with furs, but would have to use Algonquian intermediaries. As the easternmost Algonquian lands bordered on Quebec, they were able to extract trade advantages in dealing with both the Hurons and the French. It was this target that attracted attacks by the Iroquois, supported by the British. In the end, both Algonquians and Hurons would be displaced from their traditional homelands by their former European sponsors.

Cultural Impacts. The fur trade had many impacts on the material and social culture of Indians. Ecological effects (such as blocking waterways, eventual depletion of select fauna and, as a result of the latter, abnormal distribution of plant species previously controlled by omnivorous animals) are harder to reconstruct than patterns that were immediately observable by the traders themselves. For example, stereotypes concerning "simple"

Indian acceptance of exploitative terms in the fur trade do not always hold up. It is inaccurate to suggest that, when major trading sites such as those of the Hudson Bay Company or the French One Hundred Associates existed, Native Americans became hopelessly dependent on foreign goods offered for their furs. In some cases, attraction to what Europeans thought would be easy sales just did not develop, because local cultures preferred to hold fast to traditional items of value, many of which had ceremonial significance unknown to outsiders. In other widely documented cases, because of independent Indian preference for certain goods, especially quality French metal tools and weapons, frustrated traders with inferior quality or different style goods were unable to convince consumers to make deals.

This does not alter the regrettable fact that many traders took advantage of Indian unfamiliarity with either the real value of trade items, sometimes just worthless trinkets, or the dangers they ran by exchanging furs for alcohol. Omens of the troubles that afflicted later stages and different regions of the fur trade surfaced in 1642, when a number of Indian tribes, supported by Jesuit missionaries, petitioned the governor of New France to return to the higher moral standards of Champlain's days, when trade involving alcohol had been banned.

See also: Beaver Wars; Fox Wars; French and Indian War; Indian-white relations: Canadian; Indian-white relations: Dutch colonial; Indian-white relations: English colonial; Indian-white relations: French colonial; Indian-white relations: Russian colonial; Iroquois Confederacy; Lewis and Clark expedition; Manhattan Island purchase; Pontiac's Resistance; Proclamation of 1763; Red River Raids; Trade and Intercourse Acts.

Byron D. Cannon

Sources for Further Study

Brown, Jennifer, et al., eds. *The Fur Trade Revisited*. East Lansing: Michigan State University Press, 1994. Selected papers on different aspects of the fur trade from the Sixth North American Fur Trade Conference.

Francis, Daniel, and Toby Morantz. *Partners in Furs*. Montreal: McGill-Queen's University Press, 1983. A study of the Hudson Bay Company's impact on Algonquians in the Eastern James Bay.

Phillips, Paul. *The Fur Trade*. 2 vols. Norman: University of Oklahoma Press, 1961. Although somewhat dated, this general history is extremely complete for all regions and periods.

Gadsden Purchase

Date: December 30, 1853; ratified June 29, 1854
Locale: Southern Arizona, New Mexico
Tribes involved: Chiricahua Apache, Tohono O'odham
Categories: National government and legislation, Nineteenth century history, Treaties
Significance: The Gadsden Purchase resolved boundary disputes between the United States and Mexico resulting from the Mexican War but ignored consultation with affected Indians.

James Gadsden was a South Carolina railroad promoter turned diplomat. On behalf of President James Buchanan, he negotiated America's purchase of 45,535 square miles of territory from Mexico for the payment of fifteen million dollars (reduced later to ten million). A block of land nearly the size of New York State, the Gadsden Purchase lies south of the Gila River, forming part of present-day Arizona and New Mexico. The treaty embodying the purchase was signed on December 30, 1853, and ratified on June 29, 1854, settling boundary questions between the United States and Mexico left unresolved by the Treaty of Guadalupe Hidalgo at the end of the Mexican War in 1848.

The purchase was prompted by American politicians eager to build a transcontinental railroad through the Southwest. Neither the Mexican nor American governments consulted with the Tohono O'odhams (Papagos) and Chiricahua Apaches who lived in the area, and these Indians subsequently ignored boundaries that were not theirs.

See also: Guadalupe Hidalgo, Treaty of.

Clifton K. Yearley

General Allotment Act

Date: February 8, 1887
Locale: United States
Tribes involved: Pantribal in the United States
Categories: National government and legislation, Native government, Nineteenth century history
Significance: A policy of allotting land to individual Native Americans in severalty begins to dissolve the tribal nations.

When the General Allotment, or Dawes, Act became law on February 8, 1887, proponents hailed it as the Indian Emancipation Act and Secretary of the Interior L. Q. C. Lamar called it "the most important measure of legislation ever enacted in this country affecting our Indian affairs."

The law dealt primarily with Native American ownership of land. It authorized the president of the United States, through the Office of Indian Affairs in the Department of the Interior, to allot the lands on reservations to individual Native Americans, so that they would hold the land in severalty instead of the tribe's owning the land communally. Each head of a household would receive a quarter-section of land (160 acres); single persons over eighteen years of age and orphans would receive 80 acres; and other persons, 40 acres. (In 1891, an amendment to the law equalized the allotments to provide 80 acres for each individual, regardless of age or family status.) The United States government would hold the allotments in trust for twenty-five years, during which time the Native American could not sell or otherwise dispose of his or her land. At the end of that period, he or she would receive full title to it. After the process of dividing up the reservation land for allotments, the federal government could sell the surplus land (often a considerable portion of the reservation) to willing purchasers (most of whom would be European Americans). The money from such sales would go to a fund to benefit Native American education.

Effect of Allotment on Land Ownership, 1890-1970

| | Indian-Owned | | Government- | |
Year	Trust Allotted	Tribal	Owned	Total
1890	—	104,314,000	—	104,314,000
1900	6,737,000	77,865,000	—	84,602,000
1910	31,094,000	41,052,000	—	72,146,000
1920	37,159,000	35,502,000	—	72,661,000
1930	—	32,097,000	—	32,097,000
1940	17,574,000	36,047,000	1,786,000	55,407,000
1949	16,534,000	38,608,000	863,000	56,005,000
1960	12,235,000	41,226,000	4,618,000	58,079,000
1970	10,698,000	39,642,000	5,068,000	55,408,000

Note: Figures represent acres, rounded off to thousands, under Bureau of Indian Affairs jurisdiction. Dash (—) indicates unavailable data.

Source: U.S. Department of Commerce, Bureau of the Census, Historical Statistics of the United States, Colonial Times to 1970, Part 1. Washington, D.C.: U.S. Government Printing Office, 1975.

The Dawes Act also provided for Native American citizenship. Native Americans who received allotments in severalty or who took up residence apart from their tribe and adopted what European Americans considered civilized ways became citizens of the United States and subject to the laws of the state or territory in which they lived. In 1924, Congress passed the Indian Citizenship Act, granting full citizenship to nearly all Native Americans who were not already citizens, and measures in the late 1940's extended such status to Arizona and New Mexico Native Americans that the 1924 law had missed.

Proponents of the Act. Two groups of European Americans especially welcomed the Dawes Act. Land-hungry settlers who had long cast covetous eyes on the reservation lands—which, to European American thinking, were going to waste because of the lack of productive agricultural practices by Native Americans, whom they considered to be hunters and gatherers—were now able to acquire the lands left over from the allotment process. No doubt, the less scrupulous among the settlers also looked forward to the day when individual Native Americans would receive full title to their land and be able to sell, lease, or otherwise dispose of it. Then pressure, legitimate or not, would likely induce the new owner to part with the acreage.

A second group of European Americans, however, was more influential in securing passage of the Dawes Act. These were the humanitarian reformers of the day, who considered private ownership of land in severalty, U.S. citizenship, education, and consistent codification of laws to be indispensable means for the acculturation of the Native Americans and their eventual assimilation into the mainstream of U.S. society. As ministers from the several Christian denominations, educators, civil servants, politicians, and even a few military personnel, these philanthropists exerted a clout beyond their numbers. Calling themselves the Friends of the Indian, these reformers had been meeting annually since at the Catskills resort of Lake Mohonk to discuss ways to bring the tribal peoples to what the conveners deemed to be civilization.

Federal politicians had long considered private ownership of land essential to the civilizing process. Thomas Jefferson and the like-minded policymakers of his time had strongly advocated it, and in 1838 the Commissioner of Indian Affairs gave voice to a widespread view when he said, "Unless some system is marked out by which there shall be a separate allotment of land to each individual . . . you will look in vain for any general casting off of savagism. Common property and civilization cannot coexist."

It was not until the post-Civil War years, when increasing European American pressures on the Native Americans created crisis after crisis, that humanitarians and philanthropists began a concerted drive for "Indian reform." Land in severalty would be the most important factor in breaking up tribalism. The reform groups that were organized—the Board of Indian Commissioners (1869), the Women's National Indian Association (1879), the Indian Rights Association (1882), the Lake Mohonk Conference of Friends of the Indian (1883), and the National Indian Defense Association (1885), to name the most important—all strongly espoused allotment in severalty. Nor were they satisfied with the piecemeal legislation that affected one tribe at a time; the panacea they sought was a general allotment law. Although supporters argued over the speed of implementing allotment, such proponents as Carl Schurz, Herbert Welsh, and the Reverend Lyman Abbott fought energetically for such legislation. They finally won to their cause Senator Henry L. Dawes, chairman of the Senate Committee on Indian Affairs, who successfully shepherded through Congress the measure that bears his name.

Voices Against Allotment. Only a few European American voices cried out against the proposal. Congressman Russell Errett of Pennsylvania and a few others protested that the bill was a thinly disguised means of getting at the valuable tribal lands. Senator Henry M. Teller of Colorado argued that the Native Americans did not want to own land in severalty and were not prepared to assume the responsibilities that went with private property and citizenship. He denied the contention of the reformers that private ownership of land would lead to civilization. Albert Meacham, editor of *The Council Fire*, maintained that there was little enthusiasm for severalty among traditionalist Native Americans, and anthropologist Lewis Henry Morgan thought that allotment would result in massive poverty. Presbyterian missionaries apparently were disunited on the subject of allotment, and their views fell by the wayside as the juggernaut of reform plunged ahead.

Native American response to allotment has largely gone unrecorded. The Cherokee, Creek, Chickasaw, Choctaw, Seminole, Sac, Fox, and a few other tribes in Indian Territory, as well as the Seneca in New York, contended that they already mostly owned land individually and won exclusion from the act's operation. By 1906, however, Congress extended allotment to them as well. Most of the complaints came after the act's passage, when Native Americans lost land and found farming difficult under its provisions.

"February 8, 1887," one optimistic spokesman of the Board of Indian Commissioners commented, "may be called the Indian emancipation day."

Although much sincere Christian goodwill motivated passage of the Dawes Act, it turned out to be a disaster for Native Americans. The sponsors of the Dawes Act had assumed an unrealistically romantic view of the Native American. People who had had firsthand experience with tribal peoples attempted to prove to the reformers that the "noble savage" had never existed. In 1891, Congress allowed Native Americans to lease their allotments if they were not able to farm for themselves.

The allotments and the leasing moved faster and with less careful discrimination than Dawes and other promoters had intended. Instead of being a measure that turned Native Americans into self-supporting farmers, the act, through the rapid alienation of the Native Americans' lands, meant the loss of the land base on which the tribal people's hope for future prosperity depended. Tribal peoples held claim to about 150 million acres of land in 1887. The Dawes Act eventually diverted two-thirds of that acreage out of Native American ownership, down to about 48 million acres by 1934. Not until that year, with the passage of the Indian Reorganization Act (the Wheeler-Howard Act, also known as the "Indian New Deal"), did the federal government repeal the Dawes Act and encourage communal forms of ownership again, but by that time much of the former reservation land was gone as surplus sales, leases, or sales by the individual allottees.

See also: Allotment system; Friends of the Indian organizations; Indian Citizenship Act; Indian Reorganization Act.

Francis P. Prucha, updated by Thomas L. Altherr

Sources for Further Study

Coleman, Michael C. "Problematic Panacea: Presbyterian Missionaries and the Allotment of Indian Lands in the Late Nineteenth Century." *Pacific Historical Review* 54, no. 2 (1985): 143-159. Shows that the Presbyterians were not united about allotment of tribal lands.

Gibson, Arrell Morgan. "The Centennial Legacy of the General Allotment Act." *Chronicles of Oklahoma* 65, no. 3 (1987): 228-251. Examines the long-range effects of the Dawes Act on Native Americans.

Greenwald, Emily. *Reconfiguring the Reservation: The Nez Perces, the Jicarilla Apache, and the Dawes Act.* Albuquerque: University of New Mexico Press, 2002. Examines the effect of the General Allotment Act on two groups of Native Americans.

Hoxie, Frederick E. *A Final Promise: The Campaign to Assimilate the Indians, 1880-1920.* Lincoln: University of Nebraska Press, 1984. Interweaves the story of the Dawes Act with the larger assimilationist programs toward Native Americans.

Mintz, Steven, ed. *Native American Voices*. St. James, N.Y.: Brandywine Press, 1995. Contains part of the Dawes Act and a complaint by a Cherokee farmer in 1906.

Prucha, Francis Paul, ed. *Americanizing the American Indians: Writings of the "Friends of the Indian" 1880-1900*. Lincoln: University of Nebraska Press, 1973. Section 2 provides a representative sampling of primary source writings about the Dawes Act.

Washburn, Wilcomb E. *The Assault on Indian Tribalism: The General Allotment Law (Dawes Act) of 1887*. Philadelphia: J. B. Lippincott, 1975. A concise summary of the attitudes that produced the act and its repercussions for Native Americans; contains the full text of the original law.

Guadalupe Hidalgo, Treaty of

Date: February 2, 1848
Locale: Southwest
Tribes involved: Pantribal in California and the Southwest
Categories: Nineteenth century history, Treaties
Significance: This treaty ended the Mexican-American War; in it, Mexico ceded to the United States about half its national territory, and the ramifications for native peoples in the ceded territory were profound.

The Mexican-American War (1846-1848) and the treaty that ended it were largely the result of a belief that came to be called manifest destiny, the theory that white European settlers of the United States were predestined to settle and dominate the land from coast to coast. This attitude was used to justify U.S. acquisition of both Indian and Mexican territory. President James K. Polk, a leading advocate of manifest destiny, was the most important figure in the Mexican-American War and the peace negotiations that followed. In Mexico chronic instability caused by the struggle between the various political parties and leaders made waging war and negotiating peace difficult and made preserving the peace impossible.

Tension between the United States and Mexico had been increasing in the years preceding the war. Mexico was aware of, and feared, the Polk administration's desire to annex New Mexico and California. The United

Before the Treaty of Guadalupe Hidalgo, c. 1835

States was pressing claims against Mexico, and the Texas boundary dispute was becoming more critical. After fighting broke out in the disputed area along the Rio Grande, the United States declared war. Attempts to negotiate peace before and during the war were unsuccessful. Mexico saw no advantage in it, and the United States hoped to occupy more territory.

As a result of its military success, the United States was able to make acquisition of New Mexico and California a condition of peace. Polk chose Nicholas P. Trist as peace commissioner in April, 1847, and gave him a draft of a treaty which called for the cession of Alta and Baja California and New Mexico, the right of transit across the Isthmus of Tehuantepec, the Rio Grande as the Texas border, and a payment to Mexico of $15 million plus the assumption of claims of United States citizens against Mexico.

Opposition quickly developed in both Mexico and the United States to the proposed treaty. Mexico did not want an imposed peace, and the United States envisioned better terms. When Trist negotiated a peace unacceptable to Polk, the president recalled Trist. Trist remained in Mexico, however, and finally negotiated a modified treaty that Mexico accepted because of financial problems and fear of additional losses if war continued. The possibility of a successful revolution in Mexico added urgency to the peace process.

After the Treaty of Guadalupe Hidalgo, 1848

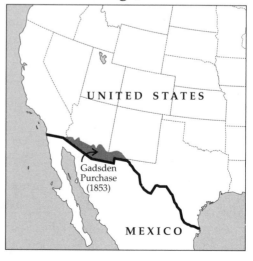

The United States dropped its demand for transit across the isthmus and agreed to stop Indian raids across the border. The treaty was signed on February 2, 1848, in Guadalupe Hidalgo, and ratification was exchanged on May 30, 1848, in Mexico City.

Although Articles IX and X guaranteed the political and property rights of Mexican citizens and Indians in the territory transferred to the United States, the Indians of California did not receive citizenship, nor were their property rights protected. As a result of violence and other factors such as disease, the Indian population declined by 100,000 within two decades. In New Mexico Territory the Indians were placed under federal protection and denied citizenship, but they did not lose their lands. Citizenship was granted to the Indians in 1869, and reservations were later created.

See also: Indian-white relations: U.S., 1775-1830; Gadsden Purchase.

Robert D. Talbott

Horseshoe Bend Treaty

Date: August 9, 1814
Locale: Alabama
Tribes involved: Creek
Categories: Nineteenth century history, Treaties
Significance: This agreement eliminated any possibility of an effective Creek alliance against U.S. expansion and thus facilitated the removal of the Creek people to the trans-Mississippi region during Andrew Jackson's presidency.

After his defeat of the Red Stick faction of the Creeks at Horseshoe Bend, General Andrew Jackson took full advantage of his authorization to secure a peace agreement. His purpose was twofold: to secure large tracts of land as compensation for the cost of his campaign and to eliminate Creek political power by isolating them. In the Treaty of Horseshoe Bend, also known as the Treaty of Fort Jackson, signed on August 9, 1814, Jackson received, on behalf of the United States, 22 million acres in south Georgia and central Alabama, or half of the Creek domain.

Cessions in the west isolated the Creeks from the Choctaws and Chickasaws, while those in the south created a buffer against the Seminoles and the Spanish. Ironically, only one Red Stick signed the treaty; the remaining signatories were Creek allies of Jackson, who lost much of their own land. Each Creek ally was allowed to keep a square mile of land as long as they or their family used it, but the United States reserved the right to build forts, trading posts, and roads on Creek lands.

See also: Creek War; Fort Mims, Battle of; Indian Removal Act; Indian-white relations: U.S., 1831-1870; Trail of Tears.

Richard B. McCaslin

Indian

Date: Fifteenth century-present
Locale: Americas and West Indies
Tribes involved: Pantribal
Categories: Terminology
Significance: In its use to refer to the native peoples of the Americas, the term "Indian" is based on historical error.

In the late fifteenth century, there was some disagreement over the size of the earth, although it had been accurately determined by the ancient Greeks many centuries earlier. Christopher Columbus and explorers who followed him believed the earth's circumference to be roughly half what it is known to be today.

The purpose of the early explorations of the Americas was to find a pathway to India by sailing west instead of east from Europe, primarily to avoid trouble with the Muslim nations that controlled the territory between Europe and India. Apparently, Columbus thought he had reached India when he landed on the island of Hispaniola (today occupied by Haiti and the Dominican Republic), named the area the West Indies, and referred to the natives as *indios* (Spanish for Indians).

While the later British and French explorers who landed in North America did not believe that Massachusetts and Quebec were India, the term was still used, translated into the appropriate languages. The term is still in wide use essentially because no better collective term has been widely accepted. Some native people find the term "Indian" deeply offensive, whereas others find it and "American Indian" acceptable and even preferable to such well-intentioned revisions as "Native American" or the less widely used "Amerind." The most accurate—and most widely accepted—

way to identify a person or tradition is simply to refer to the specific tribe or group to which the person or tradition belongs.

See also: American Indian; Amerind; Federally recognized tribes; Native American; Tribe.

Marc Goldstein

Indian Act of 1876

Date: 1876
Locale: Canada
Tribes involved: Pantribal in Canada
Categories: National government and legislation, Nineteenth century history
Significance: The Indian Act of 1876 was the first comprehensive post-Confederation law to establish Canadian policy toward Native Americans.

The British North America Act of 1867, which created the Dominion of Canada, gave the federal government sole jurisdiction in all issues related to Canadian Indians. This long-held British colonial policy had been established initially in recognition that natives treated in an inconsistent and often unscrupulous manner posed a military threat to British colonies. Even after Indians ceased to be an obstacle to British settlement, the policy was continued with the twin goals of protection and the eventual assimilation of the natives.

With the passage of the Act to Amend and Consolidate the Laws Respecting Indians, better known as the Indian Act of 1876, the government of Prime Minister John A. Macdonald continued the policies established during British colonial rule. As Canada's first prime minister, Macdonald's primary aim was nation-building—to which Canadian Indians, particularly those in the newly acquired prairies, presented an obstacle. With regard to the Indian Act, Macdonald was later quoted as saying, "the great aim of our legislation has been to do away with the tribal system and assimilate the Indian people in all respects with the other inhabitants of the Dominion." Consequently, Canadian Indian policy under Macdonald placed less emphasis on protection and more on assimilation. Ironically, the goals worked at cross purposes. Paternalistic efforts to protect natives emphasized the distinctions between them and the European Canadians, therefore discouraging assimilation. The Indian Act was amended nine times between 1914 and 1930. Nearly every change in the act placed greater restrictions on the activities of Native Canadians.

Reserve System. The Indian Act set out a series of reserved lands that were to be laboratories for training Canadian Indians in the ways of the European settlers. The first reserves were established away from areas of white settlement in an effort to protect Indians from the unsavory elements of European Canadian society. When it became clear that this policy hindered assimilation, new reserves were created near towns populated by whites, in the hope that natives would learn from their European Canadian neighbors. Another element of the Indian Act provided for the establishment of elected band councils. While these had little power, they were meant to supplant traditional native leadership. The act permitted the superintendent general for Indian Affairs or his agent to remove any elected councilor deemed unfit to serve for reasons of "dishonesty, intemperance, or immorality." The natives of British Columbia were forbidden from engaging in potlatches or any other giveaway feasts, in part because such ceremonies helped to perpetuate traditional leadership roles. This ban on ceremonies was quickly extended beyond the tribes of British Columbia and the Northwest Coast to nearly all expressions of traditional religion and culture. Canadian Indians also were prohibited from consuming alcohol.

In order to protect tribal lands from sale to nonnatives, title to those lands was held by the Crown rather than by the tribes. Reserve lands were exempt from property and estate taxes, and income earned on reserves was exempted from taxation. While these provisions have protected Canadian Indian property from seizure, they also have hindered economic development on the reserves. Because Canadian Indians have been unable to mortgage their lands, it often has been difficult for them to raise capital for development projects. Indian agents, who retained power to make nearly all economic decisions with respect to tribal lands, often resorted to harsh measures (such as withholding relief rations) in efforts to force adoption of European Canadian beliefs and practices.

While many of the provisions of the Indian Act were intended to ease Native Canadians into a European Canadian lifestyle, others were purely racist. In British Columbia, for example, natives had been denied the treaty rights and land tenure provisions afforded natives in much of the rest of Canada. In order to prevent court action to secure those rights, the Indian Act was amended to prohibit fund-raising for the purposes of pursuing land claims.

Revision of 1951. The Indian Act was significantly revised in 1951 to eliminate much of the blatant discrimination resulting from amendments to the 1876 act. Some discrimination remained, however. One onerous aspect of the Indian Act that was retained codified the category "Indian" as a legal rather than a racial or cultural designation and gave the government the legal power to determine who qualified as an Indian. It also provided that a man could surrender Indian status for himself, his wife, and his children in exchange for Canadian citizenship and a plot of land. Very few natives chose to relinquish their Indian status voluntarily, however. An Indian woman who married a non-Indian or a nonstatus Indian involuntarily surrendered her own Indian status and benefits, and her children were precluded from claiming Indian status. Non-Indian women who married status Indians, however, became status Indians themselves. This provision of the Indian Act was challenged in 1973 by Jeannette Lavelle, an Ojibwa from Manitoulin Island who had lost her Indian status through marriage. Lavelle based her case on Canada's Charter of Rights and Freedoms. Although Lavelle did not prevail in court, her case and others exposed Canada to condemnation by several international human rights organizations and led to the 1985 passage of Bill C-31, which restored to thousands of Native Canadian women (and their children) the Indian status they had lost through marriage to non-Indians.

The issue of Indian status divides native people as well. While many acknowledge that maintaining a legal status distinct from that of other Canadians creates opportunities for discrimination, others believe that they have inherent aboriginal rights that must be recognized. Despite the flaws and failures of the Indian Act, there has been only one serious attempt to discard it. In 1969, Jean Chrétien, minister of the Department of Indian Affairs and Northern Development, proposed a repeal of the Indian Act. This initiative, which became known as the White Paper, proposed eliminating many of the legal distinctions between natives and nonnatives and requiring the provinces to provide the same services to Canadian Indians that they provide to other citizens. Fearing that the provinces would be even more likely to discriminate against natives and that the federal government would abandon its responsibilities for native welfare, many native groups fought the White Paper proposals. They were withdrawn in 1971.

See also: Indian Act of 1951; Indian-white relations: Canadian; Reserve system of Canada.

Pamela R. Stern

Sources for Further Study

Dickason, Olive Patricia. *Canada's First Nations: A History of Founding Peoples from Earliest Times*. Norman: University of Oklahoma Press, 1992.

Contains several lengthy discussions of the policies generated by the Indian Act.

McMillan, Alan D. *Native Peoples and Cultures of Canada: An Anthropological Overview.* Vancouver: Douglas & McIntyre, 1988. Chapter 12 discusses both the Indian Act and issues related to the status of Canadian Indians.

Satzewich, Vic, and Terry Wotherspoon. *First Nations: Race, Class, and Gender Relations.* Scarborough, Ont.: Nelson Canada, 1993. Contains a thoughtful discussion of the impact of the Indian Act on native women in Canada.

Tennant, Paul. *Aboriginal Peoples and Politics: The Indian Land Question in British Columbia, 1849-1989.* Vancouver: University of British Columbia Press, 1990. A thorough discussion of the history of Canadian Indian policy and relations between Canadian Indians and whites in the province of British Columbia. Several sections deal specifically with the Indian Act.

Tobias, John L. "Protection, Civilization, Assimilation: An Outline History of Canada's Indian Policy." In *Sweet Promises: A Reader on Indian-White Relations in Canada,* edited by J. R. Miller. Toronto: University of Toronto Press, 1991. This article, reprinted from the *Western Canadian Journal of Anthropology,* provides a critical overview of legislation and policy making with regard to Canadian Indians.

Indian Act of 1951

Date: 1951

Locale: Canada

Tribes involved: Pantribal in Canada, including status and nonstatus Indians, Metis, Inuit

Categories: National government and legislation, Twentieth century history

Significance: The first major revision of the Indian Act in seventy-five years softened, but did not eliminate, the blatant discrimination against native peoples institutionalized by earlier legislation.

Although the Indian Act of 1951 was the first comprehensive revision of Canada's 1876 Indian Act, it did little to undo the paternalism of its predecessor. Like the previous law, it gave nearly absolute control of Indian activities to the Department of Indian Affairs and Northern Development (DIAND). This included the development of Indian lands and resources as well as oversight of band councils. The new act also retained the enfranchisement provisions of the earlier legislation, including those that denied Indian status to women who married non-Indians. In a well-known sex discrimination suit brought by Jeannette Lavelle, an Ojibwa who was denied Indian status as a result of her marriage, the Supreme Court in 1973 upheld those provisions of the act. A Maliceet woman, Sandra Lovelace, took a similar case before the United Nations in 1981. Although Canada was found to have violated international human rights covenants, the enfranchisement provisions of the Indian Act were not repealed until 1985.

The new act did, however, repeal the most blatant discrimination inherent in the Indian Act of 1876. It no longer prohibited Indian religious ceremonies, political fund-raising, or consumption of alcohol off reserve lands. Later amendments permitted the consumption of alcohol on reserves and gave Indians the right to vote in Canadian elections.

The 1951 act continued a number of benefits of the earlier legislation including the exemption of Indian lands from property and estate taxes and exemption of income earned on reserves from taxation. Although these provisions have protected Indian property from seizure, they have also hindered economic development on the reserves. Because Indians have been unable to mortgage their lands, it has often been difficult for them to raise capital for development projects.

Despite the restrictions imposed by the 1951 Indian Act, natives have fought efforts to discard it altogether. Fearing that the federal government would abandon its responsibilities to native welfare, many natives fought the 1969 White Paper proposal to repeal the Indian Act. The Indian Act was rewritten in 1985, but other than the repeal of enfranchisement provisions, it remained virtually unchanged.

See also: Department of Indian Affairs and Northern Development; Indian Act of 1876; Indian Act of 1989; Indian-white relations: Canadian; Reserve system of Canada.

Richard G. Condon

Indian Act of 1989

Date: 1989
Locale: Canada

Tribes involved: Pantribal in Canada, including status and nonstatus Indians, Metis, Inuit

Categories: National government and legislation, Twentieth century history

Significance: The Indian Act of 1989 updated and standardized Indian and government rights and responsibilities in Canada.

Because of the confusion created by a diversity of local laws in different provinces under the federal government in Canada, legislators have created certain acts that cannot vary according to locality. Such is the case of the Indian Act of 1989. In effect a compendium of earlier acts (of 1927 and 1951), it also added new laws more in keeping with contemporary conditions.

The main divisions of the act provide for the designation of reserves (land vested in Her Majesty's Crown, but "reserved for Indian use"), establishment of band councils and election of band leaders, and a comprehensive Indian Register. By the act, the sole authority of the band council to assign possession of specific reserve lands to individuals is recognized for the first time. This right of possession must be recognized by the Superintendent General of Indian Affairs, who issues a Certificate of Possession. Possessors may transfer their land rights, but only to other members within their band, or back to the band council itself.

Provisions respecting the security of reserves against government expropriation ended misunderstandings that had developed over many years. With the right of security went defined areas of band responsibility (to maintain roads, bridges, and so on) which, if unfulfilled, could lead to government charges against band councils. Common responsibility between councils and government for revenues accruing to bands (through royalties or sale of Indian produced goods) is spelled out, including the government right to use such funds to assure proper sanitary facilities and disease control.

One use of government funds on reserves reflects benevolent subsidies under the 1989 act. Schools are to be provided to all bands on an equal basis, and attendance up to a minimum age is required of all Indian children. Provisions for tax-exempt status (lands, personal property, or salaries earned in reserve areas) and taxable income earned from contacts beyond the reserves are meant to protect both Indian and government interests.

The act contains brief mention of individual rights. There is a right of testamentary wills for family security. Otherwise, where individual Indian rights might be jeopardized owing to band council inaction, government intervention is allowed (mainly to aid orphans or the mentally handicapped).

See also: Indian Act of 1876; Indian Act of 1951; Indian-white relations: Canadian; Reserve system of Canada.

Byron D. Cannon

Indian Appropriation Act

Date: March 3, 1871
Locale: United States
Tribes involved: Pantribal in the United States
Categories: National government and legislation, Native government, Nineteenth century history, Treaties
Significance: Congress unilaterally determines that Native Americans no longer belong to their own sovereign nations, ending treaty making between U.S. and tribal governments.

In 1871, Congress voted to end treaty making with Native American peoples. Since the origins of the republic, the U.S. government had dealt with tribes by recognizing each one as an independent nation living within the United States. Hence, ambassadors were sent out from Washington, D.C., to negotiate treaties, and each agreement had to be ratified by two-thirds of the Senate, as provided in the Constitution. Chief Justice John Marshall, in *Worcester v. Georgia* (1832), had determined that this process had to be followed because each tribe was self-governing and sovereign in its own territory.

The change took place because many people in the United States came to believe that the Native American nations no longer acted like sovereign states. They were too weak, post-Civil War whites believed, and many had become dependent on the federal government for their existence. Members of Congress expressed that view in a series of discussions on American Indian policy in 1870-1871. In the House of Representatives, the feeling also grew that the House was being ignored in the development of Indian policy. The only way the House could influence Native American relations would be by renouncing the treaty concept. The attack on treaty making gained strength during the debate over the money to be appropriated for the United States Board of Indian Commissioners. This agency had been created in 1869 to oversee money authorized to be spent on Indian programs.

Policy Changes. The commissioners' first report suggested major changes in Indian policy. It called for ending the treaty system and dealing with "uncivilized" native peoples as "wards of the government." Board chair Felix R. Brunot echoed the views of many U.S. citizens when he declared that it was absurd to treat "a few thousand savages" as if they were equal with the people and government of the United States. President Ulysses S. Grant supported that view, as did his commissioner of Indian affairs, Ely S. Parker, a member of the Seneca nation. Parker believed that it was a cruel farce to deal with the tribes as equals; in his view, most were "helpless and ignorant wards" of the federal government.

The resentment of members of the House of Representatives at their exclusion from Indian policy making became apparent during debates over treaties negotiated in 1868 and 1869. A May, 1868, an agreement with the Osage Nation in Kansas had ceded eight million acres of land to the government. The land then would be sold to a railroad company for twenty cents per acre. The House voted unanimously to recommend that the Senate not ratify the treaty because the land transfer had taken place outside the traditional methods of selling public property. The Senate responded to the House plea by rejecting the treaty. Later, however, the land was sold to the railroad company with the approval of the House.

The House took up the issue of treaty making again in 1869 during a violent debate over the Indian appropriation for 1870. It provided money for food, clothes, and education for tribe members living on reservations. The House refused to accept an increase in funds voted by the Senate. Representatives also began to question whether native peoples were capable of signing official treaties with the United States. Most members attacked the traditional system, although three congressmen spoke in favor of the treaty process. Representative William Windom of Minnesota argued that changing the process would be a breach of faith with the tribes. Revoking the process would create great confusion among Native Americans and add to their distrust of the U.S. government.

Representative John J. Logan, Republican of Illinois, responded for the majority, however, by declaring that "the idea of this Government making treaties with bands of wild and roving Indians is simply preposterous and ridiculous." Amid loud cheers and laughter, Logan attacked the character of native peoples and suggested that they were an inferior race that should not be treated as equal in status to the people of the United States. The House refused to approve the appropriation, and the Senate refused to compromise; therefore, no Indian appropriation bill passed Congress in 1869.

In the debate over the 1871 appropriation, both sides raised the same arguments. In the Senate, supporters of the treaty system argued that any change would severely injure any goodwill native peoples still held toward the U.S. government system. Senator Richard Yates reiterated the antitreaty sentiment, declaring that the tribes were not civilized and that making treaties with them had been a mistake. The Senate, however, passed an appropriation bill and sent it to the House. While the debate took place, many tribes were waiting for the money due to them under treaties negotiated in 1868 and 1869. Unless Congress agreed to an appropriation bill, they would receive nothing. In a compromise arranged between the two legislative branches, a sum of two million dollars was appropriated to pay off prior obligations. Debate over the appropriation for the next year bogged down in the House, however.

Agitation Against Treaties. The Board of Indian Commissioners helped the House position by calling for an end to treaty making and for abrogating all existing agreements. Only Representative Eugene M. Wilson of Minnesota spoke in favor of continuing the historic policy. If Native Americans were not protected by treaties, they would be cheated out of their lands by white speculators and end up with nothing, he argued. Debate in the Senate and the House seemed far more concerned with constitutional technicalities than with the welfare of native peoples. Once more, no bill seemed possible. On the last day of the session, President Grant urged a compromise, or, he warned, a war with the tribes was sure to break out. Under this threat, Congress agreed to put aside its differences temporarily and passed a bill.

When the new Congress opened on January 4, 1871, Representative Henry Dawes of Massachusetts led the call for change. Dawes, who in 1887 would author a major bill in the Senate drastically changing policy toward native peoples, called for a quick program of assimilation in this earlier debate. If natives were to become Americanized—a policy he supported—they should be treated as individuals rather than as members of foreign nations. Native peoples were not and never had been equal to the United States. The House passed a bill denouncing "so-called treaties."

In the Senate, an amendment to delete the words "so-called" before "treaties" led to a vigorous debate. Senator William Stewart of Nevada objected to the amendment. "The whole Indian policy of feeding drunken, worthless, vagabond Indians, giving them money to squander . . . has been a growing disgrace to our country for years." Treaties with "irresponsible tribes" were no treaties at all. Only a few senators agreed with this amendment, however, and "so-called" was eliminated. This angered the House, which refused to accept the Senate version.

Many congressmen and senators were tired of the endless debate and seemed willing to compromise. A conference committee of senators and representatives agreed that past treaties would be accepted or the integrity of the United States would be compromised. It agreed that no more treaties should be negotiated with Native Americans, however. Most conferees agreed that the tribes remaining hardly seemed like legitimate nations, as they were too small, weak, and miserable. The final compromise asserted the validity of prior agreements but provided that in the future, "no Indian nation or tribe within the territory of the United States shall be acknowledged or recognized as an independent nation, tribe, or power with whom the United States may contract by treaty." Both the Senate and the House accepted the compromise, and President Grant signed it into law on March 3, 1871. Treaties would no longer be negotiated with Native American peoples. Native Americans would, instead, become "wards of the state."

See also: Allotment system; General Allotment Act; Indian-white relations: U.S., 1871-1933; Treaties and agreements in the United States.

Leslie V. Tischauser

Sources for Further Study

Cohen, Fay G. *Treaties on Trial: The Continuing Controversy Over Northwest Indian Fishing Rights.* Seattle: University of Washington Press, 1986. Shows the continuing importance of treaties and the bitterness still evoked by pre-1871 agreements.

Heizer, Robert F. "Treaties." In *California.* Vol. 8 in *Handbook of North American Indians.* Washington, D.C.: Smithsonian Institution Press, 1978. A brief description of treaty making before 1871.

Jones, Dorothy V. *License for Empire: Colonialism by Treaty in Early America.* Chicago: University of Chicago Press, 1982. Discusses abuses of the system and how native peoples failed to understand the process.

Kvasnicka, Robert M. "United States Indian Treaties and Agreements." In *History of Indian-White Relations,* edited by Wilcomb E. Washburn. Vol. 4 in *Handbook of North American Indians.* Washington, D.C.: Smithsonian Institution Press, 1988. A short discussion of the debate over treaties and how the process was ended.

Prucha, Francis Paul. *American Indian Treaties: The History of a Political Anomaly.* Berkeley: University of California Press, 1994. The full story of treaty making and how it was ended in 1871. Index and list of treaties.

Indian Child Welfare Act

Date: November 8, 1978
Locale: United States
Tribes involved: Pantribal in the United States
Categories: National government and legislation, Twentieth century history
Significance: This act established minimum standards for placement of Indian children in foster or adoptive homes to prevent the breakup of Indian families.

The Indian Child Welfare Act, passed into law in 1978, establishes minimum federal standards for the removal of Indian children from their families and the placement of these children in foster or adoptive homes. In essence, the act restricts the placement of Indian children in non-Indian homes and gives jurisdiction to tribal courts in deciding matters of child welfare involving adoptive or foster placement. The law removes state jurisdiction in most Indian child welfare cases, even when problems occur off the reservation.

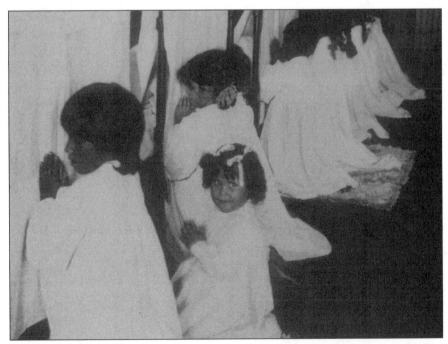

Native American children praying beside their beds at Phoenix Indian School, c. 1900. (National Archives)

The law affirms the continued existence and the integrity of Indian tribes and was specifically designed to end discriminatory practices of state and county welfare agencies which disregarded Indian extended family arrangements and placed large numbers of Indian children in non-Indian homes. Senate hearings conducted in 1974 documented evidence that as many as 25 percent of Indian children were being systematically removed from their natural families. This in turn was causing the breakup of the Indian family and a high degree of social disruption in Indian communities.

The law provides that when foster care or adoption is necessary, the child's extended family has first priority to assume custody. If no extended family member is available, a member of the child's tribe or an Indian from another tribe has priority over non-Indians.

See also: Carlisle Indian School; Tribal courts; Women of All Red Nations.

Carole A. Barrett

Indian Citizenship Act

Date: June 2, 1924
Locale: United States
Tribes involved: Pantribal in the United States
Categories: National government and legislation, Native government, Twentieth century history
Significance: Confers citizenship on all American Indians born within territorial limits of the United States, thus encouraging the dissolution of tribal nations.

American Indians hold a unique position in U.S. society and law, so the question of their citizenship was complicated. By the time of the Revolutionary War (1775-1783), it was established practice for European colonial powers to negotiate treaties with American Indian tribes, as they were considered to be independent nations, and this policy was continued by the United States. The Constitution regards tribes as distinct political units separate and apart from the United States, although not foreign nations, so as long as American Indians were members of tribes or nations that negotiated treaties with the United States government as semi-independent political units, they could not be considered U.S. citizens. Two significant rulings made it clear that an act of Congress would be required in order to grant citizenship to American Indians.

The issue of whether American Indians were citizens came into question when the Fourteenth Amendment to the Constitution was adopted in 1868. The amendment stated that "All persons born or naturalized within the United States and subject to the jurisdiction thereof, are citizens of the State wherein they reside." This amendment was intended to grant citizenship to newly emancipated slaves; however, there was a question as to whether it covered American Indians as well. In 1868, Senator James Doolittle of Wisconsin led the opposition to the extension of citizenship to American Indians under the Fourteenth Amendment. Many tribes were not yet settled on reservations, there were ongoing tribal wars in the Great Plains, and Doolittle felt strongly that the natives were not yet prepared for citizenship. There was considerable confusion in the Senate as to whether Indians living with tribal connections were subject to the jurisdiction of the United States. It was decided that Fourteenth Amendment rights did not extend to American Indians, when the Senate Committee on the Judiciary ruled, in 1870, that tribal Indians were not granted citizenship under the Fourteenth Amendment because they were not subject to the jurisdiction of the United States in the sense meant by the amendment.

Once this matter was settled, issues arose over the status of American Indians who voluntarily severed relationships with their tribe. John Elk, an American Indian who terminated relations with his tribe and lived and worked in Omaha, Nebraska, sought to register to vote in a local election. Elk met all the requirements to vote in the state of Nebraska, but he was refused the right to vote because election officials, and later the courts, ruled that as an American Indian, he was not a United States citizen. In 1884, the United States Supreme Court upheld the lower court decisions; it ruled, in *Elk v. Wilkins*, that an Indian born as a member of a tribe, although he disassociated himself from that tribe and lived among whites, was not a citizen and therefore was ineligible to vote. This ruling indicated it would take a specific act of Congress to naturalize American Indians.

Ending Tribal Sovereignty. By the 1880's, many persons in the United States sought to end tribal sovereignty, individualize Indians (end their status as tribal members), and grant citizenship to them so they eventually would be amalgamated into the general population. As a means toward this end, Senator Henry L. Dawes of Massachusetts, a leader in reform legislation for American Indian issues, sponsored the General Allotment Act, which became law in 1887. This act carried provisions for citizenship as a reward for leaving the tribe and adopting "the habits of civilized life." In part, this meant that American Indians had to accept small plots of land, successfully farm their lands, and learn the English language. Provisions in the General Allotment Act meant that eventually every American Indian could become a citizen, except members of tribes specifically excluded in legislation. Indians in Oklahoma were originally excluded from these provisions, but in 1901, a congressional act granted Indians in Oklahoma Territory citizenship. By 1917, through a variety of federal statutes, as many as two-thirds of all Native Americans were United States citizens. However, it was World War I that reopened the debate about citizenship for American Indians as a whole.

American Indians actively supported the war effort through increased food production, purchase of war bonds, contributions to the Red Cross, and most dramatically, enlistment: Between six and ten thousand Indians, many of whom were not citizens, enlisted for military service. In return for their service to the country, Representative Homer P. Snyder of New York authored the Veterans Citizenship bill, which became law on November 6, 1919. This law granted any American Indian who had received an honorable discharge from military service during World War I the right to apply for citizenship with no restriction on the right to tribal property. Still, by 1920, some 125,000 American Indians were not citizens. Many people in the United States believed that all Indians should be rewarded for their patriotism in World War I. Therefore, Snyder introduced a bill in Congress proposing to declare all remaining noncitizen Indians born in the United States as citizens. Political maneuverings began at once.

Citizenship with Sovereignty. Many people favored citizenship as a way to sever the legal relationship between the tribes and the federal government, and many American Indians were aware that citizenship could alter their tribal governments and possibly dissolve the reservation land base. In particular, full-bloods in many tribes were fearful that citizenship would end tribal sovereignty, bring them under state jurisdiction, and ultimately destroy tribal life and values. Compromise was required to resolve these conflicting views. In January, 1924, Congressman Snyder introduced House Resolution 6355, authorizing the secretary of the interior to grant citizenship to all American Indians, but ensuring that "the granting of such citizenship shall not in any manner impair or otherwise affect the right of any Indian to tribal or other property." The bill was approved by Congress, and the American Indian Citizenship Act, signed into law on June 2, 1924, by President Calvin Coolidge, made Native Americans both citizens of the United States and persons with tribal relations.

Ultimately, citizenship had little impact on American Indian life. The Bureau of Indian Affairs continued its policy of treating tribal members as wards of the government and administering affairs for American Indian citizens. The right to vote was denied to many American Indians until the 1960's, because the states had the power to determine voter eligibility and did not consider tribal members living on reservations to reside in the state. With federal protections in place, American Indians have been granted the right to vote in federal, state, and local elections, and as members of tribes, they also can vote in tribal elections.

See also: *Elk v. Wilkins;* Indian Civil Rights Act; Indian-white relations: U.S., 1871-1933; World wars.

Carole A. Barrett

Sources for Further Study

Cohen, Felix. *Handbook of Federal Indian Law.* Washington, D.C.: Government Printing Office, 1942. The most complete sourcebook for American Indian legal issues.

Debo, Angie. *A History of the Indians in the United States.* Norman: University of Oklahoma Press, 1989. A comprehensive, in-depth historical survey of Indians of the United States, emphasizing tribal relations with the U.S. government.

Olson, James S., and Raymond Wilson. *Native Americans in the Twentieth Century.* Chicago: University of Illinois Press, 1984. A good text for interpreting major trends, events, and attitudes affecting American Indian peoples, including the myriad issues involved in the citizenship debate.

Prucha, Francis Paul. *The Great Father: The United States Government and the American Indians.* Lincoln: University of Nebraska Press, 1984. A seminal work for understanding federal-tribal relationships and the development of American Indian policy. Traces the controversies surrounding citizenship for Indians.

Smith, Michael T. "The History of Indian Citizenship." In *The American Indian Past and Present.* 2d ed. New York: John Wiley & Sons, 1981. Traces the major factors that made it difficult for American Indians to obtain citizenship.

Washburn, Wilcomb, ed. *Indian-White Relations.* Vol. 4 in *Handbook of North American Indians.* Washington, D.C.: Smithsonian Institution Press, 1988. Discusses the American Indian in the complex federal-tribal context and contains information on citizenship.

Indian Civil Rights Act

Date: April 11, 1968
Locale: United States
Tribes involved: Pantribal in the United States
Categories: Civil rights, National government and legislation, Native government, Twentieth century history
Significance: A controversial but important measure is designed to guarantee Indians living under tribal governments the same rights as those of other U.S. citizens.

A significant but controversial piece of legislation designed to guarantee the rights of individual American Indians came about in special Indian titles of the Civil Rights Act signed into law on April 11, 1968. The existence of tribal governments and tribal courts had raised the issue of protection of the individual rights of American Indians living in a tribal context. Tribal governments have been considered to be inherently sovereign, because they predate the Constitution and do not derive their power to exist or to govern from either federal or state governments. Federal recognition or regulation of tribes does not make them part of the United States government or guarantee constitutional protection for tribal members. An 1896 Supreme Court case, *Talton v. Mayes*, determined that the Bill of Rights of the Constitution does not apply to tribes, because tribes derive and retain their sovereignty from their aboriginal self-governing status. The Indian Citizenship Act of 1924, which gave American Indians dual citizenship in their tribes and the United States, did not make the Bill of Rights applicable to situations involving tribal government.

There was little interest in the lack of individual rights for American Indians living a tribal existence until the 1960's, when national attention turned to civil rights. When the United States Senate began to investigate civil rights abuses throughout the nation, some attention was directed at tribal governments. In 1961, the Senate held hearings on civil rights issues on reservations, and investigators heard many examples of infringement on individual liberties and the lack of any way to redress grievances. Contributing to the problem was the fact that tribal societies emphasized the good of the group and were inclined to consider the good of the people as a whole more important than the preservation of individual rights.

An 1886 Supreme Court decision in *United States v. Kagama* determined that Congress has authority to govern the internal affairs of tribes and to make laws that directly affect American Indians. Therefore, Congress could impose restrictions on tribal governments and move toward granting greater individual protections to American Indians living on reservations.

The Civil Rights Movement. In 1968, when civil rights legislation was proposed to remedy the unequal protection of some groups in the United States, Senator Sam Ervin of North Carolina proposed bringing tribal governments under the constitutional framework of the United States. After a good deal of political maneuvering, Congressman Ben Reifel of South Dakota, a member of the Rosebud Sioux tribe, rallied support for the bill, and Public Law 90-284, the Indian Civil Rights Act, became law. This act was a set of special titles within the Civil Rights Act. It was intended to protect the rights of individual American Indians; however, it was controversial for its emphasis on individuals rather than the tribal group. The act was intended to preserve tribal autonomy while protecting the rights of individual tribal members. Largely as a result of tribal protests that the full Bill of Rights would severely upset traditional governing practices, a blanket imposition of the Bill of Rights on tribal governments was replaced by a more selective and specific list of individual rights that were to be protected. Those parts of the Bill of Rights that seemed to infringe on the special character of tribal government were omitted.

The Indian Civil Rights Act prohibits tribal governments from interfering with freedom of speech, religion, press, assembly, and petition for redress of grievances. It specifically authorizes a writ of *habeas corpus* for anyone detained by the tribe, and it grants due process. This bill also protects the right of privacy against search and seizure, using language identical to that of the Bill of Rights. The Indian Civil Rights Act does not guarantee persons free counsel in criminal proceedings nor the right of indictment by grand jury.

In addition to protecting individual freedoms, the Indian Civil Rights Act contains some provisions that impact tribal governments directly. The Indian Civil Rights Act permits tribal governments to establish an official tribal religion in order to allow the continuation of the quasi theocracies that form the basis of government in some American Indian communities. However, the act does require that individual freedom of religion be protected. The secretary of the interior is charged with the responsibility of drawing up codes of justice to be used in courts trying American Indian offenders. Assault resulting in serious bodily injury was added to the offenses on reservations that are subject to federal jurisdiction under the Major Crimes Act. In an important victory for tribal autonomy, Section 7 of Public Law 83-280 was repealed. Public Law 83-280, passed by Congress in 1953 in an attempt to abridge the rights of tribal courts, had given states the authority to extend civil and criminal jurisdiction over reservations. The passage of the Indian Civil Rights Act authorized the retrocession of jurisdiction already assumed by a state. A provision in the bill guaranteed the automatic approval of tribal contracts if the secretary of the interior did not act on a tribal request within ninety days.

Controversies and Challenges. The Indian Civil Rights Act was controversial when it was proposed and has remained so. Many American Indians view it as an attempt to impose non-Indian values on tribal societies and regard it as a violation of tribal sovereignty, because Congress unilaterally imposed the bill on tribal governments and people. This raised many questions regarding the meaning of "consent." Tribes do not seek to be protected from misuse of power, but there are questions about both the legality and cultural implications of the Indian Civil Rights Act. The fact that Congress intended to bring tribal governments more within the constitutional framework of the United States caused a good deal of controversy. Tribes have questioned the legality of permitting Congress, which basically represents states, to have a direct role in the formulation and passage of a law for tribes. No mechanism was afforded for tribes to accept or reject this legislation, although tribal cultures and customs are directly impacted by this law because it emphasizes individualism. Many tribal leaders feel the Indian Civil Rights Act restricts tribes in the exercise of their inherent sovereignty.

Since passage of the bill, numerous individual challenges to tribal authority have been litigated in federal courts, and many court decisions have favored the individual and weakened the concept of tribal sovereignty. More recent court decisions have tended to use tribal customs and traditions in interpreting the act. A landmark 1978 decision, *Santa Clara Pueblo v. Martinez*, supported a tribe's right to extend membership only to the children of male tribal members, as this was in keeping with tribal custom. The court ruled that it did not violate laws against sexual discrimination, because the Indian Civil Rights Act had a dual purpose of protecting individual rights as well as tribal autonomy.

See also: American Indian Movement; Indian Citizenship Act; Indian-white relations: U.S., 1934-2002; Major Crimes Act; Native American Rights Fund; *Santa Clara Pueblo v. Martinez*; Tribal courts; *United States v. Kagama*.

Carole A. Barrett

Sources for Further Study

Clarkin, Thomas. *Federal Indian Policy in the Kennedy and Johnson Administrations, 1961-1969*. Albuquerque: University of New Mexico Press, 2001. A groundbreaking study of federal Indian policy in the 1960's.

Deloria, Vine, Jr., ed. *American Indian Policy in the Twentieth Century*. Norman: University of Oklahoma Press, 1985. Several essays deal with the impact of the Indian Civil Rights Act on American Indian tribal governments. Also explores larger constitutional issues and tribal governments.

Deloria, Vine, Jr., and Clifford M. Lytle. *The Nations Within: The Past and Future of American Indian Sovereignty*. New York: Pantheon Books, 1984. An important discussion of the impact of legal and legislative measures on tribal autonomy and self-rule.

Olson, James S., and Raymond Wilson. *Native Americans in the Twentieth Century*. Chicago: University of Illinois Press, 1984. Examines the Indian Civil Rights Act and its assault on tribal sovereignty. Discusses numerous contemporary issues in a historical context.

Prucha, Francis Paul. *The Great Father: The United States Government and the American Indians*. Lincoln: University of Nebraska Press, 1984. Examines the relationship of the federal government and tribal governments from the formation of the United States to the 1980's. Explores the Indian Civil Rights Act in this context.

Wunder, John R. *"Retained by the People": A History of American Indians and the Bill of Rights*. New York: Oxford University Press, 1994. Chronicles the history of the relationship between American Indians and the Bill of Rights. Presents a detailed assessment of the 1968 Indian Civil Rights Act.

Indian Claims Commission

Date: Established 1946; expired 1978
Locale: United States
Tribes involved: Pantribal in the United States
Categories: National government and legislation, Organizations, Twentieth century history
Significance: The Indian Claims Commission (ICC) purported to resolve all pending Indian land claims in the United States.

The Indian Claims Commission (ICC) was established by an act of Congress in 1946. Its mandate was to review all pending territorial claims by native peoples within the forty-eight contiguous states and, where these were found to be valid, to retire them through payment of appropriate compensation.

American Indian leaders with President Harry Truman at the signing of the Indian Claims Commission bill in 1946. (Library of Congress)

Although the life of the commission was originally expected to be ten years, the sheer volume of the cases it encountered caused its duration to be repeatedly extended. When it was finally suspended on September 30, 1978, the ICC still had a docket of sixty-eight cases remaining to be heard (these were reassigned to the U.S. Court of Claims). In the interim, it had considered several hundred separate claims which, in aggregate, led it to reach some rather striking conclusions in its final report.

As Russel Barsh summarized the ICC's general findings,

> about half a country was purchased by treaty or agreement at an average price of less than a dollar an acre; another third of a [billion] acres were claimed by the United States without presence of a unilateral action extinguishing title.

Because the ICC was specifically precluded under its authorizing legislation from effecting transfers of land title where none had previously occurred, the clear implication of the last finding was that legal ownership of the land in question remained vested in American Indians. In effect, then, the United States was engaged in the illegal occupation of approximately one-third of its claimed "domestic" territoriality. There was, however, little the ICC could do to rectify the situation, even if it had been so inclined, because its authorizing legislation also prevented it from actually restoring property to its rightful owners.

For this reason Lakota scholar Vine Deloria, Jr., observed:

> [T]he Claims Commission ultimately resolved nothing. Rather, it served the useful purpose of clearing away the underbrush of confusion about who really owns what in the United States and thereby paved the way for the resolution of property rights issues at some future point. In the meantime, it assigned some degree of compensation to Indians for the historic loss of use of land to which they never relinquished title.

See also: Allotment system; General Allotment Act; Indian Reorganization Act.

Ward Churchill

Sources for Further Study

Barsh, Russel. "Indian Land Claims Policy in the United States." *North Dakota Law Review* 58 (1982): 1-82.

Clarkin, Thomas. *Federal Indian Policy in the Kennedy and Johnson Administrations, 1961-1969*. Albuquerque: University of New Mexico Press, 2001.

Ross, Norman A., ed. *Index to the Expert Testimony Before the Indian Claims Commission: The Written Reports*. Washington, D.C.: Congressional Information Service, 2001.

U.S. Indian Claims Commission. *Indian Claims Commission, August 13, 1946-September 30, 1978: Final Report*. Washington, D.C.: Government Printing Office, 1978.

Vance, John T. "The Congressional Mandate and the Indian Claims Commission." *North Dakota Law Review* 45 (1969): 325-336.

Indian Education Acts

Date: 1972, 1978
Locale: United States
Tribes involved: Pantribal in the United States
Categories: Education, National government and legislation, Twentieth century history

Significance: These acts represent the first legislative victories for Native American peoples under the policy of Indian self-determination, announced by President Richard Nixon in 1970.

The Indian Education Act of 1972, Public Law 92-318, was an attempt to remedy some of the problems in Indian education identified in the National Study of American Indian Education (carried out from 1967 to 1971) and in the hearings of the Special Senate Subcommittee on Indian Education that summarized its findings in 1969 under the title *Indian Education: A National Tragedy, a National Challenge* (also known as the Kennedy Report). Both studies found that Indian people wanted a better education for their children, wanted schools to pay more attention to Indian heritage, and wanted more say in how their children's schools were run.

The 1972 act pertained to public schools on and off reservations and provided supplemental funding for schools with ten or more Indian students in order to meet their special needs. All public schools with Indian students could get this quasi-entitlement funding and were required to involve Indian parents and communities in designing the supplemental programs. Grant money was also provided.

Part A of the act required parental and community participation in impact-aid programs (programs that provided federal money to local school districts to make up for tax-exempt federal lands such as Indian reservations). Part B authorized a series of grant programs to stress culturally relevant and bilingual curriculum materials. Part C provided money for adult-education projects. Part D established an Office of Indian Education within the U.S. Office of Education (now the Department of Education). Part E provided funds for training teachers for Bureau of Indian Affairs (BIA) schools, with preference to be given to Indians. The act also established the National Advisory Council on Indian Education.

The Indian Education Amendments of 1978 (P.L. 95-561) established standards for BIA schools, institutionalized BIA school boards, required formula funding of BIA schools, and provided for increased Indian involvement in the spending of impact-aid funds.

See also: American Indian Higher Education Consortium; Bureau of Indian Affairs; Carlisle Indian School; Indian New Deal; Indian Self-Determination and Education Assistance Act; Kennedy Report; National Congress of American Indians; National Indian Youth Council; Reservation system of the United States.

Jon Reyhner

Indian Gaming Regulatory Act

Date: October 17, 1988
Locale: United States
Tribes involved: Pantribal in the United States
Categories: National government and legislation; Native government; Reservations and relocation; Twentieth century history
Significance: Congress regulates gaming on Indian lands by dividing it into three classes and authorizing compacts between tribes and states.

The Indian Gaming Regulatory Act (IGRA), Public Law 100-497, signed into law on October 17, 1988, by President George Bush, represents an amalgamation of ideas presented in various bills introduced in Congress from 1983 through 1987 and provides a system to permit and regulate gaming on American Indian lands.

The IGRA divides gaming into three classes. Class I gaming includes social games of minimal value, as well as traditional games played as a part of tribal ceremonies or celebrations. Class I gaming is exclusively regulated by the tribes. Class II gaming includes bingo, and if played within the same location, pull tabs, lotto, tip jars, instant bingo, games similar to bingo, and certain card games. A tribe may engage in Class II games if the state in which the tribe is located permits such gaming for any purpose by any person, organization, or entity. Class III gaming includes all forms of gaming other than Class I or II, for example, banking card games like blackjack, baccarat and chemin de fer, slot machines, craps, parimutuel horse racing, and dog racing. Class III gaming is prohibited unless authorized by a tribal-state compact.

In addition to classifying games, the IGRA established a three-member National Indian Gaming Commission within the Department of the Interior. The commission chairman is appointed by the president of the United States with Senate approval; the other two members are appointed by the secretary of the interior. At least two members must be enrolled members of an American Indian tribe. The commission has the power to approve all tribal gaming ordinances and resolutions, shut down gaming activities, levy and collect fines, and approve gaming management contracts for Class II and III gaming. The commission has broad power to monitor Class II gaming by inspecting gaming permits, conducting background investigations of personnel, and inspecting and auditing books and records. Regulation and jurisdiction of Class III gaming is more complicated. Class III gaming is lawful when it is authorized by a tribal ordinance, approved by the chairman of the commission, located in a state that permits such gaming (whether for charitable, commercial, or government purposes), and conducted in compliance with a tribal-state compact that is approved by the secretary of the interior.

A tribe seeking to conduct Class III gaming must request that the state in which its lands are located negotiate a tribal-state compact governing the conduct of gaming activities. The compact may include provisions concerning the application of tribal or state criminal and civil laws directly related to gaming, the allocation of jurisdiction between the state and tribe, state assessments to defray the costs of regulation, standards for operation and maintenance of the gaming facility, and other subjects related to the gaming activity. The state is not authorized to impose a tax or assessment upon a tribe unless the tribe agrees. The state cannot refuse to negotiate a compact based on its inability to impose a tax, fee, or other assessment.

Sovereignty and Economy. The question of gaming on American Indian reservations is one that involves both sovereignty and economic issues for tribes and states alike. The IGRA grants United States district courts jurisdiction over actions by tribes. Reasons for such action include failure of a state to negotiate with a tribe seeking to enter a compact; failure of the state to negotiate in good faith; or any violation of the tribal-state compact. The IGRA provides that a federal district court may order a tribe and state to reach a compact if the state fails to meet its burden of proving that it negotiated in good faith. If no compact is forthcoming, a court may appoint a mediator to recommend a compact. In March, 1996, the United States Supreme Court ruled in *Seminole Tribe of Indians v. Florida* that Congress cannot force states into federal court to settle disputes over gambling on reservations. Federal law, through the IGRA, still permits tribes to seek help from the secretary of the interior when state officials balk at tribal plans for gaming operations.

The IGRA requires that all gaming facilities be tribally owned and that revenue from gaming operations be directed for specific tribal programs, such as education, elderly programs, or housing. Restriction of gaming to tribal governments ensures that American Indian gaming remains a government function rather than a personal endeavor.

The most controversial aspect of the IGRA involves the tribal-state compacting required for Class III gaming. Tribal sovereignty is diminished by the IGRA, because it forces states and tribes into an agreement. Most laws recognize that tribes have a government-to-government relationship with the federal government and are not under state jurisdiction unless there is prior agreement (as in Public Law 280 states). The IGRA specifically requires negotiations between tribes and states, a relationship they do not normally have.

States objected to the tribal-state compacting on the grounds that it violated their sovereignty under the Eleventh Amendment of the Constitution, which protects states from being sued in federal court against their will. In a 1996 Supreme Court decision, it was ruled that Congress cannot attempt to resolve stalled negotiations between states and tribes over on-reservation gambling by making states and their officials targets of federal lawsuits. The Eleventh Amendment rights of states were upheld.

The IGRA has been embraced by many tribes in the United States as a way to bolster reservation economies. Some of the most poverty-stricken areas in the United States are American Indian reservations, and gaming revenues give tribes income to reinvest in other business ventures. The need to generate widespread support for ballot initiatives such as California's Propositions 5 (1998) and 1A (2000), the California Indian Self-Reliance Initiative, helped Native American tribes develop more powerful political lobbies, with influence beyond issues of gambling. However, the compacting process can result in conflict of interest for some states that rely heavily on gaming revenues. In addition, the issue of untaxed revenues resulting from American Indian gaming operations is a factor in establishing compacts, and states in need of such revenue cannot act dispassionately with tribes when they negotiate those compacts. Gaming on American Indian reservations is fraught with issues of competing interests for both tribes and states.

See also: Indian-white relations: U.S., 1934-2002.

Carole A. Barrett

Sources for Further Study

Canby, William C. *American Indian Law in a Nutshell*. Minneapolis: West, 1981. Provides simple explanations of complex legal issues that inhere in dealings between the federal government, states, and tribal nations.

Eisler, Kim Isaac. *The Revenge of the Pequots: How a Small Native American Tribe Created the World's Most Profitable Casino*. Lincoln: University of Nebraska Press, 2002. A journalistic account of the effect of IGRA on one tribe.

MacFarlan, Allan A. *Book of American Indian Games*. New York: Associated Press, 1958. Discusses and describes various games, including gambling games, played by a variety of North American tribes.

Pommersheim, Frank. "Economic Development in Indian Country: What Are the Questions?" *American Indian Law Review* 12 (1987): 195-217. Explains the need for revenue in American Indian country and the possibilities gaming provides tribes.

Santoni, Roland J. "The Indian Gaming Regulatory Act: How Did We Get Here? Where Are We Going?" *Creighton Law Review* 26 (1993): 387-447. Provides a comprehensive chronology of the legislation, pertinent legal cases, suggested amendments, and a table of tribal-state compacts.

Turner, Allen C. "Evolution, Assimilation, and State Control of Gambling in Indian Country: Is *Cabazon v. California* an Assimilationist Wolf in Preemptive Clothing?" *Idaho Law Review* 24, no. 2 (1987-1988): 317-338. Explores the seminal case that influenced involvement of states in the compacting process.

Wilkinson, Charles F. *American Indians, Time, and the Law: Native Societies in a Modern Constitutional Democracy.* New Haven, Conn.: Yale University Press, 1987. Discusses tribal sovereignty as a preconstitutional right and how this inherent right can be diminished.

Wunder, John R. *"Retained by the People": A History of American Indians and the Bill of Rights.* New York: Oxford University Press, 1994. A chronicle and comprehensive history of the relationship between American Indians and the federal government. Gives detailed analysis of the tribal-federal relationship.

Indian Health Service

Date: Established 1954
Locale: United States
Tribes involved: Pantribal in the United States
Categories: Organizations, Twentieth century history
Significance: Indian Health Service (IHS) provides a broad array of health-related care to American Indian populations in fulfillment of federal trust responsibilities.

Many treaties negotiated between Indian tribes and the United States government contained provisions for health care in return for land. In part, these requests for health care during treaty negotiations came about because many tribal people had little resistance to European-American diseases. Indian populations were in decline after the earliest days of contact with non-Indians. Health care delivery to Indians by the United States was inadequate and inconsistent through all of the nineteenth and much of the twentieth century, as evidenced by high disease rates and low life expectancy of tribal people. In order to carry out its trust obligation to provide health care for American Indians, the U.S. Congress created the Indian Health Service in 1954 and placed it in the jurisdiction of the Bureau of Indian Affairs. In that same year, management of Indian Health Service was transferred to what is now the Department of Health and Human Services.

The mandate of Indian Health Service is to provide comprehensive health care, develop preventive medicine, and manage sanitation programs. Indian Health Service has clinics and hospitals located on some reservations and in urban areas where there is a significant Indian population. Poverty on reservations, coupled with inadequate Indian Health Service funding, contribute to major health care problems that persist in Indian country: lower life expectancy, substance abuse, high suicide rates, and disease.

Carole A. Barrett

See also: Bureau of Indian Affairs; Epidemics and diseases; Indian-white relations: U.S., 1934-2002; Reservation system of the United States.

Indian New Deal

Date: 1933-1945
Locale: United States
Tribes involved: Pantribal in the United States
Categories: National government and legislation, Twentieth century history
Significance: Sweeping reforms of the Bureau of Indian Affairs instituted under the directorship of John Collier.

The Indian New Deal refers to John Collier's innovative years as director of the U.S. Bureau of Indian Affairs (1933-1945). Collier was an energetic and humane visionary who sought to revolutionize federal Indian policy. The keystone of New Deal Indian reform was the Indian Reorganization Act, which ended allotment, organized tribal self-government, established revolving loan programs for tribes, and provided a mechanism for tribes to buy back lost lands. Collier also targeted Indian education and health for improvement. Day schools began to replace boarding schools, and preventive health programs reduced the incidence of certain diseases. Religious freedoms also were extended to Indian people during this time, and bans on the practice of traditional ceremonies were lifted.

Possibly the most lasting achievements in the New Deal era lay in the area of economic development. Tribes were aided in developing resources, preserving the reservation land base, and participating in a variety of public programs available to other Americans. Increasingly, Collier's revolutionary ideas were attacked, in part, because they encouraged Indian traditions and respect for Indian culture rather than assimilation of Indian people into mainstream American life. Collier resigned in 1945 amid increasing criticism, but he left a definite mark on federal Indian policy.

See also: Allotment system; General Allotment Act; Indian Reorganization Act; Indian-white relations: U.S., 1934-2002; Meriam Report.

Carole A. Barrett

Indian Offenses Act

Date: 1883
Locale: United States
Tribes involved: Pantribal in the United States
Categories: National government and legislation, Native government, Nineteenth century history
Significance: The federal government creates courts, located on reservations, run by Native Americans who were responsible for policing native cultural practices deemed offensive by European American society.

Courts of Indian Offenses were created by the Bureau of Indian Affairs in 1883. The judges of these courts were Indian men appointed by the federal agent on each reservation, and they heard only cases involving certain cultural practices, termed "Indian offenses," which were banned on the reservations. All decisions of the court were subject to the approval of the Indian agent.

Essentially, the Indian offenses were a list of common traditional practices that the government determined were "demoralizing and barbarous" and therefore should be discontinued so that Indians could become more assimilated into mainstream American culture and values. The list of Indian offenses included prohibitions against dancing, plural marriages, feasts, giveaways, and destroying the property of the dead (a funerary custom among some tribes). Additionally, and most devastating to many Indian people, traditional religious practices including sun dances, sweatlodge ceremonies, vision questing, and shamanism were strictly prohibited in the hope that Indian people would be more likely to convert to Christianity. In short, Indian offenses were an extensive body of religious and cultural practices that the federal government banned because they were deemed disruptive to the smooth functioning of reservations. When living within the reservation context, Indian people were not granted constitutional protections.

See also: Major Crimes Act; Tribal courts; Reservation system of the United States.

Carole A. Barrett

Indian preference

Date: Established 1933-1945
Locale: United States
Tribes involved: Pantribal in the United States
Categories: Civil rights, National government and legislation, Native government, Terminology, Twentieth century history
Significance: Preference in hiring Native Americans in the Bureau of Indian Affairs and other federal agencies, as well as in Indian organizations, skirts the provisions of the United States Civil Rights Act of 1964.

Title VII of the United States Civil Rights Act of 1964 prohibits employment discrimination on the basis of race, sex, national origin, color, or religion. However, this provision does not apply to Indians uniformly. During the period of reforms in the John Collier era, often referred to as the Indian New Deal (1933-1945), Indian preference in employment was instituted first in the Bureau of Indian Affairs and eventually in other federal agencies, such as the Public Health Service, which work closely with Indian people. Later, tribal governments, tribal colleges, and other Indian organizations were able to invoke Indian preference in making hiring decisions.

Commonly tribes develop criteria that give first preference to members of their own tribe, next preference to an American Indian from any tribe, and last preference to a non-Indian. When Title VII provisions are dropped, there is no uniform protection against employment discrimination. Indian preference was permitted as a way to increase the numbers of Indian people working within agencies and organizations that deal primarily with American Indian populations. It was also viewed as a way to increase the number of Indian people in the workforce significantly and so address the chronic issue of Indian unemployment.

See also: Bureau of Indian Affairs; Indian New Deal.

Carole A. Barrett

Indian Removal Act

Date: May 28, 1830
Locale: Georgia and other Southeastern states
Tribes involved: Cherokee, Chickasaw, Choctaw, Creek, Seminole
Categories: National government and legislation, Nineteenth century history, Reservations and relocation
Significance: The Indian Removal Act marked the beginning of forced resettlement of sixty thousand eastern Native Americans to lands west of the Mississippi River.

Cherokees and other members of the so-called Five Civilized Tribes—Choctaw, Chickasaw, Cherokee, Seminole, and Creek—established independent republics with successful governments. Adapting to their white neighbors, they became farmers, miners, and cattle ranchers. Some had plantations, even owning slaves. They built schools and churches, wrote constitutions, and established independent governments. They learned a bitter lesson: Whites wanted their land, not their assimilation into Euro-American society.

As a local militia leader and politician, Andrew Jackson negotiated the acquisition of fifty million acres of Georgia, Alabama, Tennessee, and Mississippi even before he became president of the United States in 1828. By then, the Cherokees had lost their land outside Georgia, and neighbors had grown increasingly jealous of Cherokee success. For generations, Cherokees had provided a textbook picture of Jefferson's ideal nation of farmers. Sequoyah, a young man of Cherokee and white blood, invented a phonetic

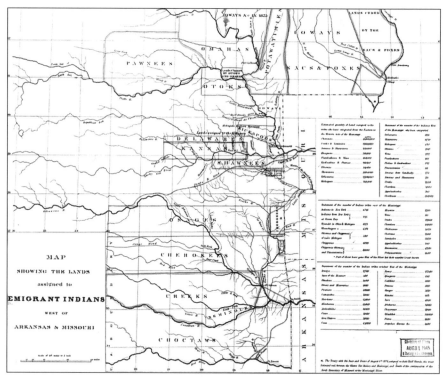

An 1836 map of Indian Territory (today, primarily the region of Oklahoma), to which the peoples of many Indian nations, named on the map, were removed after the passage of the 1830 Indian Removal Act. The tables on the right record numbers of acres assigned to tribes, numbers of Indians removed, and numbers of tribes resident east and west of the Mississippi River. (Library of Congress)

alphabet, or syllabary, that enabled almost every member of his nation to become literate within a few months. To hold their remaining land, Cherokees made the sale of any additional land to whites a capital offense.

Yet violent conflicts between whites and natives became so common that many friends and enemies alike advocated removal to protect Cherokees from white citizens who routinely attacked them. In 1817, some Cherokees exchanged land in North Carolina for space in Arkansas. Within two years, six thousand had moved voluntarily, but the move only worsened Cherokee problems. By 1821, the Cherokees were at war with the Osages who had been in Arkansas Territory already, and both groups fought whites who continued to move onto their land.

These early voluntary removals proved so disastrous that the Cherokees and Choctaws remaining in Georgia vowed to stay on their native land. Although President James Monroe proposed removal again in 1825, neither

Monroe nor his successor, John Quincy Adams, could get the measure through Congress. Only the enthusiasm of President Jackson got removal approved on a close vote in 1830. In 1829, President Jackson admitted that the five republics had made "progress in the arts of civilized life," but he said American Indians occupied land that whites could use. Beyond the Mississippi River lay enough land for Native Americans and their descendants to inhabit without interference "as long as grass grows or water runs in peace and plenty."

Meanwhile, the Georgia legislature extended its power over the Cherokee nation and stripped Native Americans of civil rights. These laws forbade anyone with American Indian blood to testify in court against a white man, annulled contracts between Native Americans and whites, and required an oath of allegiance to Georgia by white people living among American Indians. The laws also prevented Native Americans from holding meetings or digging for gold on their own land.

Legal Challenges. Instead of going to war, the Cherokees hired two prominent Washington lawyers and went to the U.S. Supreme Court. They lost their first case, challenging Georgia for hanging a Cherokee man convicted under Cherokee law. The second case (*Worcester v. Georgia*) challenged the loyalty oath designed to remove teachers, missionaries, and other whites from the reservation. The Reverend Samuel Worcester and other missionaries among Cherokees refused to sign the loyalty oath, despite public humiliation, abuse, and imprisonment.

Chief Justice John Marshall declared repressive Georgia laws unconstitutional. American Indian nations, Marshall said, were "domestic dependent nations" that could have independent political communities without state restrictions. President Jackson, who had fought American Indians in the South, suggested that Georgia could ignore the Court's decision. The president, not the Court, controlled the army.

Congress also took up Georgia's cause. The Indian Removal Act of 1830 began a process of exchanging Indian lands in the twenty-four existing states for new lands west of the Mississippi River. In 1834, Congress established Indian Territory, now much of Oklahoma, as a permanent reservation. Major Ridge and his family had been among the strongest opponents of removal, and Cherokee lobbyists, including John Ridge, celebrated their Supreme Court victory in *Worcester*. However, they had thought Whigs in Congress would prevail against Jackson's removal policy.

The federal removal law did not say that Native Americans could be forced to move, but the Ridge family and Cherokee newspaper editor Elias Boudinot began to see the move as necessary to protect Cherokees from increasing violence. Principal Chief John Ross, however, still resisted removal. Believing it in their nation's best interests, the Ridge family signed a removal treaty without approval of the tribal council.

Resistance. Many natives resisted removal from their ancient homelands. The Alabama Creeks were forcibly removed, some of them in chains. Choctaws were forced out of Mississippi in winter, with no chance to bring provisions against the cold. Some were tricked into getting drunk and signing away their possessions. Others signed away their lands, believing the promises of government officials. Forced marches of Creeks, Choctaws, and Cherokees brought sickness, starvation, and death to thousands of people throughout the 1830's.

The Cherokees faced a special horror. Georgia's repressive laws had created a climate of lawlessness. Whites could steal land, and Cherokees could not testify in court against them. In one notorious case, two white men enjoyed dinner in the home of a family whose father was part Cherokee. In the evening, the parents left temporarily and the guests forced the children and their nurse from the home and set it on fire, destroying the house and all of its contents. The men were arrested, but the judge dismissed the case because all the witnesses were part Cherokee. Only pure-blooded whites were allowed to testify in court.

Finally, Jackson's successor, President Martin Van Buren, ordered General Winfield Scott, with about seven thousand U.S. soldiers and state militia, to begin the forced removal on May 26, 1838. Soldiers quietly surrounded each house to surprise its occupants, according to James Mooney, a researcher who interviewed the participants years later. Under Scott's orders, the troops built stockades to hold people while being prepared for the removal. "From these," Mooney wrote,

> squads of troops were sent to search out with rifle and bayonet every small cabin hidden away in the coves or by the sides of mountain streams, to seize and bring in as prisoners all the occupants, however or wherever they might be found. Families at dinner were startled by the sudden gleam of bayonets in the doorway and rose up to be driven with blows and oaths along the weary miles of trail that led to the stockade.

Men were taken from their fields, children from their play. "In many cases, on turning for one last look as they crossed the ridge, they saw their homes in flames." Some scavengers stole livestock and other valuables, even before the owners were out of sight of their homes. "Systematic hunts were made by the same men for Indian graves, to rob them of the silver pendants and other valuables deposited with the dead." Some sympathetic soldiers

Indian Territory, c. 1875

By 1875, Indian nations that had once ranged over large regions of the continent were largely confined to Indian Territory (later, Oklahoma).

allowed one family to feed their chickens one last time, and another to pray quietly in their own language before leaving their home.

Within a week, the troops had rounded up more than seventeen thousand Cherokees and herded them into concentration camps. In June, the first group of about a thousand began the eight-hundred-mile journey. Steamboats took them on the first leg down the Tennessee River. The oppressive heat and cramped conditions fostered disease and caused many deaths. Then the Cherokees walked the last leg of the trip to beyond the western border of Arkansas. Because of the oppressive heat, Cherokee leader John Ross persuaded General Scott to permit them to delay the largest removal until fall. Thus, the largest procession—about thirteen thousand people—started on the long overland march in October, 1838. Most walked or rode horses; they drove 645 wagons.

Trail of Tears. Dozens of people died of disease, starvation, or exposure on each day of the journey. More than four thousand Cherokees died on the journey that the survivors named the Trail of Tears. The procession reached the Mississippi River opposite Cape Girardeau, Missouri, in the middle of winter. Most had only a single blanket to protect themselves from the winter winds as they waited for the river ice to clear. In March, 1839, they reached their destination in Indian Territory. Many were buried along the road, including Chief John Ross's wife, Quatie Ross, who died after giving up her blanket to a sick child in a sleet- and snowstorm. Her death left Ross to grieve both his wife and his nation.

In his last message to Congress, President Jackson said he had settled the Native American problem to everyone's satisfaction and saved the race from extinction by placing them "beyond the reach of injury or oppression." Native Americans would now share in "the blessings of civilization" and "the General Government will hereafter watch over them and protect them." Between 1778 and 1871, 370 treaties stipulated land cessions to whites. Jackson ridiculed the idea of making treaties with Native Americans and called the idea of treating American Indians as separate nations an absurd farce.

By the end of June, 1838, Georgians could boast that no Cherokees remained on their soil, except in the stockade. Sixty thousand members of the five republics had been removed beyond the Mississippi River. As many as fifteen thousand men, women, and children died of starvation and disease. The Choctaw had moved in 1832; the Chickasaw in 1832-1834, the Seminole in 1836, and the Creek in 1836-1840. In June, 1839, members of the Ross faction, in revenge for the law that John Ridge signed into effect, murdered John Ridge, Major Ridge, and Elias Boudinot for their signing of a removal treaty selling Cherokee land.

See also: Indian-white relations: U.S., 1831-1870; Trail of Tears.

William E. Huntzicker

Sources for Further Study

Foreman, Grant. *Indian Removal: The Emigration of the Five Civilized Tribes of Indians*. 2d ed., 1953. Reprint. Norman: University of Oklahoma Press, 1985. The classic and most comprehensive history of removal.

Green, Michael D. *The Politics of Indian Removal: Creek Government in Crisis.* Lincoln: University of Nebraska Press, 1982. Well-researched history of removal as it affected the Creek nation.

Guttmann, Allen. *States' Rights and Indian Removal: "The Cherokee Nation v. the State of Georgia."* Boston: D. C. Heath, 1965. Brief documentary history of the Cherokees' legal struggle to keep their land.

Hoig, Stanley. *Night of the Cruel Moon: Cherokee Removal and the Trail of Tears.* New York: Facts on File, 1996. An account of Cherokee removal relying on first-person accounts.

McLoughlin, William G. *Cherokee Renascence in the New Republic.* Princeton, N.J.: Princeton University Press, 1983. Cherokee history up through the removal crisis.

_____. *Cherokees and Missionaries, 1789-1839.* New Haven, Conn.: Yale University Press, 1984. Thorough, well-documented history of missionary involvement among the Cherokees in the period leading up to their removal.

Mooney, James. *Historical Sketch of the Cherokee.* Chicago: Aldine, 1975. A valuable study by a contemporary who interviewed people involved.

Moulton, Gary E. *John Ross, Cherokee Chief.* Athens: University of Georgia Press, 1978. Biography of the Cherokee leader at the time of removal.

Remini, Robert V. *The Legacy of Andrew Jackson: Essays on Democracy, Indian Removal, and Slavery.* Reprint. Baton Rouge: Louisiana State University Press, 1990. The leading biographer of Andrew Jackson reflects on his significance to these issues.

Wallace, Anthony F. C. *The Long, Bitter Trail: Andrew Jackson and the Indians.* New York: Hill & Wang, 1993. Brief overview of the removal policies, the Trail of Tears, and the implications of both for U.S. history.

Wilkins, Thurman. *Cherokee Tragedy: The Ridge Family and the Decimation of a People.* Rev. ed. Norman: University of Oklahoma Press, 1986. Discusses the prominent family of Cherokee leaders.

Indian Reorganization Act

Date: June 18, 1934
Locale: United States
Tribes involved: Pantribal in the United States
Categories: National government and legislation, Native government, Twentieth century history
Significance: One of the most important pieces of legislation affecting Native Americans reverses policies of forced assimilation and promotes tribal self-government.

The New Deal policy toward American Indians in the 1930's and early 1940's and its centerpiece, the Indian Reorganization Act, were a reaction to the controversies generated by past federal policies toward American Indians. From the 1870's through the 1920's, tribal peoples were confined to government-controlled reservations and subjected to a policy aimed at bringing them into the dominant society's mainstream through forced assimilation. Government and church-run schools attempted to eradicate native languages and religion, customs and dress, tribalism and group loyalty, and replace them with Christian values, traditions, and institutions. To foster individualism and undermine tribalism, congressional legislation allotted the tribal communal domain to small individual holdings and opened surplus land for public sale.

This ambitious social experiment did not work as its original reform-minded advocates had intended. Under allotment, American Indians lost most of their lands to whites, while the educational experience undermined or destroyed indigenous people's heritage and culture without providing a viable substitute. The common results were demoralization, loss of identity, abject poverty, poor health, and defective education. These conditions, documented by independent studies, sparked a high-level, decade-long debate in the 1920's about American Indian policy. Congress, the Department of the Interior, and the authoritarian management style of the department's Bureau of Indian Affairs (BIA) came under sharp criticism.

John Collier and the BIA. The political upheaval wrought by the Great Depression and the election of Franklin D. Roosevelt in 1932 provided reformers with an opportunity to reshape American Indian policy. In 1933, John Collier, a persistent critic of the BIA, became commissioner of Indian Affairs and directed the bureau until 1945.

Collier, a former social worker in New York City, had been introduced to the Pueblo cultures of the Southwest in 1920. Collier had experienced a native society that had maintained its communal and group traditions. Collier believed that he had discovered a "Red Atlantis," whose communal life and harmonious relationship with the natural world contained lessons and hope for the regeneration of Western society through a cooperative commonwealth.

After taking office, Collier began to reverse past government policy by initiating the Indian New Deal through executive orders and lobbying activities. In January, 1934, he forbade interference with traditional Native Americans' religious practices, declared their culture equal to all others, and encouraged the revival of native languages. Next, Collier ended forced attendance at Christian religious exercises by American Indian children at boarding schools. The commissioner persuaded Congress to repeal espionage and gag rules that restricted free speech and other civil liberties on reservations. Collier also decreased BIA controls and interference with tribal courts and tribal law. Finally, he placed a moratorium on the further sale of tribal lands.

Collier then sought to implement his goals of American Indian cultural freedom and political self-determination through legislation. He and his associates drew up a forty-eight-page document containing four sections aimed at replacing the agency's authoritarian approach with a new bilateral relationship between the tribes and the federal government. Title I dealt with the restoration of tribal self-government and economic revitalization to make tribal society viable. Tribes would petition for home-rule elections, adopt constitutions, and charter a tax-exempt corporation to set up businesses, manage property, and borrow from a federal revolving loan program. Title II, which focused on education, promoted the study of American Indian civilization and traditional arts and crafts, provided scholarships, and appropriated funds for primary and secondary education. Title III, which concerned Indian lands, ended allotments, returned previously allotted lands to tribal ownership, and restored unsold surplus reservation lands to tribal control. The federal government also was authorized to provide tribes with funds to rebuild their lost land base. Title IV proposed setting up a federal Court of Indian Affairs that would have original jurisdiction in cases involving Native Americans. In Congress, Representative Edgar Howard of Nebraska and Senator Burton K. Wheeler of Montana agreed to sponsor this initial version of what was to become the Indian Reorganization Act (IRA).

The proposed legislation immediately encountered opposition from both Indian and non-Indian sources. Few American Indians were consulted when the proposal was drawn up, which gave rise to suspicion and concern about some provisions. Those Native Americans who were most affected by assimilation policies over the last half century saw the act's provisions as taking a step backward. Some who held private allotments were concerned about losing them. Tribal leaders who viewed their sovereignty as inherent and some groups that already had constitutions or intact traditional political structures argued that the proposed BIA constitutional guidelines provided no new rights and, in fact, restricted tribal sovereignty. BIA constitutions resembled U.S. governmental bodies rather than traditional forms of tribal government. Some clergy and missionaries denounced the promotion of traditional culture as anti-Christian and pagan. A growing conservative coalition in Congress did not share Collier's radically progressive views on the restoration of traditional tribal cultures and the establishment of politically independent tribal nations.

Compromise. In the end, Collier had to compromise. Getting the legislation out of the congressional committee in which it was stalled required the strong support of both President Roosevelt and Secretary of the Interior Harold Ickes. In the bill's final version, which passed on June 18, 1934, Title II, concerning Native American culture, and Title IV, which provided for an American Indian court, were deleted. The amount of funding to assist the establishment of tribal governments was cut back significantly. Other modifications greatly reduced the number of tribal peoples to be covered under the act. Senator Wheeler insisted on subjecting tribal self-government to the approval of the secretary of the interior and excluded from the act American Indians who were not members of tribes, as well as those tribes located in Oklahoma and Alaska. Another amendment by Howard required that each tribe hold a referendum to accept or reject the IRA.

In referenda held between 1933 and 1945, 174 tribes accepted the act while 73 voted against ratification, including the largest American Indian nation, the Navajo. However, only 92 of the tribes that voted in favor adopted IRA constitutions, and 71 took the next step of incorporating for the purpose of obtaining federal economic development loans. American Indians living in Oklahoma and Alaska were placed under the IRA by legislation passed in 1936.

Collier reluctantly accepted these changes, emphasizing the breakthrough represented by those parts of his original proposal that were retained. The commissioner also attempted to implement many of his goals through administrative actions and orders. The failure of Congress to appropriate the full amounts authorized in the IRA, continuing opposition to some of Collier's goals, and the commissioner's own misjudgments and administrative shortcomings were some of the factors that prevented his dream of a Red Atlantis from becoming reality. In the decade following the New Deal era, federal American Indian policy temporarily adopted an assimilationist and antitribal orientation.

Nevertheless, the IRA was a landmark in federal American Indian policy, with some noteworthy results. Many scholars consider it the single most important piece of federal American Indian legislation. Accomplishments of the IRA and the Indian New Deal included halting the disappearance of the tribal land base and restoring several million acres to various reservations. The act permitted many tribes to assume a degree of economic and political control over their affairs. The restoration of religious freedom and traditional ceremonies were also important measures. With few exceptions, those tribes that received government loans used them to improve economic conditions on reservations and made repayment. American Indians were given preference for positions in the BIA. Many tribes have taken advantage of IRA provisions to defend sovereignty and survive. Most important, the reversal of past policies awakened hope and pride in being American Indian.

See also: Bureau of Indian Affairs; Carlisle Indian School; Indian New Deal; Indian-white relations: U.S., 1871-1933; Indian-white relations: U.S., 1934-2002; Meriam Report; Reservation system of the United States.

David A. Crain

Sources for Further Study

Deloria, Vine, ed. *The Indian Reorganization Act: Congresses and Bills*. Norman: University of Oklahoma Press, 2002. A collection of primary source documents assembled by the noted Native American legal scholar.

Fey, Harold E., and D'Arcy McNickle. *Indians and Other Americans: Two Ways of Life Meet*. Rev. ed. New York: Harper & Row, 1970. Good account of the Collier years from a pro-IRA perspective. McNickle, a Montana Blackfoot, was a BIA employee during this era.

Kelly, Lawrence C. "The Indian Reorganization Act: The Dream and the Reality." *Pacific Historical Review* 44 (August, 1975): 291-312. Balanced look at what the IRA failed to achieve in contrast to the claims of some proponents. Discusses Collier's strong points and shortcomings as American Indian commissioner during the New Deal era.

Kelly, William H., ed. *Indian Affairs and the Indian Reorganization Act: The Twenty Year Record*. Tucson: University of Arizona Press, 1954. A collection of scholarly essays on this subject.

Parman, Donald L. *The Navajos and the New Deal*. New Haven, Conn.: Yale University Press, 1976. A study of the troubled relations between the American Indian policy reformers in the Roosevelt administration and the nation's largest tribe.

Philp, Kenneth R. *John Collier's Crusade for Indian Reform, 1920-1954*. Tucson: University of Arizona Press, 1977. A detailed, objective account of Collier's achievements and shortcomings as a policy critic, activist, reformer, and administrator.

Taylor, Graham D. *The New Deal and American Indian Tribalism: The Administration of the Indian Reorganization Act, 1934-1945*. Lincoln: University of Nebraska Press, 1980. Argues that the IRA, although enlightened compared to previous policies, was weakened by its emphasis on tribal reorganization and its mistaken assumptions about contemporary American Indian societies.

Indian Rights Association

Date: Established 1882
Locale: United States
Tribes involved: Pantribal in the United States
Categories: Native government, Nineteenth century history, Organizations, Religion and missionary activities, Twentieth century history
Significance: An important and influential European American organization dedicated to assimilating Native Americans into mainstream American society is established.

The Indian Rights Association was founded in Philadelphia in 1882 by Henry Panacoast and Herbert Welsh, and it became the most important of the humanitarian groups which formed in the last two decades of the nineteenth century to seek the assimilation of Indians into mainstream American society. Welsh and Panacoast viewed the federal reservation system as a cultural and economic failure and asserted that reservations were obstacles to the civilization of Indians.

The Indian Rights Association diligently pursued its agenda to break up tribalism and bring Christian civilization to Indians by pressing for abolition of the reservation system through allotment of tribal lands, by supporting industrial education for Indians in order to encourage self-sufficiency, and by pressing for immediate citizenship for Indians so they would come under constitutional and state laws. The organization's political goals were inextricably bound to a belief in the superiority of Christian civilization. In 1886, Welsh asserted that the organization was doing God's will by guiding Indians "from the night of barbarism into the dawn of civilization."

The Indian Rights Association was successful because it was well organized and had dedicated members who pushed its agenda. The association hired a lobbyist in order to exert constant pressure on congressional committees, legislators, and Indian affairs officials. The organization also influenced public opinion by publishing pamphlets, news articles, and speeches that advanced its views. The association got much public and congressional support for its programs because it regularly sent representatives into Indian country to gather facts that gave such programs credibility. Additionally, the organization mirrored American society of the day by combining religious sentiment with patriotism in its proposals for reforming Indian policy. The association's goal was to acculturate and assimilate Indians fully into American society, and it viewed Indian culture and traditions as being un-American and pagan.

The Indian Rights Association declined in power and influence after Welsh resigned as secretary in 1902 and as federal Indian policy gradually began to support tribalism in the 1920's. The association continues to exist, although it now supports Indian self-determination and Indian groups seeking federal recognition.

See also: Allotment system; Carlisle Indian School; Friends of the Indian organizations; General Allotment Act; Indian Citizenship Act; National Congress of American Indians; National Indian Association.

Carole A. Barrett

Indian Self-Determination and Education Assistance Act

Date: 1975
Locale: United States
Tribes involved: Pantribal in the United States
Categories: Education, National government and legislation, Native government, Twentieth century history
Significance: This act marked a significant swing away from the overt assimilationist policies of the federal government and supported the basic concepts of tribalism and Native American sovereignty.

The 1970's were marked by support of federal officials for broadening Indian participation in programs that affected them and lessening the paternalism that had guided federal Indian policy for so long. The Indian Self-Determination and Education Assistance Act of 1975 marked a radical change in federal policy—the assimilationist philosophy of the federal government was replaced by policies favoring tribalism and Native American sovereignty. This law enabled and encouraged tribes to take over and run their own programs.

The act clearly endorsed Indian decision making, and the preamble declared that the United States recognized its obligation "to respond to the strong expression of the Indian people for self-determination by assuring maximum participation in the direction of educational as well as other federal services to Indian communities so as to render such services more responsive to the needs and desires of those communities." It also stated that

Congress confirms its commitment to maintain "the Federal Government's unique and continuing relationship with and responsibility to the Indian people through the establishment of a meaningful Indian self-determination policy."

The Self-Determination and Education Assistance Act consists of three major sections. In the first part, Congress outlines the basic federal policy toward native people, denounces federal paternalism, and affirms tribal rights to control their own affairs. Second, Congress asserts it will work for Indian self-determination particularly in education, while maintaining and preserving the trust relationship. Third, Indians will receive hiring preference in all federal government contracts affecting Indian tribes.

The most significant drawback to the act is that, even though decision making and administrative authority seemed to pass to tribal councils, the Bureau of Indian Affairs maintained the power to decide which tribal contracts it would accept. This reserved power included determining budget allocations provided to tribes who seek to run their own programs. Yet despite limitations placed on tribal authority, many tribes throughout the United States contract and run many programs that were formerly run by the Bureau of Indian Affairs. The most dramatic impact of the act has been in the area of education. A majority of former Bureau of Indian Affairs schools are now run by tribes, and many higher education scholarship programs are tribally run. The act is important in that it supports the basic concept of tribal self-determination.

See also: American Indian Higher Education Consortium; Carlisle Indian School; Indian Education Acts; Kennedy Report; National Congress of American Indians.

Carole A. Barrett

Indian slave trade

Date: 1671-1730
Locale: South Carolina
Tribes involved: Tuscarora, Yamasee
Categories: Colonial history
Significance: British colonists use intertribal rivalries and natives' desire for European goods to gain slaves and establish dominance over Spanish claims.

The earliest known record of Carolina natives being captured and enslaved was in 1520, when Spanish explorers took them to provide slaves for sugar plantations in Santo Domingo. In 1663, William Hilton, an Englishman, also captured natives from the Carolina coast for Caribbean slave owners. In 1670, Charleston was settled by the English. In 1671, after the defeat of Kusso warriors and the taking of numerous captives, English colonists initiated the Indian slave trade when Henry Woodward was commissioned to open trade in Indian slaves with Indians of rival tribes.

Carolina included what is now South Carolina and North Carolina until 1713, but between the 1670's and 1730, almost all of Carolina's American Indian trading was out of Charles Town, or Charleston, which was the hub of the area that became South Carolina. Agriculture and forest industries also were part of Carolina's economy, but trading with the natives became the most lucrative aspect of the Carolina economy. Deerskins, leathers, and furs were the most important exports from this trading, but slavery also became an important part of the trade. Although American Indian slaves existed in other areas (Virginia, for example), only South Carolina developed Indian slavery as a major part of its commerce. As a result, South Carolina enslaved more natives than any other English colony.

The Carolina traders had an advantage in developing a thriving trade with natives all the way to the Mississippi River for several reasons: The Carolina colony got an early start in the trade; there were no mountains blocking the westward expansion of Carolina trading; and Carolina traders could trade directly with American Indians rather than going through other natives as middlemen (in the northeastern United States, the Iroquois acted as middlemen between other American Indians and the Europeans).

Opposition to Slavery. The enslavement of natives by Carolina traders did have some opposition. From 1680 until 1730, South Carolina was under the active or nominal leadership of eight Lord Proprietors (headquartered in London) who recognized the crucial financial importance of developing trade with the natives. The Lord Proprietors knew that the enslavement of natives ultimately would hurt their general trade with Indians by leading to uprisings. A few proprietors also owned stock in the Royal African Company (begun in 1672), which was bringing slaves from Africa, and did not want competition from American Indians. Some prominent local leaders also spoke against American Indian slavery. For example, Francis Le Jau, a French Huguenot minister, publicly criticized the slave trade. In 1720, sixteen prominent businessmen issued a statement against the enslavement of American Indians. As a group, Charleston's Huguenot merchants were more opposed to native slavery, although a few did own Indian slaves. The proprietors were not opposed to slavery in principle, however, and they wavered in their opposition.

Despite some opposition, major factors encouraged slavery. The selling of captives into slavery in order to pay volunteer soldiers was an old custom in Europe, with military commanders and pirates routinely enslaving people on ships they captured. For example, some Jews escaping the Spanish Inquisition in the 1490's were captured by pirates and sold into slavery. The idea that slavery was better than death, and that the natives would murder their captives if they did not have the option of selling them, was used as a moral justification for slavery. Although this rationale was accurate in some cases, it did not take into account the great increase in natives capturing other natives because a market existed for slaves—a market made by the Europeans. Prior to European contact, slavery had been practiced by some American Indians, who frequently sold captives as slaves, but not on a large scale and generally without the harsh treatment common to European slavery. In addition, the enslavement of both American Indians and Africans got strong support in Charleston because a large number of Charleston's political and economic establishment were from the Caribbean and brought a strong tradition of slavery with them to South Carolina.

Indian Interest in European Conflict. The trade in American Indian slaves became an important part of the national conflicts involving Great Britain, Spain, and France for control of the Americas. Indians were drawn into these conflicts, often allying with a European power against other natives allied with another European power. In 1680, for example, Indians allied with the British in Carolina began raids against Indians allied with the Spanish Catholic missions in Georgia and northern Florida. The British and Spanish had attempted attacks on each other, and the English feared that the natives in Georgia and Florida would ally with the Spanish to attack Carolina. At the same time, the availability of a large number of Indians who were easy to capture because of their sedentary village life was tempting to slave traders for nondefense reasons. In 1704 under James Moore, for example, fifty British soldiers and a thousand Indians from Carolina took large numbers of Indian slaves from the Spanish areas. The French settled on the Gulf coast in 1699, putting them in proximity with natives in the lower Mississippi River area who were being threatened by attack and enslavement from Carolinian slave traders or (more likely) their Indian allies. This opposition from the French increased the risk and cost of capturing lower Mississippi River natives and, by 1720, largely ended the English slave trading.

Although the Europeans actually kidnapped or captured American Indians in the early years of the slave trade, mostly from coastal areas, they soon began to rely on other Indians to do the capturing as the slave trade increased and moved farther away from the coast. Encouraging native allies to capture other natives for slavery became a major part of the strategy of the slave dealers. In 1712, for example, the Tuscaroras of North Carolina killed some English and German settlers who had taken their land. The governor of North Carolina announced the availability of Indian slaves to induce South Carolina officials to send him military help. South Carolina expeditions—comprising mostly American Indians—killed more than a thousand Tuscaroras, mostly men, and more than seven hundred, mostly women and children, were sold into slavery. Peaceful natives along the route back to South Carolina also were captured and enslaved.

Yamasees Revolt. In 1715, the Yamasees in South Carolina revolted against the Carolina traders because of the traders' dishonest practices, such as cheating when weighing deerskins and furs. The Yamasees were defeated only because the Cherokees allied with the Carolina traders to capture Yamasees to sell as slaves, the proceeds from which they used to buy ammunition and clothing from the Carolinians. After that time, Carolina deliberately played off one tribe against another. The exposure of natives to European clothing, ammunition, rum, and other goods led to a rising desire for more European products, which further encouraged Indians to capture other Indians for exchange.

Indians comprised one-fourth of the slaves in Carolina in 1708, numbering fourteen hundred out of fifty-five hundred slaves, but the percentage generally decreased after that, for several reasons. Natives were more likely than Africans to try to escape. Although Indians had to beware of other hostile Indians, they frequently were successful in their attempts because they were in the same country as their original homes. For this reason, and because of the heavy demand for slave labor on the Caribbean sugar plantations, native slaves usually were sold to Caribbean traders. Some were also sold to New England. In addition, native slaves were more susceptible to European diseases and hence had a greater death rate than African slaves. Early writers also described American Indian slaves as being more docile than African slaves, ascribing this alleged trait to the Indians' sense of independence. For these reasons, native slaves usually were less desirable than, and cost much less than, African slaves. Because large numbers of native men were killed, a high percentage of American Indian slaves were women, partly explaining a significant mixture of African and Indian genealogies.

Although some American Indian slavery continued for several more decades, the practice basically had ended by 1730 in Carolina, with the Carolina traders turning to other trades and the English turning their American Indian slavery concerns to central America.

See also: Indian-white relations: Spanish colonial; Natchez Revolt; Pueblo Revolt; Seminole Wars; Tuscarora War; Yamasee War.

Abraham D. Lavender

Sources for Further Study

Crane, Verner. *The Southern Frontier, 1670-1732.* Ann Arbor: University of Michigan Press, 1929. A classic work on relations between European settlers and American Indians in the South.

Gallay, Alan. *The Indian Slave Trade: The Rise of the English Empire in the American South, 1670-1717.* New Haven, Conn.: Yale University Press, 2002. The first book to focus specifically on the Indian slave trade and its effects on the development of the plantation system in the American South.

Rozema, Vicki. *Footsteps of the Cherokees: A Guide to the Eastern Homelands of the Cherokee Nations.* Winston-Salem, N.C.: John F. Blair, 1995. Devotes several pages to American Indian slavery, helping to correct the previously small amount of attention given to this topic.

Waddell, Gene. *Indians of the South Carolina Lowcountry, 1562-1751.* Spartanburg, S.C.: Reprint Company, 1980. Describes how enslavement was one of several major factors in the extinction of South Carolina's lowcountry tribes.

Weatherford, Jack. *Native Roots: How the Indians Enriched America.* New York: Fawcett Columbine, 1991. One chapter is devoted to American Indian slaves, with a section describing the important part played by Charleston merchants in Indian slavery.

Wright, J. Leitch, Jr. "Brands and Slave Cords." In *The Only Land They Knew: The Tragic Story of the American Indians in the Old South.* New York: Free Press, 1981. Gives details on the Carolina slave trade in American Indians, with emphasis on historical details.

Indian trust fund lawsuits

Date: Beginning 1996
Locale: United States
Tribes involved: Pantribal in the United States

Categories: Court cases, National government and legislation, Nineteenth century history, Reservations and relocation, Twentieth century history

Significance: Beginning in 1996, class-action lawsuits by Native Americans against the Department of the Interior over land-use royalties held in trust for individual Indians attempted to hold the U.S. government accountable for more than a century of financial exploitation.

As a result of the 1887 General Allotment Act, many Indian reservations were broken up into individual holdings, usually of about 160 acres. Indians were not allowed to sell their allotments, although the allotments could be inherited by their children, and the mineral, forestry, and other natural resource rights could be leased out. Since the individual holdings were relatively small, lessors would negotiate with the Bureau of Indian Affairs for the rights to large swaths of land, and the royalties were paid into trust funds that the government held for the individual landowners. The government, in turn, was supposed to forward the payments to the landowners yearly.

Problems in the system developed early; in fact, serious flaws in the process of making trust fund payments to Indian tribes, rather than individuals, had been noted as early as 1828, nearly sixty years before the individual trust fund system was established. More complications arose as the original allotment owners died and their trust fund monies had to be divided among their heirs. The fact that many Indians did not leave wills meant that probate court hearings had to be held to determine the legal heirs. Furthermore, accounting for the trust fund monies was a low governmental priority, and record keeping was exceptionally lax.

In 1972, the Bureau of Indian Affairs announced that the accounting problem had become unfixable. A series of reports urging reform were issued over the next decade, culminating in the establishment of the Branch of Trust Fund Accounting in 1985 and the Office of Trust Fund Management in 1991 to oversee investment and accounting of trust funds. The American Indian Trust Reform Management Act of 1994 established a special trustee within the Department of the Interior to develop a management plan for the funds. Nonetheless, no real action took place.

In 1996, Elouise Cobell, the treasurer of the Blackfeet tribe in Montana and a founder of the Blackfeet National Bank, filed a class-action lawsuit against the Department of the Interior and then-secretary Bruce Babbitt demanding an accounting for all Indian trust funds dating back to 1887. *Cobell v. Babbitt* (which became *Cobell v. Norton* with the change of administration in 2001 and the appointment of Gale Norton as secretary of the interior) revealed not only the disgraceful state of government record keeping over the previous century but also that the government was destroying what records it had and making misrepresentations in court. In 1999, U.S. district judge Royce Lamberth found both Interior Secretary Bruce Babbitt and Treasury Secretary Richard Rubin in contempt of court for failing to produce trust-related documents as ordered by the court. In 2002, Interior Secretary Gale Norton was also tried for contempt of court as the government continued to drag its feet on producing documents and setting up a system to account for the mismanaged funds.

On December 21, 1999, Judge Lamberth ruled that the secretaries of the interior and treasury had breached their trust obligations to Native Americans, in phase one of the trial on reform of the trust fund system. As of spring, 2002, the trial for phase two, on accounting for the money paid into the trust funds since 1887, had not been scheduled. Some estimates placed the amount of royalties owed to over 500,000 Native Americans as in the range of $100 billion. In the meantime, the court would retain judicial oversight of the trust fund system through 2004.

Leslie Ellen Jones

See also: General Allotment Act; Indian-white relations: U.S., 1934-2002; Treaties and agreements in the United States.

Indian-white relations: Canadian

Date: 1500's-present
Locale: Canada
Tribes involved: Pantribal in Canada
Categories: Colonial history, National government and legislation, Native government, Nineteenth century history, Twentieth century history
Significance: Canadian Indian-white relations, while less confrontational than relations in the United States, have focused on the same issues of land and self-determination.

Whereas American Indian-white relations frequently focused on confrontation and hostility, Canadian relations focused predominantly on trade and legal cession of land. Though both countries followed policies of assimilation and cultural extermination at different points, Canada progressed further in its attempts to treat its native population as participants in the political process.

1500's-1700's. When French and English explorers first arrived in lands now occupied by Canada, they remarked upon the settled natives they encountered. The tribes along the Hudson River lived in large villages around which they farmed and fished. When French sailors were deposited on the shores of Hudson Bay to start a colony in 1542, they found the Indians to be quite helpful. English sailors and explorers felt equally welcomed by the Indians.

By the early 1600's, as the French began to develop permanent outposts, a trading relationship had been established between the Indians and the French. The French placed their forts in places unwanted by the Indians and relied on the Indians for agricultural support as well as trade. They built their trading posts at traditional Indian trading spots. The French generally respected traditional trading patterns. They used tribes that had always been intermediaries for trade and did not attempt to replace them with Frenchmen. This inspired trust and confidence in the French; the English in the American colonies and the Spanish refused to honor such traditional patterns. In short, the French recognized the importance of the Indians within the region.

The fur trade represented the most important aspect of European relations with the Indians. Originally based on beaver, the fur trade tied the French and English traders to the Indians, who not only trapped and killed the beaver but also treated it to be pelted. The French and English traded goods such as hatchets, cloth, and liquor for these treated pelts, while the Dutch traded muskets. These goods dramatically altered Indian life, changing everything from hunting and warfare to cooking.

The Indians also introduced new technology to the English and French. The canoe helped the French and English establish themselves in Canada. The canoe provided them with the means to transport goods through the river and lake systems. Indians also taught white traders how to survive in the wilds of Canada, which increased the interaction and interdependence between the groups.

Additionally, relations between Canadian Indians and the French remained friendly despite the arrival of Catholic missionaries in 1625. Though the French traders transported missionaries, the state did not support priests. Unlike the Spanish Catholic missionaries, they had no support from the military. While the acceptance of priests into an Indian community might be a condition for trade, the acceptance of Christianity was not a requirement for trade with the French.

Hudson's Voyage of 1610-1611

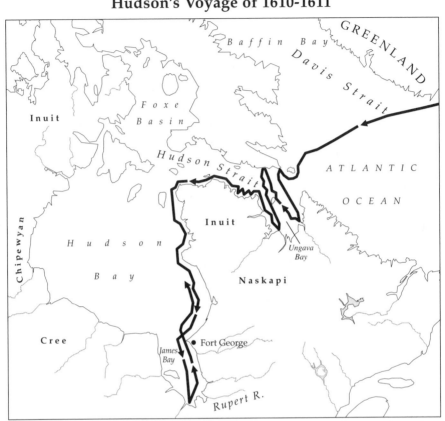

In 1610-1611, Henry Hudson searched in vain for the Northwest Passage in regions bordering the territories of Inuit, Chipewyan, Cree, and Naskapi peoples that later became part of present-day Canada.

The French, unlike their English and Spanish counterparts, tended to allow intermarriage. Many traders discovered that intermarriage strengthened the trading ties between the French and an Indian tribe, increasing profit. Many early French trappers married Indian women, creating a Metis population.

The French also encouraged alliances and peace between different tribes. They acted as intermediaries for settling disputes, which worked to their advantage. If the Iroquois refused to trade with the French because the Abenaki did, the French arranged for some sort of settlement so that both would trade with them.

When the English began to establish a foothold in Canada in the early 1700's, the calm relations between the French and the Indians forced the

English to adopt similar methods. Unlike the American colonies, where traders were almost forbidden to marry Indian women, the Hudson's Bay Company, founded in 1670, encouraged such relationships in the name of trade. An Indian or Metis wife offered a certain cachet to the rising trader.

The Hudson's Bay Company became an important definer of Indian-white relations in Canada. Built on the fur trade, it relied heavily on cordial relations with the Indians. Until the French were forced out in 1760, it was necessary to encourage friendly relations with the Indians lest they switch trade to the French. The Hudson's Bay Company also established forts at traditional trading points.

Contact between the whites and the Indians during this period was not always peaceful. Whites in Canada spread disease just as they had in Mexico and the United States. Some groups, such as the Micmacs and the Hurons, suffered greatly from epidemics which destroyed their cultures. Additionally, international tensions spilled over into Canada. The Anglo-French War (French and Indian War) and the American Revolution brought European wars onto Indian soil. Indians had to choose sides, sometimes between enemies and sometimes between trading partners. Often Indian women and children from one tribe were mistaken for those from another by the Europeans and killed for wrongly assumed alliances.

Period of Transition: 1800's. The nineteenth century radically changed the path of Indian-white relations in Canada. The British now controlled Canada and ruled it as a colony. The Hudson's Bay Company controlled the western regions of Manitoba, Saskatchewan, Calgary, and British Columbia as well as the Northwest Territories and the Yukon. Protestant and Catholic missionaries began to spread across the country to previously "undiscovered" groups of Indians. Within a hundred short years, the missionaries would alter daily life for most Indians, the Hudson's Bay Company would be gone, Canada would become an independent nation, treaties would cede much Indian land, and settlers would take much of the rest.

In the early 1800's, much remained the same in Canada as it had been for the previous three hundred years. The fur trade remained the main relation between Indians and whites. The Hudson's Bay Company controlled Indian-white relations in the west as well as trade. Intermarriage and interdependence between the whites and Indians still remained.

The nineteenth century, however, soon brought many changes to Indian-white relations. The first big alteration came with an influx of Catholic and Protestant missionaries at the beginning of the century. By the 1830's, missionaries had worked their way into western Ontario and into contact with Plains groups in Manitoba. These missionaries sought to change the Indians into white people through assimilation, agrarianism, and cultural extermination. They built churches and schools. They translated Indian languages and produced Bibles in these languages. The Protestants tried to re-create English villages, while the Catholics absorbed parts of Indian religions into Catholicism to make it more acceptable. Both Protestants and Catholics were disappointed by the conversion rates. Canadian Indian societies tended to remain closed to Christianity; many Indian groups found it interesting but not inspiring. Tensions rose between Indians and white missionaries as missionaries pushed for total acceptance of Christianity and white "civilization."

In 1837, a report presented to the British Parliament stated that frontier development was harmful to the Indians. Parliament reacted by passing the Crown Lands Protection Acts, which placed Indian lands in Crown trust. This accomplished two things. It prevented whites from squatting on Crown lands. It also, however, denied Indians any political rights based on land ownership. This set the pattern for policy after confederation in 1867.

In 1842, the Bagot Commission began to review the Indian Affairs office. It produced three recommendations for British policy regarding the Indians: First, the Indian Affairs office should develop an agricultural program for the Indians; second, schools should be created to assimilate Indian youths into Canadian society; and, finally, the state should help support religious instruction to the Indians to aid in assimilation. In 1850, the British government continued to encourage assimilation by offering citizenship to any Indians who abandoned their Indian status. Additional legislation blurred the lines between Indians and Canadian citizens. The government offered enfranchisement to any male Indian who was literate (meaning he possessed an understanding of the English language), over twenty-one, free of debt, and possessing a "good character." Though the British/Canadian government did not actually remove Indians from their land in this period, they did attempt to remove land, status, and culture from the Indians.

By the mid-1800's, the railroads had expanded into western Ontario, bringing more whites to the area. The Hudson's Bay Company remained firm in disallowing settlers within its territories. In 1867, confederation came to Canada. The Hudson's Bay Company released the western territories to Canada, changing Indian-white relations. Indians were no longer protected by their trading relationship, and white settlers and developers wanted Indian land for farms and gold. The white Canadian-born population grew from three million to almost five million between confederation and the end of the century, placing new demands on land and natural resources. During the same period, the number of acres under production rose from eighteen million to thirty million, representing the treaties that removed promising farmland from the Indians.

The newly formed Canadian government followed many of the same policies as the American government, emphasizing assimilation, agrarianism, and cultural extermination. With confederation, the government pushed for land settlements with the Indians, the creation of schools to teach them English and make them Canadian, and the introduction of farming as a means of survival. The reserve system demanded that Indians abandon traditional methods of survival and adopt "peasant" farming. Farming tied native groups to one area of land, making them available for conversion, assimilation, and government control while freeing the land for white farmers. The Canadian government did not seek to create large or profitable farms for the Indians. Instead, they sought to provide them with minimal survival with rudimentary tools and small plots.

The new Canadian government also sought to remove Indian status from the Indians. In 1868 and 1869, the government passed the Indian Act and the Enfranchisement Acts, which created a legal division between "uncivilized Indians" and "civilized whites." The Canadian government promised the same legal and political rights that whites had to any Indian who relinquished his status as an Indian. The Canadian government simply adopted the policies of the British government in erasing the Indian population, politically and legally.

Most Indian groups were not happy with the transfer of power from the Hudson's Bay Company to the Canadian government. Many did not want to surrender their land and adopt farming. One group in particular felt slighted by the arrangements made by the government: the Metis. In 1870, alarmed by government surveyors, a group of Cree Indians and Metis banded together to fight the encroachment on their land. While defending their land, they executed a man from Ontario, which hardened white Canadians against them. The government ended this first rebellion, with leader Louis Riel escaping to the United States. He returned in 1884 to begin the Northwest Rebellion, which stalled the Canadian government for several months. Riel demanded that Metis also receive land settlements. Though they eventually received these rights through the Manitoba Act, Riel was executed for treason and murder in 1885, making him a hero of the Metis and many Indians.

Between confederation and the end of the century, whites infiltrated the rest of Canada. Miners arrived in the Yukon Territory, bringing missionaries and government officials as well as disease with them. Canadians began to "settle" British Columbia from the Pacific Coast inward. The railroad began to crisscross the country, dividing traditional lands and limiting movement. By 1885, all the major land treaties had been signed. The Plains Indians, who had resisted the longest, relinquished their land as the buffalo disappeared. Only the Indians of British Columbia avoided signing treaties, though whites usurped much of their land without the treaties.

The nineteenth century ended with two notable incidents. First, the Canadian government outlawed the potlatch among the Northwest Pacific coast tribes. This law represented the last act in a war of attrition against Indian cultures. It became a battle cry in the first part of the twentieth century as Indian groups battled for political and legal rights. Second, a smallpox epidemic among the same tribes decimated them. Hundreds of lives were lost, breeding anger, distrust, and discontent among the survivors.

Twentieth Century. The twentieth century did not begin auspiciously for the Indians of Canada. Most resided on reserves, their children sent to boarding schools run by missionaries, their cultures stripped from them, and their movement restricted by laws and pass systems. Many struggled to survive on farming plots that were too small to support families, with outdated tools and equipment. Change, however, eventually came.

Beginning with World War II, Indians began to take back control of their lives. Many Canadian Indians served in World War II, gaining citizenship and political rights without losing their Indian status. This allowed them to challenge certain laws and stereotypes. Though many reserves remained mired in poverty, Indian leaders began to fight for the right to a proper education, for medical reform and access, and for representation. Indians also took control of their natural resources, including timber, oil, and other resources. Inspired by the actions of the American Indian Movement in the United States, several groups formed in Canada in the 1960's and 1970's. The most powerful of these today is the Assembly of First Nations, a coalition of recognized and unrecognized tribal groups.

The Assembly of First Nations has focused on several things since the 1970's. First, it provides political action and a political voice to various groups. Instead of every group fighting the same political and legal battles separately, the assembly helps unify and streamline these battles. Second, it supplies social support in health, business, and education. It organizes arts cooperatives, learning cooperatives and centers, and business cooperatives, centralizing these activities and making them more powerful than small individual groups could be. Finally, its leaders have sought to put Indian concerns firmly on the agenda of the Canadian government. Some of the issues they have focused on in the past are the Great Whale Project on Cree land in Northern Quebec, the lack of treaties in British Columbia, the development of Indian land as tourist attractions, and access to education for Indian men and women.

The Assembly of First Nations has been instrumental in helping make Indian rights an issue for the Canadian government. Indians today represent 5 percent of the Canadian population and are the fastest-growing segment of the population. Yet, until the 1990's, they were not represented in the government. As Canada struggled to maintain its unity and keep Quebec in the Confederation, the Assembly of First Nations and Indian leaders sought to have their concerns included. In 1989, the Canadian government sought ratification of the Meech Lake Accord, which would have allowed Quebec to remain a "distinct society." It made no mention of Indian rights as "distinct societies" or of self-determination. When the accord reached Manitoba for ratification, Elijah Harper, a Cree, stalled the vote in a traditional manner by raising one white feather and refusing comment. He effectively ended the Meech Lake Accord. By 1992, the Canadian government included the Assembly of First Nations in negotiations between provincial governors, finally allowing Indians a voice in their own destiny.

Ironically, 1992 became the unofficial "year of the Indian" in Canada. As well as the assembly being included in the council of governors, the Canadian government returned a large land mass to the Indians of Northern Quebec. An area called Nunavut became available for Indian control, allowing them to regulate hunting, fishing, and development of the land. The area represents almost a complete province in Canada.

Indian-white relations into the twenty-first century remained tense. Many contemporary Canadians see Indians as freeloaders on the government. Stereotypes of drunken Indians, Indians wealthy from annuities, and freeloading Indians abound still in Canada. Despite the more peaceful Canadian policy toward Indians, Canada and its Indian population still suffer from the same tensions as those in U.S. society.

See also: Aboriginal Action Plan; American Indian Higher Education Consortium; Beaver Wars; Declaration of First Nations; *Delgamuukw v. British Columbia*; Department of Indian Affairs and Northern Development; Fifteen Principles; Indian Act of 1876; Indian Act of 1951; Indian Act of 1989; Indian-white relations: English colonial; Indian-white relations: French colonial; Indian-white relations: Norse; International Indian Treaty Council; Meech Lake Accord; Nisga'a Agreement in Principle; Nunavut Territory; Oka crisis; Prehistory: Arctic; Prehistory: Plateau; Prehistory:

Northeast; Prehistory: Plains; Prehistory: Subarctic; Proclamation of 1763; Red River Raids; Reserve system of Canada; Riel Rebellions; Royal Commission on Aboriginal Peoples; Thames, Battle of the; Treaties and agreements in Canada; Tribe (term); White Paper of Canada.

C. L. Higham

Sources for Further Study

Carter, Sarah. *Lost Harvest: Prairies Indian Reserve Farmers and Government Policy*. Montreal: McGill-Queen's University Press, 1990. Critically exposes the agricultural policies of the Canadian government.

Dickason, Olive. *Canada's First Nations: A History of Founding Peoples from Earliest Times*. Norman: University of Oklahoma Press, 1992. An unparalleled legal, political, and social history of Canadian Indians.

Getty, Ian, and Antoine Lussier, eds. *As Long as the Sun Shines and Water Flows: A Reader in Canadian Native Studies*. Vancouver: University of British Columbia Press, 1983. Includes essays on issues of self-determination, treaty negotiation, and use of natural resources.

Grant, John Webster. *Moon of Wintertime: Missionaries and the Indians of Canada in Encounter Since 1543*. Toronto: University of Toronto Press, 1984. Examines Indian-white contact through the eyes of missionaries and through their cultural legacy.

Miller, J. R. *Skyscrapers Hide the Heavens: A History of Indian-White Relations in Canada*. 3d ed. Toronto: University of Toronto Press, 2000. An excellent study of Indians as politicians and cultural survivors.

St. Germain, Jill. *Indian Treaty-Making Policy in the United States and Canada, 1867-1877*. Lincoln: University of Nebraska Press, 2001. Explores and contrasts the "civilizing" efforts of the United States and Canada through their Indian treaty policies.

Van Kirk, Sylvia. *Many Tender Ties: Women in Fur-Trade Society, 1670-1870*. Norman: University of Oklahoma Press, 1983. Examines relations between white traders and Indian/Metis women.

Indian-white relations: Dutch colonial

Date: 1600's
Locale: Hudson Valley
Tribes involved: Lenni Lenape, Mahican, Mohawk

Categories: Colonial history
Significance: Dutch control of the Hudson Valley (1609-1664) paved the way for the takeover of the southern half of New York by European colonists.

The creation of a Dutch colonial claim to the Hudson Valley through the exploration of the river by Henry Hudson, sailing under Dutch charter in 1609, laid the foundations for the creation of a Dutch colony, New Netherland, in the Hudson Valley. The arrival of the Dutch, first as traders and then as settlers, had a disastrous effect on the Indians of the area.

The Fur Trade. Initially, the Dutch perceived the Hudson River Valley as the ideal approach to the rich fur trade of the interior. In this view, they were seeing things exactly as their rivals to the north, the French, did. Indeed, with the exception of the Pilgrims and others escaping hardship, oppression, or authorities in their homelands, the Europeans of the late sixteenth and early seventeenth centuries viewed the New World as primarily a source of wealth, to be gained by acquiring its resources and selling these on the European market. For the Spaniards to the south, the resource was gold bullion; for the French and the Dutch to the north (and even for some English traders) the resource was furs. These furs were gained by trading European goods—in the contemporary phrase, "trade goods"—to the Indians in return for their fur harvest.

After the news of Henry Hudson's exploration of the river named for him, the earliest Dutch visitors were all seeking furs. In 1614 the New Netherland Company was chartered to exploit the fur trade; it was superseded in 1621 by the West India Company, which dominated affairs in New Netherland until the English conquest in 1664. Throughout the Dutch period, the hope of those who were interested in the area was that it would be a major source of wealth, because its location offered ready access to the Indians of the interior, principally the Mohawks, the easternmost tribe of the Iroquois Confederacy.

Some of what the Dutch brought to trade with the Indians was of benefit to the Indians. From the Europeans the Indians acquired axes, hoes, and iron cooking pots, all of which enabled them more readily to secure their needs from nature. The Indians soon acquired a taste for coarse woven cloaks of a material known as "duffel." These things were positive. At the same time, however, the Dutch readily supplied the Indians with two items that had negative effects on their culture: guns and liquor. Moreover, with the passage of time the Indian taste for trade goods grew to the point where they were essentially dependent on them.

The focal point of the fur trade was Fort Orange, built near the present site of Albany in 1624. There the West India Company established its trading post, buying furs brought in by the Indians to the west. These Indians were the Mohawks; because of their access to large quantities of furs and their warlike reputation, the Dutch were always careful to maintain good relations with them. The guns furnished to them by the Dutch enabled the Mohawks to carry on vigorous warfare with the Hurons to the north and west. The Dutch were agreeable to that outcome, for it diverted to the Hudson River some of the furs that would otherwise have been sold to the French along the St. Lawrence River.

At home in the United Provinces, however, there were others who had different objectives. A group of wealthy merchants, most notably Kiliaen van Rensselaer, succeeded in breaking the monopoly of the West India Company and opening up New Netherland both to other traders in fur and to settlers. As the English settlements to the north and to the south began to fill with colonists, the Dutch saw their position threatened if New Netherland consisted solely of a few trading posts. Under the leadership of van Rensselaer, a policy of encouraging settlement began in the 1630's.

Settlement and Impact. The earliest settlements were at New Amsterdam, on Manhattan Island, purchased from the local Indians by Peter Minuit in 1626. As the number of settlers grew, frictions with the Indians grew too; many settlers allowed their livestock to roam free (fencing their cultivated fields); as the Indians did not fence theirs, the free-roaming livestock often destroyed Indian crops. As more settlers arrived, more land was needed; although the Dutch were always careful to purchase land from the Indians (sometimes the same land more than once), the Indians began to resent the Dutch presence. The Dutch authorities were also not able to control the actions of free traders, who often sought to defraud the Indians of their pelts.

Conflict peaked in the 1650's (in the Peach Wars), during which time the Dutch, through military action, effectively dispossessed the various tribal groups living around the lower Hudson. They continued to maintain good relations with the Mohawks, for they would have been unable to match the Mohawks militarily, especially after the latter were armed with European muskets. By the time the Dutch were forced to cede New Netherland to an invading British fleet in 1664, the local Algonquian tribes had been essentially wiped out.

See also: Bacon's Rebellion; Beaver Wars; Fur trade; Iroquois Confederacy; Manhattan Island purchase; Pavonia Massacre; Peach Wars; Pequot War.

Nancy M. Gordon

Sources for Further Study

Bachman, Van Cleaf. *Peltries or Plantations: The Economic Policies of the Dutch West India Company in New Netherland, 1623-1639.* Baltimore: The Johns Hopkins University Press, 1969.

Donck, Adriaen van der. *A Description of the New Netherlands.* Translated by Jeremiah Johnson. 1841. Reprint. Syracuse, N.Y.: Syracuse University Press, 1968.

Merwick, Donna. *Possessing Albany, 1630-1710: The Dutch and English Experiences.* Cambridge, England: Cambridge University Press, 1990.

Rink, Oliver A. *Holland on the Hudson: An Economic and Social History of Dutch New York.* Ithaca, N.Y.: Cornell University Press, 1986.

Trelease, Allen W. *Indian Affairs in Colonial New York: The Seventeenth Century.* Ithaca, N.Y.: Cornell University Press, 1960.

Indian-white relations: English colonial

Date: 1600's-1700's
Locale: Eastern seaboard
Tribes involved: Northeast and Southeast polities
Categories: Colonial history
Significance: Indian-English relations developed over the span of two centuries and were dominated by issues of trade, land, and religion; both sides borrowed from their adversary's culture throughout the colonial period.

Indian-English relations predate English attempts to colonize the American continent. In the Chesapeake Bay region, for example, groups such as the Powhatans had contact with Europeans in the 1580's. The experience of Don Luis (a *mamanatowick*, or paramount chief, of the Algonquian confederacy) with the Spanish provided a model for his successor, Powhatan, to draw upon when the English established their Jamestown colony in 1607. The English encountered the confederacy further when they began colonizing the Chesapeake Bay region. In New England, Squanto's ability to communicate with the Pilgrims illustrates that there was a familiarity with the English before actual colonization began.

Policies and Preconceptions. When English colonists began establishing colonies on the North American continent, they hoped to coexist with their Indian neighbors. The English assumed that their indigenous neighbors would recognize the superiority of English civilization and would try to emulate the colonists. Unfortunately for the colonists, the Indians were unwilling to accommodate these hopes. Equally distressing to the colonists, more than a few of their own found Indian culture preferable to English society. This phenomenon frightened colonial leaders, and all colonies worked to prevent their citizens from adopting Indian lifestyles. Even when introduced to Indian culture unwillingly, as prisoners of war or other captives, English colonists often preferred to stay with their Indian captors.

The treaty minutes between Native Americans and English delegates illustrate this problem. In these documents, colonial officials demand the return of English captives from the Indians. Inevitably, some of the captured colonists refused to return to colonial society. Their unwillingness to return challenged colonial attitudes of superiority throughout the colonial period. Complicating the relationship was Indian custom. Within the eastern woodlands, when two adversaries agreed to peace, they often exchanged community members, who served as visible reminders of goodwill. Once the colonists realized this, they demanded that Indian hostages remain

Contemporary depiction of a meeting between Ottawa leader Pontiac (right) and a British major named Rogers during the 1760's. (Library of Congress)

with them until the articles of peace were implemented. Some colonial officials proposed placing English orphans among the Indians. Archibald Kennedy, a member of New York's Governor's Council, argued that placing orphans among the Indians would help bind Anglo-Indian alliances.

Indian-English relations went through various phases in the colonial period. Native Americans initially worked to establish peaceful and beneficial relations with the English colonists. Only when Native Americans had reasons to fear the colonists did relations become inhospitable. Each Indian polity welcomed English colonists for different reasons. Over the course of time, each side grew more familiar with the other; familiarity did not produce harmony. Cultural biases on both sides prevented satisfactory resolutions to problems with Anglo-Indian relations. Benjamin Franklin, in his *Remarks Concerning the Savages*, reports how Iroquois leaders rejected an English request to send Iroquoian youths to colonial schools. The Iroquois spokesman declined, stating that schooling made Indian youths unfit for any future work among the Indians.

The second phase of the Anglo-Indian relationship was one of distrust and conflict. The English made it clear that they were not willing to play by traditional tribal rules. The timing of this second period of Anglo-Indian relations depended on local circumstance. In the Chesapeake and New England regions, hostilities broke out within a decade of colonial settlement. Both sides fought these wars within their traditional understandings of war. Colonists saw women and children as legitimate targets and often fought in formations better suited to European plains than American forests. Native Americans ambushed, fought skirmishes, raided, and captured women and children. As both sides learned about the other they adopted various strategies from their opponents. (From this cultural borrowing has emerged the polemical debate about which culture "invented" scalping.)

Many architects of England's early relationships with the Indians based their policy on their experiences in Ireland. Two of the first colonizers, Gilbert Humphreys and Walter Ralegh, fit this generalization. They and their families, like other Devon families, had gained their position in English society through their participation in the Irish wars. Later colonizers, such as John Winthrop and Roger Williams, brought with them the legacy of the struggles of the English Reformation. These sixteenth and seventeenth century settlers held certain convictions that contact with North America's indigenous inhabitants could not alter. English settlers viewed Algonquian society from a European perspective. Algonquian males were "lazy and indolent." Females were immodest and lived a life of drudgery. English settlers believed the Indians "uncivilized." They were convinced that the Algonquian religion was an alliance with Satan. These attitudes provided the theoretical underpinnings of Anglo-Indian relations.

Anglo-Indian relations had two specific spheres. The first sphere concerned official relations. This realm includes treaties, policy decisions, and trade negotiations. The second domain involved informal relations. This area included marriages, cultural borrowing, and cultural critiques. In addition to these spheres, four specific rubrics shaped Indian-English relations. These four areas were disease, trade, land, and religion. Although these areas are interrelated, each requires a separate examination.

Disease. The role of disease in Anglo-Indian relations has, until recently, been a little understood aspect of interaction. Scholars now think that disease was the greatest killer of Native Americans in the colonial period. A series of epidemics known as "virgin soil epidemics" were particularly devastating to Indian communities because these epidemics killed people aged fifteen to forty. This age group was most responsible for the societal tasks of food gathering, making military decisions, and procreation. Native American social practices exacerbated the disease problem, since communities did not isolate the sick originally. Disease often predated significant Anglo-Indian contact and set the parameters for the Anglo-Indian relations that followed. On at least one occasion Englishmen used disease as a weapon of war: Sir Jeffery Amherst, commander of British forces in North America, ordered that blankets infected with smallpox be given to some Delaware Indians during Pontiac's Rebellion.

Disease transformed the Anglo-Indian relationship. For Native Americans, disease meant a declining population base from which to meet European aggression. The most lethal disease that Native Americans encountered was smallpox. Other diseases that swept eastern North America in the colonial period were measles, influenza, diphtheria, typhus, and perhaps bubonic plague. The presence of a devastating disease often called for a reassessment of traditional assumptions about the world. Sometimes this reassessment provided European missionaries with the opportunity necessary to gain a foothold in native communities. Most of the time the missionaries followed the trade routes west.

Trade. From the beginning of contact, Indians and Englishmen traded. Arthur Barlow wrote of trading when he met with the Algonquians around Roanoke in 1584, and European fishermen exchanged items with Native Americans during the seasonal voyages to fishing banks off Newfoundland. From the Indians' perspective, this trade reinforced a traditional manner of integrating foreigners into an existing worldview. While the English saw trade as a simple economic exchange, it was something more complex for the Indians. They based trade on their notion of reciprocity, and reciprocity implied obligation. Both Powhatan and Squanto based their initial relationships with the colonists on the notion of reciprocity. Very quickly this reciprocal relationship became an interdependent one. Initially it was the colonists who depended on Indian trade items for survival. By the end of the colonial period, however, the Native Americans were dependent on the trade for survival.

Trade flourished partly because it initially required little adjustment for either side. English and Indian traders tapped existing trade networks. In the early colonial period Indian expectations shaped the trade; they determined which goods were traded and at what price. English traders discovered the importance of adhering to Indian cultural expectations when doing business. Some traders found marriage with a native woman a beneficial custom. It opened doors previously closed within the native community. For many native polities, a trader's marriage transformed the trader from a stranger to a family member. The trader now had special obligations to fulfill. As the colonial period progressed, English traders tried to transform such relationships to fit English expectations. They were never truly successful.

One reason that trade predated colonization is that the items both sides exchanged required little change within each cultural tradition. Algonquian males traditionally hunted for beaver in the winter, and winter pelts were what Europeans wanted when they began trading. Native peoples had processed deerskins for internal consumption before the arrival of Europeans. For their part, the Englishmen who did the trading did so at first in conjunction with their fishing expeditions. The furs were tangential to the primary purpose. Nevertheless, the trade in pelts and goods produced change.

For some Native American groups, trade with the English stimulated the process of political centralization. Even if trade did not produce political changes for Native Americans, it forced fundamental changes in labor. For the Cherokees, the processing of such large numbers of skins produced a cottage industry. This industry required more labor from the women of the community, which placed strains on Cherokee communities. Other groups experienced increased conflict as neighboring Indian polities attempted to obtain access to the English market. Interior polities sought their own relationships with the English. Various groups tried to force their way onto rivals' territories in the quest for more pelts and skins; the Beaver Wars are perhaps the most famous example of this. Other polities positioned themselves as intermediaries within the growing trade. Whatever the reason, the fur trade produced an increasing level of violence, which made peaceful Anglo-Indian relations even more difficult. For the Indians, the increasing violence made any attempt to unite against the English difficult. As a result, most Indian polities stood alone against the English when colonists sought Indian land for their own occupation.

Land. Perhaps the greatest strain on Native American-English relations concerned land. English colonists had an insatiable appetite for Indian lands. To justify their taking of Indian land, English officials and colonists relied on three specific arguments. First, they claimed land by right of discovery. Second, they claimed land by right of conquest. Third, they asserted their right to the land because they could better utilize the land than the Indians. Land was probably the single most important irritant to Anglo-Indian relations in the colonial period.

In some areas, however, disputes over land were not a major factor. A smallpox epidemic had wiped out large numbers of Massachusetts Indians on the eve of Boston's founding by the English, for example; it was only when the colonists sought more than the original land ceded them by the Indians that land became an issue. Within two decades of colonization, land was the source of Anglo-Indian conflict. The Pequot War (1636-1637), Metacom's (King Philip's) War (1675-1676), Bacon's Rebellion (1675-1676), Pontiac's Rebellion (1763-1764), and Lord Dunmore's War (1774) were some of the wars that involved, at least tangentially, English-Indian disagreements about land. So important were land issues to Indian-English relations that various attempts to restrict colonial encroachments on Indian land were tried; none of them worked. Nevertheless, the Albany Congress (1754), the creation of the Indian superintendent system, the Proclamation of 1763, and the Treaty of Fort Stanwix (1768) illustrate attempts to alleviate the problems that land created in Anglo-Indian relations.

Religion. English missionaries found their greatest success among Native American polities that had reached the nadir of their cultural existence. In New England, those Indian polities decimated by disease often turned to Christianity because traditional religion no longer explained what was happening to them. Other groups turned to Christianity after they could no longer defend themselves culturally because of lost territory. The "praying Indians" of New England processed the missionaries' message within an Algonquian framework. The songs and rituals associated with Christianity, not the message, were what primarily drew the Algonquians' attention. By the end of the colonial period, Christian Indians acted as missionaries to other Indian groups. Samson Occom, for example, a Mohegan

Indian, became a missionary to the Brothertown Indians living among the Iroquois.

The missionaries and their message often divided Indian communities. The result was an increasing level of factionalism within native politics. This factionalism further hindered the Indians' ability to withstand English pressures. The Iroquois Confederacy offers an example of how this factionalism influenced Indian-English relations. Initial Christian factions emerged in Iroquoia with the arrival of French Jesuit missionaries. They arrived at a time when the Iroquois were on the defensive in their struggles against the French and their western Indian allies. In the following years, pro-Christian Iroquois came to dominate confederacy councils. When the Iroquois turned the tables on the French, new traditionalist leaders emerged to lead the confederacy until new troubles appeared and the tide turned once again. This factional ebb and flow continued until the end of the colonial period, when Samuel Kirkland and his Oneida followers challenged the leadership position of Sir William Johnson and the Mohawks. Kirkland had converted a number of Oneida warriors to his New Light Congregationalism. Johnson was a supporter of Anglican attempts to Christianize the Indians. This religious struggle had political overtones because it became part of the colonial-imperial struggles of the 1760's and 1770's. When the American Revolution broke out, the league extinguished its council fire at Onondaga and let each nation determine which side to support: Christianity had helped splinter the Six Nations Confederacy.

Gift-Giving. One area of English-Indian interaction that has received extensive coverage is gift-giving. The use of gifts in Indian society was well established before English colonization. When the English arrived, they found they had to adapt to Indian protocol if they hoped to establish peaceful relations with their Indian neighbors. Indian gifts involved large expenditures on the part of colonial governments. New governors to New York were often presented an allowance of six hundred pounds for the purchase of gifts. Officials in South Carolina spent more than twenty-six thousand pounds on Indian affairs between 1732 and 1755, when the Crown officially took control of Indian relations. A significant portion of South Carolina's Indian expenses went to Indian gifts. These expenditures suggest that colonial and imperial officials understood the importance of gifts to Anglo-Indian relations.

Intermarriage. One area often overlooked in discussions of Indian-English relations is gender. While all European nations were concerned with blood purity, the English were perhaps the most prudish on the matter. Nevertheless, there were many cross-cultural relationships. In 1615 John Rolfe married Pocahontas. In Algonquian terms this marriage served to cement the peace. In the eighteenth century the British Indian superintendent for the northern colonies, Sir William Johnson, married an Iroquoian woman, Molly Brant. Johnson's marriage to Brant gave him an opportunity to operate within Iroquoia that he would not have had otherwise. In the southern colonies the trader Lachland McGillivray married a Creek woman, and his son Alexander became a leading figure in the Anglo-Indian dialogue. Johnson's and McGillivray's marriages provided each man with entry into his wife's community in a manner no outsider could hope to achieve. Equally important, these men were now obligated to meet certain familial and kinship expectations on the part of their wives' families.

In examining Indian-English relations it is important to remember that neither side spoke with a single voice. While scholars have repeatedly mentioned the problems Native Americans had in uniting to oppose English objectives, there has been a tendency to downplay the difficulties the colonists also had in presenting a united front to the Indians. The ramifications of the lack of unity on both sides give the study of Indian-English relations its unique character. The diversity of opinion and actions among British colonial and Indian leaders made that relationship a complex one.

See also: Indian-white relations: Canadian; Indian-white relations: Dutch colonial; Indian-white relations: French colonial; Indian-white relations: Norse; Indian-white relations: Russian colonial; Indian-white relations: Spanish colonial; Indian-white relations: Swedish colonial; Indian-white relations: U.S., 1775-1830; Indian-white relations: U.S., 1831-1870; Indian-white relations: U.S., 1871-1933; Indian-white relations: U.S., 1934-2002.

Michael J. Mullin

Sources for Further Study

Axtell, James. *The European and the Indian: Essays in the Ethnohistory of Colonial North America.* Oxford, England: Oxford University Press, 1981. Many of the essays in this book were previously published; together they provide a good introduction to the study of ethnohistory and Anglo-Indian relations in the colonial period.

Crosby, Alfred W. "Virgin Soil Epidemics as a Factor in the Aboriginal Depopulation in America." *William and Mary Quarterly* 3d ser., 33 (1976): 289-299. This essay is considered a classic examination of the effect of disease on Indian populations in North America.

Jacobs, Wilbur R. "British Indian Policies to 1783." In *History of Indian-White Relations*, edited by Wilcomb E. Washburn. Vol. 4 in *Handbook of North American Indians*, edited by William C. Sturtevant. Washington,

D.C.: Smithsonian Institution Press, 1988. As the title indicates, this essay details British policy toward the Indians. It covers the formal relations between Indians and colonists and is particularly good at examining the role of land in the Indian-English experience.

Kupperman, Karen Ordahl. *Indians and English: Facing Off in Early America.* Ithaca, N.Y.: Cornell University Press, 2000. A highly readable account of the evolutions of Indian-English relations along the East Coast of North America.

Oberg, Michael Leroy. *Dominion and Civility: English Imperialism and Native America, 1585-1685.* Ithaca, N.Y.: Cornell University Press, 1999. Focuses on English interactions with Algonquian groups in the Chesapeake Bay area.

Richter, Daniel K. *Facing East from Indian Country: A Native History of Early America.* Cambridge, Mass.: Harvard University Press, 2002. Presents early American history from an Indian perspective, focusing on the figures of Pocohontas, Blessed Catherine Tekawitha, and Metacom, a.k.a. King Philip.

_____. *The Ordeal of the Longhouse: The Peoples of the Iroquois League in the Era of European Colonization.* Chapel Hill: University of North Carolina Press, 1992. Published for the Institute of Early American History and Culture, this study of the Iroquois League demonstrates the influence of factionalism on an Indian people as they dealt with the Europeans. It synthesizes much scholarship on the Six Nations and their relationship with the French, Dutch, and English. It is particularly strong on seventeenth century relations.

Rountree, Helen C., ed. *Powhatan Foreign Relations, 1500-1722.* Charlottesville: University Press of Virginia, 1993. A series of articles written by leading scholars. The book details Powhatan relations not only with the English but also with other Indian groups in the region. The articles emphasize the complexity and difficulty of thinking about Native Americans as single-culture polities.

Indian-white relations: French colonial

Date: 1400's-1700's
Locale: Northern and eastern North America
Tribes involved: Huron, Iroquois Confederacy, Lenni Lenape, Ojibwa, Ottawa, Potawatomi, Shawnee

Categories: Colonial history, Religion and missionary activities
Significance: French colonial relations with Indian tribes displayed mutual interest in trading, useful political and military alliances, missionary schooling, and protection.

France's colonial claim on major portions of North America dates from the reign of the Valois king François I. It was François who protested the assumptions of the 1494 Treaty of Tordesillas, which claimed to divide the newly discovered Western Hemisphere between Spain and Portugal solely. Soon France would be engaged, well before the Pilgrims landed at Plymouth Rock in 1620, in exploring North American lands that were inhabited only by Indian tribes. The French labeled this new territory Gallia Nova, or New France.

Early Contacts. Historians date the earliest trading contact between French explorers and American Indians to Jacques Cartier's entry into the Gulf of St. Lawrence in 1534. The French exchanged knives and trinkets for furs offered by Micmac tribesmen. The next year Cartier sailed farther up the St. Lawrence River, first encountering Iroquois at the point where Quebec would later be established and then penetrating as far as the Indian village of Hochelaga (later Montreal).

The sequel to these earliest encounters in the area that would become known as New France was not promising for future relations. After Cartier captured Indians and transported them to France (where they died from exposure to European diseases), returning French parties were not welcome in the St. Lawrence area. Attempts by Cartier's successor, Sieur de Roberval, to found a colony failed after only three years.

The contributions made by Samuel de Champlain, founder of Quebec City in 1608, were more lasting. Champlain was very curious to know more about the origins of the St. Lawrence River, questioning Hurons who came to trade at Quebec concerning their homelands. The Hurons spoke of great interlocking expanses of water—those yet to be discovered by the Europeans and named Great Lakes. Champlain tried in vain in 1613 to journey to the Great Lakes by ascending the Ottawa River, the most direct path being blocked by hostile Iroquois tribesmen.

It was only several years later, after Champlain became a direct lieutenant of the French Viceroy and founder of what was known as Champlain's Company (composed of traders from Normandie), that a real French colony would develop. Champlain's Company was granted a monopoly of trade with the Indians of the St. Lawrence as far westward as they could succeed. Built into the organization of the chartered trading company was

Champlain and French Explorations, 1603-1616

The greatest French explorer of North America, Samuel de Champlain, spent half his lifetime making numerous voyages to the regions surrounding the Gulf of St. Lawrence and the St. Lawrence River. He founded the city of Quebec, traversed the rapids near Montreal that had barred the way to the Great Lakes, and spent months with Algonquian and Huron Indians during his explorations of the lands near Lakes Huron and Ontario.

a mandate to support the work of French missionary friars called the Recollects, who represented a reformed branch of the Franciscan Order. The Recollects claimed that they were the first to hold a formal ceremony of the Mass in Canada in June, 1615. It was a Recollect missionary, not the explorer Champlain himself, who was the first European to set foot on the easternmost shores of the Great Lakes.

Not much success was registered by the French in the Great Lakes area in this early period, partially because a decision was made to choose Huron peace and trade offers rather than to struggle to win over Iroquois friendship. This meant that the Champlain Company based in Quebec carried on more trade in the rather bleak areas to the north, rather than penetrating the more fertile regions of what would become New York and Pennsylvania, eventually areas where British colonial claims, together with complex relations with the Iroquois, would expand.

During the second half of the sixteenth century a few other French expeditions came into contact with Indian groupings, but in general they decided not to insist on fixed colonization, which inevitably involved a need for military defense and possibly sustained warfare. French expeditions preferred to develop mobile trading networks instead. The lucrative attractions of the fur trade would leave a characteristic stamp on the actions of the *coureurs de bois* ("woods runners," or trappers), who would cover vast inland areas and develop particular relations with several tribes. The nature of traders' alliances with Indians would change significantly in the eighteenth century colonial period, when military considerations in dealing with British enemies in colonial North America came to the forefront.

From Exploration to Conquest. One of the most famous *coureurs* was Nicholas Perrot, who, after beginning but then abandoning training to enter the Jesuit Order and work among tribes as a missionary, began his career at twenty-six as the interpreter for the 1670 Daumont de St. Lusson (copper exploration) expedition into the Miami tribal area around Green Bay (now Wisconsin). Eventually Perrot mastered not only Algonquian but also a dozen other Indian dialects. The most far-seeing governors-general in Quebec, notably Louis de Baude, count of Frontenac, tended to place great confidence in the judgment of *coureurs* such as Perrot and sometimes even countered instructions from Paris in favor of "commonsense" counsel offered to them by those who knew the Indians best.

When French colonial policy toward the Indians came under the influence of aggressive governors-general such as the marquis de Denonville, however, relations could worsen overnight. By the mid-1680's de Denonville was convinced that his British colonial neighbors in New York (then under the governorate of Thomas Dongan) were stirring up Iroquois hostility against the French. When clumsy efforts to deal with the problem through hostage-taking and physical duress failed, de Denonville resorted to massive armed action in 1687, mainly against the Senecas near the present site of Rochester, New York. His force of French soldiers, accompanied by Indian Christian converts and tribesmen who had more interest in fighting Seneca enemies than in Christianity, numbered almost three thousand—nearly ten times the size of any previous military expedition.

Although de Denonville's battle tactics were not strikingly successful, his remarks revealed the psychological distance already growing between official colonizers of his ilk and the commonsense "forest runner" emissaries of New France who knew the manners and customs of the Indians and how to use them to obtain desired ends without violence. When his Indian allies fell ill from overeating (booty and animals taken from the Senecas), de Denonville observed with disgust that "it is a miserable business to command savages who, as soon as they have knocked the enemy on the head, ask for nothing but to go home and carry . . . scalps they have taken off like a skullcap" (quoted in Joseph Rutledge, *Century of Conflict*, New York, 1956, p. 58).

Contributions by French Christian Missionaries. The second main thrust of French influence into American Indian homelands before 1700 was religiously motivated. Among the earliest French Jesuit missions to establish relations with the broad tribal area they called Huronia was Father Bressani. The so-called Black Robes took on special status in dealing with the Hurons not with guns (and not even by formal conversion to Christianity) but by taking on the honorific function of tribal medicine men. Tensions mounted among various factions of Indians, however, when "converts" only, not those who rejected missionary overtures, received firearms from French suppliers (not from the missionaries themselves). By 1649, deteriorating conditions between Hurons and the Five Nations of the Iroquois led to defeat of the former by Seneca and Mohawk nations of the latter. Within five years of their Huron ally's loss, however, the French Jesuits received a request from the Onondaga middle tribe of the Iroquois for the establishment of a trading and missionary post to teach converts in their midst. This new French-Indian alliance was accompanied by arms supplies to aid the Onondagas not only in their war with the Eries but also in defending themselves against hostile attacks from their fellow Iroquois, the Mohawks. The policy would prove a failure when Mohawks destroyed the Onondaga mission in 1658. This act brought a special military force from France under the marquis de Tracy, who, after burning many villages, forced the Mohawks to accept the presence of missionaries in their midst.

Thereafter, Black Robe policy toward Indian converts in the region changed. To avoid intertribal warfare, the French sent individual converts away from their tribal homelands to mission reservations near the emergent French colonial center at Montreal. Descendants of these mixed Indian Christian communities, who came to form the most reliable allies of French colonists, were called Caughnawaga Mohawks (still identifiable in late twentieth century Canada as "Kahnawake" people, who live on a reservation bearing the same name).

Missionary-Explorers. Some seventeenth century French missionaries combined two callings—that of explorer and that of bearer of Christianity for people who were often considered outright savages—when they entered Indian territories beyond established colonies. One of the best-known French missionaries was Gabriel Sagard, a lay brother (not an ordained priest) in the Recollect Order. Sagard's famous 1632 account of his journey into Huronia contained numerous suggestions that the "savage" life of the

Indians contained many positive elements that could benefit European society, including simplicity of relations and rejection of selfish hoarding of material goods.

Sagard's 1632 account of the minute details of Indian habits, including their modes of preparing various foods, their dress, and their recreations, became the first widely read popular treatise on Gallia Nova. It would be greatly expanded in a second printing only four years after it first appeared. A second widely read account of French and Indian missionary encounters would appear exactly fifty years after Sagard's famous volume. The later work, by another Recollect, Louis Hennepin, was called "Description of Louisiana," a title that suggests how far westward and southward the French had explored since Sagard's experience among the Hurons.

Much credit for this wider exploration went to the Recollects' missionary "rivals," the French Jesuits. Jesuit Father Jacques Marquette, for example, together with Louis Jolliet, a former seminarian turned fur trader, were among the first white people to explore the Mississippi River Valley in the 1670's. It was they who opened the way for the extension of New France into the vast area that would be known as Louisiana (named for King Louis XIV). Jolliet's initial interest in proceeding farther west and south of the territory under Quebec's administrative control was to establish a settlement on the Illinois River. Unsuccessful in getting support for this, Jolliet took on the commissioned task of discovering the upper Mississippi itself. A wealth of information tracing Jolliet's progress is preserved in Father Marquette's journals, which begin when the party received aid from the Mascouten Indian people, whose territory in the Fox River Valley and the Meskousing (later "Wisconsin") River zone held the key to rapid canoe transit toward confluents of the Mississippi. One of these, then called the Pekitonoui River, passed through the territory of the Illinois tribes. There Marquette would later found, on his return north after their long journey down the Mississippi to the point where it is joined by the Arkansas River, the Mission of the Conception in the tiny Indian village of Kaskaskia. He died there in 1675, only to be succeeded by generations of French missionaries and fur traders who would open the Mississippi to extensive exploration and settlement far beyond the new "capital" of St. Louis. By 1700, when Father Jacques Gravier had taken charge of Marquette's Indian mission program among the Kaskaskia of Illinois, he decided to establish a network of communications to link the Illinois mission to new French settlements as far south as Biloxi (the future state of Mississippi, settled from the New Orleans delta northward). Gravier's 1700 contacts with the Akansa (Quapaw) Indians (who had seen Marquette in 1674) were already tinged with hints of possible hostile reactions by Mississippi Valley Indians to what they feared would be increased takeover of their lands by French settlements.

By 1711 and 1712, all the way back north in the Fox River Valley, where Marquette had begun among friends in the 1670's, the hostilities later known as the Fox Wars began, and the safety of the French in a great number of previously peaceful areas would be placed in jeopardy.

The French fur traders, called *voyageurs* ("travelers") as well as *coureurs de bois*, in order to survive in relative isolation among the Indians far from colonial military forts or missionary zones, consciously chose to develop close personal ties with the tribes. They often established networks of what amounted to political as well as trading relationships with different groups by marrying Indian women and adopting many aspects of the Indian way of life. Fur trader knowledge of Indian customs, as well as the configurations of tribal alliances, would serve the needs of more official political pol-

Mississippi Valley:
The Marquette/Jolliet and La Salle Expeditions, 1673-1682

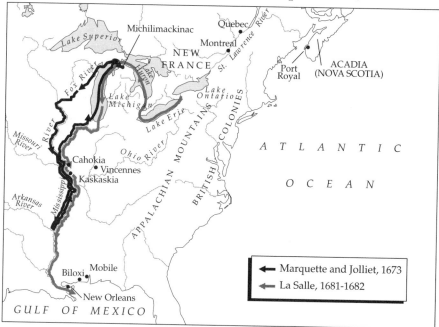

Among the many French explorations of the Mississippi River Valley, that of Jacques Marquette and Louis Jolliet is famous as the first major expedition into the region. That of René Robert Cavelier, sieur de La Salle, was the first to reach the mouth of the Mississippi River, confirming that the great midcontinental waterway emptied into the Gulf of Mexico.

icies of administrative authorities of New France when the latter faced military challenges from their main colonial rivals, the British.

Relations During the Seven Years' War. Historians often refer to the French and Indian War (1754-1763) between France and England as the North American manifestation of the Seven Years' War (the war between Frederick the Great of Prussia, aided by England, and France, aided by Austria and Russia) because of the importance of English and French alliances with Indian tribes in Canada and several of the thirteen American colonies. For the French, many of these alliances predated the formal period of war by more than half a century. One of France's long-established goals in what would become the United States was to hold the limit of British colonization to east of the Appalachian Mountains. Because so few actual French fighting units were present in the vast territories it wished to defend against British occupation, French emissaries in essence "recruited" Indian groups to fight for them against the British. The appointment in 1752 of Marquis Ange Duquesne de Menneville as France's governor-general in Quebec came with instructions to block all British attempts to penetrate the Ohio Territory, a move that could cut off north-south contact between France's Canadian and "Louisianan" colonies. As the much more serious declaration of war in Europe approached, Duquesne soon followed the example of one of his agents, Charles Langlade, who had led Ottawa, Potawatomi, and Ojibwa Indian allies in attacks against other Indians who had joined the Iroquois Covenant Chain (including the Delawares, or Lenni Lenape) and were being courted as potential allies of the British cause. When it came to struggles over control of the famous Fort Duquesne, the French attempted to rely on support from so-called Three Fires Indians, who came from points far to the west, where Indian sensitivity to threats of seizure of their lands was not yet as highly developed as it was in the Ohio Territory.

As the terms of war became even more serious, the French strategy of allying with Indians who thought they might regain lands lost to British colonizers seemed to be succeeding. Not only the Lenni Lenapes but also the Shawnees and even some Iroquois broke away from British support to help the French in their attempts to expel English colonizers from Iroquoia (New York). British General John Forbes and a Quaker colonist leader named Israel Pemberton finally succeeded in turning the tide of French and Indian superiority in 1758, when a treaty with the Delawares signed at Easton, Pennsylvania, promised to establish a firm boundary between British and Indian territory after the war. When the struggle finally ended in 1763, the French essentially lost their entire Canadian and Northeast North American colonial empire. For many of their former Indian allies, this defeat meant an unclear future. At Fort Niagara, for example, Seneca Indians were expelled from a stronghold they had held for the French. British control, although it would last only another twenty years in the thirteen colonies, rapidly brought quite different conditions for the Indian people of North America.

See also: French and Indian War; Indian-white relations: Canadian; Indian-white relations: Dutch colonial; Indian-white relations: English colonial; Indian-white relations: Norse; Indian-white relations: Russian colonial; Indian-white relations: Spanish colonial; Indian-white relations: Swedish colonial; Indian-white relations: U.S., 1775-1830; Indian-white relations: U.S., 1831-1870; Indian-white relations: U.S., 1871-1933; Indian-white relations: U.S., 1934-2002.

Byron D. Cannon

Sources for Further Study

Douville, Raymond, and Jacques Casanova. *Daily Life in Early Canada*. New York: Macmillan, 1967. Although this carefully documented study concentrates on various conditions affecting French colonial life in Gallia Nova (transportation, religious life, trapping, and trading), each chapter includes useful information on relations with Indian populations.

Hamilton, Raphael N. *Marquette's Explorations: The Narratives Reexamined*. Madison: University of Wisconsin Press, 1970. This scholarly monograph not only describes the experiences of Father Marquette before and during his famous exploration of the 1670's but also provides a critical analysis of the authenticity of manuscript sources ascribed to Marquette.

Jennings, Francis. *The Founders of America*. New York: W. W. Norton, 1993. An excellent general history of the Indian population of all regions of North America from precolonial to contemporary times. The colonial section contains essential facts of French and Indian relations.

Rutledge, Joseph Lister. *Century of Conflict*. Garden City, N.Y.: Doubleday, 1956. A comprehensive account of American Indian relations with both French and British colonial regimes from the early to the late eighteenth century, including the key Seven Years' War period.

Sagard, Gabriel. *The Long Journey to the Country of the Hurons*. Translated by Hugh H. Langton. Toronto: Champlain Society, 1939. This is a translation of the French explorer's original travel logs, published in 1632.

Sleeper-Smith, Susan. *Indian Women and French Men: Rethinking Cultural Encounter in the Western Great Lakes*. Amherst: University of Massachusetts Press, 2001. Considers the effect of Indian women married to French men upon the early colonial fur trade.

Indian-white relations: Norse

Date: 1000's-1500's
Locale: Greenland, eastern Canada, eastern seaboard
Tribes involved: Algonquian, Inugsuk, Iroquois, possibly Mandan, Thule
Categories: Pre-Columbian history
Significance: For five hundred years before Christopher Columbus's voyage to the Caribbean islands in 1492, people from Scandinavia interacted with the indigenous population of North America; the Norse traded with, influenced, and were influenced by American Indians.

Until relatively recently, most historians considered the enduring folktales concerning pre-Columbian Norse colonization of North America and contacts with its aboriginal population to be nothing more than romantic fiction. The few scholars who did take seriously the Icelandic sagas, on which the folktales were based, assumed that the alleged Norse-Indian contacts had little or no historical significance.

Despite the disinterest of the academic community, many amateur historians and archaeologists pursued the story of the pre-Columbian Norse in North America with an enthusiasm often bordering on fanaticism. Since at least the seventeenth century, sincere but often ignorant proponents of the Norse presence in North America before Columbus have put forth evidence for their claims in the form of maps, runestones, and purportedly Norse-made artifacts. Some of this supposed evidence proved to be the product of hoaxes, which cast doubt on the entire thesis of an early Norse presence in North America.

Archaeological discoveries during the last third of the twentieth century, however, showed conclusively that the Norse established permanent colonies on the North American continent. At L'Anse aux Meadows in Newfoundland, archaeologists have excavated an entire Norse village, dated by radiocarbon methods to around 1000 C.E. or a little earlier. Other archaeologists have recovered indisputably Norse artifacts from dozens of Eskimos (Inuit) sites throughout northern Canada. These discoveries have caused historians to begin reexamining the original Icelandic sources that told of the Norse movement into the area west of Greenland and other evidence of Norse-Indian interaction.

Background. Three Icelandic sagas, probably composed in the twelfth and thirteenth centuries (*Eirik's Saga, Karlsefni Saga,* and the *Graenlendinga Saga*), constitute the primary historical source material for a pre-Columbian Norse presence in North America. Other sagas contain numerous references to the subject but give little detail. The Icelandic sagas began as oral history—stories about people and events passed along orally from generation to generation. Icelandic scribes probably wrote down the stories dealing with what the Greenland Norse called "Vinland the Good" (which many scholars today believe was the coast of New England) in the late fourteenth century.

These sagas tell first of the Norse colonization of Greenland in 985-986 C.E. by Eric the Red. Shortly afterward, according to the sagas, Bjarni Herjolfsson accidentally sighted what must have been the coast of North America when a storm blew his ship off course. After hearing Herjolfsson's story, Leif Eriksson, known as Leif the Lucky, Eric's son, bought Herjolfsson's ship some years later (around the year 1000) and sailed west from Greenland searching for the land his predecessor had seen. He found several islands or promontories and gave them names during this voyage: Helluland (which many historians now believe was Baffin Island), Markland (often identified with Labrador), and finally Vinland. The sagas relate that Vinland abounded with wild grape vines (thus the name), game of all types, and fertile soil; the rivers teemed with fish. Leif and the thirty-five men who sailed with him built permanent dwellings and explored the surrounding area for almost a year. The next spring, Leif sailed back to Greenland with a cargo of timber, grapes, and grape vines.

The Norse and the Indians. Eric the Red died during the winter following Leif's return from Vinland. Leif became too engrossed in his duties as chieftain of the Greenland colony to follow up his voyage of discovery. The sagas record three more expeditions from the Greenland colony to Vinland during subsequent years. According to the sagas, the Norse encountered aborigines they called Skraelings (literally "wretches") in Vinland and interacted with them on several occasions. If the sagas are correct, the Norse both exploited the Skraelings in trade and killed them in battle and by treachery.

The sagas give no details about any subsequent Norse exploits in Vinland. Despite the anecdotal and undoubtedly embellished nature of the sagas, they have a ring of truth about them. After the archaeological discoveries at L'Anse aux Meadows, many historians have come to regard the sagas as valuable sources (although ones to be used with caution) about the first European contacts with American Indians. From the accounts in the sagas it must be concluded that the Norse exploited the Indians in trade as callously as did the Spanish, Dutch, English, and French after Columbus.

The Norse of the sagas had no more compunction about killing the Indians than did the later European explorers.

Other evidence, however, suggests that contacts between the Norse and the Indians were not always as hostile, or trade so one-sided, as portrayed in the sagas. Since 1960, archaeologists have discovered numerous artifacts in Eskimo sites throughout northern and central Canada of undoubted Norse manufacture. These objects include wrought-iron axes, iron spearheads, and carved figurines. Such finds suggest extensive trade between the Norse and American Indians. The game of lacrosse, taught by the Algonquian Indians to French and British colonists, resembles an ancient Norse game so closely that several historians are convinced it is the same game. The Norse introduced it in Vinland, they argue, and from there it spread throughout the pre-Columbian American northeast. If this theory is correct, it suggests amiable relations between the Norse and Indians over a considerable period of time.

One linguist has compiled a large collection of Northeast Indian (especially Iroquois) words that are pronounced similarly and have meanings similar to those of words in the old Norse language. The language similarity again suggests long and continued contact between the two peoples. Many anthropologists also believe that the Norse left their genes among American Indians, especially several groups of Eskimos and tribes of the interior such as the Mandans. These groups display or displayed a number of European characteristics when first encountered by post-Columbian colonists, including fair hair, light-colored eyes, exceptionally tall stature, and luxuriant beards. If this assessment is accurate, the Norse did not launch a war of extermination against the Indians, as did later waves of colonists, but rather merged their culture with those of the aborigines.

See also: Indian-white relations: Canadian; Indian-white relations: Dutch colonial; Indian-white relations: English colonial; Indian-white relations: French colonial; Indian-white relations: Russian colonial; Indian-white relations: Spanish colonial; Indian-white relations: Swedish colonial; Indian-white relations: U.S., 1775-1830; Indian-white relations: U.S., 1831-1870; Indian-white relations: U.S., 1871-1933; Indian-white relations: U.S., 1934-2002.

Paul Madden

Sources for Further Study

Enterline, James Robert. *Viking America: The Norse Crossings and Their Legacy.* Epilogue by Thor Heyerdahl. Garden City, N.Y.: Doubleday, 1972.

Magnusson, Magnus, and Hermann Palsson, eds. and trans. *The Vinland Sagas: The Norse Discovery of America.* New York: Penguin Books, 1980.

Mowat, Farley. *Westviking: The Ancient Norse in Greenland and North America*. Boston: Little, Brown, 1965.

Reman, Edward. *The Norse Discoveries and Explorations in America*. Berkeley: University of California Press, 1949.

Wahlgren, Erik. *The Vikings and America*. London: Thames & Hudson, 1986.

Indian-white relations: Russian colonial

Date: 1741-1867
Locale: Alaska
Tribes involved: Aleut, Inuit, Yupik, other western Subarctic and Northwest Coast tribes
Categories: Colonial history, Religion and missionary activities
Significance: Russia first encountered New World indigenous people while trading furs and missionizing in the area of present-day Alaska.

Russian traders made contact with many Indian tribes along the western Canadian and northwestern American coasts, from Alaska south to northern California. Their strongest influence, however, was felt in the Arctic and Subarctic areas by the Eskimos and Aleuts. There were very few early contacts between Eskimos and Europeans because of the remoteness of the Arctic region. Soon after the first encounters, which began with the Russians, the fur trade drew most European powers into the area. This led to a radical change in the nature of indigenous Arctic culture.

Historical Background. Cossacks first heard of the Aleuts when they arrived in Siberia in 1650. The Russians were continuing a policy of eastward expansion and exploration in search of pelts. The indigenous people in Siberia told of their trading with groups in the Aleutian Islands. The desire for sea otter furs, a maritime product, pushed the Russian traders farther to the east into the "Great Land." Knowledge of Europeans and their culture, therefore, reached the Aleuts more than a century before actual European contact.

Alaskan Eskimos first came into contact with Europeans in 1741, at the time of Vitus Bering's expedition on behalf of Russia. Bering was a Danish explorer whose task was to extend the fur trade that had started in Siberia. Sea otter fur obtained on the second Bering expedition precipitated the arrival of many traders in the Aleutian Islands, as they left Siberia for this lu-

Voyages to Alaska, 1728-1769

Between 1728 and 1769, the Russian government sponsored several important expeditions to explore the waters and lands across what came to be known as the Bering Strait, named after the most important of these explorers, Vitus Bering.

crative fur trade. Eskimos were hospitable to the Russian explorers, providing their guests with music, dancing, and feasting. They were also, however, skillful traders who drove hard bargains for pelts in order to obtain metal and enamel buttons, Siberian sabers, blue glass beads, and knives. In exchange, the Russians received skins of river otter, red fox, marten, and wolverine.

Traders moving from island to island through the Aleutian chain had reached the Alaska peninsula by 1762. The Aleuts were often brutalized in the process. Aleut laborers were required to pay a tax (*yasak*). In an effort to help stem the cruel treatment by traders, the Russian government made the Aleuts Russian subjects in 1766. The yasak payment was revoked in 1788. Between 1743 and 1797, dozens of Russian companies made numerous voyages along the Aleutians. These companies obtained almost 200,000 pelts worth almost eight million rubles.

Colonization. In Southern Alaska, Grigory Shelekhov and Ivan Golikov founded the first colony at Three Saints Bay, Kodiak Island. Shelekhov was granted a charter in 1799 to form the Russian-American Company as a twenty-year monopoly, although the Imperial Navy undertook an independent expedition in search of a northern path to the Atlantic. More charters were made in 1821 and 1844. The first company chief decreed that the natives must labor for the company. Natives hunted sea otter under dangerous conditions including the possibility of attack by the Tlingit Indians and the threat of bad weather. Official government policy sought to treat the Eskimos and Aleuts fairly, but local exploitation of laborers by traders was common. Each year, sea otter pelts and seal skins were shipped through Siberia to Moscow and then on to China.

There was much intermarriage between Russian hunters and native women. The children of these unions were recognized by a charter of 1821 as Russian subjects. Neither they nor their mothers could leave the colony. Intermarriage was a key factor in the radical cultural changes that took place among the natives of the Arctic region.

With the establishment of St. Michael in 1833, commercial trade became of major importance. A few years later, however, the first of a series of devastating epidemics attacked the area of Norton Sound and southern Alaska. In some parts of the south, up to 50 percent of the population perished. The Aleut population dropped from about seven thousand in 1836 to about four thousand in 1840, the year the epidemic ended. The Russians were able to contain the epidemic through a rigorous vaccination program which began in 1838.

Russian Orthodox Church. The missionaries of the Russian Orthodox church altered Aleut culture as much as the commercialization process. Virtually all Aleuts were converted to Christianity, but the more numerous Tlingits resisted missionization and commercialization. The Russian-American Company and the Russian Orthodox Church were often at odds with each other over the control of the region. Father Ivan Veniaminov was the first priest concerned with indigenous people in the northern areas; he arrived in 1829. From a mission on the Yukon River, established in 1844, priests visited the surrounding villages. After the U.S. purchase of Alaska in 1867, most clergy personnel were withdrawn, but a school in St. Michael remained active.

Much of the Aleut culture underwent radical transformation. The new form of religion was markedly different from the former traditional practice. Both the new modes of labor and the amount of intermarriage with Russians had profound effects on social organization. Disease, resettlement, and other effects of contact followed the well-known destructive pattern experienced by the indigenous peoples of the New World.

See also: Bering Strait migrations; Indian-white relations: Canadian; Indian-white relations: Dutch colonial; Indian-white relations: English colonial; Indian-white relations: French colonial; Indian-white relations: Norse; Indian-white relations: Spanish colonial; Indian-white relations: Swedish colonial; Indian-white relations: U.S., 1775-1830; Indian-white relations:

U.S., 1831-1870; Indian-white relations: U.S., 1871-1933; Indian-white relations: U.S., 1934-2002; Prehistory: Arctic; Prehistory: Subarctic.

William H. Green

Sources for Further Study

Chevigny, Hector. *Russian America: The Great Alaskan Venture, 1741-1867.* New York: Viking Press, 1965.

Gibson, James R. *Imperial Russia in Frontier America: The Changing Geography of Supply of Russian America, 1784-1867.* New York: Oxford University Press, 1976.

Kan, Sergei. *Memory Eternal: Tlingit Culture and Russian Orthodox Christianity Through Two Centuries.* Seattle: University of Washington Press, 1999.

Mangusso, Mary Childers, and Stephen W. Haycox, eds. *Interpreting Alaska's History: An Anthology.* Anchorage: Alaska Pacific University Press, 1989.

Oswalt, Wendell H. *Mission of Change in Alaska.* San Marino, Calif.: Huntington Library, 1963.

Ray, Dorothy Jean. *The Eskimos of Bering Strait, 1650-1898.* Seattle: University of Washington Press, 1975.

Sherwood, Morgan B., ed. *Alaska and Its History.* Seattle: University of Washington Press, 1967.

_____. *Exploration of Alaska, 1865-1900.* New Haven, Conn.: Yale University Press, 1965.

Indian-white relations: Spanish colonial

Date: 1492-1820's
Locale: Southern, western, and southwestern North America
Tribes involved: Apache, Apalachee, Chumash, Pueblo, Timucua, Yuma
Categories: Colonial history, Religion and missionary activities
Significance: The Spanish Empire imposed a heavy cost on the Indian peoples of North America from the 1570's until its collapse in the 1820's, in spite of Native Americans' valiant efforts to deal with its demands peacefully.

The Indians of North America escaped the violence and disruption of the early Spanish conquest only to encounter later imperial thrusts that contained the seeds of conflict. From the arrival of Christopher Columbus in 1492 to Hernán Cortés's victory over the Aztecs in 1521, the Spanish established their control of the Caribbean area. The riches of the Aztecs inspired expeditions southward to conquer the Inca Empire, but probings into North America failed to locate concentrations of gold or large urban centers. Yet the 3,000-mile stretch of territory from Florida to California became a vital but vulnerable frontier for the Spanish. They wanted to defend the lifeline of their New World empire, which stretched from Mexico to Hispaniola and on to Spain, by the establishment of settlements along the southern fringe of what is now the United States. Relations between the Indians of North America and the colonists and institutions of the empire were characterized by periods of tentative harmony under Spanish domination followed by the growth of tension and distrust among the natives, which often resulted in alienation, rejection, and, in a few cases, open rebellion.

Before the arrival of the Spanish, the Native American peoples along the southern rim of North America had evolved a large variety of languages and cultures that, while lacking the urbanization and centralization of the Aztecs, had internal strengths of their own. From the Apalachees of what is now northern Florida to the Chumash along the California coast, life usually centered on the extended family and villages with various combinations of hunting, gathering, and small-scale agriculture to supply material needs. All was not harmony in pre-conquest North America, however, as the strained relationship between the Pueblos and Apaches revealed. The Pueblos of the upper Rio Grande Valley lived a sedentary existence in their multistory stone and adobe houses. Their agricultural practices gave them a fairly stable source of food in contrast to their neighbors, the Apaches, who were wandering hunter-gatherers. When the Apaches' supplies ran short, they would sometimes raid the villages of the more prosperous Pueblos.

Spanish Institutions. These Apache-Pueblo conflicts were of limited duration, but the arrival of the Spanish brought major disruptions that would permanently change the lives of the Indians. The Spanish transplanted institutions previously established in Mexico, Peru, and other imperial centers. The *encomienda*, a type of land grant, was for many years their chief method of commanding Indian labor. The *encomendero* (holder of the *encomienda*) controlled Indian workers in exchange for a commitment to protect and to provide for them. A second system of labor supervision was the *repartimiento*, in which colonial officials assigned native workers to a particular settler for a certain amount of time. Although in theory these situations were regulated by colonial officials, in practice *encomenderos* and settlers took advantage of their Indian charges by requiring them to work beyond the original agreements. In addition to the *encomienda* and *repartimiento*, the Spanish enslaved natives as personal servants or as laborers in their agricultural or trading enterprises.

These labor practices, often harsh and exploitative, drew the protests of Catholic missionaries. The priests assigned to frontier areas from Florida to California brought with them an awareness of the ideals of Bartolomé de Las Casas, who, from the 1520's until his death in 1566, campaigned against the mistreatment of Native Americans. These missionaries, usually members of the Franciscan order along the North American frontier, attempted to convert the Indians to Christianity. Their missions often served the natives as havens from the demands of *encomenderos*, settlers, and even government officials.

The presidio, a small fort manned by a detachment of soldiers, generally accompanied the mission. The original purpose of these frontier forts was to protect the missionaries, settlers, and friendly natives from attacks by European rivals such as the British and the French and their Indian allies. As internal institutional and political disputes arose, however, these soldiers were sometimes deployed against the mission Indians to serve the demands of settlers and officials for additional land or native laborers.

Historical records of the interaction of the Indians and the Spanish tend to emphasize institutions such as the mission and the presidio, but the native response to the arrival of the Spanish was much more subtle than early studies limited to archives reveal. Spanish friars reported massive conversions of Indians to Christianity in remarkably short periods of time, but these apparent conversions may have been simply the natives' way of attempting to develop good relations with the Europeans rather than the profoundly religious experiences often described in the reports. The Indians did not passively accept Spanish dominance but rather found ways to accommodate demands for conversion and for labor while, at the same time, preserving much of their own autonomy and tradition.

Florida. The Franciscans began their work in Florida in 1573 and within eighty years had erected more than thirty missions extending northward and westward in two chains from their base in St. Augustine. The Franciscans used music, paintings, and colorful ceremonies to attract the natives' attention. They claimed that twenty-six thousand converts had accepted Christianity by 1655 (this claim is disputed by many historians). The Apalachees, Timucuas, and other nearby tribes were receptive to the missionaries in the early years in part as a response to the Franciscan appeals; however, the Indians also saw strategic advantages in an alliance with the missionaries for protection against Spanish settlers and soldiers. The na-

Nineteenth century painter Frederic Remington's fanciful depiction of Francisco Vásquez de Coronado's march through Colorado in 1541 in search of a kingdom known to him as Gran Quivira. Much of what drove the early Spanish explorers was a search for gold and other riches. (Library of Congress)

tives' selective acceptance of Catholicism was indicated by their placement of Christian images among their traditional religious symbols.

The tensions in the Indian-Spanish relationships exploded in the early 1700's under additional pressures from British settlements to the north. The British founded Charleston in 1670 and began to push to the interior, thereby posing a threat to the mission-presidio system stretching out from St. Augustine. The Charlestonians recruited nonmission Indians and welcomed the alienated natives who left the Spanish. The Indians, caught in the struggle between the two European powers, found it necessary to take sides or abandon the area. One Apalachee chief, Patricio de Hinachuba, urged Spanish officials to end their abusive policies in order to hold the support of his people and other nearby tribes. Patricio, a perceptive leader, attempted to represent the interests of the Apalachee while remaining within the Spanish orbit. Through personal diplomacy with the British in 1706, he managed to spare his village from attack and then led his followers toward St. Augustine for sanctuary. His hopes were dashed, however, when a group of pro-British Indians attacked his band just outside the large stone fortifications of St. Augustine. Patricio de Hinachuba perished along with his Apalachee community.

The defeat of the Spanish in the early 1700's was a symptom of the decline of the missions. The British military attacks were important factors in the Spanish loss, but the defection of many of the mission Indians in this time of crisis was also important. As Patricio de Hinachuba attempted to explain to the Spanish, the onerous burdens of *repartimiento* and slavery weighed heavily on many Native American communities. Apparently many Indians joined the British as an act of rebellion against the Spanish. Only a few Indians remained with the missions at the stronghold of St. Augustine and a handful of sites scattered across the northern part of Florida. These defections, however, brought few if any improvements for the Indians: The British also resorted to enslavement of the able-bodied natives and proved as aggressive as the Spanish in usurping land.

New Mexico. While different in many details, the Spanish colonial effort along the upper Rio Grande in what is now New Mexico and western Texas bore a resemblance to the rise and fall of the mission-presidio system in Florida. Although the New Mexico project may appear to have been a logical extension of Spanish settlements in northern Mexico, the expedition of explorer of Juan de Oñate in 1598 marked a significant leap for the Spanish across rugged deserts and through hostile Indian territory. New Mexico, like Florida, was isolated from the core areas of the empire and constituted not only an effort to bring Christianity and European civilization to the Native Americans but also a barrier to the occupation of the region by European rivals.

Oñate's settlements took hold, and by the 1620's New Mexico seemed to be a healthy and prosperous colony; particularly impressive was the work of the Franciscan missionaries. By 1629 they had established fifty missions that on a map formed the pattern of a cross running northward up the Rio Grande to the settlement in Taos; the arms of the cross extended westward to the Zuñi and Hopi pueblos and eastward to Pecos. Father Alonso de Benavides' report that the Franciscans had baptized eighty-six thousand Indians circulated not only in Mexico City but also in Madrid and Rome.

The actual relationship between the Pueblo Indians and the Franciscans was less dramatic than these early reports indicated. The Pueblos probably turned to the missionaries and the accompanying Spanish soldiers for security against their long-time neighbors and periodic adversaries, the Apaches. The Pueblos were impressed by the church's religious ceremonies, the support that the clerics received from military and government officials, and the Franciscans' presentation of Christian doctrine. The Pueblos, however, much like the Apalachees and Timucuas of Florida, accepted portions of the missionaries' messages while retaining significant components of their own beliefs and customs.

Inevitably, the arrival of the Spanish took a toll on the natives. The initial excitement gave way to the more practical problems of work, food, and clothing. Oñate secured imperial approval for *encomiendas* for himself and a few of the prominent early settlers. These grants placed certain Indian villages under a legal obligation to pay tribute (a tax) to the *encomenderos*. Soon colonial officials established the *repartimiento* as a means of supplying young Indians to work for settlers. Colonial governors of New Mexico often used the *repartimiento*—and even illegal slave labor—in agricultural and commercial enterprises to augment their salaries. Pueblo communities, with this loss of the labor of many of their vigorous males and females, experienced not only an indignity but also a growing difficulty in feeding themselves.

The natives' frustrations with these conditions erupted in small rebellions as early as 1632 at Zuñi and 1639-1640 at Taos, but the Spanish seemed to ignore these ominous signs. Crop losses from bad weather in the 1660's and 1670's and intensified Apache raids added to the Pueblos' difficulties. A leader capable of unifying Indian resistance appeared in the person of Popé, a Pueblo religious mystic punished by the Spanish for alleged sorcery. In August and September of 1680, Popé led a large portion of the seventeen thousand Pueblos in an uprising that killed more than four hundred of New Mexico's twenty-five hundred Spanish settlers and sent the survivors fleeing down the Rio Grande to El Paso. After the expulsion of the Spanish, the native leadership openly rejected Christianity and discouraged the use of the Spanish language. Although the Spanish returned to New Mexico in the early 1690's, the growth of the colony was slow, and its reputation as a center for peaceful conversion was discredited.

Frontier Struggles of the Eighteenth Century. The Indians' defections and rebellions in Florida and New Mexico did not force the Spanish to abandon the northern edge of their American empire, but these events dramatized the need for new approaches in their relations with American Indians. Also, the 1763 acquisition of the vast territory of Louisiana placed new pressures on Indian-Spanish relations. Imperial defense policy called for control of the Apaches and other mobile tribes of Texas because they threatened access to Louisiana by land from northern Mexico.

The Apaches roamed the large area between New Mexico and the small group of missions precariously planted around San Antonio in eastern Texas. The basic unit of Apache social organization was the extended family, and for their material existence, they relied on hunting and gathering, limited agriculture, and, when shortages developed, raids on nearby sedentary Pueblos. In their small, migratory groups, the Apaches confused the confounded Spanish officials, who, in spite of the efforts of missionaries and soldiers, found it impossible to bring them into the colonial system.

The most intensive effort to deal with the Apaches came in the initiatives of José de Gálvez, a powerful colonial official in the 1770's and 1780's. Gálvez continued military actions against the Apaches but also incorporated the French and British strategies of stimulating trade with the natives along the northern frontier to undermine tribal autonomy. Gálvez authorized the sale of alcohol and poorly made firearms to the Apaches. The alcohol was intended to create a dependency among the natives on their merchant-suppliers, and the firearms would require frequent repair and replacement. Historian David J. Weber summarized the new policies as the adoption of "tried and true English and French practices to destroy the basis of native culture" in order to achieve with "the iron fist and the velvet glove what missionaries had been unable to do through less violent and cynical means." Gálvez's changes came too late for the Spanish Empire, however; within a generation, the expansion of the United States and the independence of Mexico would remove Spanish control from the borderlands area.

California. Gálvez also pushed Spanish settlements into Alta California (the present state of California) in response to the rumored encroachments of the Russians moving down the Pacific coast from Alaska. Gálvez did not like the flawed mission-presidio system, but financial problems forced him to implant a variation of this approach in California in 1769. Franciscans led by Junípero Serra recaptured some of the enthusiasm of the first generations of missionaries in Florida and New Mexico. Within five years they had nearly five thousand Indians living on their missions. Mission life for the Chumash and other tribes, while pleasant at first, became another disastrous encounter with Europeans. Epidemic diseases and crowded living quarters brought high infant mortality rates and a rapid decline in the Indian population of California, from about 300,000 in 1769 to perhaps 200,000 in 1821. Many natives eventually fled the missions, but except for the Yumas' attack on the settlements along the California side of the lower Colorado River in 1781, Indian violence against the Spanish was rare. Although these desertions and the decline of the native population strained the Indian-Spanish relationship, the missions enjoyed some prosperity and were among Spain's most viable settlements in California in 1821 when Mexican independence brought an end to the empire in the borderlands.

While Indian-Spanish relations were generally dominated by the Europeans, the natives were resourceful in many of their earlier efforts to limit foreign influences. They had their greatest successes with subtle, diplomatic adjustments to the peaceful methods of the missionaries. The influence of these missionaries, however, survived for only a few decades. Eventually the trauma of epidemic diseases and the burdens of forced labor, tribute payment, and cultural-religious impositions kindled hostile reactions among many native groups. In the borderlands areas, the Spanish were often motivated by strategic factors in response to the expansive actions of their European rivals. These strategic concerns frequently placed military policies at the forefront in Indian-Spanish relations, especially in response to native unrest and rebellion. The ultimate outcome of the clash between Native Americans and the Spanish favored the latter; Native Americans paid an immense price in terms of life, culture, and property.

See also: Acoma, Battle of; California missions; Epidemics and diseases; Gadsden Purchase; Guadalupe Hidalgo, Treaty of; Indian-white relations: English colonial; Indian-white relations: French colonial; Indian-white relations: Russian colonial; Pima uprisings; Prehistory: California; Prehistory: Southwest; Pueblo Revolt; Taos Rebellion; Zuñi Rebellion.

John A. Britton

Sources for Further Study

Hanke, Lewis. *The Spanish Struggle for Justice in the Conquest of America*. Boston: Little, Brown, 1965. Historical study of the Spanish debate concerning the treatment of Indians, with emphasis on the work of Bartolomé de Las Casas.

Hann, John. *Apalachee: The Land Between the Rivers*. Gainesville: University Presses of Florida, 1988. An in-depth synthesis of a crucial area in Indian-Spanish relations based on thorough research and thoughtful analysis.

Jackson, Robert H., and Edward Castillo. *Indians, Franciscans, and Spanish Colonization: The Impact of the Mission System on California Indians*. Albuquerque: University of New Mexico Press, 1995. An ethnohistory of Indian life under the mission system.

John, Elizabeth A. H. *Storms Brewed in Other Men's Worlds: The Confrontation of the Indians, Spanish, and French in the Southwest, 1540-1795*. College Station: Texas A&M University Press, 1975. Readable overview of the confrontations involving the Indians, Spanish, and French in the American Southwest from 1540 to 1795. Heavy emphasis on the Native Americans' responses.

McAlister, Lyle. *Spain and Portugal in the New World, 1492-1700*. Minneapolis: University of Minnesota Press, 1984. Includes a clearly written account of Spain's general imperial policies such as the *encomienda* and the *repartimiento*.

Sandos, James. "Junípero Serra's Canonization and the Historical Record." *American Historical Review* 93 (December, 1988): 1253-1269. An important article on the controversies surrounding the early California missions.

Spicer, Edward H. *Cycles of Conquest: The Impact of Spain, Mexico, and the United States on the Indians of the Southwest, 1553-1960*. Tucson: University of Arizona Press, 1962. Broad study of the impact of several generations of outside cultural, economic, and military invasions on the Indian peoples. Somewhat dated by more recent research but contains much useful material.

Todorov, Tzvetan. *The Conquest of America: The Question of the Other*. Translated by Richard Howard. Norman: University of Oklahoma Press, 1999. Investigates the cultural clash between Spanish and Native American mentalities and explores the European conquest of North America as a semiotic process.

Weber, David J. *The Spanish Frontier in North America*. New Haven, Conn.: Yale University Press, 1992. Excellent detailed synthesis of Spanish imperial efforts from Florida to California based on a comprehensive survey of the research in the field. Includes historical, ethnographic, and archaeological sources to provide a balance of European and Native American points of view. Extensive footnotes and lengthy bibliography provide the reader with valuable citations for further research.

Indian-white relations: Swedish colonial

Date: 1600's
Locale: Delaware River Valley
Tribes involved: Asseteque, Lenni Lenape, Mingo, Nanticoke
Categories: Colonial history
Significance: Swedish colonial ventures to the Delaware River Valley during the seventeenth century had a lasting impact on the American Indians who inhabited the region, particularly the Lenni Lenape and the Mingo; Swedish occupation, although relatively peaceful, caused the Indians' removal from the area.

Contact between American Indians and Europeans in North America during the seventeenth century embodied a wide range of experiences. One component often overlooked is the Swedish venture into the Middle Atlantic region. Although their official occupation was relatively brief—1638 to 1655—they had a lasting impact on the area and the Indians that they encountered. Their officials set the stage for later English negotiations with the Indians of the area, and their colonists contributed to the ethnic diversity of the region. The Swedes and their Dutch allies concentrated their colonial ventures in the region south of the Susquehanna River and north of the Potomac. These endeavors stretched from 1638 through the middle of the century and established the pattern of colonial contact in the area.

Prehistoric Background. Prior to European contact in the late 1630's, the Indians of the Delaware Valley represented two major linguistic and ethnographic groups. The first, the Lenni Lenape, were Algonquian speakers and were closely related to the Asseteque and the Nanticoke that surrounded them. This group, whom the English later referred to as the Delaware, were subdivided into three contingents: the Munsi, the Unami, and the Unalachtigo. According to the oral tradition of the Lenni Lenape, the *Walam Olum*, this tribe migrated into the region from the northwest to cross the Mississippi River and then east over the Appalachian Mountains. The other component consisted of Iroquoian speakers, the Mingo (or Minqua), who were loosely affiliated with the Iroquois Confederacy. The Mingo were later arrivals to the region and were an invasive force aligned with the powerful Iroquois tribes to the north and the west. Both groups were fairly typical of the Northeast Woodlands culture zone which they inhabited. They tended toward political decentralization, with the greatest emphasis placed on tribal integrity. Leadership generally resided with a chief or *sachem*. Economically these peoples depended on agriculture, supplemented by hunting and gathering. They also engaged in extensive trade networking.

Colonial Contact. Swedish colonial enterprise resulted from the monarchy's interest and trade in the Netherlands during the early seventeenth century. Swedish settlement in the Delaware Valley during the 1630's occurred as an extension of the already established Dutch interests in the New Netherlands to the north. In March, 1638, with the aid of the Dutch envoy, Peter Minuit, the Swedish negotiated with local natives for the land that became the Swedish settlement Christina (present-day Wilmington). These settlements then expanded to Passayung (Philadelphia) in the north

Nineteenth century depiction of Peter Minuit helping Swedish colonists buy Indian land for New Sweden in 1638. (Library of Congress)

and to Fort Casmir (New Castle). The Swedes, some three to four hundred strong, concentrated their settlement on the west side of the Delaware River and lived on individual farms in log houses of the sort they inhabited in Sweden. This association focused primarily on the trade of European manufactured goods for animal pelts obtained by Indians and was conducted by representatives of the Swedish government. In the 1640's the Swedish power and influence in the region reached its peak, and the relationships between the settlers and their native counterparts remained relatively peaceful. Officials suggested that the colonists learned from the Indians methods of adapting to their "primitive existences" in New Sweden. By 1650, when the Dutch had attempted to reassert their control over the region, approximately one thousand Swedes and ethnic Finns resided under the protection of the Swedish crown in the Delaware Valley. During that decade, the interests of the Swedish monarchy and the Dutch traders in the region faded, and support for the venture declined. The colonists found themselves in increasingly marginal situations; their abilities to trade and to defend themselves waned.

Indian Relations. When the Swedes entered the region in 1638 they approached peoples, the Lenni Lenape and the Mingo, already at odds with each other. The Swedish presence exaggerated each group's concerns about the access to land and the local balance of power. Initial negotiations treated the various tribes generically. Later Swedish discussions, however, resulted in a trade alliance that favored the Mingo, whom the Swedes described as "special friends." According to Johan Rising, Swedish governor, by 1655 the situation in the colony had grown ominous, with the "Renappi [*sic*] threatening not only to kill our people in the land . . . but also to destroy even trade with the Minques [*sic*] and the other savage nations." The trade with the Mingo persisted until Swedish trade goods ran out and the beaver trapped by the Indians disappeared. By the end of the 1660's the official Dutch and Swedish presences in the region disappeared, and the English replaced them. The Lenni Lenape had begun a forced retreat to the west. The combination of encroachment on the land by the Swedes, the impact of European disease, and the predations of the hostile Mingo forced them from the valley. The Mingo survived the Swedish occupation but not that of the English who succeeded them.

See also: Indian-white relations: Canadian; Indian-white relations: Dutch colonial; Indian-white relations: English colonial; Indian-white relations: French colonial; Indian-white relations: Norse; Prehistory: Northeast.

Martha I. Pallante

Sources for Further Study

Acrelius, Israel. *A History of New Sweden*, 1759. Reprint. Translated by William M. Reynolds. Philadelphia: The Historical Society of Pennsylvania, 1874.

Cochran, Thomas C. *Pennsylvania: A Bicentennial History*. New York: W. W. Norton, 1978.

Munroe, John A. *History of Delaware*. 2d ed. Newark: University of Delaware Press, 1984.

Sachese, Julius F. *History of the German Role in the Discovery, Exploration, and Settlement of the New World*. Reprint. *Germany and America, 1450-1700*. Edited by Don H. Tolzman. New York: Heritage Books, 1991.

Weslager, C. A. *Delaware's Buried Past: A Study of Archaeological Adventure*. Rev. ed. New Brunswick, N.J.: Rutgers University Press, 1968.

Wuorinen, John H. *The Finns on the Delaware, 1638-1655: An Essay in Colonial American History*. Philadelphia: University of Pennsylvania Press, 1938.

Indian-white relations: U.S., 1775-1830

Date: 1775-1830
Locale: United States
Tribes involved: Pantribal in the United States
Categories: Eighteenth century history, National government and legislation, Native government, Nineteenth century history, Treaties, Wars and battles
Significance: Following the Declaration of Independence, the fledgling United States was confronted with designing an Indian policy that combined two contradictory objectives: protecting Indians while aiding westward movement of white settlers.

During the two centuries of colonization prior to American independence, Indians had been ineffectual in halting the encroachment of white settlers on tribal lands. Disease, demoralization, alcohol addiction, and wars had tragically diminished native populations. Moreover, Indians lost their principal ally as the French suffered defeat in the French and Indian War (1754-1763), thereafter subjecting Indians to their British enemies as well as to the virtually unchecked and seemingly relentless land hunger of English settlers.

American Revolution. Both the Americans and the British initially sought to ensure Indian neutrality during the American Revolution, for both sides claimed to fear Indian "savagery" in battle. Their policies of neutrality were quickly abandoned, however, as both the Americans and the British sought aid from the powerful Indians still remaining on their eastern tribal lands. The turning point occurred in 1776 as the Cherokees, angered by incessant American intrusions, launched a series of raids on American settlements. Believing them to have been armed by the British, Congress accordingly authorized General Griffith Rutherford to undertake a retaliatory strike against the Cherokees. Rutherford and his troops subsequently rampaged through Cherokee land, razing thirty-six Indian villages, including their crops and stores. The Cherokee War served as a deterrent against further southern Indian involvement in the revolution, as other tribes feared similar retribution would be visited upon them should they elect to participate.

A similar fate befell the powerful Iroquois of New York, whose alliance was courted by both the Americans and the British. A majority of the Iroquois Confederacy joined the British, who sponsored a series of Iroquois attacks intending to sever American supply lines through New York's Mohawk Valley. In response, American commander-in-chief George Washington authorized General John Sullivan to lead a sizable punitive expedition against the Iroquois in 1779. Sullivan's troops mercilessly burned and pillaged, destroying twenty-eight Iroquois villages, along with their stores and crops. Economically the Iroquois never recovered from the Sullivan campaign. In addition, the centuries-old Iroquois Confederacy was destroyed when some Tuscaroras and Oneidas, encouraged by the influential missionaries Eleazar Wheelock and Samuel Kirkland, joined the Patriot cause against the British.

During the revolution most Indians ultimately allied themselves with the British, and at war's end they were once again at the mercy of their enemies; this time, however, their enemies were the Americans.

Indian Rebellions. From the initial Powhatan rebellion in Virginia in 1622 through the pantribal alliance of Pontiac in 1763, Indian tribes had endeavored to safeguard their land rights as the white population advanced at an alarming rate. After the American Revolution, aided by government policy which treated Indian lands as forfeit because of the Indian and British alliance, European Americans viewed their victory as license for uninhibited westward expansion. In the north, Americans made no distinction between

An illustration from Lewis and Clark's journal (published in 1812) provides insight into the attitudes of at least some Euro-American settlers who were encroaching upon Native American lands in the trans-Mississippi West. (Library of Congress)

Patriot and Loyalist Indians; all Indian land was subject to confiscation. Thus, during the Confederation period (in which the U.S. government was operating under the Articles of Confederation), Indians were forced to sign treaties which forfeited their land titles. The Confederation government proved incapable of enforcing treaties that failed when challenged by Indian resistance. In the south, federal treaties were negotiated for Indian protection. Those treaties were not upheld either. One problem was that some southern states, notably Georgia, repudiated Confederation authority. As American settlers vigorously resumed their unremitting westward drive, Indians responded with rebellions.

With British defeat in 1783, steadily increasing numbers of settlers moved into the Old Northwest territory (around the Great Lakes). United by a war chief, Little Turtle, Indians of that region participated in numerous raids on white settlers between 1783 and 1790. Although President George Washington in 1790 ordered armed resistance, Indian raids continued nearly unimpeded. In 1794, a force of three thousand rigorously drilled and highly disciplined troops under the command of General "Mad" Anthony Wayne earned a decisive victory against Little Turtle at the Battle of Fallen Timbers. The following year, Indians signed the Treaty of Fort Greenville, ceding virtually all of their lands in the Northwest Territory.

The spirit of rebellion persisted, however; in the early 1800's, the visionary Shawnee leader Tecumseh organized a pan-Indian alliance and sought to create a united Indian confederation. He traveled from north to south (from New York to Florida) and westward to present-day Iowa seeking allies among Indian tribes. His resistance was aborted, however, when his brother, spiritual leader Tenskwatawa (the Shawnee Prophet), led a premature, ill-fated attack on November 11, 1811, against the forces of William Henry Harrison at Tippecanoe. His warriors were defeated, resulting in disillusionment and then defections from the alliance. Many tribes pursued rebellions in their own territories, but Tecumseh was thereafter unable to organize a united Indian front. During the War of 1812, he joined forces with the British, proving himself a capable ally. Several other tribes that Tecumseh had courted, however, chose to ally with the Americans.

In the south, Indians invoked Spanish aid against American encroachments. With General Andrew Jackson's victory against the Creeks at the Battle of Horseshoe Bend, March 27, 1814, however, expectations of an ultimate Indian victory were extinguished.

Trade. In the aftermath of Little Turtle's War, President Washington and his secretary of war, Henry Knox, both principled men, sought a policy to ensure peace between Indians and the federal government. To that end, on April 18, 1796, Congress established the "factory system" for the regulation of Indian trade. It was designed to make peace rather than to generate profit. Government trading posts, known as factories, were designated across the frontier as centers for Indian trade. At the government-regulated factories, Indians were assured equitable trade. The factory system persisted until 1822 but failed to withstand the machinations of independent and frequently dishonest American and British Canadian traders.

After the War of 1812, additional measures known as the Trade and Intercourse Acts were enacted to regulate trade and establish a licensing system. These laws were designed to safeguard Indian lands and to provide for the extradition of criminals and the punishment of crimes committed by whites on Indian land. They formed the basis for the Trade and Intercourse Act of 1834.

Civilization. By 1819, through the efforts of the humanitarian reformer Thomas L. McKenney, aided by missionaries' lobbying of the federal government, a new federal Indian policy was initiated. The goal, which was to be accomplished through education, was the assimilation of Indians through Christianization and introduction to white agricultural techniques. Under the Civilization Fund Act, passed in 1819, which allocated ten thousand dollars for establishing schools on Indian tribal lands, Indians were to be taught American culture. Theoretically, civilization would result in the assimilation of Indians into white America, thereby eliminating threats of violence as well as freeing Indian land for white usage. Most Indians, however, continued to resist white culture, preferring to retain their tribal traditions. The minority who were indoctrinated as youths faced racial prejudice if they attempted to live as members of white society.

In the 1820's American encroachment on Indian lands was virtually uninhibited, and regulation of Indian trade, despite the best intentions embodied in the factory system and the Trade and Intercourse Acts, was largely ineffectual. Furthermore, many, including state officials, found assimilation through acculturation intolerably slow. Consequently, federal Indian policy evolved toward a final resolution to the "Indian problem" in the form of relocation of Indians to the newly created Indian Territory (present-day Oklahoma).

Removal. Indian removal, or the exchange by treaty of eastern land for lands west of the Mississippi, had several proponents, including humanitarian reformers concerned with safeguarding Indian culture through resettlement beyond the pale of white America, thereby relieving pressures on Indian tribal lands. Others were motivated by the base expectation of settlement on rich Indian lands. Georgia, coveting the sizable territory of the Cherokee Nation, eventually forced the issue to resolution. Ironically, the Cherokee Nation had become the most "civilized" of the Indian tribes, having adopted sedentary agriculture, a Cherokee syllabary, a written constitution, and a legal system patterned after that of the United States.

The spread of cotton agriculture and the discovery of gold on Cherokee lands, as well as the specter of a foreign nation within the state's boundaries, lent impetus to Georgia's eagerness to annex Indian lands. After the passage of Georgia's statutes extending the state's laws to the Cherokee Nation and disallowing Cherokee land claims, the Cherokee Nation appealed to the United States Congress. Meantime, President Andrew Jackson, elected in 1828, proved unsympathetic to Indian protests. He initiated, and saw to fruition, plans for Indian removal.

On May 28, 1830, Jackson signed into law the Indian Removal Act, by which all eastern Indians were to exchange their ancestral lands for land in the new trans-Mississippi Indian territory. Land exchanges were intended to be peaceably negotiated with Indian tribes. In practice, however, removal was frequently enforced against protesting Indians through both legal and illegal methods. Although 90 percent of the Cherokees resisted removal, for example, the intractable Jackson negotiated a removal treaty with a friendly minority faction. The Cherokee Nation, although disavowing this patently spurious document, was nevertheless bound to it and forced to move westward.

Indian removal eliminated the last obstacles to white expansion east of the Mississippi River. While the benefits to the states were obvious, removal for the eastern Indians was disastrous. Their new lands, often marginal and geographically dissimilar to their homelands, rendered their hunting and agricultural practices obsolete. A number of tribes were moved several times before their final settlement; others were located on land already inhabited by hostile tribes. Moreover, relentless white pressures for Indian lands continued as American settlers pushed their settlements ever farther westward. The process of dispossession begun early in the seventeenth century continued unabated until the end of the nineteenth century.

See also: Bureau of Indian Affairs; *Cherokee Phoenix*; Creek War; Dancing Rabbit Creek, Treaty of; Epidemics and diseases; Fallen Timbers, Battle of; Fort Greenville Treaty; Fort Mims, Battle of; Fort Stanwix Treaty; Fort Wayne Treaty; Horseshoe Bend Treaty; Indian Removal Act; Indian-white relations: Dutch colonial; Indian-white relations: English colonial; Indian-white relations: French colonial; Indian-white relations: Swedish colonial; Indian-white relations: U.S., 1831-1870; Iroquois Confederacy-U.S. Congress meeting; Kickapoo Resistance; Lewis and Clark expedition; Little Turtle's War; Lord Dunmore's War; Northwest Ordinance; Seminole Wars; Tecumseh's Rebellion; Thames, Battle of the; Tippecanoe, Battle of; Trail of Tears; Treaties and agreements in the United States; Tuscarora War; Wabash, Battle of the; Winnebago Uprising.

Mary E. Virginia

Sources for Further Study

Graymont, Barbara. *The Iroquois in the American Revolution.* Syracuse, N.Y.: Syracuse University Press, 1972. An excellent, highly detailed account of the Iroquois during the American Revolution.

O'Donnell, James H. *Southern Indians in the American Revolution.* Knoxville: University of Tennessee Press, 1973. Focusing on the Cherokees, Chickasaws, Creeks, and Choctaws, O'Donnell describes the attitudes of both the British and the Americans toward their Indian allies and Indian enemies. Indexed, annotated, with bibliography.

Prucha, Francis Paul. "Andrew Jackson's Indian Policy: A Reassessment." *Journal of American History* 56, no. 3 (1969): 527-539. A discussion of Jackson's Indian policy from a sympathetic viewpoint, describing the pressures leading to Indian removal.

_____. *The Great Father: The United States Government and the American Indians.* 2 vols. Lincoln: University of Nebraska Press, 1984. An extensive, fully annotated, indexed, and illustrated history of Indian-white relations from the founding of the United States to the 1980's by one of the premier authorities on Indian-white relations.

Remini, Robert V. *Andrew Jackson and His Indian Wars.* New York: Viking, 2001. An acclaimed biography of Jackson in the context of his ideas about and policies toward Indians. Attempts to show the underlying motives for Indian removal.

Satz, Ronald N. *American Indian Policy in the Jacksonian Era.* Lincoln: University of Nebraska Press, 1975. A thorough treatment of Andrew Jackson and Indian removal. Annotated, indexed, with bibliography.

Tyler, S. Lyman. *A History of Indian Policy.* Washington, D.C.: Government Printing Office, 1973. A brief chronological guide to Indian policy. Illustrated, containing maps, time lines, and bibliography.

Utley, Robert Marshall, and Wilcomb E. Washburn. *Indian Wars.* Boston: Houghton Mifflin, 2002. A comprehensive survey of the wars, battles, and conflicts between European Americans and Indians, written by two well-respected historians.

Viola, Herman J. *Thomas L. McKenney: Architect of America's Early Indian Policy, 1816-1830*. Chicago: Sage Books, 1974. Informative biography of McKenney, superintendent of Indian trade and the first director of the Bureau of Indian Affairs, and description of his Indian policy under the administrations of presidents James Madison, James Monroe, John Quincy Adams, and Andrew Jackson. Illustrated and indexed. Bibliography.

Washburn, Wilcomb E., ed. *History of Indian-White Relations*. Vol. 4 in *Handbook of North American Indians*. Washington, D.C.: Smithsonian Institution Press, 1988. An invaluable reference source containing articles on all aspects of Indian-white relations. Includes biographical dictionary. Fully annotated. Bibliography and illustrations.

Indian-white relations: U.S., 1831-1870

Date: 1831-1870
Locale: United States
Tribes involved: Pantribal in the United States
Categories: National government and legislation, Native government, Nineteenth century history, Treaties, Wars and battles
Significance: In the 1830's, U.S. policy toward Native Americans changed from treating tribes as "separate nations" to forcing integration into white society.

The nineteenth century represents a pivotal point in Indian-white relations. Indian tribes went from being independent nations to being treated as wards of the United States. The U.S. government reduced Indian rights and freedoms until they almost disappeared.

1830's. During the 1830's, the U.S. government and its citizens generally viewed Indians as a disposable nuisance. Despite the acculturation of the Five Civilized Tribes, many whites viewed them as dispensable "savages" who failed to utilize "properly" the land under their control. Many Indian groups suffered from white misconceptions. Where whites once searched for the "noble savage" or the Indian with whom they could discuss politics and religion, now whites viewed Indians as "wretched" and as an annoyance.

U.S. policy reflected these changes in attitudes. In 1830 Congress passed the Indian Removal Act, and soon thereafter the U.S. government forcibly removed the Five Civilized Tribes of the southeast (Cherokee, Chickasaw,

Western Indian-White Conflicts, 1831-1870

Four Lakes (1858)

Kildeer Mountain (1864)

Big Mound (1863)

Hayfield (1867)

Whitestone Hill (1863)

Birch Coulee (1862)

New Ulm (1862)

Bear River (1863)

Fetterman Defeat (1866)

Wood Lake (1862)

Fort Ridgely (1862)

Pyramid Lake (1860)

Platte Bridge (1865)

Bluewater (1855)

Beecher's Island (1868)

Sand Creek (1864)

Canyon de Chelly (1864)

Washita (1868)

Adobe Walls (1864)

Soldier Spring (1868)

Apache Pass (1862)

Creek, Choctaw, and Seminole). The government no longer treated tribes as independent foreign nations; they became "domestic, dependent nations." This meant that treaties could be made with them but that the government treated the land as being held in escrow for the Indians. The Five Civilized Tribes were moved to Oklahoma (then known as Indian Territory) and made to live in a different climate from the one they knew. Forced to leave behind their farms, tools, and buildings, they faced death and disease in their new homes.

The U.S. government considered removal the best policy for settling disputes between whites and Indians. During the 1830's, the U.S. government removed the Winnebagos from Wisconsin, the Potawatomi from Indiana, and the Sauk and Fox from Wisconsin, as well as removing the Five Civilized Tribes from the Southeast. Removed Indians lost their land, their ways of life, and their political freedoms. Tribal factions erupted over whether to accept removal. Tensions arose again after removal over how to cope with the change. Removal attacked Indian autonomy.

Removal also increased intertribal tensions. Tribes from the east were moved into lands already occupied by western tribes. This meant that more tribes vied for the same resources. Removal upset the tribal balance of power that had existed in the Plains. Eventually, whites joined the fray over the land in the west.

Americans aggressively pursued the policy of manifest destiny, taking the Oregon Territory from the British in the 1830's. Missionary Marcus Whitman, his wife Narcissa, and the H. H. Spauldings accomplished this by leading settlers into Oregon Territory with congressional approval. Though originally sent to Christianize the Cayuse Indians, they focused instead on populating the region so that it could be claimed by the United States. The Cayuse and other groups in the area resented this intrusion by settlers. The British had simply traded with the Indians; they had not brought settlers. Clashes over land and animals erupted constantly as the two groups tried to live together. Tensions rose steadily throughout the 1830's.

1840's and 1850's. Attitudes toward the Indians changed dramatically during the 1840's. Indians were considered a threat and an impediment to American development of the west. Two incidents particularly influenced this change in attitude: the Whitman Massacre and the Mexican-American War.

The Arapaho Ghost Dance as depicted by artist Mary Irvin c. 1910, based on photographs by James Mooney. The Ghost Dance religion was begun by the prophet Wovoka, who preached a vision of Indian resurgence and resurrection. Such movements were a response to white oppression. (National Archives)

By 1845, five thousand settlers a year were moving into the Oregon Territory. The Indians in this region watched as whites subdivided the land with fences and houses. In 1847, frustrated with the tide of white settlers and disease, the Cayuse rose up and massacred the Whitmans and several other whites. Spaulding, who missed the attack, became an opponent of the Indians. The massacre shocked and horrified Americans in the East. It brought back colonial period images of the Indians as bloodthirsty savages. All Indians west of the Mississippi suffered from this characterization.

After the Mexican-American War (1846-1848), according to the Treaty of Guadalupe Hidalgo, the western border of the United States jumped from the Mississippi to the Pacific coast. It destroyed what the government considered the "Indian barrier" of the Mississippi, opening the western half of the U.S. to white "civilization" and settlement. This altered Indian-white relations on the Plains, in the Southwest, and on the Pacific coast. Until the end of the Mexican-American War, most of the Indian groups west of the Mississippi had avoided subjugation to the Spanish and had traded with the French. They did not expect to be subjugated by the Americans. The introduction of whites interested in settlement into western territory increased tensions between Indians and whites.

During the 1840's and 1850's, the Bureau of Indian Affairs (BIA) shared the responsibility of defining policy with the military. The BIA represented one of the most mismanaged of government offices. It was a favorite spot for placing beneficiaries of the spoils system—newly elected senators and congressmen placed their political allies in the BIA as a reward for service. Graft and corruption existed at every level, from the agents in the field to the commissioners in Washington. Additionally, these administrators turned over with every new election. Yet the U.S. government placed the BIA in charge of defining long-term Indian policy.

To aid westward expansion, the BIA sought to extinguish Indian land titles during this period. As whites took over more and more western land, it became apparent that removing Indians to unoccupied land would no longer be feasible. The BIA considered treaties and annuity payments to be the fastest and most efficient way to end titles. Often BIA negotiators lied to Indian representatives to get them to sign the treaties. They withheld annuities from previous treaties to force Indian leaders to sign new treaties. In addition, Congress changed the treaties before ratifying them. Such deceptions led to poor relations between whites and Indians.

The paying of annuities for relinquished land created more tension. Many agents embezzled parts of the annuity payments. Moreover, there was often confusion about who was to receive the payments, a specific chief or each individual Indian in that tribe. Agents also sometimes acted as traders, overcharging for goods so that the goods always equaled the annuity payments. These policies increased the tension between Indians and whites.

As more whites moved west, the "taming of the Indian" became an integral part of manifest destiny. To enforce this concept, the military became the second executor of Indian policy. Military protection had to be provided for white citizens moving west. Despite friendly or indifferent receptions by Indians on most parts of the trail, the few incidents of Indian attack appeared in newspapers and books everywhere. Many westward settlers considered the trail to be full of "bloodthirsty savages" looking for scalps and white women. The settlers demanded protection. The U.S. government established forts across the frontier to be able to control and eliminate the perceived Indian menace.

Civil War. The Civil War (1861-1865) changed Indian-white relations. First, the U.S. government withdrew the army regulars from the frontier and replaced them with volunteers who resented serving on the "Indian frontier." President Lincoln kept these troops in the West to protect the gold routes and the whites moving westward. Many tribes saw the Civil War as a sign of weakness in the American government. The Sioux, the Five Civilized Tribes, and others chased missionaries and Indian agents from their territory.

Two incidents during this period damaged Indian-white relations for the next several years: the decision by the Five Civilized Tribes to join the Confederacy and the Sioux Uprising of 1862. The Five Civilized Tribes sided with the Confederacy after being convinced that it would treat them as equals after the war. Some leaders, such as John Ross of the Cherokee, feared Northern reprisals if the South lost. Unfortunately, the Indian units were accused of committing savage atrocities during battles such as that at Pea Ridge, which reinforced negative attitudes toward them. The Sioux Uprising of 1862 frightened western settlers, as newspapers portrayed it as an unprovoked massacre of innocent women and children. (In reality, BIA politics and poor management ignited the conflict.) The aftermath influenced generations of western settlers who remembered only the women and children murdered by Indians.

Tensions between whites and Indians increased during the Civil War. White settlers distrusted the volunteers who had replaced the army regulars and expected the Indians to take advantage of the lack of men and muscle on the frontier to chase the settlers out. Indians also distrusted the volunteers, who were unprepared for conflict on the Plains. They were unused to guerrilla warfare. Between the lack of trust of the army and the reinforced fear of the "savage Indians," tensions increased on the frontier.

Post-Civil War. After the Civil War, the War Department and the military fought to gain control of the BIA in order to exterminate the Indians, but the cost of a military solution deterred Congress from this policy. Reformers, including missionaries, moved in to try to take control of the policy and to pacify the Indians.

In 1867, a Senate report changed policy for one year. The report stated that the Indian population was declining rapidly because of disease, war, and malnutrition. Additionally, it accused the military of starting most conflicts with the Indians, thereby reinforcing the idea that military officers were inadequate as agents of peace. The report suggested that the reservation system was the only humane policy. It would allow the Indians to become integrated into American society by teaching them farming and the rules of white society. It would also protect them from the military and from each other.

As punishment for siding with the Confederacy, the U.S. government forced the Five Civilized Tribes to surrender their westernmost lands, abolish slavery, grant the railroads rights-of-way through their territory (which would inevitably bring whites into the territory), establish U.S. military posts, and allow the creation of U.S. territorial governments within their territory. Exhausted after the war, the tribes accepted the terms of surrender.

In 1868, as new battles between Indians and the military raged in the West, the Indian Commission announced that it was no longer necessary to recognize tribes as "domestic dependent nations." This effectively meant the end of treaty negotiations. Additionally, the BIA was transferred back to the War Department, temporarily giving the military more control of policy. These policy changes resulted from the violence that existed on the Plains both during and after the Civil War. The government now considered all tribes untrustworthy and limited their rights accordingly. As the 1870's approached, Indian policy and Indian-white relations entered a new and dangerous phase: war and open extermination.

See also: Adobe Walls, Battles of; Apache Wars; Bear River Campaign; Black Hawk War; Bozeman Trail War; Bureau of Indian Affairs; Cayuse War; Cherokee legal cases; *Cherokee Phoenix*; Fort Atkinson Treaty; Fort Laramie Treaty of 1851; Fort Laramie Treaty of 1868; Gadsden Purchase; Guadalupe Hidalgo, Treaty of; Indian Removal Act; Indian-white relations: U.S., 1775-1830; Indian-white relations: U.S., 1871-1933; Keetoowah Society; Kickapoo Resistance; Kickapoo uprisings; Long Walk; Medicine

Lodge Creek Treaty; Minnesota Uprising; Navajo War; Reservation system of the United States; Sand Creek Massacre; Seminole Wars; Sioux War; Snake War; Taos Rebellion; Trade and Intercourse Acts; Trail of Tears; Treaties and agreements in the United States; Walla Walla Council; Washita River Massacre; Yakima War.

C. L. Higham

Sources for Further Study

Berkhofer, Robert F., Jr. *Salvation and the Savage*. Lexington: University Press of Kentucky, 1965. This work focuses on how missionaries portrayed white culture to the Indians and on the policy behind these presentations.

Brown, Dee. *Bury My Heart at Wounded Knee*. New York: Henry Holt, 1970. This work represents the Indian perception of Indian-white relations in the nineteenth century.

Dippie, Brian. *The Vanishing American*. Middletown, Conn.: Wesleyan University Press, 1982. Dippie examines the concept of the extinction of the Indian in the nineteenth century.

Hoxie, Frederick E., James Merrell, and Peter C. Mancall, eds. *American Nations: Encounters in Indian Country, 1850-Present*. New York: Routledge, 2001. A series of essays on aspects of Indian-U.S. relations and cultural encounters.

Kelley, Robert. *American Protestantism and United States Indian Policy*. Lincoln: University of Nebraska Press, 1983. Discusses how Protestant reformers influenced Indian policy and Indian-white relations.

Utley, Robert M. *The Indian Frontier*. Albuquerque: University of New Mexico Press, 1984. Examines, through vignettes and traditional narrative, Indian-white relations on the military and political frontiers.

Utley, Robert Marshall, and Wilcomb E. Washburn. *Indian Wars*. Boston: Houghton Mifflin, 2002. A comprehensive survey of the wars, battles, and conflicts between European Americans and Indians, written by two well-respected historians.

Indian-white relations: U.S., 1871-1933

Date: 1871-1933
Locale: United States
Tribes involved: Pantribal in the United States

Categories: National government and legislation, Native government, Nineteenth century history, Treaties, Twentieth century history, Wars and battles

Significance: This period saw the last of the Indian wars, significant changes in white attitudes toward Native Americans, and important attempts to regularize the legal status of American Indians by new acts of law.

In the period between 1871 and 1933, the last of the tragic Indian wars were fought, and several attempts were made by the federal government to re-form Indian policy. The attempts at reform were often wrongheaded, and they ultimately had to be reversed, but they demonstrate the popular perception that the existing policy could not be sustained indefinitely.

Indian Wars. A series of serious Indian wars characterized the period between 1871 and 1890. Some of these were precipitated by the desire of whites for Indian lands or by the desire of white settlers to eliminate the Indians be-

Western Indian-White Conflicts, 1871-1890

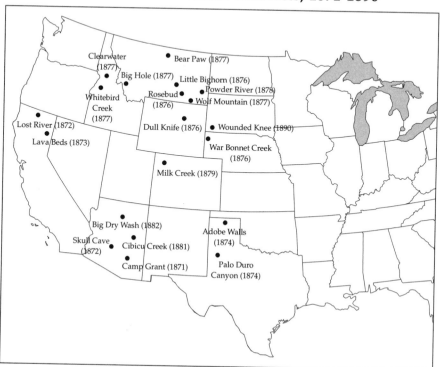

cause of prejudice or fears of attack. Others seem primarily to have been the result of the inability of many tribes and tribal leaders to accept confinement on reservations, which were often composed of extremely poor land. Confinement also flew in the face of traditional patterns of Indian life.

In 1871, the Kiowas rose up in Texas under Satanta, Satank, Big Tree, Eagle Heart, and Big Bow, engaging in a campaign that included the ambush of a wagon train on Salt Creek Prairie. In the period 1872-1873, the Modoc War erupted as the Modocs, a Northern California tribe, resisted resettlement in Indian Territory. The war ended with the trial and execution of Captain Jack, the Modoc leader. The years 1874-1875 saw the outbreak of the so-called Red River War, with the U.S. Cavalry under General Philip Sheridan and Nelson A. Miles and the Texas Rangers battling an alliance of Comanche, Cheyenne, and Kiowa warriors under Big Tree, Lone Wolf, and Satanta. The war ended with the surrender of Quanah Parker, the feared Comanche chief.

The famous campaign known as the pursuit of the Nez Perce occurred in 1877. It began when young braves resisting a forced march to reservation land led a substantial group of the tribe in flight, with General Oliver O. Howard in pursuit. Led by Chiefs Joseph the Younger and Looking Glass, the Nez Perce evaded army pursuit across Idaho and Wyoming, fighting battles at White Bird Canyon, Clearwater, Big Hole River, Camas Meadows, Billings, and Bear Paw Mountain. They reached a point only 100 miles from their goal of Canadian sanctuary before surrendering.

In 1878-1879, the campaign of the pursuit of the Northern Cheyenne followed the pattern of the Nez Perce campaign, but in less spectacular form. Chiefs Dull Knife and Little Wolf led three hundred braves off the reservation, pursued by regular army troops and civilian volunteers. Dull Knife's faction surrendered at Camp Robinson but then refused to proceed to the reservation. In a fight with the troops, half of Dull Knife's followers were killed. Little Wolf's band surrendered later.

The Bannock War commenced in 1878. Bannocks, under Chief Buffalo Horn, began raiding in southern Idaho and Oregon. Paiutes under Chief Egan and the medicine man Oytes broke out from the Malheur Reservation and joined the Bannocks, pursued by General Howard. The Indian confederates were defeated at the Battle of Birch Creek, and during their subsequent flight Chief Egan was killed by Umatilla warriors through a trick involving a war council with the Umatillas to discuss an alliance.

The year 1879 contained two complete Indian wars. The Sheepeaters War involved a band of renegade Shoshones and Bannocks who raided throughout Idaho and neighboring areas. The Ute War occurred in Colorado when Indian agent Nathan Meeker telegraphed for aid against restive

Utes. Relieving forces were put under siege after the Battle of Milk Creek, and additional forces were required to subdue the Utes.

Less confined in time were the Sioux and Apache wars, which stretched out over many years. In 1872, a band of Yavapais Apaches died at the Bat-

tle of Skull Cave in Salt River Canyon; after the subsequent Battle of Turret Peak, many Apaches returned to the reservation. When the Apaches were ordered to the hated San Carlos Reservation in Arizona in 1876, however, the war reignited. There followed several years when Geronimo and Victorio broke from their reservations, raided, and crisscrossed the Mexican border at will. For a decade, until 1886, Geronimo would be a constant problem for the army and for the government.

Finally, in 1876, the Sioux reacted against orders to move from the Black Hills to the San Carlos Reservation in Arizona. Battles included Sitting Bull's attack on General Crook's column at Rosebud Creek, the defeat of Colonel George Armstrong Custer and the Seventh Cavalry at the Battle of the Little Bighorn, the Battle of Slim Buttes, the Battle of Wolf Mountains, and the Battle of Muddy Creek. Sitting Bull fled into Canada with his warriors but returned to surrender to U.S. forces in 1881.

Sitting Bull in 1885, nine years after Rosebud Creek, probably about the time he participated in William Cody's wild west shows. His death at the hands of reservation police during the Wounded Knee Massacre and the subsequent surrender of the Sioux signaled the end of the Indian Wars. (Library of Congress)

In the latter days of 1890, a sad sequel to the Sioux wars was enacted. The Ghost Dance

Uprising and the Battle of Wounded Knee (the Wounded Knee Massacre) ended the era of the Indian wars. The prophet Wovoka preached a vision of Indian resurgence and resurrection based on the use of the magical Ghost Dance. Sitting Bull was killed by reservation police at the Standing Rock Reservation. At the camp of Chief Big Foot at Wounded Knee, three hundred Indians were slaughtered in what has become known as the Wounded Knee Massacre. The surrender of the Sioux the next year at White Clay Creek ended the era of direct warfare between the whites and Indians.

Legal Status and Governmental Policy. When Ulysses S. Grant became president in 1869, a new "peace policy" was adopted in U.S. relations with the Indian tribes. Under the new policy, new appointments of Indian agents would be made from among the religious groups who sent missionaries among the tribes, and extraordinary efforts would be made to get the Indians to adopt white ways—living in houses, practicing agriculture, and so on.

Many other developments in Indian affairs filled the Grant years. In 1871, in the *Cherokee Tobacco* case, the Supreme Court upheld the principle that new acts of Congress supersede prior treaties, including those with the Indian nations, when they contradict. The next year saw the complete abandonment of treaty making in regard to the tribes, with all future agreements replaced by statutes and executive orders. Partly this represented the desire of the House of Representatives to have a say in such agreements, and partly it represented a reaction to the fact that treaties, after the *Cherokee Tobacco* case, offered no enhancement of protection over simple statute. Some reservations were established by treaty, others by statute, but beginning in the 1870's, executive orders were also employed.

In 1874, the Report of the Indian Commissioner proposed major changes in the status of the Indians and their way of life. Citizenship was proposed for any Indian who desired it. It was also proposed that the protection and obligations of white law be extended to Indian Territory and that reservation land be held in individual plots—called "allotments in severalty"—rather than communally by tribes. This would promote agriculture and the improvement of land.

In 1879, the case *Standing Bear v. Crook*, decided by Judge Elmer S. Dundy of the U.S. Circuit Court, District of Nebraska, declared Indians to be "persons" under the Constitution and extended the writ of *habeas corpus* to them to protect their liberty.

In 1883, Secretary of the Interior Henry M. Teller instigated "courts of Indian affairs" (after the Indian Offenses Act was passed in 1883) on reservations to create a rule of law on tribal lands. The drive to bring Indians under white law suffered a major setback in the 1883 Supreme Court case *Ex parte Crow Dog*, wherein the Brule Sioux Chief Crow Dog's conviction and death sentence for the murder of Spotted Tail was overturned on the grounds that there was no federal jurisdiction over the crime of an Indian against another Indian on Indian land. Further separating Indians from white governance was the 1884 Supreme Court case *Elk v. Wilkins*, whereby the Court refused to enforce a franchise right for the plaintiff, who had severed his ties to his tribe and lived among whites.

These moves away from white law began to be reversed in 1885 with Congress's passage of the Major Crimes Act, which placed seven serious felonies under federal law if committed on reservations or other Indian territory in order to avoid situations such as that in the *Crow Dog* decision. In 1886 in *United States v. Kagama*, the high Court upheld the constitutionality of the act.

Assimilation of the Indians into white society became the stated solution to all problems in white-Indian relations, and indeed, to all problems of Indian society. Politicians rushed to embrace this solution, as did many of those who regarded themselves as friends and defenders of the "red man." In 1884, the Lake Mohonk Conference of Friends of the Indian issued a program which called for assimilation by bringing the Indians under territorial law, private individual ownership of land, and other forms of white civilization. Groups such as this were torn between their recognition of the potential loss of Indian culture and the need to prevent further depredations by white society.

In 1887, the General Allotment Act (Dawes Act) provided for allotments in severalty for reservation Indians, providing citizenship for Indians on such allotments. In that year as well, Commissioner J. D. C. Atkins ordered that, in all schools on reservations, all instruction was to be in the English language to aid in assimilation. Two years later, the government moved to establish a system of government-run Indian schools. By 1889, Commissioner Thomas J. Morgan was calling for the conscious destruction of the tribes as the ultimate means of assimilation of the Indians into the dominant culture.

In 1892, Indian courts were authorized to punish as offenses such Indian practices as traditional dances, polygamy, and the practices of medicine men as well as standard criminal offenses such as destruction of property, fornication, and drunkenness. Truancy of children enrolled in government schools was also an offense. The inclusion of several Indian cultural and religious practices as "offenses" struck sharply at the Indian way of life.

In 1898, upon the failure of the Dawes Commission to achieve agreement with the Five Civilized Tribes and the other tribes of the Indian Territory, Congress imposed the Curtis Act, which essentially applied the provisions of the Dawes Act to that territory, destroying tribal government. The Supreme Court upheld the act in *Stephens v. Cherokee Nation* (1899).

Twentieth Century. In *Lone Wolf v. Hitchcock* (1903), the Supreme Court upheld the plenary power of Congress over Indian affairs and established the right of Congress to abrogate treaties. By 1905, however, the government was having second thoughts about its wholesale reforms. Commissioner Francis E. Leupp issued a report to Congress which endorsed attempts to institute Indian self-sufficiency and called for presentation of aspects of Indian culture.

In 1906, the Burke Act provided for discretion in the length of trust periods for allotments and provided that citizenship should come at the end rather than at the beginning of such periods. The Lacey Act (1907) further struck at the tribal system by providing for allotment of tribal funds to individuals under specified conditions.

In 1919, as an acknowledgment of its gratitude for war service, Congress passed an act providing U.S. citizenship to Indian veterans of World War I upon request. In 1928, the Institute for Government Research issued the Meriam Report, which dealt systematically with the general problems facing Indians in the nation and was critical of U.S. government policies. It would lead to milestone legislation in 1934, the Indian Reorganization Act.

See also: Adobe Walls, Battles of; Alaska Native Brotherhood and Alaska Native Sisterhood; All-Pueblo Council; Allotment system; American Indian Defense Association; Apache Wars; Bannock War; Bison slaughter; Burke Act; Carlisle Indian School; *Cherokee Tobacco* case; *Elk v. Wilkins; Ex parte Crow Dog;* Friends of the Indian organizations; General Allotment Act; Indian Appropriation Act; Indian Citizenship Act; Indian Offenses Act; Indian Rights Association; Indian-white relations: U.S., 1831-1870; Indian-white relations: U.S., 1934-2002; Kickapoo uprisings; Little Bighorn, Battle of the; *Lone Wolf v. Hitchcock;* Major Crimes Act; Meriam Report; Modoc War; National Indian Association; Nez Perce War; Red River War; Reservation system of the United States; Rosebud Creek, Battle of; Society of American Indians; *Standing Bear v. Crook;* Treaties and agreements in the United States; Tribal courts; *United States v. Kagama;* Wild west shows; Wolf Mountains, Battle of; World wars; Wounded Knee Massacre.

Patrick M. O'Neil

Sources for Further Study

Axelrod, Alan. *Chronicle of the Indian Wars: From Colonial Times to Wounded Knee*. New York: Prentice Hall General Reference, 1993. This work provides a useful and detailed overview of the armed struggles of the Indians and the whites.

Faulk, Odie B. *Crimson Desert: Indian Wars of the American Southwest*. New York: Oxford University Press, 1974. Faulk presents a fine and detailed description of the campaigns of this region.

Hoxie, Frederick E., James Merrell, and Peter C. Mancall, eds. *American Nations: Encounters in Indian Country, 1850-Present*. New York: Routledge, 2001. A series of essays on aspects of Indian-U.S. relations and cultural encounters.

Jackson, Helen. *A Century of Dishonor: A Sketch of the United States Government's Dealings with Some of the Indian Tribes*. 1880. Reprint. New York: Barnes & Noble, 1993. This volume is a reprint of an 1880 history of Indian-white relations from earliest colonial times through 1871, with many excellent quotations from official documents.

Marshall, Samuel L. A. *Crimsoned Prairie*. New York: Charles Scribner's Sons, 1972. Details the Indian campaigns of the West. The author is an excellent military historian, although slightly biased in the direction of preserving the honor of the military.

Prucha, Francis Paul, ed. *Documents of United States Indian Policy*. 3d ed. Lincoln: University of Nebraska Press, 2000. Reprints major documents in the history of U.S. policy toward native peoples.

St. Germain, Jill. *Indian Treaty-Making Policy in the United States and Canada, 1867-1877*. Lincoln: University of Nebraska Press, 2001. Explores and contrasts the "civilizing" efforts of the United States and Canada through their Indian treaty policies.

Shattuck, Petra T., and Jill Norgren. *Partial Justice: Federal Indian Law in a Liberal Constitutional System*. New York: Berg, 1991. This study carefully analyzes the relationship of U.S. Indian law and policy to the U.S. constitutional order and governmental administrative policy.

Tyler, Lyman S. *A History of Indian Policy*. Washington, D.C.: Government Printing Office, 1973. This work sets out accurately and in great detail the development of the Indian policy of the United States.

Utley, Robert Marshall, and Wilcomb E. Washburn. *Indian Wars*. Boston: Houghton Mifflin, 2002. A comprehensive survey of the wars, battles, and conflicts between European Americans and Indians, written by two well-respected historians.

Wilkinson, Charles F. *American Indians, Time, and the Law: Native Societies in a Modern Constitutional Democracy*. New Haven, Conn.: Yale University

Press, 1987. This treatise traces Indian law and rights through court cases, primarily U.S. Supreme Court cases.

Williams, Robert A., Jr. *The American Indian in Western Legal Thought: The Discourses of Conquest.* New York: Oxford University Press, 1990. This book deals with earlier times in white-Indian relations but is vital reading for anyone who wishes to understand the philosophical and traditional bases of American Indian law.

Indian-white relations: U.S., 1934-2002

Date: 1934-2002
Locale: United States
Tribes involved: Pantribal in the United States
Categories: National government and legislation; Native government; Twentieth century history
Significance: During the period since 1934, three stages led from open displacement of Indian rights to self-determination policies.

The landmark Indian Reorganization Act of 1934, which remained the legislative model for relations between the U.S. government and Indian tribes until the mid-1950's, was based on a massive 1928 report entitled *The Problem of Indian Administration*, commonly called the Meriam Report. This report had been requested by Secretary of the Interior Hubert Work. It was intended to reexamine the effects of the General Allotment Act of 1887. Briefly stated, the 1887 act had provided for allotment to each Indian family a specific plot of land within their tribe's "traditional" holdings. Under this law, after titles had been held for twenty-five years, families would gain full property rights, including the right to sell their land. Any tribal land that was left after plot allotment to families was to be sold to the government for homesteading. It is estimated that, when the Indian Reorganization Act came into effect in 1934, Indians held legal rights to only one-third of the land they had had before the General Allotment Act. This fact, coupled with a number of other critical factors pointed out in the Meriam Report (including inferior conditions in the areas of health care and education), led to the policy changes embodied in 1934's Indian Reorganization Act. Most of the responsibility for implementing these changes rested with President Franklin D. Roosevelt's appointee to the post of commissioner of Indian affairs, John Collier.

Indian Reorganization Act. In addition to slowing the loss of Indian lands, the 1934 act brought a new philosophy to the Bureau of Indian Affairs (BIA). It proclaimed a need to reverse a long-standing policy of forced assimilation of Indians into "mainstream" America and to build stronger bases for the retention of local Indian cultures. In Collier's words, it aimed at "both the economic and spiritual rehabilitation of the Indian race."

In the first domain, plans were laid to appropriate funds to buy back for the tribes Indian land that had been lost since 1887. The BIA also initiated a program to spread knowledge of land and timber conservation technology to receptive tribes and began steps to provide local development loans. Although the deepening of the Great Depression soon made special appropriations impossible, much surplus government land that had not gone to homesteading was returned. In its bid to encourage a greater sense of local tribal identity, the 1934 act also offered aid for drawing up and implementing tribal constitutions as the basis for their own local government.

World War II. In the period between 1934 and the next major redefinition of BIA policy in 1953, many domestic policy factors intervened to affect what Roosevelt's policymakers had seen as the long-term goals of the BIA. The greatest single factor affecting tens of thousands of Indian lives during the decade of the 1940's, however, was initially set in play by forces far beyond the reservations: This factor was military service in the U.S. forces during World War II. More than twenty-five thousand Native Americans served between 1941 and 1945. Many thousands more left reservations to work in war-related industrial factories. Indian women were also welcomed as volunteers in the army nurses' corps and the Red Cross.

Whatever their experiences in the ranks of the armed forces, still strictly segregated along racial lines, clear problems confronted thousands of returning Indian veterans at the end of the war. Part of the dilemma stemmed from continuing economic underdevelopment on the reservations they left. Equally debilitating, thousands of returning American Indian veterans felt alienated from their own people after experiencing life off the reservation.

Problems such as these impelled U.S. lawmakers to consider once again whether assimilation, rather than "protected separation," was the best policy to pursue in Indian affairs. Parties supporting the former, including outspoken conservative Republican senator Arthur Watkins from Utah, introduced what became, in House Concurrent Resolution 108, the policy of "termination and relocation."

Native American relocatees standing in front of their low-cost home in Winner, South Dakota. (National Archives)

Termination Act of 1953. When HCR 108 became law in mid-1953, it pledged

> to make Indians . . . subject to the same laws and entitled to the same privileges and responsibilities as . . . other citizens . . . and to end their status as wards of the United States.

Even as HCR 108 was about to become law, a number of Indian spokespersons for the first tribes scheduled for termination (which meant stopping various forms of federal government "protective" intervention in their affairs) openly questioned Senator Watkins's claims that, since there were multiple sources to develop potential wealth on their reservations, the tribes should be able to "go it better alone."

Menominee leader Gordon Keshena was not alone in expressing worries that, if BIA supervision over local Indian affairs ended, the tribes' lack of experience would produce deterioration of many Indian material interests. Some congressional supporters of the general principles behind HCR 108 also admitted that the government might find itself spending large amounts of money trying to prepare the weakest and poorest Indian groups to know what forms of local autonomy might suit them best.

In fact, just as local termination bills began to appear in 1954, President Dwight D. Eisenhower seemed prepared to increase budgetary allocations to encourage the establishment of new industries in or near tribal areas. For example, by 1956, $300,000 of tribal funds formerly held in trust were earmarked to induce industrial plant owners to locate on the fringes of Navaho territory. Two companies constructed factories, one manufacturing baby furniture, the other making electronic equipment, near Flagstaff, Arizona.

In 1957 the Indian Vocational Training Act was intended to provide job skills needed for Indian applicants to be attractive to potential employers, even if such jobs meant relocating off reservations. More than a hundred different occupations were included in the curriculum of free schools located in twenty-six states. This ambitious program continued to expand even as economic recession worsened in 1956 and 1957. Indian policymakers seemed convinced that the overall objectives of the 1953 termination laws would be best served if Indians who could not expect to gain employment on economically backward reservations relocated in off-reservation towns. Ideally, such a movement of families would also ease pressures on the limited economic means of their respective homelands.

Relocation. A separate budget for relocation came by the mid-1950's, to avoid negative consequences for Indians who left the reservations without adequate security. Statistics showed that, of the nearly 100,000 Indians who left reservations between 1945 to 1958, some 75,000 had relocated without federal assistance, sometimes causing familial disasters. Thus, job training and relocation funds expended in 1957 doubled in one year, reaching $3.5 million. In the same year, seven thousand Indians moved from their reservations. Controversy soon developed over shortcomings in the relocation program.

Realistic prospects for employment fell short of demands; moreover, job layoffs left many Indians "stranded" and unemployed in unsympathetic white-dominated environments. At the same time, there were very high dropout rates in BIA-sponsored vocational schools. Nurse's aide programs for women registered the lowest percentage of dropouts (21 percent), while rates for less challenging factory-type programs for men were very high (a 50 percent dropout rate for sawmill workers and a rate as high as 62 percent among furniture factory trainees).

As the 1960's approached, critics of the effects of termination and relocation, including Sophie Aberle, formerly responsible for the United Pueblos
Agency, warned Indian Commissioner Glenn Emmons of trouble ahead.
Emmons tried to defend his office by reiterating a philosophy that was not
accepted by all—that whatever successes were occurring usually stemmed
from individual initiative, whereas groups that fell back on the security of
"communal lifestyle" tended to accept status quo conditions. Emmons
cited gains that were not so easily measured in paychecks, such as advances in tribal health programs and in education. The number of Indians
going beyond high school by this date (the 1958-1959 school year) showed
an increase of more than 65 percent in only three years.

Toward Self-Determination: 1960's and 1970's. Despite the fact that the Eisenhower administration's last BIA budget (for fiscal year 1960) was the
largest ever ($115,467,000), it was during the 1960 presidential campaign
that controversy over Indian policy began to come to public attention.
Party platform committees actually heard testimony from tribal leaders
such as Frank George, a Nez Perce who asked not for abandonment of termination but for improvement in its procedures for aiding needy tribes.
Other claims, such as the Miccosukee Seminole demand for all of Florida to
reconstitute their sovereignty, received less sympathy. The new tide that
was coming was best expressed by La Verne Madigan of the Association on
American Indian Affairs, who stated that Indians should have the right to
choose freely between assimilation and "life in cultural communities of
their own people."

In general, the Kennedy-Johnson Democratic years (1960-1968) witnessed a continuation of termination actions despite the views of Lyndon
Johnson's interior secretary, Stewart Udall. It was Udall's insistence that
the BIA should do more to secure better conditions of relocation that led to
the replacement of Commissioner Philleo Nash by Wisconsin Oneida Indian Robert Bennett in 1966. Under Bennett's influence, the president began, in the troubled political climate of 1967, to declare the nation's need to
end the termination policy. Soon thereafter, Johnson urged passage of the
Indian Civil Rights Act (1968).

The 1970's, under Presidents Richard Nixon, Gerald Ford, and Jimmy
Carter, brought what has been described as the "self-determination" policy, emphasizing the development of tribal resources on restored reservations. Perhaps the most dramatic example of reversal of what many perceived to be the harmful effects of termination occurred in 1973, when the
Menominee tribe was told that (as the tribe had requested) its twenty-year
experience of termination was over and that its entire reservation was to be

restored to it as "unencumbered Menominee property." Yet despite pronouncements of "better intentions" coming from Washington and the BIA, the cumulative effects of decades of misunderstanding were not to be dispelled easily. In the same year that the Menominees regained tribal control over their own destiny, a breakdown in relations between federal troops and Lakota Sioux during a seventy-one-day siege on the Pine Ridge Reservation ended in an assault that the Lakotas call "Wounded Knee II." Similar confrontations with threats of violence came in different regions, pressing government authorities to review its Indian policy yet again.

In May, 1977, the congressional American Indian Policy Review Commission, which included five Indian members for the first time, made more than two hundred recommendations, most of which aimed at confirming all tribes' power to enact laws within the confines of their own reservations. On the heels of this symbol of intended reform, the U.S. Congress passed the 1978 American Indian Religious Freedom Act, which guaranteed freedom for tribes to practice their own traditional religions. This act ended the mixed legacy of several centuries of insistence that missionary conversion and education following Christian principles were vital aspects of Indian-white relations in the United States.

1980's Through 2001. During the Ronald Reagan and George Bush (Sr.) Republican presidencies (1980-1992), budgetary cuts seriously affected the continuity of existing programs of assistance to Indian tribes. In 1981 alone, one-half of the prior budget for health services was cut, while funding for Indian higher education was reduced from 282 million to 200 million dollars. By the mid-1980's, the education budget had been cut further, to 169 million dollars.

Despite alarming cutbacks in BIA funding and looming questions of Indian demands for restoration of their sovereignty, the Republican administration of George Herbert Walker Bush made one major contribution by enacting the Native American Languages Act, which allowed tribal use of (formerly banned) traditional languages in BIA schools.

The issue of Indian land claims was prominent throughout the 1980's and early 1990's. In 1980, the U.S. Supreme Court (in *United States v. Sioux Nation*) upheld a $122 million judgment against the United States for having taken the Black Hills from the Sioux illegally. In 1986, a federal court awarded each member of the White Earth Chippewa group compensation for land lost under the 1887 General Allotment Act. A significant piece of legislation regarding land claims was the 1982 Indian Claims Limitation Act, which limited the time period during which land claims could be filed against the U.S. government.

The issue of Indian sovereignty and the related issue of gambling on Indian lands created considerable controversy among Indians and non-Indians in the early 1990's. The 1988 Indian Gaming Regulatory Act legalized certain types of gambling on reservations, and the vast amounts of income that could be generated appealed to many tribes struggling with widespread poverty. Gambling engendered protests by some non-Indians, however, and created tribal divisions that occasionally turned violent; in 1990, violence between gambling and antigambling contingents on the St. Regis Mohawk Reservation caused state and federal authorities to intervene. In California, Indian efforts in 1999 to pass Proposition 5, the California Indian Self Reliance Initiative (which promoted casinos as a source of independent income) had the side effect of creating an increasingly powerful political interest group—powerful enough to be accused of having undue influence on President Bill Clinton in the series of scandals attending his last months in office. An important court decision involving another aspect of sovereignty was handed down in 1990: The U.S. Supreme Court decided in *Duro v. Reina* that tribes do not have criminal jurisdiction over non-Indians living on reservation lands.

In 1992, a number of American Indian groups protested the celebrations planned for the five hundredth anniversary of Christopher Columbus's arrival in the Americas. Two events in 1994 symbolized both an increasing respect for, and the continuing problems of, American Indians. The first facility of the National Museum of the American Indian, a new part of the Smithsonian Institution, opened in New York (funding had been approved by Congress in 1989). On the other hand, the National Congress of American Indians and the National Black Caucus announced an alliance, stating that American Indians and African Americans continued to face similar forces of political and economic oppression.

Over a century of mismanagement of Indian trust funds was brought to public attention with the filing of a class-action lawsuit against the Department of the Interior by Elouise Cobell, treasurer of the Blackfeet in Montana, *Cobell v. Babbitt*, in 1996. (The lawsuit changed to *Cobell v. Norton* with the appointment of Gale Norton as interior secretary in 2001.) The suit charged that $100 billion of trust funds for land-use royalties, administered by the Department of the Interior since the break-up of reservations under the Dawes Act of 1887, was missing and the paperwork that would track the funds was in shambles. By 2002, three cabinet members from two administrations had been found in contempt of court for blocking or delaying the turning over of records.

See also: Alaska Native Claims Settlement Act; Alcatraz Island occupation; American Indian Higher Education Consortium; American Indian

Movement; American Indian Policy Review Commission; American Indian Religious Freedom Act; *Colliflower v. Garland*; Council of Energy Resource Tribes; Determined Residents United for Mohawk Sovereignty; *Duro v. Reina; Employment Division, Dept. of Human Resources of the State of Oregon et al. v. Smith*; Federally recognized tribes; Fish-ins; Indian Child Welfare Act; Indian Citizenship Act; Indian Civil Rights Act; Indian Claims Commission; Indian Education Acts; Indian Gaming Regulatory Act; Indian Health Service; Indian New Deal; Indian preference; Indian Reorganization Act; Indian Self-Determination and Education Assistance Act; Indian-white relations: U.S., 1871-1933; International Indian Treaty Council; Keeler Commission; Kennedy Report; Longest Walk; *Lyng v. Northwest Indian Cemetery Protective Association*; Maine Indian Claims Act; Menominee Restoration Act; National Congress of American Indians; National Indian Education Association; National Indian Youth Council; *Native American Church v. Navajo Tribal Council*; Native American Graves Protection and Repatriation Act; Native American Rights Fund; Navajo-Hopi Land Settlement Act; Navajo Rehabilitation Act; Nisga'a Agreement in Principle; Nunavut Territory; Oka crisis; Oklahoma Indian Welfare Act; *Oliphant v. Suquamish Indian Tribe*; Pine Ridge shootout and Peltier killings; Public Law 280; *Santa Clara Pueblo v. Martinez*; Termination Resolution; Trail of Broken Treaties; Treaties and agreements in the United States; *United States v. Washington; Winters v. United States*; Women of All Red Nations; World wars; Wounded Knee occupation.

Byron D. Cannon

Sources for Further Study

Chamberlain, Kathleen P. *Under Sacred Ground: A History of Navajo Oil, 1922-1982*. Albuquerque: University of New Mexico Press, 2000. An ethnography and history of the effect of oil production on the formation and expansion of Navajo tribal government.

Clarkin, Thomas. *Federal Indian Policy in the Kennedy and Johnson Administrations, 1961-1969*. Albuquerque: University of New Mexico Press, 2001. A groundbreaking study of federal Indian policy in the 1960's.

Falkowski, James E. *Indian Law/Race Law: A Five-Hundred-Year History*. New York: Praeger, 1922. Places the subject of U.S. government policy toward Indians in a wider context both of historical and contemporary international legal models.

Fixico, Donald L. *Termination and Relocation: Federal Policy, 1945-1966*. Albuquerque: University of New Mexico Press, 1986. This is a study of the phase of BIA policy that existed from 1953 to 1960, involving presumed "self-help," including working away from home reservations.

_____. *The Urban Indian Experience in America*. Albuquerque: University of New Mexico Press, 2000. An ethnography of the urban Indian experience, especially in third- and fourth-generation urban dwellers who are increasingly distanced from the reservation experience.

Hoxie, Frederick E., James Merrell, and Peter C. Mancall, eds. *American Nations: Encounters in Indian Country, 1850-Present*. New York: Routledge, 2001. A series of essays on aspects of Indian-U.S. relations and cultural encounters.

Peroff, Nicholas C. *Menominee Drums*. Norman: University of Oklahoma Press, 1982. A case study of one of the most important examples of tribal termination actions.

Prucha, Francis Paul, ed. *Documents of United States Indian Policy*. 3d ed. Lincoln: University of Nebraska Press, 2000. General policy and issues for specific tribes.

International Indian Treaty Council

Date: Established 1974
Locale: United States and Canada
Tribes involved: Pantribal
Categories: Native government, Organizations, Treaties, Twentieth century history
Significance: Promoted international rights of indigenous peoples; established indigenous presence at the United Nations.

The International Indian Treaty Council (IITC) was founded during a conference convened on the Standing Rock Reservation (North Dakota) during July, 1974. Its initial mandate, conveyed by the Lakota elders, was to "take the 1868 Fort Laramie Treaty and place it before the community of nations." AIM leader Russell Means, asked to assume responsibility for IITC, accepted by agreeing to serve as "Permanent Trustee." Jimmie Durham, a Cherokee AIM member, became IITC's founding director.

By 1975, Means and Durham had established an office in New York and expanded the mission of the "international diplomatic arm of AIM" to include advocacy of the rights of all indigenous peoples, worldwide. Durham then set about organizing the first major forum on indigenous rights in the history of the United Nations.

This resulted in the "Indian Summer in Geneva," an assembly of delegates from ninety-eight indigenous nations throughout the Western Hemisphere at the Palace of Nations in Geneva, Switzerland, during July, 1977. As the coordinating entity, IITC became the first indigenous Non-Governing Organization (NGO; Type-II, Consultative) ever recognized by the United Nations.

The assembly stimulated the U.N. to establish a formal body, the Working Group on Indigenous Populations, under its Economic and Social Council (ECOSOC) for purposes of receiving annual reports on the grievances of the world's native peoples. The Working Group's broader charge was to make the studies necessary to prepare a Draft Declaration on the Rights of Indigenous Peoples for ratification by the U.N. General Assembly as international law.

With this established, Durham resigned in 1981 to pursue a career as an artist. He was replaced by Russell Means's younger brother, Bill, who proved a far less appropriate director. Almost immediately, the younger Means initiated a policy of aligning IITC with a range of leftist governments, many of them oppressing indigenous peoples within their borders. The result was a steady erosion of native support for IITC.

By 1986, disputes over IITC's support of Nicaragua's Sandinista regime in its drive to subordinate the Miskito, Sumu, and Rama peoples of the country's Atlantic coast led to a purge. "Indigenists," such as Harvard-trained Shawnee attorney Glenn Morris, were summarily expelled from IITC. The Lakota elders' original mandate was negated, Russell Means was displaced from his permanent trusteeship, and IITC was structurally separated from AIM by its incorporation under U.S. law.

Thereafter, although Bill Means continued to speak of "representing more than a hundred indigenous nations," IITC's isolation and decline accelerated. By the early 1990's, it was increasingly encumbered by the fundraising requirements of supporting its staff. Fortunately, many of the peoples whose rights it had once championed had by then learned to represent themselves internationally.

See also: American Indian Movement; Fort Laramie Treaty of 1868.

Ward Churchill

Sources for Further Study

Deloria, Vine, Jr. *Behind the Trail of Broken Treaties: An Indian Declaration of Independence.* 2d ed. Norman: University of Oklahoma Press, 1987.

Morris, Glenn T., and Ward Churchill. "Between a Rock and a Hard Place: Left-Wing Revolution, Right-Wing Reaction, and the Destruction of Indigenous People." *Cultural Survival Quarterly* 11, no. 3 (1987): 17-24.

Weyler, Rex. *Blood of the Land: The U.S. Government and Corporate War Against the First Nations*. 2d ed. Philadelphia: New Society Publishers, 1992.

Irish Potato Famine

Date: 1847
Locale: Oklahoma, Ireland
Tribes involved: Choctaw
Categories: Nineteenth century history, Reservations and relocation, Twentieth century history
Significance: The Irish people commemorate the Choctaw people of Oklahoma for raising funds for Irish famine relief in 1847, only a few years after the Choctaw Trail of Tears.

The Choctaw Indian nation originated and lived in Mississippi and Alabama. In 1819, the United States government, following up on Thomas Jefferson's policy of the Americanization of native peoples, began seeking the removal of the Choctaw from their rich Mississippi territory to the largely inhospitable lands of Oklahoma. On September 15, 1830, the Treaty of Dancing Rabbit Creek dictated that the move become a reality. Between 1830 and 1834, during the presidency of Andrew Jackson, the Choctaw made the five-hundred-mile journey from Mississippi to Oklahoma. The trek was made by three successive groups in three successive years, each in the middle of winter. The Choctaw were ordered to leave their possessions and livestock behind and were not provided with tents, supplies, or medical assistance on the journey.

Army guides unfamiliar with the terrain became lost. Temperatures dropped below freezing, and many of the people died of disease and starvation. Since the cold winter precluded digging graves, the dead were burned by the roadside. Some fourteen thousand Choctaws perished along what has come to be known in Choctaw lore as the Trail of Tears.

Halfway around the world the Irish people would likewise experience starvation and removal only a dozen or so years later, in the tragedy now known as the Irish Potato Famine.

Famine in Ireland. Ireland of the mid-nineteenth century was a bleak place. The famine, caused by the fungus *Phytophthora infestans*, ravaged the Irish potato crop for five years. The fungus that caused the blight had found its way into Ireland from North America. The blight was a particular disaster for laborers in Ireland, who dependended on the potato for daily sustenance. It was also a catastrophe for the British government, which was ill-prepared to cope with the challenge of administering relief to a population of approximately eight million people. At its first appearance in September of 1845, local newspapers mentioned the blight, but public reaction was divided by political difference or allegiance, and the looming disaster was denied proper attention. While politicians and others bickered over which group—medical, commercial, or administrative—was most competent or obliged to deal with it, famine swept across Ireland and devastated its people. In the long run, between 1.1 and 1.5 million persons died of starvation; at least 500,000 had been evicted from their homes by landlords; some 3 million people (about 40 percent of the population) were on some form of official relief; more than 1 million were crammed into poorhouses; and between 1845 and 1855, more than 2.1 million Irish (about 25 percent of the population prior to the famine) emigrated overseas, nearly 1.9 million of them to North America. Naturally, the immigrants shared their story with their neighbors in the new country. Some of these were the Choctaw.

The Choctaw-Ireland Connection. Following up on Irish appeals for international relief from famine and starvation, a great meeting of the Choctaw nation was held near Skullyville, Oklahoma, in 1847 to consider the merits of the cause. In the long run, the Choctaw, in conjunction with traders, missionaries, and Indian agency officials, contributed $170 (some sources indicate $710) to buy food for Irish famine relief. The lesser sum is estimated at around the equivalent of $10,000 in 2002 dollars. Among the distributors of relief would have been the Belfast Ladies' Association, the Society of Friends (Quakers), and the British Relief Association. The Irish never forgot the Choctaw gift, and in May, 1995, Mary Robinson, then president of Ireland, formally thanked the Choctaw nation from the steps of the Tribal Complex building for its act of generosity some 150 years prior. In Choctaw, President Robinson said: *Chohta i yakne ala li kut na sa yukpa.* ("I am glad to have come to Choctaw country.") Chief Hollis E. Roberts thanked her for recognizing the Choctaw Nation for what was done in the past and looked forward to what could be done in the future.

The Ties That Bind. Like the Irish diaspora in America, the modern Choctaw have grown strong in numbers and resolve. Today, the Oklahoma and Mississippi tribal networks offer community, social, medical, and educational assistance to members. They sponsor an annual walk along the Trail of Tears to honor the memory of the ancestors. Likewise, a group of Irish activists from the Dublin-based Action From Ireland completed a commemorative five-hundred-mile walk from Oklahoma to Mississippi, the Trail of Tears in reverse, to raise famine funds for Somalia. In September, 1997, an intertribal group from North America landed in Ireland to do its Irish leg of a "sacred run," with 58,000 miles completed since 1978. Once again, as in 1847, hands and hearts have reached across the ocean in solidarity.

Arthur Gribben

Sources for Further Study

Angie, Debo. *The Rise and Fall of the Choctaw Republic.* 2d ed. Reprint. Norman: University of Oklahoma Press, 1989. The history and cultural development of the Choctaw from earliest times.

Carson, James T., ed. *Searching for the Bright Path.* Lincoln: University of Nebraska Press, 1999. Mississippi Choctaws from prehistory to removal.

Fitzpatrick, Marie-Louise. *The Long March.* Dublin: Wolfhound Press, 1999. For younger audiences, tells the story of Choona, a young Choctaw who must make his own decision about answering the Irish people's plea for help.

Gribben, Arthur, ed. *The Great Famine and the Irish Diaspora in America.* Boston: University of Massachusetts Press, 1999. Interdisciplinary collection of essays on the consequences of the famine from perspectives of anthropology, ethnomusicology, political science, and more.

See also: Trail of Tears.

Iroquois Confederacy

Date: c. 1500-1777

Locale: Hudson River west to Lake Michigan and St. Lawrence River south to the Cumberland Gap and the Ohio River

Tribes involved: Iroquois Confederacy (Mohawk, Oneida, Onondaga, Cayuga, Seneca, Tuscarora)

Categories: Colonial history, Native government

Significance: The Haudenosaunee, or People of the Longhouse, controlled northeastern North America for three centuries.

The Iroquois are the prime example of the level of cultural evolution that American Indian tribes attained when they stayed in one place for a long time. Archaeologic evidence places the predecessors of the Iroquois in New York State for one thousand to fifteen hundred years prior to the emergence of the Iroquois Confederacy. A subsistence culture called Owasco preceded the Iroquois, which in turn was preceded by the Hopewell culture. Both cultures left traceable influences in Iroquois culture. By 1400, contemporary-style Iroquoian villages existed; by 1600, all the units of the confederacy were calling the larger group Haudenosaunee, the People of the Longhouse.

The Haudenosaunee lived in fortified, stockade villages, were agrarian and matrilineal (that is, passed property from mother to daughters), and banded together through a strong political and religious system, in which ultimate power was vested in the hands of the oldest "sensible" woman of each clan. The foundation of the culture was called the fireplace, or hearth. Each hearth—a mother and her children—was part of a larger extended family, or *owachira*. Two or more owachiras made a clan; eight clans made a tribe.

The purposes of the Iroquois Confederacy, League of the Iroquois, or League of Five Nations, which was established as early as 1500, were to unite and pacify the infighting Iroquois and to gain strength in numbers in order to resist the opposition of Huron- and Algonquian-speaking neighbors. (The word *iroquois*, as spelled by the French, is probably from the Algonquian enemy name *iriokiu* or "spitting snake.") The confederacy, if later dates of its inception are accepted, may have formed as a response to the fur trade. Before the consolidation of the confederacy, wars, primarily revenge feuds, were constant among the Iroquois, who had no mechanism to bring the strife to an end. The consolidation of the confederacy was primarily a result of the efforts of the Mohawk chief Hiawatha and the Onondaga chief Atotarho, historical figures who based the religious and political principles of the confederacy on the teachings of Deganawida (the Peacemaker), whose historical authenticity is contested. The political rules and regulations, the cultural model, and the spiritual teachings and religious model all attributed to Deganawida were later qualified and codified by Handsome Lake, a Seneca visionary prophet responding to the pressures of Christianity after the Revolutionary War.

Social Organization. The League of the Iroquois included the Mohawk, Oneida, Onondaga, Cayuga, Seneca (the Five Nations), and, after 1722, the Tuscarora (the Six Nations). The league was based on a carefully crafted constitution. The "faithkeeper," or central religious leader, called a yearly council to recite the constitution and its laws and resolve differences. The council retained the roles of the leaders, which were defined from ancient

Native Peoples of Eastern North America c. 1600

times by clan system relationships. Fifty chiefs made up the council and served for life but could be removed from office by the clan mothers if they violated moral or ethical codes.

Religious life was organized according to the teaching of the Peacemaker. Three men and three women supervised the keeping of the ceremonies. The cosmology was well defined, and the origin stories are detailed and sophisticated. Curing illnesses was a central part of daily religious life. The Iroquois had a profound sense of the psychology of the soul and understood dreams and divinations to be communications between one's personality and one's soul.

At the time of the arrival of the Europeans, the coastal regions of the Northeast were occupied by Algonquian-speaking peoples and the inland waterways were occupied by Iroquoian-speaking people. The entire area was crisscrossed by the trails of a vast trading network that reached to the Subarctic. Storable foods were traded for furs, nuts, obsidian, shells, flints, and other items. Wampum belts of shells and, later, beads described symbolically and mnemonically almost all dealings politically among and within tribes.

Impact of the Fur Trade. The fur trade and European economics changed the lives of the Iroquois drastically. Acquisition, exploitation, and competition became normal for Northeastern tribes. The confederacy created a combined military force of more than a thousand men that, in the mid-seventeenth century, effectively destroyed the Huron, Erie, Petun, and Illinois tribes as players in the fur trade.

The ever-increasing encroachment of the French and the British presented the Iroquois with three options: compromise; adoption of the ways of the Europeans, including their economics and religion; or use of violence to reject the wave of invaders. The Iroquois drew from all three options: They compromised whenever necessary to keep their neutrality and the peace; adopted the religions and much of the trade economy (thus becoming dependent upon metal items), but not the political and societal structures, of the Europeans; and chose to fight violently against the French and the tribal allies of the French.

The nations of the confederacy had a crucial role in U.S. history. After 1609, when a war party of Mohawks met a group of French and Huron soldiers under Samuel de Champlain and lost six Mohawk warriors to the muskets of the French, the Mohawks carried a dogged hatred of the French forward into alliances—first with the Dutch, from whom they obtained their firearms, and then with the British, from whom they obtained all forms of trade items and by whom they were converted to the Anglican version of Christianity. Thus the Hudson and Mohawk River Valleys were opened to the British, and the French were locked out. The subsequent British dominance of the New World was made much easier by Iroquois control of the waterways from the east coast into the interior of the continent.

The Iroquois Constitution. In 1677, the Five Nations of the Confederacy met in Albany and wrote into history their memorized, mnemonically cued Great Law, best described as a constitution. At the end of the seventeenth century, the Iroquois had mastered the artful politics of their pivotal position. They played the various European traders one against the other, kept their neutrality with level-headed diplomacy, and maintained their control of the riverine system and the Great Lakes with intimidating success. Their hegemony included the territory from Maine to the Mississippi River, and from the Ottawa River in Canada to Kentucky and the Chesapeake Bay region.

In the eighteenth century, the Iroquois had more power than any other native nation in North America. Colonial delegates from all the states of the Americas traveled to Albany to learn about governing from the Iroquois. The longhouse sachems urged the colonists to form assemblies and to meet and discuss common interests. In 1754, the first intercolonial conference was held at Albany, and Iroquois delegates were in attendance.

The Iroquois maintained their power in spite of the assault of European culture and religion during the eighteenth century. Until about the end of the French and Indian War, the Iroquois were united in their resolve to stay neutral and not be drawn into the imperial wars between the French and the English. By the time of the American Revolution, however, the league's ability to stay neutral and to influence its members had lessened. During the Revolutionary War, the Seneca, Cayuga, and Mohawk fought with the British; the Onondaga tried to remain aloof; the Oneida and Tuscarora sided with the Americans.

The American Revolution ended the power of the Iroquois. By 1800, only two thousand survived on tiny reservations in western New York. Another six thousand had fled to Canada. Despite the conflicts and contacts with European cultures, the Iroquois have retained their society and many of their cultural practices, including kinship and ceremonial ties.

See also: Albany Congress; Beaver Wars; Code of Handsome Lake; Fort Greenville Treaty; Fort Stanwix Treaty; Indian-white relations: French colonial; Iroquois Confederacy-U.S. Congress meeting; Northwest Ordinance; Paxton Boys' Massacres; Prehistory: Northeast; Prophetstown; Tecumseh's Rebellion; Walking Purchase.

Glenn Schiffman

Sources for Further Study

Fenton, William Nelson. *The Great Law and the Longhouse: A Political History of the Iroquois Confederacy.* Norman: University of Oklahoma Press, 1998. A massive work—over eight hundred pages—on the history and culture of the Iroquois Confederacy.

Graymont, Barbara. *The Iroquois*. New York: Chelsea House Press, 1988. Graymont is an expert on the Haudenosaunee or Iroquois; this precise, concise text is essential for scholars of the Longhouse culture.

Henry, Thomas R. *Wilderness Messiah: The Story of Hiawatha and the Iroquois*. New York: W. Sloane, 1955. Defines the line between legend and history in the founding of the Iroquois league, and in the stories of Hiawatha, Deganawida, and Atotarho.

Jennings, Francis. *The Founders of America*. New York: W. W. Norton, 1993. An accurate history of special value to high school teachers.

Lyons, Oren, et al. *Exiled in the Land of the Free*. Santa Fe, N.Mex.: Clear Light Publishers, 1992. Lyons, faithkeeper of the Six Nations Confederacy, is distinctive in his understanding of the role of the American Indian in U.S. history.

Taylor, Colin F., ed. *The Native Americans: The Indigenous People of North America*. New York: Smithmark, 1991. Companion book to a 1990's televised series on Native Americans.

Iroquois Confederacy-U.S. Congress meeting

Date: May 24 and June 11, 1776

Locale: Finger Lakes Region, Mohawk River Valley, Albany, Boston, Philadelphia

Tribes involved: Iroquois Confederacy (Mohawk, Oneida, Onondaga, Cayuga, Seneca, Tuscarora)

Categories: Eighteenth century history, National government and legislation, Native government

Significance: The Six Nations of the Iroquois Confederacy attempt to secure neutrality during the Revolutionary War but ultimately dissolve, losing control of the Northeast riverine trade.

The withdrawal of the French in 1763 from the New World was a watershed event for the Six Nations (the Iroquois Confederacy). Between 1640, when the Iroquois established their hegemony over the fur trade, and the end of the French and Indian War in 1763, the Iroquois were profoundly involved in the imperial rivalries between the English and the French and were pivotal in the balance of power in the New World. When the French left, the Iroquois lost the fulcrum on which they kept the balance.

The British government's Proclamation of 1763 provided that all territory between the crest of the Alleghenies and the Mississippi River and from Florida to 50° north latitude were closed to settlers and land speculators and reserved "for the present" to American Indians. This proclamation, however, served the British agenda, not the needs of either natives or settlers. Britain wished to protect the valuable furbearing animals' habitat from encroaching colonists. Guaranteeing boundaries, moreover, did not guarantee sovereignty.

In fact, the British were less accommodating of the Indians than the French had been. Native resistance flared with Pontiac's Resistance (1763-1766), in which the Six Nation Senecas fought on the side of Pontiac, while the Mohawks supported the British. When that rebellion failed, the Senecas were punished by William Johnson and were forced to cede some of their land to the British. In 1775, the Senecas successfully negotiated with the Americans at Pittsburgh to remain neutral in the frontier battles and the impending Revolutionary War, as long as the Americans stayed out of Iroquois territory. This negotiation was approved by the full governing council of the Six Nations. It was the last significant action that exhibited that the council still had control of its warriors.

In that Pittsburgh agreement, American settlers who encroached on Mohawk territory were supposed to be punished by Americans. However, encroachment of the farmers and frontiersmen called the Albany Group near the Mohawk River Valley never abated; thus the Mohawks, led by Joseph Brant, grew more dependent on the British to help defend against American encroachment.

English Agreements During the Revolution. During 1775 and into the spring of 1776, the British expended considerable effort to create military allegiances with all the tribes of the Six Nations. So great was their influence among the Mohawks that Joseph Brant and several other warrior chiefs sailed to England in November, 1775, professedly to secure Iroquois sovereignty in exchange for allegiance to the British during the war. By 1776, the American Congress wanted desperately for the Iroquois to join the fight on the side of the colonies, but they did not have the financial ability to dispense the gifts of food, ammunition, clothing, and other necessities that the Iroquois expected when asked to fight as mercenaries. The American alternative was a proclamation of friendship and the stated desire that the Six Nations remain neutral.

In England, King George III guaranteed Joseph Brant the boundaries of the Iroquois homelands, but this was no concession to the key word, "sovereignty." It is believed that Joseph Brant misunderstood the British attitude toward territorial *sovereignty* and territorial *occupancy*. It is known that Brant believed the Americans' goal was to overrun the continent at the expense of all American Indians. Brant decided the Iroquois' future lay with the British. In England, Joseph Brant was commissioned a colonel in the British colonial militia.

Up to this time, the Americans had done no violence to the Iroquois and, with the exception of the Albany Group, were careful to avoid trespassing on Iroquois territory. After acting Indian Commissioner John Johnson attempted to arrest the patriot missionary Samuel Kirkland at Oriskany, the Oneida stronghold, the Albany Group entered Mohawk territory to arrest Johnson. Both actions failed in their objectives, although Kirkland was momentarily muzzled and Johnson had to flee to Canada with a significant force of Mohawk warriors.

The Americans Court the Iroquois. With this backdrop, an Iroquois delegation of twenty-one members representing four of the Six Nations traveled to Philadelphia to be presented to Congress on May 24 and again on June 11. Brant was still in England. The delegates were presented to "the great warrior chief" George Washington on May 24 and to the full Congress on June 11. While in Philadelphia, they boarded in a room directly above the meeting room of the Congress. Washington had spent the previous two weeks persuading the Continental Congress to break the Pittsburgh agreement and allow him to recruit an Indian militia. On May 25, the Congress resolved that it would be expedient to engage American Indians in the service of the colonies. The significance of this was twofold: Congress was ignoring or nullifying the sovereignty of the Council of the Confederacy that had approved the Pittsburgh agreement, and Congress was ignoring the purpose of the Iroquois delegation, which was to assure the sincere and serious effort by the Iroquois to hold fast to the neutrality agreement.

George Washington knew the path to either a British or American victory led through Iroquois land. The strategic importance of that land could not be ignored. Congress did not tell the Iroquois delegates that Washington was about to recruit Iroquois as soldiers; as the minutes of June 11 show,

> We shall order our warriors not to hurt any of your kindred, and we hope you will not allow any of your young brothers to join with the enemy . . . we desire you accept these few necessaries as tokens of our good-will . . . we hope the friendship between us will be firm as long as the sun shall shine and the waters run, that we be as one people.

While saying these words, Congress did not understand the disastrous implications of their efforts to recruit American Indians.

The word to recruit was passed through patriot channels to the Reverend Kirkland and the Oneida and Tuscarora, and also to General Philip Schuyler of the Albany Group. Schuyler was asked to recruit two thousand Iroquois to be paid a reward of one hundred dollars for every British officer killed or taken prisoner and thirty dollars for every enlisted man. Schuyler was dubious not only of the policy but also of the numbers—there were not two thousand Iroquois men available, much less warriors, who were not already aiding the British. The Oneida, however, decided to send five hundred warriors to help protect the American Fort Stanwix near Utica, New York. This action would breach the Iroquois Confederacy.

The Revolutionary War brought what was thought to be impossible to the Iroquois nations: Their Covenant Chain broke. In 1777, the league chiefs "covered their fire." For the first time within living memory, Iroquois fought and killed Iroquois, and their league shattered. The Treaty of Paris in 1783 said nothing about the American Indians. Those who allied with Britain were abandoned to the care of the Americans. Joseph Brant's pledge to the king in exchange for Brant's understanding of a pledge of sovereignty was particularly bitter when he discovered that the British had ceded all Mohawk land to the Americans. That the Mohawks were given a reserve in Canada was little consolation.

See also: Albany Congress; Beaver Wars; Code of Handsome Lake; Fort Greenville Treaty; Fort Stanwix Treaty; Indian-white relations: French colonial; Iroquois Confederacy; Northwest Ordinance; Paxton Boys' Massacres; Prehistory: Northeast; Prophetstown; Tecumseh's Rebellion; Walking Purchase.

Glenn Schiffman

Sources for Further Study

Graymont, Barbara. *The Iroquois*. New York: Chelsea House Publishers, 1988. A useful book by a recognized expert on the subject.

_____. *The Iroquois in the American Revolution*. Syracuse, N.Y.: Syracuse University Press, 1972. The author is considered to be the foremost authority on the subject matter of this work.

Jennings, Francis. *The Founders of America*. New York: W. W. Norton, 1993. This exceptional history of the events around the American Revolution is accessible to both casual readers and scholars.

Josephy, Alvin M., Jr. *Five Hundred Nations: An Illustrated History of North American Indians*. New York: Alfred A. Knopf, 1994. Companion book to the CBS television series *Five Hundred Nations*, written by one of America's foremost authorities on American Indian culture.

Stone, William L. *Life of Joseph Brant*. Albany, N.Y.: J. Munsell, 1864. A source for quotations of early colonial documents. Contains some historical inaccuracies; for example, this is the source of the erroneous information that Brant was in North America at the time of the Philadelphia meeting.

Wise, Jennings C. *The Red Man in the New World Drama*, edited by Vine Deloria, Jr. New York: Macmillan, 1971. The key words "new world drama" provide a clue to the American Indian perspective of this author and editor.

Jay's Treaty

Date: November 19, 1794
Locale: Canada, United States
Tribes involved: Pantribal in the United States
Categories: Colonial history, Eighteenth century history, National government and legislation, Treaties
Significance: Jay's Treaty, signed between Great Britain and the United States, was concerned with trade and issues of peace; among other provisions, it permitted Native American people to travel freely across the border between Canada and the United States.

The Treaty of Paris (1783), which ended the American Revolutionary War and made peace between Britain and the United States, contained no mention of Indians and totally ignored questions about the status of their lands. Many eastern tribal groups were fragmented during the revolution. Some pledged loyalty to the British, who, in return for that loyalty, promised to support the tribe's land claims and continue generous trading provisions. Other tribes favored the colonists. In the end, all tribal groups were disregarded in the peace negotiations. Prior to the American Revolution, many tribes had negotiated treaties with Great Britain and these contained provisions for reserved land bases. The Americans generally disregarded those treaties because they were made with Britain, and further, the Americans rejected a proposal to establish an aboriginal state.

Serious problems arose in the Old Northwest as American settlers pushed farther west. Hostilities escalated to the point that the newly formed American government realized it was necessary to begin negotiating treaties with Indians as well as to protect their lands. Nonetheless, fierce attacks between frontiersmen and Indians persisted. Compounding problems in the Northwest was the fact that the British refused to evacuate western military forts as provided in the Treaty of Paris. Indians continued to seek refuge with the British, who, in turn, encouraged Indian attacks on American settlers. Pressure on the U.S. government to address these issues was increased when Indians won a stunning victory on November 4, 1791, over General Arthur St. Clair's troops near the headwaters of the Wabash River.

Quelling Hostilities. Hostilities with the British escalated on all fronts and the United States requested American statesman John Jay to negotiate an agreement between the United States and Great Britain. Once ratified, this agreement became known as Jay's Treaty. Among other provisions which related to shipping and trade, the British agreed to evacuate Northwestern posts by June 1, 1796, and to grant free trade between Canada and the United States. The provisions of the treaty meant that Indians faced increasing American settlement in their lands. Controversy swirled around the provision that permitted traders from Canada to operate unrestricted in American territory, because there was fear these traders, who always enjoyed a close relationship with the Indians, would encourage the Indians to continue hostilities against the American frontiersmen. To add to these fears, the treaty permitted Indians to travel freely between Canada and the United States. This guarantee is still in effect, and though no longer a threat to American security, restrictions imposed by both Canada and the United States have caused Indians to protest them as a breach of the treaty.

Carole A. Barrett

See also: Fallen Timbers, Battle of; Fort Wayne Treaty; Indian-white relations: Canadian; Indian-white relations: English colonial; Indian-white relations: U.S., 1775-1830; Little Turtle's War; Northwest Ordinance; Proclamation of 1763; Treaties and agreements in Canada; Treaties and agreements in the United States.

Keeler Commission

Date: Established 1961
Locale: United States
Tribes involved: Pantribal in the United States

Categories: National government and legislation, Twentieth century history

Significance: This commission's report helped end the termination policy that began in 1953.

The intent of federal Indian policy from 1953 to 1962, as set forth in the Termination Resolution of 1953, was to dissolve government obligations and responsibilities toward Native Americans in order to bring about assimilation. This disastrous program was called "termination." It undermined tribal governments and resources, eroded ethnic identities, and impoverished groups such as the Klamath of Oregon and Menominee of Wisconsin. By the end of the decade, so much criticism had been generated by these developments that a new political consciousness concerning Indian problems began to emerge.

John F. Kennedy, elected president in 1960, affirmed that Indian land would be protected, that self-determination would be promoted, and that steps would be taken to avoid undermining the cultural heritage of any group. Secretary of the Interior Stewart Udall appointed a special task force on Indian affairs in February of 1961 with an eye toward reorganizing the Bureau of Indian Affairs (BIA) in order to carry out this mandate.

William Wayne Keeler, a top-level executive with Phillips Petroleum Company and principal chief of the Cherokee Nation, was appointed chairman of the task force. Other members included Philleo Nash, an anthropologist and former lieutenant governor of Wisconsin who had participated in the Menominee termination plans; James Officer, a University of Arizona anthropologist; William Zimmerman, Jr., assistant commissioner of the BIA from 1933 to 1950; and consultant John Crow. After hearings and field trips to western reservations, the commission filed its seventy-seven-page report on July 10, 1961. Nash also included a summary of the report in the *Annual Report of the Commissioner of Indian Affairs* for 1961.

The commission's main finding was that future BIA policy should emphasize development rather than termination. Recommendations included the attraction of industries to reservations, along with job training and placement services. Loan programs were encouraged, rapid settlement of Indian Claims Commission cases was urged, and increased efforts to educate the general public about Indian culture were promoted. The commission report also stressed the need for Indian participation in government programs.

In the 1960's, Congress granted authorization for Indian loans, tribal resources increased, and development of reservation resources replaced the focus on assimilating Indians through relocation to the cities. The Keeler

Commission played a small but noticeable role in the shift away from the termination policy.

See also: Bureau of Indian Affairs; Termination Resolution.

Gary A. Olson

Keetoowah Society

Date: Established 1859
Locale: United States
Tribes involved: Cherokee
Categories: Nineteenth century history, Organizations
Significance: The Keetoowah Society was founded in an effort to advance the interests of full-blooded Cherokees.

The Keetoowah Society was founded by two white clergymen in 1859. The men were abolitionists, and their goal, ostensibly, was to organize Cherokee opposition to slavery. Members of the order were full-bloods, and some called themselves "Pin Indians," wearing crossed pins on their left lapels. The Keetoowah Society evolved from simple support of abolition to a group whose purpose was the protection of Cherokee interests. Society goals were taken from the ancient Anti-Kutani, designed to oppose adoption of European American ways. "Pin Indians" were Christians who wished to syncretize their religion with ancient tribal rites.

The Keetoowah Society was popular and at one time had a membership of more than two thousand men. It was fiercely loyal to the Union during the Civil War (1861-1865). That fact threatened the Confederacy, which impressed society members into military service. Stories abound of men who were forced to serve the South and deserted at the first opportunity.

Following the Civil War, the Keetoowah Society remained active in Cherokee political and social life. It opposed the Dawes Commission in the 1890's, insisting on the observance of treaty obligations, a guarantee of self-government, and freedom from territorial organization. When the Cherokee delegation reached agreement with the Dawes Commission in 1900, the full-blood Keetoowah Society urged its members to boycott the agreement. In 1906, the Dawes Commission agreement prevailed. The society then functioned as a political party (the Union Party) and fraternal lodge. The Keetoowah Society is viable to this day and is the only fraternal lodge in the United States whose principal emblem is the United States flag.

See also: Cherokee legal cases; *Cherokee Phoenix*; *Cherokee Tobacco* case; Cherokee War.

David N. Mielke

Kennedy Report

Date: 1967
Locale: United States
Tribes involved: Pantribal in the United States
Categories: Education, National government and legislation, Twentieth century history
Significance: The result of a Senate Subcommittee investigation into Native American education, which led to the Indian Education Act of 1972.

In 1967, the United States Senate created the Special Subcommittee on Indian Education. Senator Robert F. Kennedy chaired the committee, which held hearings and authorized studies of educational programs for Native Americans. His brother Edward "Ted" Kennedy was the chair when the subcommittee released its final report in November, 1969. Entitled *Indian Education: A National Tragedy, a National Challenge*, but more commonly called the Kennedy Report, the study concluded that "national policies for educating American Indians are a failure of major proportions." The report blamed efforts to force Indian children to accept cultural values other than their own as one of the major flaws in Indian education and as a leading cause of high dropout rates. The subcommittee offered sixty recommendations for improving Indian education, which included emphasizing Indian culture and history and increasing funding for existing programs. Although government officials responsible for Indian education rushed to defend their programs, the Kennedy Report raised serious questions in the minds of many Americans concerning the government's management of Indian affairs. The report's findings helped promote passage of the Indian Education Act of 1972, which implemented some of its recommendations.

See also: American Indian Higher Education Consortium; Carlisle Indian School; Indian Education Acts; Indian Self-Determination and Education Assistance Act; National Congress of American Indians.

Thomas Clarkin

Kennewick Man controversy

Date: Beginning July 28, 1996
Locale: Washington State
Tribes involved: Colville, Nez Perce, Umatilla, Wanapum, Yakima
Categories: Court cases, National government and legislation, Pre-Columbian history, Twentieth century history
Significance: The debate over the ancient skeletal remains known as Kennewick Man raised a number of historical and contemporary questions about Native American identity and about conflicts between tribal traditions and modern scientific activities.

The people who lived in the Americas before the arrival of Europeans in the fifteenth century are commonly identified as Native Americans or American Indians. Most scientists maintain that Native Americans are descended from groups of people who crossed the Bering Strait from Siberia. Some Native Americans believe that their first ancestors came into existence on the American continents. Claims that Kennewick Man resembled Europeans more than contemporary Native Americans therefore challenged both standard scientific views and Native American traditions.

In addition, the discovery revived long-standing disagreements between Native Americans and parts of the American scientific establishment. For most of American history, the remains of the Native American dead were frequently deposited in museums and laboratories. This was resented by living Native Americans, whose traditions taught that their dead should be treated with respect. In 1990, the U.S. Congress passed the Native American Graves Protection and Repatriation Act (NAGPRA), which recognized the rights of Native American groups to the remains of their ancestors. When some anthropologists and archaeologists attempted to claim the right to keep and study the Kennewick bones, Native Americans saw this as disrespect for their dead and as another attack on Native American culture. Those who were against handing the remains over to contemporary Native Americans argued that scientific values required studying the remains and that it was not clear which tribe or nation, if any, could claim Kennewick Man as an ancestor.

The Discovery. The Kennewick Man controversy began when two young men attending annual hydroplane races found a skull in the Columbia River near Kennewick, Washington, on July 28, 1996. The discoverers turned the skull over to local police authorities, who investigated and found more skeletal remains. The county coroner recognized that the remains were too old to be the result of a recent crime and he asked an anthropologist, James C. Chatters, to examine them. On July 29, Dr. Chatters had the bones X-rayed and CAT-scanned. Chatters came to two conclusions that would create both publicity and controversy. First, he decided that some of the features of the skull were not those of contemporary Native Americans. He maintained that the skull had "Caucasoid" characteristics, or characteristics usually associated with people whose ancestors were from the area of Europe. Second, with further investigation, he came to the conclusion that the bones were more than eight thousand years old.

After the initial discovery, the area of the find was carefully examined, and investigators found more bones during August, 1996. Since the remains had been found on land owned by the federal government, Chatters informed the Army Corps of Engineers of the discovery. One of the bone fragments was sent to the University of California, Riverside, where a test that involved destroying part of the bone indicated that the remains were about 8,400 years old.

Publicity and Controversy. On July 30, 1996, The *Tri-City Herald*, an eastern Washington newspaper, reported that the newly discovered skull apparently belonged to someone of European descent, possibly an early pioneer settler. A month later, on August 28, the *Tri-City Herald* gave a more detailed and more intriguing account, based on a more complete examination of the fragments, on scientific tests, and on speculation. The newspaper reported that the skeleton was taller and thinner than the skeletons of most Native Americans and that the skull was not flattened by boards in infancy, as was commonly the practice among ancient American Indians in the region. In the right hip of the skeleton, found after the skull, there was a spear point of the type used between five thousand and nine thousand years earlier. The newspaper observed that the University of California test supported the view that Kennewick Man lived in very early times.

These newspaper reports drew widespread attention. Representatives of Native American groups became concerned with the treatment of the pre-Columbian skeleton. In the August 28 article of the *Tri-City Herald*, Jerry Meninick, the vice chairman of the Yakima Nation's tribal council, said that Native Americans would regard Kennewick Man's remains as sacred and as deserving burial. Other Native American leaders and activists also began to object to Chatters's possession of Native American remains.

Jeff Van Pelt and other representatives of the Umatilla Reservation, Alan Slickpoo of the Nez Perce, and Bobby Tomanowash of the Wanapum opposed Chatters's work with the remains and voiced their concerns to the Army Corps of Engineers.

On September 2, 1996, the Army Corps of Engineers took control of the bones. Soon afterward, the five Native American tribal groups in the area claimed the bones under NAGPRA. In response, the Corps recognized the claims of the these groups and, on September 17, published the "Notice of Intent to Repatriate" required by the act. The publicity surrounding the discovery and scientific interest in it made it impossible for the Army Corps of Engineers to quietly hand over the remains to representatives of any tribe or set of tribes. A Portland, Oregon, attorney named Alan Schneider wrote the Corps at the end of September, offering his view that since Kennewick Man was apparently not an ancestor of any existing tribe, the remains were not covered by NAGPRA. On October 16, Robson Bonnichsen and seven other anthropologists represented by attorney Schneider filed suit in the U.S. Magistrate Court in Portland. In their suit, the anthropologists maintained that they would be deprived of their rights to study the remains if these were given to the Native American groups.

The controversy drew other interested parties. Not long after the anthropologists filed their suit, another Portland attorney filed a suit asking that the remains be turned over to his clients, the Asatru Folk Assembly. The group consisted of Americans of European descent who had revived the worship of the old Norse gods Odin and Thor. According to the Asatru Folk Assembly, if the skeleton could be shown to be more similar to Europeans than to Native Americans, then the remains should legally belong to the worshipers of the Norse gods.

The members of the Asatru Folk Assembly dropped their claim to Kennewick Man in January, 2000, asserting that the legal system was biased against them. Still, the ancient man continued to find others claiming descent from him. In July, 2001, a man of Samoan ancestry, Joseph P. Siofele, filed suit for custody of the remains, claiming that Kennewick Man was a relative of the ancient Polynesians.

Movements and Status of the Remains. The status of Kennewick Man under NAGPRA was unclear in the eyes of many people. In 1997, Doc Hastings, a member of the U.S. House of Representatives from Washington, drafted a bill intended to clarify NAGPRA and to permit scientists to continue with their studies of the bones. However, the administration of President Bill Clinton joined with Native American groups in opposing the bill. The U.S. government told the court that the remains would have been automatically handed over to a Native American tribe if the discovery had occurred in territory that was recognized as American Indian land by the Indian Claims Commission. Since the place of discovery was not recognized as tribal land, though, right of possession was open to question. At the end of October, 1998, the bones of Kennewick Man were moved to the Thomas Burke Memorial Washington State Museum at the University of Washington in Seattle. At the Burke Museum, scientists would be allowed to continue some studies until the court reached a final legal decision, but the remains would have to be treated in a respectful manner.

The case took on a new twist in late 1998, when an anthropologist from the Smithsonian Institution who examined the remains reported that several major pieces of the bones had disappeared. The mystery of these missing bone fragments was never solved. To complicate matters, in late 1999 scientists appointed by the U.S. Department of the Interior to study the remains concluded that Kennewick Man was not similar to either modern Native Americans or modern European Americans. Instead, the Interior Department scientists reported, the remains showed resemblances to natives of southeastern Asia, such as the Ainu of Japan and the Polynesians.

On July 13, 2000, Frank McManamon, consulting archaeologist of the U.S. Department of the Interior and chief archaeologist of the National Park Service, announced that Kennewick Man was between 9,320 and 9,510 years old. McManamon indicated that this age, along with some skeletal evidence, meant that the remains should be regarded as Native American and should be dealt with according to NAGPRA. If researchers had been able to obtain deoxyribonucleic acid (DNA) from the remains, this would have enabled them to establish any relationship with possible modern descendants. However, laboratories failed at obtaining DNA. In September, 2000, U.S. Secretary of the Interior Bruce Babbitt announced that the location of the discovery and the oral traditions of Native Americans were enough to establish a link between Kennewick Man and contemporary Native Americans. Therefore, Secretary Babbitt stated, the bones should be handed over to the Native American groups that were claiming them.

The announcement by the Interior Department did not resolve the controversy. Dr. Bonnichsen and his associates vowed to fight on in court. Representative Hastings said that he hoped the Department of the Interior's announcement would lead to reconsideration of his bill to make NAGPRA friendlier to science. Many concerned Native Americans continued to feel that their dead and their traditions had been treated with a lack of respect.

See also: Bering Strait migrations; Indian-white relations: U.S., 1934-2002; Native American Graves Protection and Repatriation Act; Prehistory: Northwest Coast.

Carl L. Bankston III

Sources for Further Study

Bonnichsen, Robson, and Alan L. Schneider. "Battle of the Bones." *The Sciences* 40, no. 4 (July/August, 2000): 40-46. An article by one of the anthropologists involved in the Kennewick Man litigation and by a lawyer who presents the controversy as a conflict between tradition and science.

Chatters, James C. *Ancient Encounters: Kennewick Man and the First Americans.* New York: Simon and Schuster, 2001. The anthropologist who was one of the central actors in the controversy tells the story of the discovery of the remains, the legal quarrels over them, and the evidence and theories regarding prehistoric North Americans.

Downey, Roger. *Riddle of the Bones: Politics, Science, Race and the Story of Kennewick Man.* New York: Copernicus, 2000. A history of the Kennewick discovery and controversy that is critical of Dr. Chatters and other anthropologists.

Garrett, Kenneth. "Hunt for the First Americans." *National Geographic* 198, no. 6 (December, 2000). A description of how recent discoveries, including that of Kennewick Man, have changed scientific theories about the earliest Americans.

Owsley, Douglas W., and Richard L. Jantz. "Archaeological Politics and Public Interest in Paleoamerican Studies: Lessons from Gordon Creek Woman and Kennewick Man." *American Antiquity* 66, no. 4 (2001): 565-575. Discusses legal and social issues surrounding Kennewick Man and other remains and argues that discussions of biological connections to present-day populations are relevant to the treatment of archaeological remains.

Thomas, David Hurst. *Skull Wars: Kennewick Man, Archaeology, and the Battle for Native American Identity.* New York: Basic Books, 2000. A history of American archaeology that looks at the changing relationship between Native Americans and archaeology and places the Kennewick Man controversy in the context of this changing relationship.

Kickapoo Resistance

Date: 1819-1834
Locale: Illinois
Tribes involved: Kickapoo
Categories: Nineteenth century history, Treaties, Wars and battles
Significance: Two separate bands of Kickapoo repudiated treaties of 1819 calling for all Kickapoo to move west; not until 1834 did the last band finally do so.

The 1819 Treaties of Edwardsville and Fort Harrison required the Kickapoo to vacate their lands in Illinois and move west. Two renegade bands of about 250 Indians each repudiated the treaties and remained, but by very different means.

The band led by Chief Mecina resisted by looting, rustling, shooting livestock, and terrorizing settlers. William Clark, area superintendent of Indian affairs, used persuasion rather than force, and in 1829 Mecina and about 150 tribal members left. About a hundred members joined Black Hawk's band of Sauk and Fox Indians in their ultimately unsuccessful efforts to recover tribal lands by force. Black Hawk was defeated in 1832, after which his supporters also moved west.

The band led by the warrior Kennekuk enjoyed friendly and peaceful relations with whites. Consequently, Kennekuk was able to resist passively and delay leaving. In 1833, however, Clark lost patience and gave Kennekuk an ultimatum to leave or be considered an enemy. In spring of 1834 Kennekuk finally left, leaving the Kickapoo wholly removed from their original lands.

See also: Black Hawk War; Kickapoo uprisings.

Laurence Miller

A Kickapoo warrior thought to be Babeshikit in 1894. (National Archives)

Kickapoo uprisings

Date: 1865-1873
Locale: Southern Texas
Tribes involved: Kickapoo
Categories: Nineteenth century history, Reservations and relocation, Wars and battles
Significance: This war of retribution against southern Texans wreaked havoc, caused bitter controversy with Mexico over the sanctity of borders, and marked the beginning of reservation life for some Southern Kickapoos.

During a migration of seven hundred Southern Kickapoos from Kansas to Mexico, the Indians were attacked by four hundred soldiers of the Texas Confederate Army on January 1, 1865. The Kickapoos won a decisive victory at the Battle of Dove Creek, but they lost fifteen dead and numerous supplies.

Enraged by this unwarranted attack and considering it an act of war, the Kickapoos unleashed a relentless, merciless, and highly effective campaign of terror, vengeance, and destruction against Texans and their property along the Rio Grande over the next decade.

Unable to persuade the Southern Kickapoos to cease hostilities and return to the United States, the government resorted to force and crossed the border into Mexico without permission in 1873. On May 18, the U.S. Fourth Cavalry killed and captured many women and children at Nacimiento. Desiring to be reunited with their families, 317 Kickapoos agreed to return to Indian Territory in the United States in 1873, with the rest (about 280) remaining in Mexico.

See also: Indian-white relations: U.S., 1871-1933; Kickapoo resistance.

Laurence Miller

Lewis and Clark expedition

Date: May 14, 1804-September 23, 1806
Locale: Trans-Mississippi West
Tribes involved: Blackfeet, Cheyenne, Chinook, Crow, Flathead, Klatsop, Mandan, Minnataree, Nez Perce, Osage, Pawnee, Shoshone, Sioux, Spokane, Tillamook, Yakima

Categories: Nineteenth century history

Significance: The westward expedition of Lewis and Clark not only expanded European American knowledge of the North American continent, but also was the first contact many Native American groups had with Europeans and had long-lasting reverberations for their traditional ways of life.

Meriwether Lewis, William Clark, and their companions were the first Europeans to cross the western half of North America within the present limits of the United States. During their journeys, they traveled through the future states of Missouri, Kansas, Nebraska, South Dakota, North Dakota, Montana, Idaho, Washington, and Oregon. Their exploration was the concluding act in the long and fruitless search for a water route through the continent—a Northwest Passage—that had begun soon after Christopher Columbus discovered the New World.

The instigator of the exploration was Thomas Jefferson, the third president of the United States. He had first thought of such an undertaking about the time the United States achieved independence in 1783, and during the succeeding decade he twice tried unsuccessfully to launch a transcontinental exploring party. Not until he assumed the presidency in 1801, however, was Jefferson in a position to have his plan implemented.

On January 18, 1803, the president asked Congress for authorization and for an appropriation of twenty-five hundred dollars to send a military expedition to explore along the Missouri River to its source in the Rocky Mountains, and then down the nearest westward-flowing streams to the Pacific Ocean. Jefferson gave two reasons for the proposed mission: to prepare the way for the extension of the American fur trade to the tribes throughout the area to be explored, and to advance geographical knowledge of the continent.

When he sent his message to Congress, none of the territory Jefferson wanted to be explored lay within the United States. The area between the Mississippi River and the Rocky Mountains, called Louisiana, belonged to France, while the Pacific Northwest was claimed by Great Britain, Spain, and Russia, as well as by the United States. While he was developing his plans for the transcontinental exploring expedition, however, the president also was conducting negotiations with the French government of Napoleon Bonaparte, which resulted in the purchase of the Louisiana territory from France—not the region of the modern state of Louisiana but rather a huge area that spanned nearly half of the trans-Mississippi West and effectively doubled the size of the United States. A treaty was signed on May 2, although antedated to April 30, 1803. Thus, in ascending the Missouri River, the expedition would be exploring new U.S. territory, while by completing the journey to the Pacific Ocean, it would be strengthening the United States' claim to the region beyond the mountains.

To command the expedition, Jefferson chose his private secretary, Captain Meriwether Lewis. With the president's concurrence, Lewis then invited his longtime friend William Clark to be his co-leader. After making initial preparations in the East, Lewis traveled to Wood River, Illinois, opposite the mouth of the Missouri River. Clark and several recruits joined him on the way down the Ohio River. Lewis and Clark spent the winter of 1803-1804 at Camp Wood River recruiting and training their men, gathering additional supplies and equipment (including fourteen bales of trade goods), and collecting information about the Missouri River from traders and boatmen. The permanent party that was organized included twenty-seven young, unmarried soldiers; a mixed-blood hunter and interpreter named George Drouillard; Clark's black slave, York; and Lewis's big Newfoundland dog, Scammon. In addition, a corporal, five privates, and several French boatmen were to accompany the expedition during the first season and then return downriver with its records, sketches, and scientific specimens.

The Expedition Sets Forth. The Corps of Discovery began its historic journey on May 14, 1804. It started up the Missouri River in a fifty-five-foot keelboat and two pirogues, or dugout canoes. Averaging about fifteen miles a day, by the end of October, the corps had reached the villages of the Mandans and Minnatarees near the mouth of the Knife River in the future state of North Dakota.

A statue of Sacagawea in Portland, Oregon, commemorates the Shoshone who carried her two-month-old son with her as she guided the Lewis and Clark expedition. For her services, she received less than 0.01 percent of the total cost of the expedition. (Library of Congress)

After ending their sixteen-hundred-mile trek, the explorers built a log stronghold called Fort Mandan and went into winter quarters. During the long, frigid winter, Lewis and Clark made copious notes in their journals, drew maps of their route, and counseled with numerous Native American visitors. From the Minnatarees, especially, they obtained invaluable information about the course of the Missouri River and the country through which it ran. The contributions of these and other Native Americans to the success of the exploration cannot be exaggerated.

On April 7, 1805, the expedition resumed its journey. The party now numbered only thirty-three persons. It included, besides the permanent detachment, interpreter Toussaint Charbonneau, his young Shoshone wife Sacagawea, and her two-month-old son Jean Baptiste, nicknamed Pompey. On August 17, after passing through country never before visited by Europeans, the expedition reached the navigable limits of the Missouri River.

With Sacagawea's help, Lewis and Clark purchased horses from her brother Cameahwai of the Shoshone tribe and began their journey through the Rocky Mountains. Sacagawea had been captured three years before by a Minnataree raiding party and carried back east to the prairies, where Charbonneau had purchased her for his wife. The chance meeting of Sacagawea and her brother, who had become the chief of their clan, was a convenient opportunity for the expedition. Along with the horses, Lewis and Clark were given travel instructions and lent a guide, called Toby, to assist them through the mountains. After crossing the mountains, the explorers descended the Clearwater, Snake, and Columbia Rivers to the Pacific, where they arrived in mid-November.

The Road Home. After a dreary winter at Fort Clatsop (named for a neighboring tribe) south of the Columbia River, the explorers started for home on March 23, 1806. Other than fighting to keep warm and searching for food, the highlight of their stay was a visit to the remains of a dead beached whale, from which they obtained three hundred pounds of blubber and oil. They were anxious to start back east, as they had seen the sun only six days during their stay at Fort Clatsop. En route, they divided temporarily; Lewis and a small party explored the Marias River, while Clark and the rest of the men descended the Yellowstone River. Reuniting below the mouth of the Yellowstone, they hurried on down the Missouri and arrived in St. Louis on September 23, 1806.

The Lewis and Clark expedition had accomplished its mission with remarkable success. In only twenty-eight months, it had covered more than eight thousand miles. On the entire journey, only one member of the expe-

Western Expeditions of Lewis and Clark (1804-1806) and Pike (1806-1807)

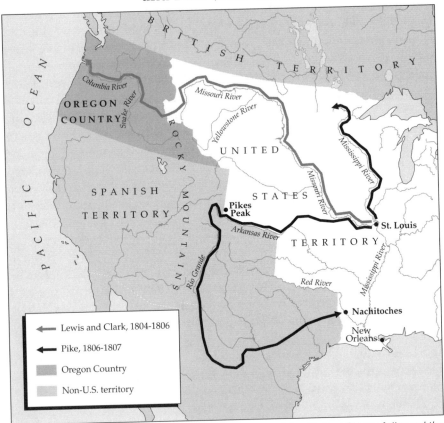

A new era in westward exploration and expansion of the United States followed the Louisiana Purchase of 1803. President Thomas Jefferson charged his private secretary, Meriwether Lewis, to undertake a northwestern reconnaissance expedition to explore the new lands. At about the same time, Zebulon Pike of the Western Army of the United States conducted several expeditions that led him deep into Spanish territory in the Southwest. Such expeditions opened the door to white settlers and devastating incursions into Native American homelands.

dition, Sergeant Charles Floyd, lost his life, probably because of a ruptured appendix. Although they met thousands of Native Americans, the explorers had only one violent encounter with them. This violence occurred while Lewis was high up the Marias River, and it resulted in the death of two Piegans, members of the Blackfoot Confederacy. The total expense of the undertaking, including the special congressional appropriation of $2,500, was $38,722.25. Charbonneau collected $500.33 for his and Sacagawea's services. At this small cost Lewis and Clark and their companions took the first giant step in opening the West to the American people.

See also: Indian-white relations: U.S., 1775-1830; Prehistory: Northwest Coast; Prehistory: Plateau.

John L. Loos, updated by Russell Hively

Sources for Further Study

Bakeless, John. *Lewis and Clark: Partners in Discovery.* New York: William Morrow, 1947. One of the most reliable sources on Meriwether Lewis and William Clark. Based on both of their journals.

Biddle, Nicholas, and Paul Allen, eds. *History of the Expedition Under the Command of Captains Lewis and Clark.* 2 vols. Philadelphia: J. B. Lippincott, 1961. Prepared by Biddle, a young Philadelphia lawyer, between 1810 and 1814, this work is based on both Lewis's and Clark's journals.

De Voto, Bernard. *The Journals of Lewis and Clark.* Boston: Houghton Mifflin, 1953. A one-volume condensation of the *Original Journals of Lewis and Clark Expedition.* Includes maps.

Dillon, Richard. *Meriwether Lewis: A Biography.* New York: Coward-McCann, 1965. A full-length study of Meriwether Lewis's life.

McGrath, Patrick. *The Lewis and Clark Expedition.* Morristown, N.J.: Silver Burdett, 1985. A simple but complete telling of the Lewis and Clark adventure for younger readers.

Ronda, James P. *Lewis and Clark Among the Indians.* Bicentennial edition. Lincoln: University of Nebraska Press, 2002. A detailed look at the Indian cultures encountered by the Lewis and Clark expedition.

Salisbury, Albert, and Jane Salisbury. *Two Captains West.* Seattle: Superior Publishing, 1950. Descriptions of the Lewis and Clark trail, with maps and photographs. Designed for the lay reader.

Tourtelott, Jonathan B., ed. "Meriwether Lewis/William Clark." In *Into the Unknown: The Story of Exploration.* Washington, D.C.: National Geographic Society, 1987. A thirty-four-page chapter devoted to the Lewis and Clark expedition.

Little Bighorn, Battle of the

Date: June 25-26, 1876
Locale: Little Bighorn River, Montana
Tribes involved: Arapaho, Arikara, Crow, Northern Cheyenne, Sioux

> **Categories:** Nineteenth century history, Wars and battles
> **Significance:** The stunning defeat of the Seventh Cavalry unleashed re-
> lentless pursuit of the victorious Indians, culminating in their surren-
> der, their exile to reservation life, and the end of traditional Plains
> culture.

The Treaty of Fort Laramie (1868) guaranteed the Sioux a permanent reservation that encompassed all of present South Dakota west of the Missouri
River and from which encroaching white settlers were forbidden. The
Sioux were also guaranteed the right to hunt in a larger unceded territory,
also closed to whites. About three thousand free-roaming Sioux lived on
these lands and despised the thought of reservation life. Crazy Horse and
Sitting Bull were the most famous of these Sioux.

Background to the Battle. The terms of the treaty, however, were blatantly
violated. From 1871 to 1874, surveying parties with army escort trespassed
on both the reservation and unceded territory, charting routes and finding
gold in the sacred Black Hills. By mid-1875 hordes of white prospectors
and adventurers were poised to invade Sioux territory, held back only by
the army.

The government tried through persuasion and threats to induce the
Sioux to sell the Black Hills but were unequivocally rebuffed. This led President Ulysses S. Grant to devise a plan to justify a war against the Sioux.
Their defeat would remove the free-roaming Sioux from the unceded territory and place them on the reservation. The Black Hills and unceded territory would be opened for settlement and prospecting. The plan began with
a decision not to enforce the ban on prospectors entering the Black Hills.
Lies about Sioux misdeeds and crimes were publicly circulated. Then in
December, 1875, the government gave an ultimatum to the free-roaming
Northern Cheyenne and Sioux to surrender at their agencies by January 31,
1876, or be forced there by military action.

The Indians bitterly resented this ultimatum. It violated the 1868 treaty,
and the free-roaming groups were determined to maintain their traditional
way of life and not go to reservations. Resentment was further fueled by a
famine on the reservation caused largely by negligence and graft in the distribution of guaranteed rations. In addition, the sale of firearms to hunt
needed food was prohibited. The Platte Sioux had been arbitrarily removed from their reservation to save on freight charges for their rations.

Annihilation of Custer's Forces. The Indians ignored the ultimatum, and
the army was ordered to capture or disperse them. On June 24 the Sev-

Rain in the Face, one of the Sioux leaders at Little Bighorn, is believed to have dealt the deathblow to General Custer in the Battle of Little Bighorn. (National Archives)

enth Cavalry, under the command of General George Armstrong Custer, found an Indian camp (predominantly Sioux but including some Northern Cheyenne and Arapaho) on the south bank of the Little Bighorn River. In the afternoon of June 25, 1876, the Battle of the Little Bighorn commenced. Major Marcus Reno and his three companies of 175 soldiers and Indian scouts attacked the southern end of the camp. Reno aborted the attack, however, when he realized the number of Indians he would engage. He took cover in timber along the river but was forced to withdraw to a more defensible hilltop on the bluffs across the river when set upon by an overwhelming force of Indians. The withdrawal turned into a panic and a rout. Seven officers and 84 men made it to the hill. Forty were killed, 13 were wounded, and several were missing.

Custer observed Reno's charge from Weir Point, a high bluff. He searched for an opening that would permit him and his 210 troops to join the battle as soon as possible. Custer made contact with the Indians at around 3:45 P.M., near the river. What then happened is not exactly clear, but Custer moved away from the river and ended up on Custer Hill, about four miles from Reno's hill. Almost two thousand Indians attacked Custer's force and completely surrounded it. Within about an hour Custer and all his men were annihilated.

The third unit of Custer's force, 5 officers and 110 soldiers, was commanded by Captain Frederick Benteen. Benteen was under orders to search for hostiles to the left of Custer's force and then hurry back and join Custer. Benteen, however, contrary to orders, dawdled behind, probably in the belief that there were no Indian warriors in the area. Benteen did not get to the battlefield in time to help Custer. The fourth unit of Custer's force, the pack train carrying supplies, was manned by 2 officers and 134 soldiers. It languished in the rear and could not be of assistance when Custer was attacked.

When Benteen and the pack train arrived at the Little Bighorn, they joined Reno on Reno Hill. This total force of 367 was able to withstand Indian attacks on the morning of June 26, with a loss of 7 killed and 40 men wounded. The Indians were gone by June 27, and the battle was over. Total army casualties numbered 263 killed and 59 wounded.

The army's defeat was the result of several factors. Inadequate intelligence led Custer to underestimate the strength and temper of his foe: Two thousand battle-tested warriors resolved to defend their way of life against 597 cavalry. Custer's troops were divided into four units, only two of which fought, and then at different times and places and against overwhelming odds. Another factor was the strength of the Indians' leadership; Crazy Horse, Gall, and Rain in the Face were all actively involved in the fighting.

The Indians' victory was short-lived. An angry American public, Congress, and military demanded revenge. The Indians were relentlessly pursued in 1877, and by the end of the 1870's nearly all Plains Indians had been killed or confined to reservations; the traditional Plains culture passed into history.

See also: Fort Laramie Treaty of 1868; Indian-white relations: U.S., 1871-1933; National Indian Association; Rosebud Creek, Battle of; Sioux War; Washita River Massacre.

Laurence Miller

Sources for Further Study

Dillon, Richard H. *North American Indian Wars.* New York: Facts on File, 1983.

Gray, John S. *Centennial Campaign.* Ft. Collins, Colo.: Old Army Press, 1976.

Green, Jerome A., ed. *Lakota and Cheyenne: Indian Views of the Great Sioux War, 1876-1877.* Norman: University of Oklahoma Press, 2000.

Rosenberg, Bruce A. *Custer and the Epic of Defeat.* University Park: Pennsylvania State University Press, 1974.

Russell, Don. *Custer's Last.* Fort Worth, Tex.: Amon Carter Museum of Western Art, 1968.

Vaughn, Jesse W. *Indian Fights.* Norman: University of Oklahoma Press, 1966.

Little Turtle's War

Date: October 18, 1790-July, 1794
Locale: Ohio Valley
Tribes involved: Chippewa, Lenni Lenape, Miami, Ottawa, Potawatomi, Shawnee, Wyandot
Categories: Eighteenth century history, Wars and battles
Significance: Native Americans inflict the worst battlefield defeat on U.S. Army troops during the Indian wars.

On November 4, 1791, Little Turtle was one of the principal chiefs among a coalition of Shawnees, Miamis, Lenni Lenapes (Delawares), Potawatomis, Ottawas, Chippewas, and Wyandots in the Old Northwest (Ohio Country) that defeated an army of 1,400 soldiers under General Arthur St. Clair. About 1,200 warriors rallied by Little Turtle, aided by the element of surprise, killed or wounded nearly 950 of St. Clair's force, the largest single battlefield victory by an American Indian force in U.S. history. The victory was short-lived, however; in 1794, "Mad" Anthony Wayne's forces defeated Little Turtle and his allies at the Battle of Fallen Timbers. On August 3, 1795, the American Indians gave up most of their hunting grounds west of the Ohio River, by signing the Treaty of Greenville.

Little Turtle was known as a master of battlefield strategy. Born to a Miami chief and a Mahican (or Mohican) mother, Little Turtle became a war chief of the Miamis because of his extraordinary personal abilities; under ordinary circumstances, the matriarchal nature of the culture would have prohibited a leadership role for him. In 1787, the hunting grounds of the Miamis and their allies had been guaranteed in perpetuity by the U.S. Congress. The act did not stop an invasion of settlers, and by the early 1790's, Little Turtle had cemented an alliance that foreshadowed later efforts by Tecumseh, who assembled an alliance of several native nations a generation later.

Little Turtle's principal allies in this effort were the Shawnee Blue Jacket and the Lenni Lenape Buckongahelas. This alliance first defeated a force of a thousand troops under Josiah Harmar during October, 1790. Harmar dispatched an advance force of 180 men, who were drawn into a trap and annihilated on October 18. On October 19, Harmar dispatched 360 more troops to punish the natives, but the Americans were drawn into a similar trap, in which about 100 of them were killed. The remainder of Harmar's force then retreated to Fort Washington, on the present-day site of Cincinnati.

Indian Successes. Harmar's defeat stunned the Army, whose commanders knew that the Old Northwest would remain closed to settlement as long as Little Turtle's alliance held. General Arthur St. Clair, who had served as president of the Continental Congress in the mid-1780's, gathered an army of two thousand troops during the summer of 1791 and marched into the Ohio Country. About a quarter of the troops deserted en route; to keep the others happy, St. Clair permitted about two hundred soldiers' wives to travel with the army.

On November 4, 1791, Little Turtle and his allies lured St. Clair's forces into the same sort of trap that had defeated Harmar's smaller army near St. Mary's Creek, a tributary of the Wabash River. Thirty-eight officers and 598 enlisted men died in the battle; 242 others were wounded, many of whom later died. Fifty-six wives also lost their lives, bringing casualties close to 950—nearly four times the number killed at Little Bighorn in 1876 and the largest defeat of a U.S. Army force in all of the Indian wars. After the battle, St. Clair resigned his commission in disgrace. Dealing from strength, Little Turtle's alliance refused to cede land to the United States.

In 1794, General "Mad" Anthony Wayne was dispatched with a fresh army, which visited the scene of St. Clair's debacle. According to Wayne,

Five hundred skull bones lay in the space of 350 yards. From thence, five miles on, the woods were strewn with skeletons, knapsacks, and other debris.

Little Turtle had more respect for Wayne than he had had for Harmar or St. Clair, calling Wayne "the chief who never sleeps." Aware that Wayne was unlikely to be defeated by his surprise tactics, Little Turtle proposed that the Indian alliance talk peace. A majority of the warriors rebuffed Little Turtle, so in late June or early July he relinquished his command to a Shawnee, Blue Jacket (although some scholars say it was Turkey Foot). In April, 1790, Blue Jacket had refused to attend treaty councils that he feared would cost his people their lands. His forces were defeated by Wayne at the Battle of Fallen Timbers. Afterward, Blue Jacket signed the Treaty of Greenville (1795) and the Treaty of Fort Industry (1805), ceding millions of acres of native land.

Aftermath. Stripped of their lands, many of Little Turtle's people sank into alcoholic despair. The aging chief continued to lead them as best he could. In 1802, Little Turtle addressed the legislatures of Ohio and Kentucky, urging members to pass laws forbidding traders to supply natives with whiskey. He said that whiskey traders had "stripped the poor Indian of skins, guns, blankets, everything—while his squaw and the children dependent on him lay starving and shivering in his wigwam." Neither state did anything to stop the flow of whiskey, some of which was adulterated with other substances, such as chili peppers and arsenic.

Little Turtle died July 14, 1812, at his lodge near the junction of the St. Joseph River and St. Mary Creek. He was buried with full military honors by Army officers who knew his genius. William Henry Harrison, who had been an aide to Wayne and who later defeated Tecumseh in the same general area, paid Little Turtle this tribute:

"A safe leader is better than a bold one." This maxim was a great favorite of [the Roman] Caesar Augustus . . . who . . . was, I believe, inferior to the warrior Little Turtle.

For almost two centuries, local historians placed the site of the Battle of Fallen Timbers along the Maumee River floodplain near U.S. Highway 24, near present-day Toledo, Ohio. A monument was erected at the site, even as Native Americans contended that the battle had really occurred a mile away, in what had become a soybean field. In 1995, to settle the issue, G. Michael Pratt, an anthropology professor in Ohio, organized an archaeological dig in the soybean field. Teams of as many as 150 people excavated the site, which yielded large numbers of battlefield artifacts, indicating conclusively that the Native American account of the site was correct.

See also: Fallen Timbers, Battle of; Fort Greenville Treaty; Indian-white relations: U.S., 1775-1830.

Bruce E. Johansen

Sources for Further Study

Carter, Harvey Lewis. *The Life and Times of Little Turtle: First Sagamore of the Wabash.* Urbana: University of Illinois Press, 1987. Includes a detailed description of the battle with St. Clair's troops from Little Turtle's perspective.

Hamilton, Charles, ed. *Cry of the Thunderbird.* Norman: University of Oklahoma Press, 1972. Extensive quotations from some of Little Turtle's speeches.

Porter, C. Fayne. *Our Indian Heritage: Profiles of Twelve Great Leaders.* Philadelphia: Chilton Books, 1964. Little Turtle is one of the twelve leaders discussed.

Sword, Wiley. *President Washington's Indian War: The Struggle for the Old Northwest, 1790-1795.* Norman: University of Oklahoma Press, 1985. Discusses the battles that the U.S. Army fought with Little Turtle's alliance, in the context of United States politics of the time.

Winger, Otho. *Last of the Miamis: Little Turtle.* North Manchester, Ind.: O. Winger, 1935. Concise sketch of Little Turtle's life and his attempts to forge a Native American confederation in the Ohio Valley.

Young, Calvin M. *Little Turtle.* 1917. Reprint. Fort Wayne, Ind.: Public Library of Fort Wayne and Allen County, 1956. A sketch of Little Turtle's life, including the St. Clair battle.

Lone Wolf v. Hitchcock

Date: January 5, 1903
Locale: United States
Tribes involved: Pantribal in the United States
Categories: Court cases, Twentieth century history
Significance: The U.S. Supreme Court decides that Congress has plenary power over Native American property and may dispose of it at its discretion.

In 1887, after years of agitation and controversy, Congress passed the General Allotment Act (also known as the Dawes Act or Dawes Severalty Act). Under the terms of the legislation, the president was authorized to allot all tribal land in the United States to individual Native Americans. The standard share was 160 acres to each head of a family, with smaller amounts to unmarried men and children. Negotiations were to be carried on with Native American tribes for the sale to the federal government of the land remaining after the allotments were made and for its opening to European American settlement.

The allotment policy, dominating United States-Native American relations for more than fifty years, proved to be disastrous for Native Americans. It transformed Native American landownership from collective to individual holdings, thus severing the Indians' connection with communal tribal organizations, exposed them to wholesale exploitation by land speculators, pushed them onto land that was often arid and unproductive, and led ultimately to a loss of control over two-thirds of their lands. Deceit, duplicity, and coercion undermined the honest, but naïve, objectives of the U.S. reformers who espoused allotment prior to its enactment.

Tribal sovereignty, the allotment policy, and Native American treaty rights came before the United States Supreme Court in *Lone Wolf v. Hitch-*

cock in 1902. In 1867, the Medicine Lodge Creek Treaty had been signed with the Kiowas and Comanches, whereby the two tribes relinquished claims to 90 million acres in exchange for 2.9-million-acre reservations in Western Oklahoma. A separate treaty placed the plains Apaches on the same reservation. Article XII of the Medicine Lodge Creek Treaty provided that no further cession of any part of the new reservation could be made without the written consent of three-quarters of the adult male members of the three tribes. The commitment to Article XII of the Medicine Lodge treaty lasted twenty-five years. In 1892, the Jerome Commission, composed of a former governor of Michigan and two judges, was able—through fraud and counterfeit signatures—to secure the necessary three-quarters consent to an agreement for the allotment of land to individual tribesmen and for the purchase of 2.15 million acres of what was denominated as surplus land at a price of approximately ninety-three cents per acre.

Almost immediately after the signing of the new agreement, representatives of the Kiowas, Comanches, and Plains Apaches claimed that assent had been obtained by fraudulent misrepresentation of its terms by the interpreters, and that three-quarters of the adult males had not consented to the cession. Their argument was ignored by the United States House of Representatives, which voted to execute the agreement, but was more sympathetically received by the Senate, which defeated the bill in January, 1899.

In July, 1900, however, Congress passed an act that allowed the United States to take title to 2,991,933 acres of the Kiowa, Comanche, and Plains Apache reservation. After 480,000 acres were set aside as common grazing lands, 445,000 acres allotted to individual members of the three tribes, and 10,000 acres committed to agency, schools, and religious purposes, 2 million acres were left to be purchased by the federal government and opened to white settlement.

The Kiowa Challenge. Although some Native Americans approved of the act, Lone Wolf, a Kiowa chief, and others were intent upon challenging the act's constitutionality. They retained William McKendree Springer, formerly chief justice of the Court of Appeals for the Indian Territory, to litigate their case before the federal courts.

Springer argued that the congressional act violated the property rights of the three tribes and was, therefore, repugnant to the due process clause of the Fifth Amendment of the Constitution. After losing in the Supreme Court of the District of Columbia and in the Court of Appeals for the district, Springer appealed to the United States Supreme Court.

Lone Wolf v. Hitchcock was argued in the Supreme Court in October, 1901, and reargued the following year. The decision was handed down in January, 1903. In the Court, Springer was joined by Hampton L. Carson, a prominent member of the Indian Rights Association; the Department of the Interior was represented by Willis Van Devanter of Wyoming, who later became a Supreme Court justice.

The unanimous decision of the Supreme Court, written by Associate Justice Edward White of Louisiana, was characterized by a later commentator as the "Indian's *Dred Scott* decision," and January 5, 1903, as "one of the blackest days in the history of the American Indians." Justice White spoke in condescending terms. He called Native Americans an "ignorant and dependent race," "weak and diminishing in number," and "wards of the nation." These contemptuous phrases were not original to White; they were epithets that had long been used in the opinions of Supreme Court justices in relation to Native Americans. More important, White ruled that Congress possessed a paramount authority over Native American property "by reason of its exercise of guardianship over their interests." In exercising such power, Congress could abrogate provisions of a treaty with a Native American tribe.

Justice White then went on to argue that the congressional act of 1900 represented only "a mere change in the form of investment of Indian tribal property from land to money" even though the price paid was below the market value. White held that Congress had made a good-faith effort to compensate the Kiowas for their lands; therefore, there was no violation of the Fifth Amendment. "If injury was occasioned," White concluded, "which we do not wish to be understood to imply by the use made by Congress of its power, relief must be sought by an appeal to that body for redress and not to the courts."

Even before the Supreme Court had ruled in *Lone Wolf v. Hitchcock*, President William McKinley issued a proclamation opening the Kiowa lands to white settlement on August 6, 1901. Lone Wolf watched with chagrin as thousands of potential settlers camped on Kiowa lands near Fort Sill, waiting to register for a lottery; during a two-month period, 11,638 homestead entries were made at the land office.

Legitimating Broken Promises. The importance of the Supreme Court decision in *Lone Wolf* should not be underestimated. Justice White's opinion legitimized the long history of broken promises, of treaties made and treaties ignored, and of Congress's assertion of plenary authority over Indian lands. The opinion justified the alienation, between 1887 and 1934, of eighty-six million acres of Native American property; it also denied to Native Americans recourse to the courts to seek redress for the coerced separation from their lands and its purchase at bargain prices.

In *Lone Wolf*, Justice White told the Kiowas and associated tribes that they would have to seek relief for their alleged injuries in Congress, and the Kiowas had no alternative but to go to the federal legislature to secure redress. It was not until 1955 that the Indian Claims Commission awarded the Kiowas, Comanches, and plains Apaches $2,067,166 in compensation for the lands taken under the congressional act of 1900. It was not until 1980, in *United States v. Sioux Nation*, that Justice Harry Blackmun, in a majority opinion, held that the *Lone Wolf* doctrine was "discredited" and "had little to commend it as an enduring principle."

See also: Allotment system; General Allotment Act; Indian Rights Association; Indian-white relations: U.S., 1871-1933; Treaties and agreements in the United States.

David L. Sterling

Sources for Further Study

Clark, Blue. *"Lone Wolf v. Hitchcock": Treaty Rights and Indian Law at the End of the Nineteenth Century*. Lincoln: University of Nebraska Press, 1994. A short but comprehensive study of the background and implications of the most significant turn-of-the-century Native American court case.

Hagan, William T. *The Indian Rights Association: The Herbert Welsh Years, 1882-1904*. Tucson: University of Arizona Press, 1985. An account of the organization that participated in the litigation of the *Lone Wolf* case.

Highsaw, Robert B. *Edward Douglass White: Defender of the Conservative Faith*. Baton Rouge: Louisiana State University Press, 1981. An analysis of the judicial record of the writer of the Supreme Court opinion in *Lone Wolf v. Hitchcock*.

Legters, Lyman, and Fremont J. Lyden, eds. *American Indian Policy: Self-Governance and Economic Development*. Westport, Conn.: Greenwood Press, 1994. A series of articles detailing current trends in Native American life and law.

Prucha, Francis Paul. *American Indian Treaties: The History of a Political Anomaly*. Berkeley: University of California Press, 1994. An exhaustive examination of the legal relationship between Native American tribes and the United States, from the American Revolution to the present.

Wilkins, David E. *American Indian Sovereignty and the U.S. Supreme Court: The Masking of Justice*. Austin: University of Texas Press, 1997. Close analysis of legal cases that Wilkins argues "mask questionable federal and administrative activities against tribes and individual Indians."

Long Walk

Date: August, 1863-September, 1866
Locale: Arizona and New Mexico
Tribes involved: Navajo
Categories: Nineteenth century history, Reservations and relocation
Significance: Forced to walk from their ancestral lands to an arid reservation three hundred miles away, the Navajo lose their home and many of their people.

Perhaps the most significant event in Navajo history occurred during and immediately after the U.S. Civil War, when U.S. Army troops, under the authority of Colonel Christopher "Kit" Carson, methodically raided and subdued the various bands of Navajos who lived between the three rivers (the Colorado, Rio Grande, and San Juan) that encircled the Dinetah, Navajo ancestral lands in present-day Arizona and New Mexico. This event is significant in U.S. history, because it is one of the last major episodes in Carson's public life, one of the earliest federal attempts to pilot an American Indian reservation policy, and the final military conflict between the Navajo people and the U.S. Army.

After Civil War hostilities began in April, 1861, the West was drained of most of its U.S. Army regulars. During the same month, Kit Carson, serving as the Ute Indian agent in Taos, raised the Stars and Stripes in the town plaza, signifying his allegiance to the Union. Carson was commissioned as a colonel in the First New Mexican Volunteers, and there is every indication that he intended to fight against the Confederate Army. However, Colorado volunteers, in the Battle of Valverde on February 21, 1862, drove Confederate forces back from the Rio Grande, and there were no further Confederate incursions in the New Mexico Territory for the balance of the war.

Meanwhile, Brigadier General James H. Carleton, who had assumed the position of commander of the Department of New Mexico in 1861, was obsessed with the idea of resettling the natives of the New Mexico Territory. As U.S. settlers had entered the region in greater numbers after 1846, relations deteriorated as a result of thievery and cultural misunderstanding. Among the Navajo, the *ladrones* (poor in sheep and possessions) usually perpetrated the raids on the settlers, while the *ricos* (comparatively wealthy) suffered the reprisals. Initially, most *ladrones* were of the war party, while the *ricos* were peace-seeking. However, years of suffering from counter-raids and reprisals drew even the *rico* Navajos into accepting the inevitability of armed conflict with New Mexican settlers.

As late as December, 1862, eighteen Navajo *ricos* traveled to Santa Fe to seek peace with General Carleton. Carleton rebuffed them, preoccupied at the time with exiling the Mescalero Apache to a barren stretch of the Pecos River Valley in eastern New Mexico known as Bosque Redondo ("round grove of trees"). This strategy was the beginning of Carleton's dream of a "Fair Carletonia," peopled with American Indians who would forgo their pagan habits and accept Christianity and a European American lifestyle.

Carleton's Ultimatum. Once the Apaches were resettled, Carleton, in April, 1863, was willing to talk peace with Navajo chiefs Barboncito and Delgadito, but only on his terms: removal to Bosque Redondo or a fight to the death. The Navajo chiefs apparently tried to explain to Carleton that voluntarily leaving their land would violate their deepest religious beliefs, but Carleton would not relent. In June, 1863, Carleton set July 20, 1863, as a deadline: All Navajos should present themselves at Fort Canby or Fort Wingate; those Navajos remaining at large would be considered as hostiles.

Only a handful of Navajos complied with this ultimatum, and Carleton responded by authorizing Colonel Carson to begin scouting expeditions in August, 1863, to capture or kill Navajos, plunder their crops, and seize their livestock. Carson led a number of scouting expeditions and authorized a number of his officers to do the same. Carson also employed Utes as both guides and warriors in hunting the Navajo.

Actual military skirmishes between the First New Mexican Volunteers and the Navajo were rare throughout the remainder of 1863. By the end of the year, Carson reported seventy-eight Navajos killed and forty wounded. Perhaps more significant was that more than five thousand sheep, goats, and mules belonging to the Navajo had been confiscated, and more than seventy-five thousand pounds of wheat were destroyed or seized. The Navajo could hide from the scouting expeditions of volunteers, but they left behind their hogans and rancheros for the troops to plunder and seize. While the Navajo tribe was not decimated by war, Carson's scorched-earth policy laid the foundation for the threat of mass starvation and, therefore, the likelihood of ultimate surrender.

In January, 1864, two scouting parties, one led by Carson and the other by Captain Albert Pfeiffer, left Fort Canby, taking parallel routes through the Canyon de Chelly area north of the fort. Each party exchanged gunshots for the Navajo arrows that rained down on them from the upper reaches of the sheer red sandstone walls and ancient Anasazi ruins where the Navajo ensconced themselves. The entire joint expedition resulted in only twenty-three Navajos being killed, but two hundred Navajos surren-

Long Walk of the Navajos

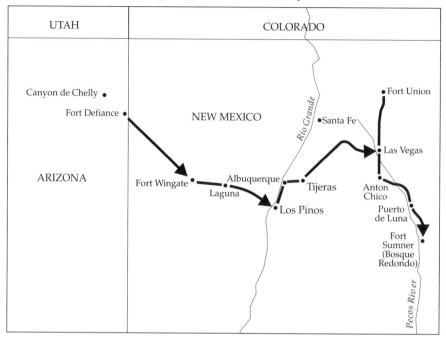

UTAH	COLORADO

Canyon de Chelly •

Fort Defiance •

NEW MEXICO

ARIZONA

Fort Wingate •

Laguna

Albuquerque •

Tijeras

Los Pinos

Rio Grande

•Santa Fe

Las Vegas

Anton Chico

Puerto de Luna

Fort Union •

Fort Sumner (Bosque Redondo)

Pecos River

dered, and at least two hundred head of livestock were seized. The peach orchards along the canyon floor were also destroyed. Once the troops returned to Fort Canby, great numbers of surrendering Navajos followed. They were starving, freezing, and dying from exposure. Carson's march along the length of the floor of Canyon de Chelly seems to have proven that the Navajo could remain in relative safety along its ledges, but that the troops could destroy their crops and orchards and seize their livestock, thereby leaving them to starve or surrender.

The Long Walk Commences. By March, 1864, there were six thousand Navajos at Forts Canby and Wingate, several thousand more than even Carleton had expected. The first of a series of Long Walks commenced at this time. Although the U.S. Army provided a limited number of carts and horses, those conveyances generally carried blankets and provisions rather than people. Most of the Navajo walked the entire three hundred miles, a journey that took anywhere from eighteen to forty days, while Carleton's plans provided for only eight days of government rations for the journey. There was actually a series of Long Walks from Fort Canby to Fort Sumner (Bosque Redondo), although the first, in March, 1864, was the largest. Although there is no Army record of such deeds, many stories in Navajo oral tradition recount atrocities whereby the old or infirm or pregnant who could not keep up were summarily shot by soldiers.

The Navajo never received the full promise of ample food, clothing, and shelter at Bosque Redondo. Carleton planned to make farmers of the hunter-gatherer Navajo, but there was not enough tillable land in arid eastern New Mexico to support more than eight thousand Navajos and the Mescalero Apaches who were already at Fort Sumner. There was not enough grass for the herds of sheep and goats, leading to frequent raids of the government stock by Kiowas and Comanches. The few crops that were raised were attacked by insects and suffered from flood, drought, and hail. Government rations were meager and of poor quality—the flour the Navajo received often was full of bugs—and the food was foreign to the Navajo, who did not consider bacon a satisfactory substitute for beef. In addition, the Navajo had to live in close quarters with the Mescalero Apaches, their old enemies, and there was a bureaucratic war between the War Department and the Department of the Interior. Indian Agent Lorenzo Labadie was ordered not to take charge of the Navajo under the aegis of the Department of the Interior, since technically, they were prisoners of war and should be quartered by the War Department. The Navajo suffered from hunger and cold, while bureaucrats bickered.

Carleton sent Carson to Bosque Redondo later in 1864 to serve as supervisor there, but Carson left in disgust after three months, disappointed and embarrassed at the failure of the federal government to provide the stipulated terms of surrender. Carson resigned his commission and returned to Taos, where he died in 1868.

Individual bands of the Navajo remained in the Dinetah, most notably one led by Manuelito, withstanding famine, military attack, bad weather, and Navajo treachery. Finally, after repeated attacks by Utes and Hopis deputized by the U.S. Army, Manuelito and twenty-three followers surrendered at Fort Wingate on September 1, 1866.

It soon became evident that Carleton's dream of a "Fair Carletonia" was an abject failure. Carleton was relieved of his command in April, 1867, although it was not until April, 1868, that Manuelito, Barboncito, and other Navajo headmen traveled to Washington, D.C., to ask President Andrew Johnson for permission to return to their ancestral lands. Johnson agreed only to establish a peace commission.

The Taylor Peace Commission arrived at Bosque Redondo in May, 1868, with the expectation of offering the Navajo land in Indian territory (now Oklahoma) to the east. Ironically, General William T. Sherman, the architect of his own scorched-earth policy in Georgia several years earlier, was the

Taylor Commission member who first became convinced that the Navajo should be allowed instead to return home.

On June 1, 1868, the Treaty Between the United States of America and the Navajo Tribe of Indians was signed, and the westward Long Walk began by the middle of the month. The initial treaty stipulated only 3.5 million acres for the Navajo (the present-day size of the reservation is 15 million acres) but consecrated Canyon de Chelly as sacred ground to be administered solely by the Navajo tribe. Thus, the Navajo returned to their once and future home, after four years in exile. They never again engaged in military conflict with the U.S. Army.

See also: *Native American Church v. Navajo Tribal Council*; Navajo-Hopi Land Settlement Act; Navajo Rehabilitation Act; Navajo War; Pueblo Revolt; *Santa Clara Pueblo v. Martinez*.

Richard Sax

Sources for Further Study

Amsden, Charles. "The Navajo Exile at Bosque Redondo." *New Mexico Historical Review* 8 (1933): 31-50. A dated but still significant article concerning the Navajo on the Bosque Redondo reservation.

Frink, Maurice. *Fort Defiance and the Navajos*. Boulder, Colo.: Pruett, 1968. This text is directed toward a middle school or high school audience. Chapter 7, "Lost Cause, Long Walk," covers the relocations.

Kelly, Lawrence C. *Navajo Roundup: Selected Correspondence of Kit Carson's Expedition Against the Navajo, 1863-1865*. Boulder, Colo.: Pruett, 1970. A collection of personal letters and U.S. Army general orders, especially those of General E. R. S. Canby, Brigadier General James Carleton, and Colonel Kit Carson.

McPherson, Robert S. *The Northern Navajo Frontier, 1860-1900: Expansion Through Adversity*. Albuquerque: University of New Mexico Press, 1988. A well-documented study of the clash of cultures in the Four Corners area.

Trafzer, Clifford. *The Kit Carson Campaign: The Last Great Navajo War*. Norman: University of Oklahoma Press, 1982. The definitive text on the Long Walk of the Navajos. Well researched and thoroughly annotated, although with some turgid language, especially when describing landscape. Three maps and sixty-eight illustrations.

Utley, Robert M. *The Indian Frontier of the American West, 1846-1890*. Albuquerque: University of New Mexico Press, 1984. Chapter 3 includes a good partial discussion of the events leading to the Long Walk.

Longest Walk

Date: February 11-July 15, 1978
Locale: From San Francisco, California, to Washington, D.C.
Tribes involved: Pantribal in the United States
Categories: Native government, Protest movements, Twentieth century history
Significance: The Longest Walk, one of the several major Indian protest movements of the 1970's, was an attempt to persuade the U.S. government to recognize and protect Indian treaty rights and Indian sovereignty.

The Longest Walk was a five-month cross-country demonstration by Indian people to protest federal bills in Congress that were seen as destructive of the Indians' very existence. About two hundred Native Americans began the walk from the once Indian-occupied Alcatraz Island, in San Francisco Bay. Thousands of Indians participated along the way, ultimately arriving in the nation's capital on July 15, 1978. One of the demonstrators was Russell Means of the American Indian Movement. The protesters set

A modern manifestation of pantribal solidarity was the Longest Walk—a protest march that began in San Francisco in 1978 and ended in Washington, D.C., where Indian leaders lobbied the federal government to recognize its existing treaty obligations. (Library of Congress)

up a camp at the National Mall, hoping to convince lawmakers not to pass the bills.

The pending legislation would have weakened Indian rights to land, resources, and self-government. For example, one bill proposed to limit Indian water rights, while others threatened to cancel Indian hunting and fishing rights and terminate all treaties between the United States and Indian tribes.

Congressional supporters and others assured the Indians that the anti-Indian bills would not pass. Nevertheless, they agreed with the Indian demonstrators that Congress and the American public should be aware that such legislation had been proposed. The Longest Walk was a symbolic victory for Indian people. It also demonstrated a solidarity among Indians.

See also: American Indian Movement; Trail of Broken Treaties.

Raymond Wilson

Lord Dunmore's War

Date: April 27-October 10, 1774
Locale: Ohio River region
Tribes involved: Shawnee
Categories: Colonial history, Eighteenth century history, Wars and battles
Significance: Frontier Virginians and Marylanders battle Shawnees, resulting in relocation of the latter as settlers moved into Kentucky.

Lord Dunmore's War (named for John Murray, fourth earl of Dunmore, governor of Virginia) was a struggle between the Shawnees and Virginians in the spring and summer of 1774. It represents the culmination of events dating back to Pontiac's Resistance (1763-1766). For both the American Indians and the colonists, the war carried important ramifications. The victor would control what is now Kentucky. In order to understand how the conflict arose, one must understand the unsettled state of Anglo-Indian relations after 1763.

Following Pontiac's Resistance, British officials had tried to create an alliance with the natives of the Ohio and Illinois region. Using the French model, Britain's Indian superintendent for the northern colonies, Sir William Johnson, tried to create a mutually intelligible world that would allow colonists and American Indians to conduct diplomatic and economic activities. Two problems undermined the superintendent's efforts. The first problem confronting the relationship was the emergence of colonial communities west of the Appalachian Mountains. Colonists had settled the region in direct violation of the Proclamation of 1763. Although British soldiers often drove them back across the mountains, the settlers often returned. Outside the range of governmental control, these settlers caused tensions with the native communities of the region. The second problem was the British government's desire to curtail expenditures relating to Indian affairs. The Crown first tried to reduce its commitment by passing some of the costs off on the colonies, but these attempts did not work. As a result, Johnson's office was unable to meet even the basic necessities for conducting Indian affairs after 1770. Taken together, colonial settlement along the frontier and reduced expenditures meant a worsening of Anglo-Indian relations in the years preceding Lord Dunmore's War.

The Shawnees' relationship with the British reached its nadir with the completion of the Treaty of Fort Stanwix in 1768. As a result of this treaty, the Six Nations of the Iroquois ceded much of the territory south and east of the Ohio River to land speculators. The ceded land had belonged to the Shawnees, Lenni Lenapes (Delawares), Cherokees, and Mingos, not the Six Nations. The treaty resulted in a series of confrontations between the Shawnees, who rejected the treaty, and the British. Beginning in 1769, skirmishes between the tribes and the frontier colonists became commonplace. These skirmishes continued not only because of reduced expenditures on American Indian affairs but also because of the withdrawal of British soldiers from the colonial frontier. By 1774, British soldiers were stationed at only Kaskaskia, Detroit, and Michilimackinac. Without British soldiers or Indian agents, the Ohio region became a battleground.

As tensions between the two sides escalated, Sir William Johnson worked to isolate the Shawnees from their allies. By the spring of 1774, he had isolated the Shawnees from their previous confederates, the Hurons, Miamis, and Potawatomis. His activities broke the Shawnee league. Colonists appreciated the importance of Johnson's actions when war broke out in April, 1774. For his part, British commander Thomas Gage expressed no surprise when Dunmore's War began. He had long suspected Virginia's colonial elites of supporting the frontiersmen in their move west.

The Yellow Creek Massacre. The war began on April 27, 1774. On this date, Daniel Greathouse and his followers lured an Iroquois hunting party into a trap at the mouth of the Yellow Creek. Greathouse and his men killed nine people. Those killed at Yellow Creek were followers of the Mingo war chief Tachnechdorus, also called John Logan, the Great Mingo. Logan recruited supporters and retaliated. By July, he and his followers had claimed thirteen scalps and the Great Mingo proclaimed himself avenged. Because Virginians were settling on Shawnee lands, Logan focused his reprisals on Virginians in particular rather than colonists (such as Pennsylvanians) in general.

If Logan's actions had been only an isolated response to a massacre, it is doubtful that war would have erupted. However, Logan's actions were not unique. Further down the Ohio River, Michael Cresap and his associates—who were trying to develop land for future settlers—received a message from John Connolly, Virginia's resident administrator for the Monongahela region. Connolly's message implied that a colonial war with the Indians had begun. Situated hundreds of miles beyond colonial settlements, Cresap and his men acted as if war were a reality. They attacked a canoe carrying Lenni Lenape and Shawnee traders. After scalping the Indians, Cresap and his men sought protection in the community of Wheeling.

Following the Yellow Creek Massacre, and while Cresap and his men were seeking the shelter of Wheeling, Connolly participated in a condolence ceremony for the victims of Greathouse's attack. Held at Pittsburgh, the ceremony mollified the Indians' civil leadership. It did not, however, appease the warriors on either side of the cultural divide. Logan continued his attacks against squatters, and Cresap tried to raise a volunteer unit for military service against the natives. Their actions illustrated how young men on both sides of the cultural divide often dictated the actions of their elders.

Attacks Against the Shawnees. As late as June, 1774, it was still possible to avert full-scale war. In July, however, Virginia's militia moved westward. Their aims were to destroy the Shawnees and open Kentucky for Virginian settlement. Virginian major Angus McDonald led four hundred Virginians across the Ohio River and destroyed five Shawnee villages, including Wakatomica, in early August. Later that month, Dunmore arrived at Pittsburgh. When Shawnee warriors refused his request to meet with him, Dunmore decided to lead an expedition against the Shawnees located along the Scioto River.

While marching to its new base of operations at Camp Charlotte, a militia detachment burned the Mingo town at the Salt Licks. In order to prevent the Virginians from invading the Scioto region, nine hundred Shawnees and their allies attacked twelve hundred Virginians at their fortifications at the mouth of the Kanawha River on October 10, 1774. This attack—the Battle of Point Pleasant—resulted in the Shawnees' defeat.

Before the battle at Point Pleasant took place, the traditional leaders of the Shawnee and Lenni Lenape had sought a negotiated settlement with

Governor Dunmore. He refused to deal with the Shawnee representative, Cornstalk. Dunmore did meet with Cornstalk's Lenni Lenape counterparts, Captain Pipe and George WhiteEyes, who tried to mediate the problem. Their efforts resulted only in limiting the war, not preventing it. After the Battle of Point Pleasant, however, Cornstalk again tried to negotiate a settlement with Dunmore. The result was the Camp Charlotte Agreement of 1774.

The Camp Charlotte Agreement. Governor Dunmore dictated the terms of this agreement. He required the Shawnees to accept Virginia's interpretation of the Treaty of Fort Stanwix. He also required that the Shawnees and Mingos give him hostages as a promise of future good behavior. He demanded that the natives give up their right to hunt on the south side of the Ohio River. In exchange for their promise, Dunmore promised to prohibit Virginians from intruding on Indian lands north of the Ohio River.

While Dunmore and Cornstalk discussed peace terms, Logan refused to attend the council. He did, however, send a statement to the council through the trader John Gibson. "Logan's Lament," as it came to be known after Thomas Jefferson included it years later in his *Notes on the State of Virginia*, justified Logan's actions in the preceding months:

> Col. Cresap, the last spring, in cold blood, and unprovoked, murdered all the relations of Logan. . . . There runs not a drop of my blood in the veins of any living creature. . . . Who is there to mourn for Logan?—Not one.

In response to Logan's speech, Dunmore ordered a detachment of troops to attack the Mingos at Salt Lick Town. The attack resulted in the death of five Indians and the capture of fourteen prisoners.

Following the Virginians' attack, Lord Dunmore's War became fused with the American Revolution. American patriots believed Dunmore really was not interested in claiming Kentucky for settlement; they concluded that Dunmore's real intent was the formation of an army for use against them. By 1775, colonists had turned against Governor Dunmore. As a result, the final treaty ending Lord Dunmore's War, the Treaty of Pittsburgh, was delayed until October, 1775. Following Lord Dunmore's War, Shawnee population centers in the Ohio Valley began to change. Most Shawnees left the Muskingum region and moved southwest toward the Scioto and Mad River areas.

See also: Indian-white relations: English colonial; Pontiac's Resistance; Proclamation of 1763.

Michael J. Mullin

Sources for Further Study

Jacob, John J. *A Biographical Sketch of the Life of the Late Captain Michael Cresap.* Cincinnati: J. F. Uhlhorn, 1866. John Jacob worked for Michael Cresap and later married Cresap's widow. His book challenges the notion that Cresap was responsible for the Yellow Creek Massacre.

McConnell, Michael N. *A Country Between: The Upper Ohio Valley and Its Peoples, 1724-1774.* Lincoln: University of Nebraska Press, 1992. Discusses colonial expansion from the eighteenth century Native American perspective. McConnell sees the Treaty of Fort Stanwix as a deciding factor in the coming of Lord Dunmore's War.

Mayer, Brantz. *Tah-Gah-Jute, or Logan and Cresap, an Historical Essay.* Albany: Munsell, 1867. The most famous study of the Cresap-Logan controversy written in the nineteenth century.

Tanner, Helen Hornbeck, ed. *Atlas of Great Lakes Indian History.* Norman: University of Oklahoma Press, 1987. This monograph traces Shawnee history through cartographic evidence. Contains a discussion of Lord Dunmore's War.

White, Richard. *The Middle Ground: Indians, Empires, and Republics in the Great Lakes Region, 1650-1815.* New York: Cambridge University Press, 1991. Discusses how both Europeans and American Indians sought accommodation and common meaning. Places Lord Dunmore's War within this context in his analysis of the event.

Lyng v. Northwest Indian Cemetery Protective Association

Date: 1987
Locale: California
Tribes involved: Karok, Tolowa, Yurok
Categories: Court cases, Twentieth century history, Religion and missionary activities
Significance: A U.S. Supreme Court decision raises questions about the enforceability of the American Indian Religious Freedom Act.

In 1982, the United States Forest Service prepared an environmental impact report for construction of a paved road through federal lands in the Six Rivers National Forest in California. The study reported a section of this land was historically used for religious purposes by Yurok, Karok, and

Tolowa Indians, and because the site was integral to the religious practices of these people, it recommended the road not be completed. That same year, despite its own report, the Forest Service decided to build the road. After exhausting administrative remedies, a coalition of Indian organizations filed suit in federal court, challenging the decision based on the right to free exercise of religion under the First Amendment and on similar guarantees in the American Indian Religious Freedom Act (1978).

In 1987, the U.S. Supreme Court ruled against the Indian coalition even though the Court admitted the road would severely affect tribal religious practices. The Court declared that although the free exercise clause affords individual protections, it does not afford an individual right "to dictate the conduct of the government's internal procedures." Additionally, it ruled that the American Indian Religious Freedom Act has no enforcement mechanisms that could compel the government to halt construction on the road. This case severely reduced both the intent of the American Indian Religious Freedom Act and the protections it afforded Indian people, and it raised questions about basic protections afforded American Indian citizens of the United States.

See also: American Indian Religious Freedom Act.

Carole A. Barrett

Maine Indian Claims Act

Date: October 10, 1980
Locale: Maine
Tribes involved: Maliseet, Passamaquoddy, Penobscot
Categories: National government and legislation, Reservations and relocation, Treaties, Twentieth century history
Significance: Beginning in the 1960's, tribes in the eastern United States alleged that state governments had illegally taken their lands; the Maine Indian Claims Act prompted a number of eastern tribes to settle similar claims rather than go through the courts.

In 1964, the Passamaquoddy Tribe, recognized by the state of Maine but not the federal government, sought protection from what it determined were illegal incursions on their lands. Both state and federal governments refused to assist the tribe. The Passamaquoddy, joined by the Penobscots, initiated a lawsuit in which they asserted protection under the Trade and Intercourse Act of 1790, which prevented tribes from selling lands unless approved by Congress. The basis of the lawsuit was that their land transfers never received such approval. The tribes won a series of lower court cases, and so the United States was obliged to bring suit against Maine for illegal purchase of Indian land. The court decisions left 1.25 million acres, two-thirds of Maine, under clouded land titles. The Maliseet Tribe also joined the lawsuit. Maine agreed to settle out of court rather than face complicated, expensive legal negotiations. The settlement extinguished all Indian claims to land. In return, the United States provided $27 million in a trust fund for the tribes, and another $54.5 million was set aside for the tribes to purchase land. The tribes also received federal recognition.

Carole A. Barrett

See also: Indian Claims Commission; Reservation system of the United States; Trade and Intercourse Acts; Treaties and agreements in the United States.

Major Crimes Act

Date: 1885
Locale: United States
Tribes involved: Pantribal in the United States
Categories: Court cases, National government and legislation, Native government, Nineteenth century history, Reservations and relocation
Significance: The Major Crimes Act gave the U.S. government, rather than tribal courts, criminal jurisdiction to prosecute fourteen major crimes committed by one reservation Indian against another.

The Major Crimes Act gave the U.S. government jurisdiction over serious crimes committed by Indians on tribal lands. Congress reacted strongly to the *Ex parte Crow Dog* (1883) decision, in which an Indian who killed another Indian was released by the federal government because it lacked federal jurisdiction in Indian country. Two years after the Crow Dog incident, Congress passed the Major Crimes Act, which gave the United States the right to prosecute Indians for seven crimes: murder, manslaughter, rape, assault with intent to kill, arson, burglary, and larceny. This law applied to any Indian who committed a crime against another Indian on a reservation.

Over the years, the list of criminal offenses expanded to include kidnapping, maiming, assault with a dangerous weapon, assault resulting in bodily injury, incest, theft, and sexual abuse. Indians accused of lesser crimes are tried in tribal court. However, federal court decisions narrowed the act so it covers only enrolled Indians who commit crimes on their own reservations. This act transformed the relationship between tribes and the federal government by limiting tribal sovereignty and the power of tribal courts and making it nearly impossible for tribes to deal with serious crimes committed on their reservations.

Carole A. Barrett

See also: *Duro v. Reina; Ex parte Crow Dog; Oliphant v. Suquamish Indian Tribe;* Public Law 280; Tribal courts; *United States v. Kagama.*

Manhattan Island purchase

Date: May 6, 1626
Locale: Manhattan Island, New Netherland
Tribes involved: Algonquian
Categories: Colonial history
Significance: The Dutch gain a stronghold in North America that they will relinquish to the British four decades later.

In the early seventeenth century, the Netherlands, like other nations of northern Europe, sent out explorers to search for a sea route around North America to the riches of eastern Asia. The principal explorer for the Dutch was Henry Hudson, an Englishman, who, in 1609, explored the river that bears his name. When Hudson and other navigators failed to find the Northwest Passage, the Dutch, like other Europeans, decided to claim the lands that they had found in the Americas and exploit their resources. While hoping to discover gold and silver, as the Spanish had done to the south, the Dutch soon found that furs were the most readily exploitable resource of the middle Atlantic coastal region that they claimed. The Dutch could obtain these furs by trading with the Native Americans, who would do most of the trapping in exchange for European goods. The demand for pelts was so great in Europe that one shipload could make its investors wealthy.

In the interests of further discovery and to stimulate trade, the Dutch legislative body, the States-General, granted to its traders and explorers the exclusive right to make four voyages to any new lands that they might explore. Under this grant, in 1614, five ships visited the Hudson River, which the Dutch then called Mauritius. Later that same year, these traders combined as the United New Netherland Company and received a monopoly on the trade of the Hudson Valley from the States-General. Ignoring Manhattan Island, these early traders sailed up the Hudson River to the site of present-day Albany, where they erected Fort Nassau on Castle Island as a base of operations. There they exchanged their goods for furs with the Mohican tribal peoples. Following the expiration of the charter of the United New Netherland Company in 1618, a succession of different companies plied the Hudson River fur trade.

Dutch Colonization Begins. In 1621, a number of influential merchants obtained from the States-General a charter for the Dutch West India Company with the sole right to trade on the Atlantic coasts of Africa and North and South America for twenty-four years. Although the new company organized primarily to challenge Spanish control of Latin America, it also was interested in the Hudson River area. In 1624, the company dispatched Captain Cornelius May with a shipload of thirty families to settle in North America. Opposite Castle Island, the group founded a trading post they named Fort Orange; to the south, they formed a settlement on the Delaware

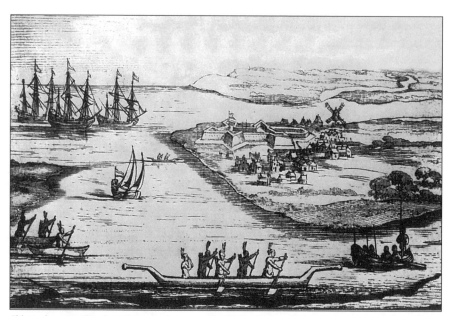

"New Amsterdam" at the southern end of Manhattan Island, in an erroneously reversed engraving from a Dutch book of 1651. (Library of Congress)

River. They also may have established a trading house on Governor's Island, in what would become New York City's harbor. Coastal Algonquian tribes probably were in the process of forming a coalition when the Dutch arrived and disrupted that maneuver.

The first two governors of New Netherland, Cornelius May and Willem Verhulst, lived at the Delaware River site and administered the colony from there. Peter Minuit, the third governor and first director-general of New Netherland, shifted his center of operations to Manhattan Island. A native of Wesel, then in the Duchy of Cleves, he was probably of French or Walloon descent. He impressed many as a shrewd and somewhat unscrupulous man.

One of his first acts after arriving on Manhattan Island early in 1626 was to buy the rights to the island from an Algonquian tribe, the Canarsee, for trinkets worth about sixty guilders, or about twenty-four dollars. There is some debate whether Minuit actually arranged the purchase himself or if his predecessor, Verhulst, did, but a May, 1626, letter revealed Minuit's intentions to buy it. Controversy also surrounds the morality of the purchase. Tradition commonly calls the sale an unconscionable steal or a tremendous bargain. However, some historians suggest that the conversion to twenty-four dollars is too low and that, refiguring the payment in 1986 dollars, the Dutch paid $31 billion. Moreover, the Canarsee certainly placed a different value on the beads, other trade goods, and land than did the Europeans; the concept of land "ownership" did not exist among most indigenous people or, at least, it had a meaning completely different from that of Europeans. Because the Manhattan tribe, whose name the island reflected, had a better claim to it than did the Canarsee, Minuit later apparently also bought the island from them. Through this, their first major land purchase from the Native Americans, the Dutch secured a semblance of a legal title to Manhattan. At the time of the purchase, it was a beautiful island, covered with a great forest and abounding with wildlife and wild fruits.

Minuit made New Amsterdam, at the southern tip of Manhattan, the nucleus of Dutch activity in the area. A large fort, pentagonal in shape, surrounded on three sides by a great moat and fronting on the bay, was one of the first structures built. When it was complete, Minuit brought several families from Fort Orange to settle in the town. He also ordered the evacuation of Fort Nassau on the South River, near present-day Gloucester, New Jersey, and transferred the garrison to New Amsterdam. Despite his vigorous administration of the colony, the parent country recalled him for examination in 1632 and dismissed him from the Dutch West India Company's service.

Land Grants and Native Relations. In the meantime, in 1629, the director-ate of the company, with the approval of the States-General, had issued a Charter of Freedoms and Exemptions that provided for the grant of large estates, called patroonships, to those members of the company who would recruit at least fifty settlers more than fifteen years of age to settle their lands within four years. These grants ostensibly were to promote farming in New Netherland, but their primary intention was to encourage settlers to go up the Hudson River to settle and make additional contacts with the Native Americans and thereby extend the fur trade. Traders presumably would ship the furs down the river to New Amsterdam, from where the Dutch West India Company had the sole right to export them. With one ex-ception, Rensselaerwyck, these patroonships never measured up to Dutch expectations.

Relations with the Native Americans remained mostly harmonious and the fur trade continued to prosper until 1641, when hostilities broke out. The fighting, called Kieft's War after Governor Willem Kieft, resulted from his attempt to collect taxes from the Algonquian tribes for Dutch "protection." The conflict ended with a treaty on August 29, 1645, but it had already dis-rupted the fur trade and forced Kieft to relinquish some of his arbitrary power to advisory bodies to obtain popular support for the prosecution of the war. In 1647, Peter Stuyvesant succeeded Kieft and became the last Dutch governor or director-general of New Netherland. It was he who sur-rendered the colony to the British in 1664. The brightness of the early prom-ise of New Netherland, lustrous with the purchase of Manhattan in 1626, faded within the half century. Although the Dutch would retain significant economic and cultural influence in the renamed New York, the English would benefit even more from one of the world's best harbors.

See also: Indian-white relations: Dutch colonial.

William L. Richter, updated by Thomas L. Altherr

Sources for Further Study

Brasser, Ted J. "The Coastal New York Indians in the Early Contact Period." In *Neighbors and Intruders: An Ethnohistorical Exploration of the Indians of Hudson's River*, edited by Laurence M. Hauptman and Jack Campisi. Ottawa: National Museums of Canada, 1978. Argues that the coastal Algonquians were probably in the process of forming a coalition when the Dutch purchased Manhattan.

Condon, Thomas J. *New York Beginnings: The Commercial Origins of New Netherland.* New York: New York University Press, 1968. Monograph examining the Dutch purchase decision as part of a wider commercial policy.

Francis, Peter, Jr. "The Beads That Did Not Buy Manhattan Island." *New York History* 67, no. 1 (January, 1986): 4-22. Asserts that the trinkets the Dutch paid for the island were much more valuable than common assumptions hold.

Gehring, Charles. "Peter Minuit's Purchase of Manhattan Island: New Evidence." *De Halve Maen* 54 (Spring, 1980): 6ff. Discusses a letter from Minuit suggesting his intention to buy Manhattan Island.

Rink, Oliver A. *Holland on the Hudson: An Economic and Social History of Dutch New York.* Ithaca, N.Y.: Cornell University Press, 1986. Argues strongly for Minuit's mastery in establishing New Amsterdam.

Trelease, Allen W. *Indian Affairs in Colonial New York: The Seventeenth Century.* Ithaca, N.Y.: Cornell University Press, 1960. Places the Dutch purchase in the context of other relations with Native Americans around New Netherland. Argues that the money paid was worth more to the Canarsee tribal people than usually is presumed.

Weslager, C. A. "Did Minuit Buy Manhattan Island from the Indians?" *De Halve Maen* 43 (October, 1968): 5-6. Questions whether Minuit actually purchased the island and suggests that Verhulst did instead.

Medicine Lodge Creek Treaty

Date: October 21, 1867
Locale: Southwestern Kansas, Texas
Tribes involved: Arapaho, Comanche, Kiowa, Kiowa-Apache, Southern Cheyenne
Categories: Nineteenth century history, Reservations and relocation, Treaties
Significance: Tribes of the Great Plains enter an agreement that ultimately results in total submission to the U.S. government.

For many years, five Native American tribes—the Comanche, the Kiowa, the Kiowa-Apache, the Southern Cheyenne, and the Arapaho—roamed the vast area of the southern Great Plains, following huge buffalo herds. This area became parts of Texas, Oklahoma, New Mexico, Colorado, and Kansas. Northern Cheyenne, Sioux, and other tribes lived a similar life on the northern Great Plains. Warfare was a part of the daily life of these tribes, generally as a result of intertribal rivalries and disputes concerning control of certain sections of the plains. This traditional life began to change when the first Europeans began to arrive on the Great Plains in the sixteenth century. Until the early nineteenth century, however, the changes were limited to the acquisition of steel knives, guns, and other products from European traders. The tribes soon became dependent on these items, but their day-by-day life changed very little.

The dominant leaders of the region were the Comanches, called the Lords of the Southern Plains. Joined by the Kiowas, with whom they established friendly relations about 1790, they controlled the smaller Kiowa-Apache tribe and all land south of the Arkansas River. Their chief rivals north of the Arkansas River were the southern Cheyenne. In 1840, the Comanches and Cheyennes established a fragile peace that also included the Arapaho, the less numerous allies of the Cheyenne. This peace came at the beginning of a decade that would change forever the face of the southern Great Plains. In 1846, the United States annexed Texas. The end of the Mexican War in 1848 added New Mexico, Arizona, and other areas of the Southwest to the United States. For the next half century, the fragile Native American peace of 1840 became a strong bond of brotherhood for the southern plains tribes as they fought to defend themselves and their land against European American settlers, railroads, buffalo hunters, soldiers, and other intruders.

With the acquisition of Texas, the United States inherited a long and bloody conflict between Texans and Comanches, who were described by some as the best light cavalry in the world. The Comanches had long hunted from the Arkansas River to the Rio Grande. In 1821, the government of Mexico began giving land grants in west Texas to settlers from the United States. These settlers immediately challenged the Comanches for control of the area.

Comanche Reservations. The first attempt to confine the Comanches to reservations was a May, 1846, treaty that created two small reservations on the Brazos River. The few Comanches who settled on them soon yearned for the free-spirited life on the vast plains. By 1850, discoveries of precious metals from the southern Rocky Mountains to California were drawing numerous wagon and pack trains through the southern plains. These were soon followed by stagecoach lines and, later, railroads. The increase in traffic was paralleled by increased confrontation with the tribes, who were accustomed to unhindered pursuit of the buffalo.

Between 1846 and 1865, several treaties were signed between the Native Americans of the southern plains and the government of the United States. Lack of confidence, sarcasm, and open contempt on both sides doomed these treaties to failure. The frustration felt by the Native Americans in-

Arapaho and Comanche council at Medicine Lodge Creek in 1867, where the tribes' leaders signed a treaty with the U.S. government designed to end wars on the southern Plains. (Library of Congress)

creased when cholera and other diseases carried by Europeans began rapidly decreasing the native populations.

In March of 1863, a party of Native American chiefs from the southern plains went to Washington, D.C., and met with President Abraham Lincoln. Returning home loaded with gifts, these leaders were convinced that coexistence with European Americans was possible. This confidence was hard to maintain after the bloody and unprovoked massacre of Cheyennes at Sand Creek, in Colorado, the following year. Nevertheless, Ten Bears of the Comanche, who had met President Lincoln, Black Kettle of the Cheyenne, who had escaped from Sand Creek, and other chiefs still felt that peace was their best protection and was possible to achieve.

Treaties and Peace Commissions. The next effort toward peace was the Little Arkansas Treaty in October, 1865. Representatives of the five southern plains tribes met with U.S. commissioners at the mouth of the Little Arkansas River near Wichita, Kansas. The government wanted to end native American hindrances to movements in and through the plains. The treaty, little more than a stopgap measure, committed the tribes to reservations—the Cheyenne and Arapaho in northern Indian Territory (Oklahoma) and the Comanche, Kiowa, and Kiowa-Apache in western Texas and south-western Indian Territory. These boundaries were impossible to enforce and did not end the violence, but the treaty set the stage for a more important meeting two years later.

In July, 1867, Congress created a peace commission to establish perma-nent settlements of grievances between Native Americans and European Americans on the Great Plains. The commission was led by Commissioner of Indian Affairs Nathaniel Taylor and included a senator and three gener-als. The group chose to meet representatives of the southern plains tribes on the banks of Medicine Lodge Creek in southwestern Kansas. Joining them there were more than four thousand Native Americans representing all five tribes, but not all bands of the tribes. Noticeably absent was the Quahadi, a Comanche band that wanted no peace with the United States government.

The council opened on October 19, 1867, with Senator John B. Hender-son giving the opening remarks. Under a large brush arbor, he referred to reservation homes, rich farmland, livestock, churches, and schools for all Native Americans. Although most tribal leaders accepted the promises as positive, the idea of being restricted to reservations covering only a frac-tion of their beloved Great Plains was sickening. The Kiowa chief Satanta, or White Bear, lamented, "I love to roam over the prairies. There I feel free and happy, but when we settle down we grow pale and die." The Yam-parika Comanche chief Ten Bears gave one of the most eloquent state-ments, declaring,

I was born where there were no inclosures and where everything drew a free breath. I want to die there and not within walls. . . . when I see [soldiers cutting trees and killing buffalo] my heart feels like bursting with sorrow.

In spite of such emotional appeals, Ten Bears and other Comanche chiefs signed the Treaty of Medicine Lodge Creek on October 21, 1867, thereby committing their people to life on the reservation. Black Kettle, with the horrors of the 1864 Sand Creek Massacre fresh in his mind, represented the Cheyenne at the council. He would not sign the treaty until other Cheyenne chiefs arrived on October 26. Although less happy with the treaty than the Comanche and Kiowa leaders, the Cheyenne chiefs signed, primarily to get ammunition for their fall buffalo hunt. The Arapaho chiefs soon did like-wise. At the end of the council meeting, Satank rode alone to bid farewell to the Peace Commission. He expressed his desire for peace and declared that the Comanche and the Kiowa no longer wanted to shed the blood of the white man.

The Treaty of Medicine Lodge Creek restricted the five southern Plains tribes to reservations in the western half of Indian Territory. However, vague terminology and unwritten promises made the treaty impossible to understand or to enforce. Violence soon erupted on the southern plains. One year after Medicine Lodge Creek, Black Kettle was killed in a confrontation similar to the Sand Creek Massacre, this time on the Washita River in Indian Territory. The violence escalated for several years, then dwindled to isolated incidents before ending at Wounded Knee in 1890.

A poignant illustration of the ultimate effect of the treaty occurred on June 8, 1871, when the seventy-year-old Satank—who along with Satanta and a young war chief named Big Tree had been arrested for attacking a mule train carrying food that the ration-deprived Indians sorely needed— was being transported to Texas to stand trial for murder. Chewing his own wrists in order to slip out of his manacles, Satank then attacked a guard and was shot dead, fulfilling a prophecy that he had uttered only minutes before to fellow prisoners: "Tell them I am dead. . . . I shall never go beyond that tree."

See also: Sand Creek Massacre; Washita River Massacre; Wounded Knee Massacre.

Glenn L. Swygart

Sources for Further Study

Brown, Dee. *Bury My Heart at Wounded Knee*. New York: Holt, Rinehart and Winston, 1970. Places the Treaty of Medicine Lodge Creek in the context of Native American history in the western United States.

Grinnell, George Bird. *The Fighting Cheyennes*. 1915. Reprint. Norman: University of Oklahoma Press, 1956. An author who observed the Cheyenne at first hand presents their history up to 1890.

Hagan, William T. *United States-Comanche Relations*. New Haven, Conn.: Yale University Press, 1976. The most complete coverage of the council and treaty at Medicine Lodge Creek.

Josephy, Alvin M., Jr. *Five Hundred Nations: An Illustrated History of North American Indians*. New York: Alfred A. Knopf, 1994. A well-illustrated history of North America from its original inhabitants' viewpoint; pages 371-374 cover the treaty, including direct quotations from Indian leaders.

Mooney, James. *Calendar History of the Kiowa Indians*. 1898. Reprint. Washington, D.C.: Smithsonian Institution Press, 1979. Provides a chronology of the tribe.

Rollings, Willard H. *The Comanche*. New York: Chelsea House, 1989. Describes the change in Comanche life after the Medicine Lodge Creek Treaty.

Meech Lake Accord

Date: Proposed 1987; defeated June, 1990
Locale: Quebec
Tribes involved: Pantribal in Canada
Categories: National government and legislation, Native government, Treaties, Twentieth century history
Significance: A coalition of native organizations rallied support around an Indian politician and successfully prevented the passage of a constitutional provision that failed to recognize aboriginal rights.

Fears that Quebec might break away from the rest of Canada led Canadian prime minister Brian Mulroney and the ten provincial premiers in 1987 to propose a set of amendments to the 1982 Constitution Act. The proposal, known as the Meech Lake Accord after the site of the meeting, recognized French-speaking Quebec as one of the founding nations of Canada and as a distinct society with its own language and culture. The accord, however, granted no such courtesy to the aboriginal peoples of Canada. In order for the accord to become law, it required ratification by all ten provinces before June 23, 1990.

An additional provision of the Meech Lake Accord dealt with admission of a new province to the Confederation. That provision required the unanimous consent of the ten existing provinces in order to establish a new province. Since many of the provinces have territorial desires to extend their borders north, this virtually ensured that the Yukon and Northwest territories, as well as the proposed Nunavut Territory, would be precluded from ever achieving provincial status. Unlike the rest of Canada, the two regions have overwhelmingly native populations.

Native organizations fought bitterly against ratification of the accord. Their leaders insisted that native cultures were no less distinct than Quebec's and that aboriginal rights also deserved formal recognition in the body of the Constitution. Since the courts had held that despite the addition of the Charter of Rights and Freedoms to the Constitution, aboriginal rights were not assured, the natives' concerns were well justified. The leaders further demanded guarantees that they would be given a role in all future First Ministers' conferences affecting natives. George Erasmus, national chief of the Assembly of First Nations, was especially vocal.

Thinking that a looming deadline would help assure passage, Prime Minister Mulroney delayed pushing for ratification of the accord until the very end of the ratification period. That delay proved fatal to the proposal.

It allowed Elijah Harper, Manitoba's only native legislator, to prevent consideration of the Meech Lake Accord by the Manitoba Legislative Assembly. Supported by native organizations, Harper exploited a procedural error made by Manitoba premier Gary Filmon. Manitoba law required unanimous consent of the legislators to begin public hearings on any issue with less than a forty-eight-hour notice. Harper withheld his consent, and the deadline for ratification passed without the Meech Lake Accord ever being considered by the Manitoba Legislative Assembly.

See also: Indian-white relations: Canadian; Nunavut Territory.

Richard G. Condon

Menominee Restoration Act

Date: December 22, 1973
Locale: Wisconsin
Tribes involved: Menominee
Categories: National government and legislation, Protest movements, Reservations and relocation, Twentieth century history
Significance: The federal policy of termination, which sought to dissolve the government's special legal relationship with tribes, was effectively destroyed when the Menominee tribe was restored to full federal status.

In June, 1954, the United States terminated its relationship with the Menominee tribe of Wisconsin, in part because the tribe was so successful in managing its resources. The Menominee owned their own sawmill and operated a hospital and utility company on their reservation. The government decided the Menominee could be self-sufficient. Termination caused an abrupt change of fortune for the tribe. The reservation became Menominee County. Property taxes were high, unemployment rose, and the hospital and utility companies closed. Most devastating, while the tribal lands, assets, and sawmill were formed into a corporation composed of all former tribal members, non-Indian shareholders, who managed the shares of minors and incompetents, dominated the corporation. The corporation began to sell valuable Menominee lakefront property and mismanaged the sawmill operation, and soon Menominee County became the poorest county in Wisconsin. In 1969, Menominee activists organized DRUMS, Determination of Rights and Unity for Menominee Shareholders, to prevent further land sales and to seek restoration of federal recognition. Both the State of Wisconsin and Congress supported restoration. In 1973, Congress passed Public Law 93-197, which repealed termination, granted federal status to the Menominee, and returned their lands to full trust status.

Carole A. Barrett

See also: Federally recognized tribes; Public Law 280; Termination Resolution; Trail of Broken Treaties; Tribe.

Meriam Report

Date: 1928
Locale: United States
Tribes involved: Pantribal in the United States
Categories: Education, National government and legislation, Twentieth century history
Significance: This report documented the failures of the Bureau of Indian Affairs to help Indian people and thus helped lead to the 1930's reforms of John Collier's Indian New Deal.

In 1926, Secretary of the Interior Hubert Work asked the Institute for Government Research (Brookings Institution) at The Johns Hopkins University to conduct a nonpolitical investigation of Indian affairs. Work's goal was to counter the harsh criticisms of John Collier and other Indian Office critics. The results of the Brookings study were published in 1928 as *The Problem of Indian Administration*, popularly known as the Meriam Report after Lewis Meriam, who headed the investigation. The report condemned the allotment policy that had been instituted with the passage of the General Allotment Act of 1887, as well as the poor quality of services provided Indian people by the Bureau of Indian Affairs (BIA). It urged protection for Indian property and recommended that Indians be allowed more freedom to manage their own affairs.

The Meriam Report emphasized the BIA's educational role and called for higher academic standards in BIA schools. W. Carson Ryan, Jr., a prominent figure in the progressive education movement, wrote most of the education section of the Meriam Report, with help from Henry Roe Cloud (a Winnebago). The education section was influenced by the teachings of John Dewey and other progressive educators.

In 1921, all Indian schools had their appropriations for food and clothing cut 25 percent. These cuts were a result of government debts from World War I. This underfunding of BIA schools continued through the 1920's. In one extreme case, a Red Cross investigator found students to be subsisting on a diet of bread, black coffee, and syrup for breakfast; bread and boiled potatoes for dinner and supper; and a quarter cup of milk with each meal. In general, the Meriam Report found the food in boarding schools to be "deficient in quantity, quality and variety." The poor food made Indian students more susceptible to tuberculosis and trachoma, which were endemic in Indian communities. Half-day student labor allowed the government to save even more money educating Indians, and the Meriam Report noted that some of the work required of students violated state child labor laws. Among other activities, students raised crops, worked in dairies, made and mended their own clothes, and cleaned their schools.

Flogging and other severe forms of punishment existed at some schools. The Meriam Report found that most BIA schools had locked rooms or isolated buildings used as "jails"; in some schools, children were forced to "maintain a pathetic degree of quietness."

To quell the growing criticism of the government's Indian policy, President Herbert Hoover in 1929 appointed a fellow Quaker and president of the Indian Rights Association, Charles J. Rhoads, to be commissioner of Indian affairs. Rhoads got Ryan to become director of Indian education. Rhoads and Ryan began to implement the recommendations of the Meriam Report, including an end to a uniform BIA curriculum that stressed only white cultural values.

See also: Allotment system; American Indian Higher Education Consortium; Bureau of Indian Affairs; Carlisle Indian School; General Allotment Act; Indian Education Acts; Indian Self-Determination and Education Assistance Act; Kennedy Report; National Congress of American Indians.

Jon Reyhner

Metacom's War

Date: June 20, 1675
Locale: New England colonies
Tribes involved: Narragansett, Nipmuck, Pocasset, Sakonnet, Wampanoag

Categories: Colonial history, Wars and battles
Significance: The first large-scale conflict between New England colonists and Native Americans.

Metacom's War, also known as King Philip's War, began on June 20, 1675, when Wampanoag, or Pokanoket, warriors began looting English houses in southern Plymouth Colony (now Massachusetts) on the edge of Wampanoag country. Serious fighting began at Swansea on June 24.

The causes of the conflict were both economic and cultural. Through a series of treaties, much native land had passed into the hands of English settlers, and the remaining Wampanoag homeland, Mount Hope Peninsula on Narragansett Bay, was in danger of being completely surrounded by English settlements. This expansion of English-controlled territory had brought many Indians under English political control, with the imposition of alien social mores. English courts, for example, sometimes sentenced tribesmen to fines or whippings for violating the Sabbath by such activities as firing a gun on Sunday. There also was growing pressure on Native Americans to convert to Christianity. Tribal chiefs (called sachems in New

An engraver's depiction of Wampanoag chief Massasoit meeting settlers of Plymouth Colony in 1621. Increasing numbers of colonists caused goodwill between English and Wampanoags to deteriorate to the point of war in 1675, led by Massasoit's son Metacom. (Library of Congress)

England) and religious leaders (powwows) strongly opposed conversion, because it tended to weaken their traditional influence.

Massasoit (renamed Ousamequin late in life), the paramount sachem of the Wampanoags and an ally and friend of the English since 1621, had died about 1661, and after his death, tensions rapidly mounted. Massasoit's eldest son, Wamsutta, called Alexander by the English, became sachem on his father's death. Wamsutta died in 1661, shortly after being required by English authorities to explain rumors that he was considering an uprising. Then another son, Metacom or Metacomet, known to the English as King Philip, became sachem, and the next few years witnessed a series of disputes. By 1671, friendly Native Americans were warning Puritan authorities that Philip was organizing an alliance of tribes to join with the Wampanoags in a war of extermination against the English.

War Breaks Out. While the evidence for such a conspiracy is strong, war, sparked by the trial and execution at Plymouth of three Wampanoags for murder, seems to have broken out before Metacom's alliance was perfected. In January, 1675, a Christian Wampanoag named John Sassamon, who had just warned Plymouth of Metacom's plans, was found murdered. On the testimony of an Indian who claimed to have witnessed the deed, three Wampanoags, including an important counselor of Metacom, were convicted and hanged on June 8. Metacom apparently was unable to restrain the rage of his warriors, and violence broke out before he was ready.

The war quickly spread to Connecticut and Massachusetts Bay colonies, and later to Rhode Island, as other tribal groups, drawn in by Metacom's diplomacy or angered by threats from colonial authorities, went on the attack. The Wampanoags were joined by the related Sakonnet and Pocasset bands to the east of Narragansett Bay, by Nipmucks from the interior of Massachusetts, by the Narragansetts of present-day Rhode Island, and by smaller groups such as the river tribes of the Connecticut Valley.

The English colonists were supported by American Indians who often were the traditional enemies of tribes in Metacom's alliance, so Indian New England was not united in Metacom's War. The Mohegans and Pequots of southern Connecticut served with the English, as did hundreds of Christian Indians from the "praying towns" of Massachusetts Bay Colony. The Niantics of southern Rhode Island remained neutral. Metacom sought the assistance of the Mohawks of New York Colony to the west, but the Mohawks aided the English by attacking their old Wampanoag enemies.

Ambush Warfare. In the early months, the Wampanoags and their allies, well armed with trade muskets, were too skillful and aggressive for the English. They repeatedly ambushed parties of colonial militiamen and assaulted and burned outlying English towns. Unskilled in forest warfare and distrustful of friendly tribesmen, the colonists were unable to pin down the enemy. The English usually had no inkling of the town chosen for attack, so hostile chiefs concentrated their forces and often greatly outnumbered the defending garrison. By using Indian allies as scouts, English militia officers learned to avoid ambush and to operate more effectively in the forest. Eventually, special colonial units that could remain in the field for weeks were used to pursue American Indian bands; disease, cold, and starvation aided the colonists in wearing down the tribes. The most effective such unit was a small, mixed force of English militia and Indian allies commanded by Captain Benjamin Church of Plymouth Colony. It was Church's company that eventually ran down Metacom and the handful of Wampanoags still with him, directed by a surrendered Wampanoag to a swamp where they had taken refuge. Metacom was killed, shot by an Indian while trying to slip away once more, on August 12, 1676. By this time, as starving groups of Indians straggled in to surrender, the war was dragging to a close. The much larger population and economic resources of the English had won out. In spite of the warriors' initial successes, it had become clear that there was no real prospect of driving the English into the sea. To the northeast in New Hampshire and Maine, where the Abenaki peoples had risen against the English, the war continued into 1678.

Both sides used ruthless methods, often killing women, children, and the elderly. Indian attackers regularly attempted to burn colonists' houses with the inhabitants inside them, and sometimes tortured prisoners. Perhaps the most strikingly ruthless act committed by the English took place in the Great Swamp Fight, December 19, 1676. A force of a thousand militiamen marched into a frozen swamp deep in the Rhode Island forest, led there by a Narragansett turncoat, and attacked perhaps a thousand Narragansetts sheltered in a log-walled fort. Forcing their way inside, the English set the fort afire. As many as six hundred Narragansetts, many of them women and children, perished in the blaze. Some eighty Englishmen were killed or died of wounds.

Metacom's War has been called the bloodiest war, proportionally, in the nation's history, with some nine thousand of the eighty thousand people in New England killed. Of these, one-third were English and two-thirds Indians. Of New England's ninety towns, fifty-two were attacked and seventeen completely burned. The frontier of settlement was pushed back many miles. The military power and the independence of the tribal people of southern New England had been crushed forever. Hundreds of Native American captives, including Metacom's wife and small son, were sold into slavery by the colonial governments to help defray the war's cost. Other captives, considered to be important war chiefs or those responsible for particular atrocities, were tried and publicly executed.

See also: Bacon's Rebellion; Indian-white relations: English colonial; Pequot War; Pontiac's Resistance; Powhatan Wars; Prehistory: Northeast.

Bert M. Mutersbaugh

Sources for Further Study

Bourne, Russell. *The Red King's Rebellion: Racial Politics in New England, 1675-1678*. New York: Oxford University Press, 1990. A detailed treatment of the war that is especially critical of the motives and acts of the colonists. Maps, illustrations, and index.

Leach, Douglas Edward. *Flintlock and Tomahawk: New England in King Philip's War*. New York: Norton Library Edition, 1966. This elegantly written study, long considered the standard modern account of the war, indicts English land hunger as a cause of the war. Maps, illustrations, and index.

Lepore, Jill. *The Name of War: King Philip's War and the Origins of American Identity*. New York: Random House, 1999. A very well-received history of Metacom's war, arguing that the conflict between Europeans and Indians served to crystallize a sense of American self-identity on the part of the colonists.

Lincoln, Charles A., ed. *Narratives of the Indian Wars, 1675-1699*. New York: Scribner's, 1913. Reprint. New York: Barnes & Noble Books, 1941. Contains a number of contemporaneous accounts of the war, including *The Soveraignty & Goodness of God . . . the Captivity and Restoration of Mrs Mary Rowlandson*, Rowlandson's account of her capture in the attack on Lancaster, Massachusetts, in 1676. Her often reprinted classic is the earliest American captivity narrative. Rowlandson reports firsthand exchanges with Metacom, who at times traveled with the mixed band that held her prisoner.

Malone, Patrick M. *The Skulking Way of War: Technology and Tactics Among the New England Indians*. Baltimore: The Johns Hopkins University Press, 1991. Study of Native American military tactics and their evolution under the influence of European weapons and methods. Argues that New England's natives adopted the more ruthless methods of total war through English influence and example. Map, illustrations, and index.

Schulz, Eric, and Michael Tougias. *King Philip's War: The History and Legacy of America's Forgotten Conflict*. Woodstock, Vt.: Countryman, 1999. A detailed history of Metacom's war, as well as a guide to the sites of conflict.

Slotkin, Richard, and James K. Folsom, eds. *So Dreadful a Judgment: Puritan Responses to King Philip's War, 1676-1677*. Middletown, Conn.: Wesleyan University Press, 1978. Six contemporaneous accounts, including Rowlandson's narrative and the liveliest, best contemporary description of the fighting, Thomas Church's *Entertaining Passages Relating to Philip's War* (1716), based on the recollections of his father, Captain Benjamin Church.

Minnesota Uprising

Date: August-December, 1862
Locale: Minnesota Valley, Minnesota
Tribes involved: Eastern (Santee) Sioux
Categories: Nineteenth century history, Reservations and relocation, Wars and battles
Significance: The Minnesota Uprising was a result of the reservation policies forced upon the Eastern Sioux by the U.S. government.

Deprived of their annual distribution of annuities during the summer of 1862, the Eastern (Santee) Sioux—Mdewakanton, Wahpekute, Wahpeton, and Sisseton—grew angry and indignant. Warehouses were full of food and other supplies, but Thomas Galbraith, the Indian agent, refused to give it to the Indians until the cash annuities arrived. The agent feared he would not receive his customary monetary kickback.

Once an independent, self-sufficient group, the Eastern Sioux had become dependent on annuities for their survival. When Minnesota became a territory, a census indicated that Eastern Sioux outnumbered the six thousand white settlers by more than two to one. When Minnesota became a state in 1858 and the number of white settlers increased, Indians ceded much of their land. The treaties of 1851 and 1858 saw the Sioux cede 28 million acres to the whites in exchange for annuities and reservation life.

Faced with the starvation of his people, Little Crow—an unusually articulate leader—tried to persuade Galbraith to distribute the food to his hungry people. His arguments fell on deaf ears. The attitude of the white trader Andrew Myrick typifies the lack of concern toward the Indians' condition: If the Indians were hungry, let them eat grass or dung.

The Indians' anger over Galbraith's decision, years of mistreatment by white officials, and the threat of starvation came to a head when four young warriors murdered five white settlers on August 17, 1862. As a result of these actions, militant Mdewakanton and Wahpekute chiefs persuaded Little Crow to lead an assault on the whites. On August 18, 1862, they attacked the Redwood Agency, killing twenty men and taking twelve women captive. Among the dead was Myrick, his body mutilated and his mouth stuffed with grass as an answer to his callous remark. After this attack, the Indians swept throughout the countryside plundering, looting, killing, and raping. The white settlement at New Ulm, for one, suffered staggering losses but repelled the attackers.

The Indians were decisively defeated by General Henry Sibley's troops at the Battle of Wood Lake on September 23. This battle virtually ended Sioux resistance. On December 26 of 1862, 38 out of 303 Sioux were tried and convicted of rape and murder. They were sentenced to death by mass hanging. Little Crow, who fled west, was killed during the summer of 1863 by a Minnesota farmer.

As a result of the uprising, between four hundred and eight hundred whites were killed. In addition, the Eastern Sioux were forced to relocate to reservations in present-day South Dakota.

See also: Indian-white relations: U.S., 1831-1870; Sioux War.

Raymond Wilson and Sharon K. Wilson

An 1863 engraving of the mass execution at Monkato of participants in the Minnesota Sioux uprising of 1862. (Library of Congress)

Modoc War

Date: November 29, 1872-June 1, 1873
Locale: Boundary of Northern California and southern Oregon
Tribes involved: Klamath, Modoc
Categories: Nineteenth century history, Reservations and relocation, Wars and battles
Significance: The Modoc War was another example of attempted Indian resistance to the loss of their homelands.

In 1864, the Modocs signed a treaty in which they agreed to leave the Lost River Valley, in Northern California and southern Oregon, and live on a reservation with the Klamaths. By 1872, Kintpuash, called Captain Jack by the whites, and other Modocs found reservation life and policies unacceptable. They missed their homeland and could no longer endure sharing a reservation with the Klamaths, who outnumbered them and made life extremely difficult for them.

Kintpuash and a group of Modocs decided to return south to the ceded lands at Lost River. White settlers, whose numbers had continued to increase, refused to accept them and demanded that the Modocs return to the reservation. Government officials tried in vain to persuade the Modocs to do so. On November 29, 1872, troops attacked Kintpuash's camp at Lost River. The Indians fled, crossed Tule Lake, and strategically entrenched themselves in the Lava Beds, a natural fortress on the lake's southern shore. For four months, Kintpuash skillfully defended the area with about sixty men against forces that numbered nearly a thousand.

The government again tried negotiation, creating a peace commission headed by General Edward R. S. Canby, a Civil War hero. Kintpuash favored negotiating for a settlement, but other Modoc leaders such as Hooker Jim and Curley-Headed Doctor forced Kintpuash to accept a plan to kill the peace commissioners at a meeting that was to take place on Good Friday, April 11, 1873. At this meeting, Kintpuash and other Modocs drew their hidden weapons and attacked. Two of the four commissioners were killed, including General Canby, who thus became the only regular army general killed in the Indian wars.

This rash action provoked a national outcry for revenge. More troops and officers were sent. Meanwhile, factionalism intensified among the Modocs. In May of 1873 the army defeated a Modoc band, and some of the defeated Modocs agreed to help the army catch Kintpuash. He was finally

Late nineteenth century sketch of an 1873 skirmish in the Modoc War. (Library of Congress)

captured on June 1. All the Modoc prisoners were taken to Fort Klamath, Oregon.

Kintpuash and several other Modocs were tried and found guilty of the murders of the two peace commissioners. Kintpuash and three others were hanged on October 3, 1873, with two other Modocs receiving life sentences at Alcatraz. The executed Modocs' heads were severed and sent to the Army Medical Museum in Washington, D.C. The other Modocs were removed to the Quapaw Agency in Oklahoma; in 1909, they were allowed to return to the Klamath Reservation.

The Modoc War lasted seven months and cost more than $500,000. The war seriously weakened the Indian Peace Policy, a program under the Grant administration that attempted to use reservations as a panacea for the "Indian Problem."

See also: Indian-white relations: U.S., 1871-1933.

Raymond Wilson

Natchez Revolt

Date: 1729
Locale: Natchez, Mississippi
Tribes involved: Natchez
Categories: Colonial history, Wars and battles
Significance: The Natchez Revolt gave rise to the French policy of encouraging enmity among the different Indian groups in order to forestall future uprisings.

The Natchez Revolt occurred on November 28, 1729. The main factor underlying this event was the ineptness of French colonial rule, which controlled this region from the late seventeenth century. The Natchez were first encountered by the French on the eastern shore of the Mississippi River, at the location of the modern town of Natchez, Mississippi. In 1713, the French built a trading post there, evidence of their desire to control the region. Skirmishes between the Natchez and the French resulted in the 1716 construction of Fort Rosalie and in colonial settlement in its vicinity. After the fort was built, there were two additional small Natchez uprisings, although each was swiftly quelled.

Commandant de Chepart, placed in control of Fort Rosalie in 1728, marred his command with drunkenness and other abuses as well as with his insensitivity toward the Natchez. Within a year, de Chepart antagonized the Indian community with his proposal to establish his own plantation on fertile lands of the Natchez White Apple village. He proposed the use of force to assist in the relocation of the aboriginal inhabitants. In response, the Natchez planned war; their ceremonial preparations lasted for several months, culminating in a November attack on the French. They killed more than two hundred settlers, and they captured approximately fifty colonists and three hundred slaves.

On January 27, 1730, Sieur Jean-Paul Le Seur led a five-hundred-strong Choctaw force against the Natchez in retaliation. They managed to rescue most of the surviving women and children, plus approximately a hundred slaves; in the process they killed about the same number of Natchez. A week later, the French force received reinforcements from New Orleans, and they laid siege to the Natchez, who agreed to surrender on February 25.

In punishment, approximately four hundred Natchez were enslaved by the French and shipped to the West Indies. An indeterminate number escaped and sought refuge with the Chickasaw. This ensured Chickasaw animosity toward both the French and their powerful Choctaw allies. The Natchez never recovered, and their culture was soon lost.

See also: Indian-white relations: French colonial.

Susan J. Wurtzburg

National Congress of American Indians

Date: Established 1944
Locale: United States
Tribes involved: Pantribal in the United States
Categories: Civil rights, Education, Organizations, Twentieth century history
Significance: The National Congress of American Indians was formed to fight for the rights of Native Americans, including education and preservation of traditional values.

The National Congress of American Indians (NCAI) is a coalition of sovereign nations recognized by the United States through treaty and executive agreement. Its purpose is to protect the rights of American Indians as citizens of nations and tribes within the boundaries of the United States. It is supported through annual membership dues and special fundraising endeavors. It is organized as a congress, with American Indian governments voting to participate and selecting delegates and alternates to represent them in the NCAI convention and executive council, where they have blocks of votes.

The NCAI was organized in 1944. American Indian delegates representing fifty tribes with homes in twenty-seven western states met in Denver, Colorado. Its initial stated goals included pursuit of American Indian rights within the United States, expansion and improvement of Indian education, preservation of Indian values, and equitable settlement of Indian claims. During the 1950's, it aided in the struggle against termination and relocation. It has been in the forefront of the struggle for Native American cultural rights legislation, which has brought on more reasonable approaches to repatriation of Indian remains and artifacts.

See also: American Indian Defense Association; American Indian Higher Education Consortium; American Indian Movement; Indian Civil Rights Act; Indian Rights Association; Indian-white relations: U.S., 1934-

2002; National Council of American Indians; National Indian Association; National Indian Education Association; National Indian Youth Council; Society of American Indians; Termination Resolution.

Howard Meredith

National Council of American Indians

Date: Established 1926
Locale: United States
Tribes involved: Pantribal in the United States
Categories: Organizations, Twentieth century history
Significance: The National Council of American Indians was important in the 1920's and 1930's as a Red Progressive movement and in developing Indian voting and supporting John Collier's "Indian New Deal" reforms.

In the early part of the twentieth century, a movement known as the Red Progressive movement called for American Indians to assimilate to the general American lifestyle. It was led by Indians who were well-educated and had achieved success in mainstream American society. Among its leaders were Henry Roe Cloud, Thomas L. Sloan, Arthur C. Parker, physicians Charles Eastman and Carlos Montezuma, and Gertrude Simmons Bonnin, a Sioux writer and musician.

The Red Progressives united at first under the Society of American Indians (SAI), but by the early 1920's that organization had split into several rancorous factions. A number of new organizations appeared, including the National Council of American Indians, founded in 1926 by Gertrude Bonnin and her husband. The organization was closely aligned with the General Federation of Women's Clubs, a mostly white and black organization of successful women. Bonnin had served as secretary of the Society of American Indians and in 1924 had coauthored *Oklahoma's Poor Rich Indians: An Orgy of Graft and Exploitation of the Five Civilized Tribes—Legalized Robbery*, a muckraking expose of graft and greed involving Oklahoma lawyers, judges, and politicians.

The slogan of the National Council of American Indians was "Help the Indians help themselves in protecting their rights and properties." Its major early emphasis was promoting voting and participation in politics after the passage of the Indian Citizenship Act in 1924. It was most successful in

An 1899 photograph of Gertrude Bonnin, founder of the National Council of American Indians, in traditional Sioux attire. (National Archives)

these efforts in Oklahoma and South Dakota. The organization also advocated banning peyote use and the Native American Church; it took a moderate stance toward the Bureau of Indian Affairs.

In January, 1934, representatives of several organizations were called together in Washington, D.C., to confer with Franklin Roosevelt's commissioner of Indian affairs, John Collier, on reforms needed to ameliorate the living conditions of Indians. The Bonnins represented both the National Council of American Indians and the General Federation of Women's Clubs. They strongly supported the Indian Reorganization Act, which was adopted by Congress the same year. The council successfully pushed for a requirement for majority rule elections for tribal offices.

The National Council of American Indians, like its predecessors, was torn by factionalism; the Bonnins were its major support. With the coming of World War II, the council faded from existence, but it left behind a strong heritage of Indian political participation.

See also: Bureau of Indian Affairs; Indian Citizenship Act; Indian New Deal; Indian Reorganization Act; Indian-white relations: U.S., 1934-2002; Society of American Indians.

Fred S. Rolater

National Indian Association

Date: Established 1879
Locale: United States
Tribes involved: Pantribal in the United States
Categories: Nineteenth century history, Organizations
Significance: The National Indian Association was one of several orga-
nizations that composed the Friends of the Indian lobbying group,
seeking to ameliorate Indian living conditions and help Indians as-
similate into American society.

After the Civil War (1861-1865), a series of groups devoted to Indian "reform" arose in the eastern United States. Events leading up to and during the culminating period of 1876-1878, including the defeat of General
George Armstrong Custer in 1876 at the Battle of the Little Bighorn, the
Nez Perce escape attempt of 1877, and the Bannock War and the tragic
Cheyenne escape attempt in 1878, led to the establishment of several influential organizations. Five of these became the core of the Friends of
the Indian movement. One was the U.S. government's Board of Indian
Commissioners, founded in 1869 and consisting of private citizens who
served without pay. Two others, established in 1879, were the Boston Indian Citizenship Commission and the National Indian Association (also
known as the Women's National Indian Association), established by a
group of Protestant churchwomen in Philadelphia. The Indian Rights Association and the National Indian Defense Association followed in the
early 1880's.

Between 1879 and 1886, the National Indian Association established
eighty-three branches in cities across the nation. It published a monthly pe-
riodical, *The Indian's Friend*, often presented petitions to Congress and the
president protesting the mistreatment of Indians, stridently pushed for reform of the Bureau of Indian Affairs, and—more than any other group—
demanded that the U.S. government follow the provisions of its treaties
with the Indians with "scrupulous fidelity." Its other major issues included
improving delivery of education for Indians (with regard to the number
and quality of schools), extending citizenship to all Indians, and dividing
Indian lands into private homesteads for each family.

The association participated yearly in the Lake Mohonk Conference of
the Friends of the Indian and the annual meeting of the Board of Indian
Commissioners. These agencies shared responsibility for helping persuade
the government to pass the General Allotment Act (Dawes Severalty Act),

enacted in 1887, which subdivided the majority of Indian reservations into individual allotments. This act was ultimately disastrous for Indians, as the National Indian Defense Association had feared. The National Indian Association failed to influence the government's honoring of treaties. The association's other major success was increasing the number of schools available to Indians.

See also: Allotment system; Bannock War; Friends of the Indian organizations; General Allotment Act; Indian Rights Association; Little Bighorn, Battle of the; Nez Perce War; Rosebud Creed, Battle of; Treaties and agreements in the United States.

Fred S. Rolater

National Indian Education Association

Date: Established November, 1969
Locale: Minneapolis, Minnesota
Tribes involved: Pantribal in the United States
Categories: Education, National government and legislation, Organizations, Religion and missionary activities, Twentieth century history
Significance: The National Indian Education Association (NIEA) was organized in Minnesota with the broad goal of improving Indian education to enable Native learners to become contributing members of their communities.

During the 1960's, United States federal Indian policy increasingly focused on correcting the poor quality of education and low student achievement that existed in most reservation schools. As federal controls on the schools loosened, Indian parents and educators sought ways to participate more fully in the development of new initiatives in Indian education and to develop curriculum that reflected tribal languages and histories. In order to promote and achieve these goals, Indian educators formed the National Indian Education Association in Minneapolis in 1969. The organization supports traditional Native cultures and values, advocates for Native control of educational institutions, and provides technical assistance to educators in the field. NIEA actively monitors legislation affecting Indian education and, in order to advocate more effectively, now has its offices to the Washington, D.C., metropolitan area. The organization sponsors an annual national conference to showcase effective educational programs, honor tribal traditions, and encourage innovative teaching and improved resources for American Indian students. Native Hawaiians, who also seek preservation and education about their indigenous culture, began participating as board members in the 1990's.

Carole A. Barrett

See also: American Indian Higher Education Consortium; Boarding and residential schools; Carlisle Indian School; Indian Education Acts; Indian Self-Determination and Education Assistance Act; Kennedy Report; Meriam Report.

National Indian Youth Council

Date: Established 1961
Locale: United States
Tribes involved: Pantribal in the United States
Categories: Organizations, Twentieth century history
Significance: Provides Native American youth with knowledge about tribal communities and traditions; develops leadership, employment, and civil liberties.

Ten Native American college students gathered to form the National Indian Youth Council (NIYC) in August, 1961, at Gallup, New Mexico. Two months earlier, these students had met at the National Congress of American Indians (NCAI) conference at the University of Chicago. After hearing the discussions encouraging self-determination and denouncing termination, the students decided to start their own group.

The foundation for the NIYC had been laid in 1953 when Herbert Blatchford (Navajo) initiated the first intertribal student group, the Kiva Club, at the University of New Mexico. In expanding his visions for native youth, Blatchford was the founding director of the NIYC. At the August meeting, Mel Thom (Paiute) was elected the chairperson; Clyde Warrior (Ponca), president; Shirley Witt (Mohawk), vice president. The NIYC's founding group came from different tribes and interests, but they had a common bond: a spirit to recover native rights and respect. Differing from the NCAI, the NIYC focused on the voices of the youth and employed strategies that were more aggressive and activist.

During its first decade, NIYC targeted problems with Native American education and discrimination. Members editorialized their opinions through NIYC's first publication, *American Aborigine*, edited by Blatchford. In 1963 the NIYC began publishing its long-running newspaper, *ABC: Americans Before Columbus*. The following year, the NIYC took its first step of direct action by going to Washington State to hold a series of "fish-ins." Members defied state law by fishing in rivers that had been closed to native fishing even though treaty language had reserved for the tribes permanent fishing rights. During this time of national unrest, other activist groups banded together to assist NIYC's "Washington Project."

With national support, NIYC members stepped into the political arena. Mel Thom encouraged a 1964 Washington, D.C., audience to stand up for self-determination. At a Memphis, Tennessee, poverty conference in 1967, Clyde Warrior delivered his passionate speech, "We Are Not Free." When Warrior died the following year, the NIYC initiated the education-based Clyde Warrior Institute in American Indian Studies. Another educational project was a 1967 Carnegie Foundation program that researched educational methodology and addressed acculturation. With this growth, the NIYC in 1970 had opened chapters on several college campuses and reservations to serve more than two thousand members.

In expanding its political involvement, the NIYC then undertook lawsuits against irresponsible mining companies on reservation lands and instituted native employment and training programs. Other NIYC projects range from conducting voting surveys to creating an all-native film company, Circle Film. To help preserve native sacred lands and to protect native rituals, the group appealed to the United Nations and was granted recognition as an "official and non-governmental organization." From its headquarters in Albuquerque, New Mexico, the NIYC hosts international native conferences that create strong networks of indigenous views.

See also: Fish-ins; National Congress of American Indians.

Tanya M. Backinger

Native American

Date: Twentieth century
Locale: North America
Tribes involved: Pantribal
Categories: Terminology
Significance: One of many terms used to refer to the peoples of North America whose cultures predate European colonization.

The term "Native American" is commonly used to refer to the many peoples of North America whose cultures existed on the continent when Europeans first arrived. It does not eliminate the possibility of foreign origin in an earlier era. It was coined as a collective name for the native peoples of the Americas (primarily North America) that would not carry the obvious falseness and the historically racist overtones of such terms as "American Indian" and "Indian." Yet, as is the case with virtually any collective term suggested, there are problems inherent in the term; for example, literally speaking, anyone of any ethnicity born in the Americas could be considered a "native American."

Beginning in the 1970's, the term Native American lost favor among activist groups and many others concerned with American Indian politics. Nevertheless, the term is still widely used, and some still prefer it to American Indian (although by the 1990's, the latter had become more common or at least more widely accepted). Some American Indians find the offensiveness of all such collective terms to be about the same. All are generalizations that deny the unique, tribal-specific cultural heritage and political legacy of the many original inhabitants of the Americas. At the same time, the names of many pantribal organizations—such as the American Indian Movement or the National Congress of American Indians—attest to the convenience of such collective terms.

See also: American Indian; Amerind; Federally recognized tribes; Indian; Tribe.

M. W. Simpson

Native American Church v. Navajo Tribal Council

Date: 1959
Locale: United States
Tribes involved: Navajo
Categories: Civil rights, Court cases, Religion and missionary activities, Twentieth century history
Significance: A U.S. Supreme Court decision finds that since Native American tribal governments predate the U.S. Constitution, they are not bound to uphold its guarantees.

In 1958, the Navajo Tribal Council, in an effort to limit activities of the Native American Church on its reservation, enacted an ordinance making it illegal to bring peyote onto the Navajo Reservation. Navajo members of the Native American Church filed a suit against the tribe in federal court charging the ordinance violated their First and Fourteenth Amendment rights. They claimed their rights to freedom of religion and to protection against arbitrary and oppressive ordinances were totally disregarded.

In 1959, the United States Court of Appeals heard the case and sided with the Navajo tribe, ruling that tribal councils existed prior to the establishment of the United States and so were not bound to uphold the United States Constitution unless "they have expressly been required to surrender [their sovereign powers] by the superior sovereign, the United States." The decision upheld tribal sovereignty and the right of tribes to manage their own internal affairs without interference. However, the decision also caused many in Congress to perceive a need to lessen tribal authority and extend certain basic constitutional protections to individuals living under tribal governments. *Native American Church v. Navajo Tribal Council* influenced passage of the Indian Civil Rights Act (1968) by Congress, which, in part, requires tribes to guarantee an individual's freedom of religion when living under tribal governance.

See also: American Indian Religious Freedom Act; *Employment Division, Dept. of Human Resources of the State of Oregon et al. v. Smith*; Indian Civil Rights Act; Indian-white relations: U.S., 1934-2002; National Council of American Indians.

Carole A. Barrett

Native American Graves Protection and Repatriation Act

Date: November 16, 1990
Locale: United States
Tribes involved: Pantribal in the United States
Categories: National government and legislation, Twentieth century history
Significance: This act changed the relationship between American Indians and mainstream museums and academic institutions by insisting

that rights of scientific inquiry do not supersede basic human rights with respect for the dead.

By the middle of the nineteenth century, Americans were fascinated with the science of phrenology, a process of measuring skulls to determine intelligence. The so-called science operated on the premise that racial minority groups, including American Indians, were inferior to Europeans, and that this inferiority was detectable in their physical appearance. Indian graves were looted to provide skulls for study. Later in the nineteenth century, the U.S. surgeon general allowed Indian remains to be collected from battlefields and other areas, and these were shipped to the Army Medical Museum in Washington, D.C., for study. Eventually, the remains were transferred to the Smithsonian Institution for exhibit and study. By the 1880's, Indians were considered a vanishing race and there was a rush to collect Indian remains and artifacts. Many graves were looted to build museum collections. In 1906, Congress passed the Antiquities Act, which made it illegal to excavate Indian grave sites on public lands without a permit. However, Indian remains and funeral objects were categorized as "natural resources," and universities and museums readily obtained permits. In the 1930's, Indian artifacts became popular art collectibles and looting became a major way of supplying the market.

In the 1960's and 1970's, Indian activists began to seek return of remains and artifacts, but their requests were ignored. In the mid-1980's, Indian people sought congressional support to draft legislation for return of skeletal remains and funeral objects. In Indian belief, the remains of the dead should be returned to Mother Earth to complete their journey into the spirit world. However, the museum and scientific communities opposed return of any remains or grave items, stating these were necessary objects for study. Indians countered that all other Americans were protected against grave robbing and human remains were not property to be taken and studied at will.

In 1990, Indian groups and the scientific and museum communities worked to craft compromise legislation known as the Native American Graves Protection and Repatriation Act (NAGPRA). This law states that all agencies who receive federal funds must notify tribes of all human remains, funeral artifacts, and sacred objects in their collections, including objects of cultural patrimony, or objects that have ongoing importance to the tribe. Indian graves on federal lands are protected, and the sale of human remains and funeral objects is forbidden. NAGPRA permits tribes to negotiate for return of artifacts. Human remains are to be returned to the proper tribe for burial. A review committee appointed by the secretary of the interior mediates disputes; however, dissatisfied parties can go to court. The Smithsonian Institution is exempt from NAGPRA regulations, but the national museum does work closely with tribes on return of human remains. NAGPRA, though it has some loopholes, is an important piece of legislation, because it recognizes the sanctity of tribal religious teachings and honors the rights of American Indians to oversee and maintain cultural continuity from generation to generation.

Carole A. Barrett

See also: Kennewick Man controversy.

Native American Rights Fund

Date: Established 1970
Locale: United States
Tribes involved: Pantribal in the United States
Categories: Native government, Organizations, Twentieth century history
Significance: NARF, established to represent Native American legal interests, has become a well-known and respected, if sometimes criticized, organization in the arena of American Indian rights and politics.

The Native American Rights Fund (NARF) is a nonprofit, public-interest legal organization that was founded in 1970. It was established to represent tribal clients in litigation in state and federal courts and to strengthen tribal governments. Operations are supported by federal funds as well as by private and corporate contributions. Its attorneys are mostly Native Americans; the group's headquarters are in Boulder, Colorado, with satellite offices in Washington, D.C., and Anchorage, Alaska. One of the organization's primary activities is to handle cases involving "federally recognized tribes" that cannot afford the full financial burden of litigation in U.S. courts. A staff of sixteen attorneys (in the early 1990's) handles about fifty cases at any given time. NARF also acts as a consultant in the drafting of federal Indian policy.

NARF's objectives include preservation of tribal existence and independence, protection of tribal resources, promotion of human rights such as education and the equitable treatment of Indian prisoners, and development of Indian law to improve tribal legal resources. The Indian Law Support Center and the Carnegie-sponsored National Indian Law Library are components of NARF, working in conjunction with its Legal Services Corporation. The law library houses a collection of more than six hundred tribal codes.

NARF has taken on a number of well-known cases involving tribal land and water interests. The group gained national notice and respect for its handling of the 1982 land rights case brought by the Penobscot and Passamaquoddy against the state of Maine. The tribes were awarded $27,000 plus the money to purchase 300,000 acres of land. (An important footnote is that, although the case was regarded as a success story, the money did not go very far for some recipients. In addition, many such cases, even when legally successful, become bogged down by governmental bureaucracy.) NARF has been involved in litigation to strengthen aspects of the 1978 American Indian Religious Freedom Act dealing with the repatriation of ancestral bones and archaeological artifacts. NARF also assists nonfederally recognized tribes in attempts to gain official tribal recognition, which may involve the restoration of at least some tribal homelands. It has litigated successfully for the Menominee of Wisconsin and the Siletz of Oregon.

NARF has not been without its critics. Some have argued that, because the organization is not self-sufficient and must rely on federal funding, it cannot truly be an effective advocacy group. From this perspective it may appear to be an extension of the federal system. Another criticism leveled against the group is that it has never attempted to challenge the European American legal paradigm by insisting on complete internal sovereignty for a client; rather, its negotiations seek negotiation, consensus, and settlement.

See also: American Indian Religious Freedom Act; Federally recognized tribes.

M. A. Jaimes

Sources for Further Study

Deloria, Vine, Jr., and Clifford M. Lytle. *American Indians, American Justice.* Austin: University of Texas Press, 1983.

_____. *The Nations Within: The Past and Future of American Indian Sovereignty.* New York: Pantheon Books, 1984.

Native American Rights Fund. *Annual Report.* Boulder, Colo.: Author, 1993.

_____. *Legal Review* 19, no. 1 (Winter/Spring, 1994).

Navajo-Hopi Land Settlement Act

Date: December 22, 1974
Locale: Arizona
Tribes involved: Hopi, Navajo, San Juan Southern Paiute
Categories: National government and legislation, Native government, Reservations and relocation, Twentieth century history
Significance: This act was designed to settle land disputes between the Hopi and Navajo; it triggered tremendous controversy surrounding the removal and relocation of several thousand Navajos.

The Navajo-Hopi Land Settlement Act was enacted by Congress in 1974 primarily to clarify rights of the Navajo and Hopi tribes in the 1882 "Executive Order Reservation" established by President Chester A. Arthur. This executive order set aside 2,472,095 acres "for the use and occupancy of the Moqui [Hopi] and such other Indians as the Secretary of the Interior may see fit to settle thereon." At the time, both Hopis and Navajos were living in the set-aside area. Disputes increased as the Navajo population in the area expanded.

In 1934 Congress consolidated the boundaries of the Navajo Reservation without altering the 1882 Executive Order Reservation. The Bureau of Indian Affairs then established grazing districts on both reservations. District 6, exclusively for Hopi use, consisted of about 25 percent of the 1882 reservation. The remainder was occupied largely by Navajo stock raisers. Disputes between members of the two tribes continued.

In 1958 Congress authorized a lawsuit to settle conflicting claims to the 1882 reservation. In 1962 a federal court, in *Healing v. Jones*, held that for the area outside District 6, the Hopi and Navajo had "joint, undivided and equal interests." Because the Navajos occupied most of the area, however, they controlled the most surface resources in the Joint Use Area (JUA).

Negotiations between the two tribes concerning management of the JUA were unsuccessful. In the early 1970's the Hopis sought and obtained a court order for livestock reduction in the area. The continuing controversy stimulated congressional interest, and the Navajo-Hopi Land Settlement Act was enacted in 1974.

The act was comprehensive. It directed that a mediator make recommendations to the district court, which would then partition the surface rights of the JUA. In 1977 each tribe received half of the JUA. Money was appropriated for livestock reduction and boundary fencing. The act, and a 1980 amendment, allowed for the transfer of some federal lands to the Navajos to help offset lost JUA land. In 1983 about 370,000 acres of "new lands" along the southern edge of the Navajo Reservation were selected.

The act required the removal of members of one tribe living on lands transferred to the other tribe. This involved a relatively small number of Hopis but thousands of Navajos. An independent commission was created to administer the relocation program, but it was inept, contributing to the hardships of relocatees. The $52,000,000 initial appropriation was inadequate. Congress belatedly responded in the 1980's, amending the act to restructure the commission and authorizing hundreds of millions of additional dollars for relocation.

As a final touch of irony, one section of this legislation, designed to resolve controversy over the 1882 reservation, allowed the tribes the right to sue to settle rights in lands within the 1934 Navajo Reservation. In 1992 a federal district court decided that the Hopis and San Juan Southern Paiutes (who had intervened in the lawsuit) had rights in portions of the Navajo Reservation long used by tribal members.

See also: Indian-white relations: U.S., 1934-2002; Navajo Rehabilitation Act.

Eric Henderson

Navajo Rehabilitation Act

Date: April 19, 1950
Locale: Arizona and New Mexico
Tribes involved: Hopi, Navajo
Categories: National government and legislation, Twentieth century history
Significance: In an attempt to improve conditions in one of the most impoverished areas of the United States, this act funded the construction of roads, schools, and other developments on the Navajo and Hopi reservations.

The Navajo-Hopi Long Range Rehabilitation Act of 1950 (Public Law 81-474) was passed by Congress to construct basic facilities on the Navajo and Hopi reservations. Passed in response to more than twenty years of deteriorating economic conditions on the Navajo Reservation, the act authorized funding for school construction, roads, and other projects.

In the 1930's the federal government had initiated a range-management program on the Navajo and Hopi reservations. Central to the program was reducing the amount of livestock on the range. This devastated the Navajo sheep-based pastoral economy. The full effects of stock reduction were partially obscured during World War II, when thousands of Navajos joined the service or worked in war-related industries. When these people returned home, however, livestock regulations and insufficient resources prevented a renewal of the pastoral economy. Unusually harsh winters added to the distress and drew national attention to the impoverished conditions among the more than sixty thousand Navajos residing in Navajo country.

Reservation schools could accommodate only about 25 percent of the student-age population. All-weather roads were practically nonexistent on the reservations. Inadequate roads contributed to health, education, and economic problems. Infant mortality was high and school enrollments low. After passing minor emergency relief measures, Congress considered a more comprehensive approach.

A 1949 bill to fund improvements on the Navajo and Hopi reservations, reflecting a resurgent congressional interest in limiting tribal sovereignty, also included a provision that extended the jurisdiction of state law over the two reservations. Citing this provision, President Harry Truman vetoed the bill.

In 1950 the president signed the Navajo Rehabilitation Act, which emerged from Congress without the offending jurisdictional provision. This version also provided expanded opportunities for Hopi participation in projects. The act appropriated $88,570,000. The largest portion, $25 million, was for school construction, followed by $20 million for roads and $19 million for rangelands and irrigation projects. Lesser amounts were appropriated for health and water facilities, industrial development, and other projects. More than $9 million was allocated for relocating and resettling individuals away from the two reservations. There were also provisions for loans and leases. Finally, one provision (ignored for more than thirty years) authorized the Navajo tribe to adopt a tribal constitution.

In 1958, Public Law 85-740 provided an additional $20 million to complete road construction. By 1962, more than 80 percent of the total appropriation had been expended, including nearly all the dollars targeted for roads and schools.

The major benefit of the act was the substantial improvement in roads and schools on the reservation. All-weather roads have provided greater access to job locations and markets. School attendance increased dramatically through the 1950's and 1960's, as did the overall educational attainment of the population.

See also: Indian-white relations: U.S., 1934-2002; Navajo-Hopi Land Settlement Act.

Eric Henderson

Navajo War

Date: September, 1863-November, 1866
Locale: New Mexico
Tribes involved: Navajo
Categories: Nineteenth century history, Wars and battles
Significance: Disputed grazing lands helped lead to this conflict, which resulted in Navajo relocation to the barren Bosque Redondo.

Disputed grazing lands near Fort Defiance were a major factor leading to the 1863-1866 war. The site was favored for rendezvous by Navajo medicine men who collected herbs there. For generations, these lands were also used as pasture for Navajo livestock. Shortly after the establishment of Fort Defiance on September 18, 1851, soldiers who wanted to pasture their horses on these lands shot the Navajo-owned horses. Revenge was swift: Navajos raided army herds to replace their losses.

Through the decade, the raids continued and the army retaliated until, in 1859, army troops attacked and destroyed the home, crops, and livestock of the Navajo clan leader, Manuelito. In 1860, Manuelito—aided by leaders of other clans—assaulted Fort Defiance and nearly captured it, but was driven back. The army pursued the attackers into the Chuska mountains but was demoralized by the hit-and-run

Manuelito, leader of his people in the Navajo War, as depicted by artist E. A. Burbank. (National Archives)

tactics of the Navajos. In January of 1861, the Navajos met with army representatives and agreed to work for peace. The uneasy truce was broken when, in September of 1861, a riot broke out over a horse race. Artillery was used to quell the disturbance, killing ten Navajos.

Raids for plunder and revenge increased, and the army responded. On September 6, 1863, Colonel Christopher "Kit" Carson was chosen to lead a campaign of "pacification." In the following months, Carson's scorched-earth offensive burned Navajo corn fields, orchards, and hogans; livestock was confiscated and destroyed. Tribes unfriendly to the Navajos were encouraged to attack and harass them. Navajo tribe members surrendered or were rounded up and relocated to Bosque Redondo (Round Forest) in the barren plains of eastern New Mexico. Some clan leaders and their followers held out as long as possible, but by the end of 1864 about 8,000 half-starving Navajos surrendered and were marched to Bosque Redondo. Some two hundred people died on the grueling three-hundred-mile march known as the Long Walk. Manuelito and twenty-six followers surrendered in September of 1866. When another clan leader, Barboncito, surrendered in November of 1866 with twenty-one followers, the Navajo War of 1863-1866 was over.

See also: Long Walk; *Native American Church v. Navajo Tribal Council;* Navajo-Hopi Land Settlement Act; Navajo Rehabilitation Act; Pueblo Revolt; *Santa Clara Pueblo v. Martinez.*

Moises Roizen

Nez Perce War

Date: June 15-October 5, 1877
Locale: Oregon, Idaho, and Montana
Tribes involved: Nez Perce
Categories: Nineteenth century history, Reservations and relocation, Wars and battles
Significance: Chief Joseph, leader of the Wallamwatkins (Nez Perce tribe), led his people in retreat through Oregon, Idaho, and Montana almost 1,500 miles on one of the most remarkable and respected Indian war campaigns in U.S. history.

During the nineteenth century the Nez Perce occupied various areas of the Northwest, including Washington, Idaho, and Oregon. There were five separate groups, each under the leadership of an autonomous chief. One group occupied Oregon Territory in the Imnaha and Wallowa Valleys and was under the leadership Old Chief Joseph. In 1855, Governor Isaac Stevens of the Oregon Territory signed a celebrated treaty with Old Chief Joseph and numerous other Nez Perce leaders, allowing the Indians ownership of all the land in the Imnaha and Wallowa Valleys. The treaty was ratified by the United States Senate.

The treaty of 1855 proved short-lived, however, as the Civil War and discovery of gold at Orofino, Idaho, in 1860 led to an ever-increasing surge of immigration of white settlers into the valleys and territories claimed by the Nez Perce. Because of increasing tensions between the whites and Indians, in 1863 a new treaty was negotiated. The new terms excluded the Imnaha and Wallowa Valleys as well as other vast areas of land that had been dedi-

Frederic Remington's depiction of Nez Perce chief Joseph surrendering in northern Montana in 1877. After fighting U.S. cavalry troops for months and leading his people in a retreat across and Continental Divide from their relentless pursuit, Joseph vowed, "I will fight no more forever." (Library of Congress)

cated to the Indians in 1855. The revised treaty was signed by James Reuben and Chief Lawyer, but chiefs Old Joseph, White Bird, and Looking Glass refused to ratify it. Thus the Nez Perce became recognized as having "treaty Indians" and "non-treaty Indians."

In 1871, Old Chief Joseph died, leaving the leadership of his band (the Wallamwatkins) to Young Joseph (Chief Joseph). The continuing influx of white immigrants into the Nez Perce lands caused increasing problems between Indians and whites. In 1876, a commission was appointed to investigate complaints, and it was decided that the non-treaty Nez Perces had no standing and that all groups should go to designated reservations. In 1877, the U.S. Department of the Interior issued instructions to carry out the recommendations of the assigned commission. Preparing for the transition, a council was arranged to meet with Indian leaders and U.S. government officials on May 3, 1877. Chief Joseph and his brother, Alokut, represented the Nez Perce, while General Oliver O. Howard represented the U.S. government. The final understanding was that the non-treaty Indians would be on the designated reservations by June 14, 1877.

The Wallamwatkins Attack. On June 15, 1877, word was received at Fort Lapwai, Idaho, that the Wallamwatkins had attacked and killed several settlers around Mount Idaho, Idaho. U.S. Army troops were sent from Fort Lapwai under the command of Captain David Perry to counterattack. The Wallamwatkins, aware of the soldiers coming, moved their camp approximately 8 miles to Whitebird Creek. The next day, troops began pursuit into Whitebird Canyon and engaged in a terrifying encounter with the Wallamwatkins. The U.S. Army suffered resounding losses, losing thirty-four troops and numerous horses. The Nez Perce, numbering only seventy warriors, suffered only four wounded in the battle.

General Howard assembled troops at Fort Lapwai and hurried to reinforce the remaining troops at Mount Idaho. The battle was joined—Chief Joseph and his entire tribe (including women and children), totaling approximately four hundred, against the U.S. Army. By July 13, after numerous skirmishes with Captain Perry's and General Howard's troops, Chief Joseph led his people eastward toward the Lolo Trail in the Bitterroot Mountains and began a remarkable retreat march into Montana. Chief Joseph kept track of Howard's position and was able to stall and frustrate Howard's advancement. As a result, Chief Joseph led the Wallamwatkins through Lolo Trail and into the Missoula area. General Howard subsequently contacted Colonel John Gibbon at Fort Shaw, Montana, and instructed him to take up the pursuit. Gibbon was able to muster 146 men of the Seventh Infantry and 34 civilians.

Route of the Nez Perce, June 15–October 5, 1877

CANADA

Bear Paw Mountains

MONTANA

Cow Island
Fort Shaw

Colonel Miles

WASHINGTON

Fort
Keogh

NORTH
DAKOTA

Nez Perce
Reservation

Fort Missoula
Stevensville

Clearwater ● Big Hole Canyon Creek ●

Colonel Sturgis

Wallowa
Valley

Whitebird
Creek

Bozeman

SOUTH
DAKOTA

Camas Creek

IDAHO

WYOMING

OREGON

Retreat and Surrender. Chief Joseph crossed the Continental Divide and camped his weary followers in the Big Hole Valley, unaware of Colonel Gibbon's pursuit and position. On August 9, Gibbon's troops made a surprise attack on Chief Joseph's camp and engaged in a long and difficult battle. Losses on both sides were substantial, but Chief Joseph was able to gather his warriors, recover lost ground, recapture his large herd of ponies, and make good his retreat.

By August 27, Chief Joseph had led the Wallamwatkins into Yellowstone Park, with General Howard and his troops in continuing pursuit. By September 6, Chief Joseph made his retreat through the northeast corner of Yellowstone Park. Continuing north, Chief Joseph led his people up through the Snowy Mountains and finally into the northern foothills of the Bear Paw Mountains, an easy day's ride to the Canadian border. Unknown to Chief Joseph, however, Colonel Nelson A. Miles, having been notified by General Howard, was in pursuit from Fort Keogh and was paralleling Chief Joseph's trail. On September 30, Colonel Miles's troops made a surprise attack on the Wallamwatkins' camp. The fighting was intense, the army losing fifty-three men and the Indians eighteen warriors. On the night of October 4, General Howard rode into Miles's camp and provided the reinforcements that would ensure a final surrender from Chief Joseph. On October 5, at 2:20 P.M., all firing ceased. At 4:00 P.M., Chief Joseph offered one of the most famous surrendering speeches ever documented. Turning to the interpreter, Chief Joseph said:

Tell General Howard I know what is in his heart. What he told me before, I have in my heart. I am tired of fighting. Our chiefs are killed. Looking-Glass is dead. Tulhulhutsut is dead. The old men are all dead. It is the young men who say yes or no. He [Alokut] who led on the young men is dead. My people, some of them, have run away to the hills and have no blankets, no food; no one knows where they are—perhaps freezing to death. I want to have time to look for my children and see how many of them I can find. Maybe I shall find them among the dead. Hear me, my chiefs. I am tired; my heart is sick and sad. From where the sun now stands I will fight no more, forever.

Thus ended the Nez Perce War, one of the most remarkable and respected Indian war campaigns of U.S. history.

See also: Indian-white relations: U.S., 1871-1933; Prehistory: Plateau; Walla Walla Council.

John L. Farbo

Sources for Further Study

Adkison, Norman B. *Indian Braves and Battles with More Nez Perce Lore.* Grangeville: Idaho County Free Press, 1967.

_____. *Nez Perce Indian War and Original Stories.* Grangeville: Idaho County Free Press, 1966.

Beal, Merrill D. *I Will Fight No More Forever: Chief Joseph and the Nez Perce War.* Seattle: University of Washington Press, 1963.

Chalmers, Harvey, II. *The Last Stand of the Nez Perce.* New York: Twayne, 1962.

Fisher, Don C. *The Nez Perce War.* Thesis. Moscow: University of Idaho, Department of History, 1925.

Thompson, Scott. *I Will Tell My Story: A Pictorial Account of the Nez Perce War.* Seattle: University of Washington Press, 2000.

Nisga'a Agreement in Principle

Date: 1996
Locale: Canadian Pacific Northwest
Tribes involved: Nisga'a
Categories: National government and legislation, Native government, Twentieth century history
Significance: This agreement, dealing with an aboriginal group from the Pacific coast of Canada, covered many areas, including land and

reserves, access to the land, fisheries, wildlife, environmental assessment and protection, Nisga'a government, fiscal matters including taxation, and cultural heritage protection.

The Nisga'a Agreement in Principle, published in February, 1996, attempted to lead to the "full and final settlement of Nisga'a aboriginal title, rights, and interests." Under the agreement, the Nisga'a were defined as an aboriginal people under the constitution with all the charter rights, benefits, and obligations of other Canadians; they did not by this agreement acquire any special rights or privileges. The criminal code of Canada continued to govern them, and they continued to pay taxes. In time, the tax-exempt status for Nisga'a citizens was to be eliminated as the Nisga'a began to assume more power for taxation.

The agreement stipulated that the Nisga'a govern themselves in a democratic manner with four village governments and an overall Nisga'a government with its own constitution. This government was empowered to make laws governing cultural, linguistic, social, educational, vocational, environmental, and related matters. In addition, this government, with provincial approval, administered justice through provision of police services and a Nisga'a court with jurisdiction over its own lands. The agreement made the Nisga'a the owners of about nineteen hundred square kilometers of land in the area of the lower Nass River, including the four villages of New Aiyansh, Canyon City, Greenville, and Kincolith. These lands, however, were to remain accessible to the general public for recreation, hunting, and fishing. All existing legal interests on the lands were to be maintained, and the roads in them were to be governed and maintained by the province.

The agreement stipulated that a financial transfer of $190 million, in addition to $11.5 million for the purchase of commercial fishing vessels and licenses, was to be paid over a period of years. The Nisga'a would receive an annual quota of salmon and other fish to be caught and were expected to conserve the stocks. Overall management was shared between the Nisga'a and the federal and provincial governments. The Nisga'a received permission to hunt wildlife subject to existing restrictions and laws of conservation. The Nisga'a were made responsible for overall environmental protection and were required to meet or exceed existing federal and provincial requirements.

See also: Indian-white relations: Canadian; Nunavut Territory; Treaties and agreements in Canada.

Gregory Walters

Northwest Ordinance

Date: July 13, 1787

Locale: Ohio, Indiana, Illinois, Michigan, and Wisconsin

Tribes involved: Chippewa, Fox, Iroquois, Lenni Lenape, Miami, Ottawa, Potawatomi, Sauk, Shawnee, Winnebago, Wyandot (Huron)

Categories: Eighteenth century history, National government and legislation

Significance: Although it was considered the greatest achievement of the Confederation Congress because it provided terms for the creation of new states in the Old Northwest, the ordinance set a tragic precedent by denying Indian rights.

By the Peace of Paris with Britain (1783), the United States acquired a vast inland empire bounded by the Appalachians, the Mississippi River, the Great Lakes, and the Gulf of Mexico. The task of disposing of this territory fell to the government as it was organized under the Articles of Confederation (1781-1789). Conflicting claims of states, settlers, land companies, and American Indians confused the issue. Lands south of the Ohio River were settled separately from those north of it. The Old Northwest, including the present-day states of Ohio, Indiana, Illinois, Michigan, and Wisconsin, was claimed by Virginia, Connecticut, and Massachusetts. Thomas Jefferson chaired a committee that, in 1784, proposed to Congress the creation of a temporary government for the Northwest and the area's eventual division into sovereign states eligible to join the Confederation on terms equal to the original members. Though the plan was not enacted, it did provide a model for the Northwest Ordinance and facilitated the cession of western lands by Virginia (in 1784), Massachusetts (1784-1785), and Connecticut (1784-1786) to the national government.

If state claims were resolved, those of Native Americans were refused. Under British rule, by the Proclamation of 1763, the entire West had been set aside as Indian Country, starting at the Appalachian Divide. The pressure for white settlement of the region had been a contributing cause of the American Revolution, a lesson the Confederation had learned. As settlers from New England, Pennsylvania, and the South pressed toward the Ohio Country, Indian claims were extinguished. By the Treaty of Fort Stanwix (1784) the Iroquois, exhausted by war, surrendered their claims to western New York and Pennsylvania. The next year, major Ohio tribes relinquished their claims to most of the future state, with the exception of the southwest shores of Lake Erie. Formal concession came within a decade in the Treaty of Fort Greenville (1795), when, for a ten-thousand-dollar annuity, twelve tribes relinquished the southwest portion of the Old Northwest (Ohio and Indiana).

Utilizing Jefferson's plan, the Congress of the Confederation (1787), even as the Constitutional Convention was meeting, established the Northwest Ordinance, by which those lands would be organized as a territory, with a nationally appointed governor, secretary, and judges. It stated that when five thousand free white males resided there, a bicameral legislature was to be created. Eventually three to five states were to be formed (with a minimum of sixty thousand free white inhabitants needed for statehood), each to be admitted to the United States and to be equal in standing to the original states. Freedom of religion, the right to jury trial, public support of education, and the prohibition of slavery were to prevail. While this legislation is traditionally regarded as the greatest achievement of the Confederation Congress, it set a tragic precedent by riding roughshod over the rights of Native Americans.

See also: Fort Greenville Treaty; Fort Stanwix Treaty; Indian-white relations: U.S., 1775-1830; Proclamation of 1763.

C. George Fry

Nunavut Territory

Date: 1993
Locale: Canadian Northwest
Tribes involved: Inuit
Categories: National government and legislation, Treaties, Twentieth century history
Significance: The Canadian government gives control over half of the former Northwest Territories to the native Inuit.

In 1993, the Nunavut Land Claims Agreement was signed with Canada's federal government. It stated that, on April 1, 1999, the Northwest Territories would be divided and the eastern region would become Nunavut Territory. "Nunavut" comes from the Inuit language Inuktitut and means "our land." The Inuit have inhabited these lands for thousands of years, and they made up 80 percent of the population in the late 1990's. The Inuit have long desired a territory of their own, and the agreement gave the Inuit control over more than 350,000 square kilometers of land, mineral rights, and financial aid. This agreement is designed to give the Inuit people control over their own education, health, social services, and many other provincial-type responsibilities.

The government of the territory is to be democratically elected to represent all residents of the territory: about twenty-two thousand people, seventeen thousand of whom are Inuit. The agreement placed the seat of government in Iqualuit and described the territory as containing twenty-eight villages or communities, including Iqualuit, which is located on Baffin Island.

See also: Indian-white relations: Canadian; Nisga'a Agreement in Principle; Prehistory: Arctic; Prehistory: Subarctic; Treaties and agreements in Canada.

Gregory Walters

Oka crisis

Date: 1990
Locale: Quebec
Tribes involved: Mohawk
Categories: National government and legislation, Native government, Protest movements, Reservations and relocation, Twentieth century history
Significance: A conflict over Mohawk land claims leads to an armed confrontation between Indians and the Surreté du Québec.

The conflict that erupted in early July, 1990, at Oka in Quebec was the result of long-standing problems both within the Mohawk community in Canada and between that community and various other, mainly governmental, bodies. It was brought on in large measure by disputes regarding the ownership of the relevant lands at Oka that dated back to the early eighteenth century.

The lands at Oka do not fit the usual pattern of disputed territory, and for this reason, a 1975 land claim presented to the federal government was rejected outright. The Mohawk community nonetheless continued to make a claim based on territorial sovereignty, treaty rights, the Royal Proclamation of 1763, unextinguished aboriginal title under common law, and land rights from obligations imposed by order of the King of France in the eighteenth century.

More recent origins of the conflict date back to 1987 and pertain both to internal conflicts in the Mohawk community over issues of governance and legitimacy of leadership in the community and to external conflicts with various governments, chiefly local, about disputed land known as "the Pines." By the late 1980's, the Municipality of Oka had proposed to allow expansion of a local golf course onto the disputed lands and followed the lead of the federal government in refusing to consider a Mohawk land claim against the "the Pines." Mohawk protest ensued in the form of barricades, which the Municipality asked the Surreté du Québec to dispense with in restoring law and order. It was the move on July 11, 1990, by the Surreté that brought about the armed conflict and resulted in the death of a Surreté officer. As the report of the Parliamentary Standing Committee on Aboriginal Affairs stated,

> Eventually the controversy over land use in the Pines became symbolic of Mohawk land rights in general. This pattern of escalating conflict continued until the shaky state of peace that managed to hold from 1987 was completely shattered by the events of July 11, 1990.

Those events would unite the previously fractured Mohawk community and would galvanize public opinion in general in favor of a solution to the land claim problem provided violence was not again used. This public support prompted the standing committee, in its fifth report, *The Summer of 1990*, to set forth several recommendations. The committee did not explore all the historical and other details of the conflict but concluded its report with a series of recommendations to resolve aboriginal issues in general and the Mohawk-Oka conflict in particular. Those recommendations included the formation of a royal commission; a review of the National Defense Act, under which Quebec was able to ask and receive from the federal government the use and support of the army in resisting the Mohawk standoff; and a better process for federal land claims and dispute resolution. More specifically, they proposed that there be an independent inquiry into Quebec's handling of native issues and of the Surreté in responding at Oka; the appointment of a mediator to resolve the conflict around land claims; and a process of healing and compensation begun in order to build a better future for all concerned.

See also: Indian-white relations: Canadian.

Gregory Walters

Oklahoma Indian Welfare Act

Date: June 26, 1936

Locale: Oklahoma

Tribes involved: All in Oklahoma except those in Osage County

Categories: National government and legislation, Native government, Twentieth century history

Significance: This act made provision for all Indian tribes, bands, or groups in Oklahoma to adopt a constitution allowing for self-government, allowed the secretary of the interior to purchase land to be held in trust for all Oklahoma Indians, and allowed small groups of Indians to form a local cooperative association and receive interest-free loans from the Revolving Loan Fund for Indians.

A major reform of U.S. policy toward American Indians resulted in the Indian Reorganization Act (IRA, or Wheeler-Howard Act), enacted by Congress on June 18, 1934. With this act, further allotment of tribal lands to individual Indians was prohibited, purchase of additional lands for Indians by the secretary of the interior was authorized, and a fund (the Revolving Loan Fund for Indians) was established that could be used for tribal enterprises. The IRA allowed and encouraged the tribes or groups to adopt written constitutions allowing for self-government, gave Indians applying for positions in the Bureau of Indian Affairs preference over other applicants, and called for very strict conservation practices on Indian lands. Oklahoma, however, was excluded from the IRA because the IRA was essentially a system of reservation government, and it was deemed inappropriate for Oklahoma because, at the time of statehood, the Five Civilized Tribes had given up their autonomy.

In 1936, the benefits of the IRA were extended to Oklahoma by way of a separate statute, the Oklahoma Indian Welfare Act. This act authorized the secretary of the interior to purchase, at his discretion, good agricultural and grazing land, from within or without reservations, to hold in trust for the tribe, band, group, or individual Indian for whose benefit the land was acquired. Title to all lands was to be taken in the name of the United States and held by the United States. All land was exempt from any and all federal taxes, but the state of Oklahoma could levy and collect a gross production tax upon all oil and gas produced from the land. The secretary of the interior was responsible for overseeing the payment of these taxes to Oklahoma. Any tribe or band in the state of Oklahoma was given the right to organize for its common welfare and could adopt a constitution and bylaws;

these had to follow the rules and regulations set forth by the secretary of the interior. Any ten or more Indians, as determined by the official tribe rolls, or Indian descendants of such enrolled members, in convenient proximity to each other, could be chartered as a local cooperative association for the following purposes: credit administration, production, marketing, consumers' protection, or land management. Funds from the Revolving Loan Fund for Indians could be used to provide interest-free loans to these groups.

See also: Indian Reorganization Act.

Lynn M. Mason

Oliphant v. Suquamish Indian Tribe

Date: 1978
Locale: Washington State
Tribes involved: Suquamish
Categories: Court cases, Native government, Twentieth century history
Significance: On March 6, 1978, the U.S. Supreme Court in the case of *Oliphant v. Suquamish Indian Tribe* decided that tribes do not have jurisdiction over non-Indians who commit crimes on reservations.

In 1978, during a tribal celebration, two non-Indian residents of the Port Madison Reservation of the Suquamish Tribe (Washington) violated tribal laws. Mark Oliphant was arrested for assaulting tribal police officers and resisting arrest, and Dan Belgarde was arrested for hitting a tribal police car in a high-speed chase. The two argued the Suquamish tribe had no criminal jurisdiction over non-Indians, and they took their case to federal court.

The Supreme Court agreed with them and determined that non-Indians, even those residing on a reservation and charged with a crime, are not subject to the jurisdiction of tribal courts. This ruling dealt a major blow to tribal sovereignty and the authority of tribal courts because it determined that tribes lack the power to enforce laws against all who come within its borders. This ruling created serious and important law-and-order problems on reservations. Some tribes have approached the problem by cross-deputization with local and county police or by arranging for non-Indians on the reservation to submit voluntarily to tribal authority.

See also: Tribal courts.

Carole A. Barrett